BLACK'S
GUIDE
TO
SCOTLAND

Published by Collins
An imprint of HarperCollins Publishers
Westerhill Road
Bishopbriggs
Glasgow G64 2QT
www.harpercollins.co.uk

1st edition 2017

Originally published in 1840 as Black's Picturesque Tourist Guide of Scotland

A catalogue record for this book is available from the British Library

ISBN 978-0-00-825114-7 10 9 8 7 6 5 4 3 2 1

Printed in China at RR Donnelley APS. Co. Ltd

This facsimile edition is sourced from the National Library of Scotland's original copy of Black's Picturesque Tourist Guide of Scotland, 1840 – NE.19.a.2
www.nls.uk

MIX
Paper from
responsible sources
FSC™ C007454

FSC™ is a non-profit international organisation established to promote the responsible management of the world's forests. Products carrying the FSC label are independently certified to assure consumers that they come from forests that are managed to meet the social, economic and ecological needs of present and future generations, and other controlled sources.

Find out more about HarperCollins and the environment at
www.harpercollins.co.uk/green

PUBLISHER'S NOTE
Plans and drawings which appear as pull outs throughout the original text have been moved to a section after the main book, with the exception of the Map of Scotland which is published as a separate product. (ISBN 978-0-00-825115-4)

BLACK'S

PICTURESQUE TOURIST

OF

SCOTLAND.

ENGRAVED CHARTS AND VIEWS OF THE SCENERY;

PLANS OF EDINBURGH AND GLASGOW;

AND A COPIOUS ITINERARY.

EDINBURGH:

ADAM AND CHARLES BLACK, 27, NORTH BRIDGE,

BOOKSELLERS AND PUBLISHERS TO THE QUEEN.

M,DCCC,XL.

BEN LOMOND & LOCH LOMOND.

T. CONSTABLE, PRINTER, THISTLE STREET, EDINBURGH.

PREFACE.

The plan and execution of the present volume will be found, in an important respect, to differ from any other work upon the same subject. In the compilation of Guide Books, it appears to the Publishers that much eloquence has often been unnecessarily expended in elaborate eulogiums on the beauty or grandeur of natural scenery, of which no adequate idea can be conveyed to the mind by any written description, however graphic and minute. In the present work, therefore, the author has refrained from the ambitious attempt to write up to the attraction of his subject. He has contented himself with giving a plain and intelligible account of the scenery most worthy of the attention of strangers, without dictating the amount of admiration, with which any given prospect is to be contemplated. Instead of the fine writing thus suppressed, it will be found that he has enriched his pages with a large amount of traditionary, historical, and literary illustration, by which it is conceived, a recollection of the scenery will be more permanently fixed in the memory of the Tourist, than by any description of its features which the author could himself have given. Much labour has been bestowed to give the work the greatest possible degree of accuracy. With this view many of the sheets have passed through the hands of individuals conversant with the topography of the respective districts, while the descriptions of Edinburgh and Glasgow have been wholly contributed by natives of these towns. The Itinerary at the end of the volume will be found peculiarly valuable, as it not only gives the distances, but also contains brief marginal notices of the interesting objects along the several roads. The Tourist, by inspecting this portion of the work as he passes along, may thus ascertain, without the trouble of enquiry, the names of all the objects of interest on both sides of the road.

To those desiring a more minute knowledge of the northern part of Scotland, the Guide to the Highlands, by George and Peter Anderson, Esquires, occasionally quoted in the following pages, may be recommended as a manual equally interesting and accurate.

EDINBURGH,
27, NORTH BRIDGE.

CONTENTS.

Page

SIXTH TOUR.

SEVENTH TOUR.

EIGHTH TOUR.

NINTH TOUR.

TENTH TOUR.

ELEVENTH TOUR.

TWELFTH TOUR.

THIRTEENTH TOUR.

Page

FOURTEENTH TOUR.

ITINERARY.

TABLE OF THE DISTANCES

OF THE PRINCIPAL TOWNS IN SCOTLAND FROM EACH OTHER AND FROM LONDON, GENERALLY CALCULATED BY THE MAIL ROADS.

	Edinburgh	Aberdeen	Arbroath	Ayr	Banff	Berwick-on-Tweed	Campbelton	Cupar Fife	Dunbarton	Dumfries	Dundee	Elgin	Falkirk	Fochabers	Forres	Fort Augustus	Glasgow	Greenock	Haddington	Hamilton	Inverary	Inverness	Jedburgh	John o' Groat's House	Kelso	Kirkcudbright	Lanark	Montrose	Paisley	Peebles	Perth	Port Patrick	St. Andrews	Stirling	Thurso	Wick	Wigton	Distance from London
EDINBURGH																																						392
Aberdeen	109																																					501
Arbroath	60	49																																				452
Ayr	77	177	128																																			394
Banff	154	45	94	222																																		546
Berwick-on-Tweed	55	164	115	132	209																																	337
Campbelton	177	276	233	60	283	232																																529
Cupar Fife	30	79	30	107	124	85	181																															422
Dunbarton	58	150	106	47	195	113	108	81																														410
Dumfries	71	180	131	59	240	108	205	101	86																													338
Dundee	43	66	17	116	111	98	181	13	89	114																												435
Elgin	169	63	99	206	34	224	231	125	180	240	112																											561
Falkirk	24	127	84	56	159	79	156	54	37	88	67	157																										416
Fochabers	160	54	90	212	25	215	240	116	186	231	103	9	163																									552
Forres	156	75	101	200	46	211	220	131	174	227	118	12	151	21																								548
Fort Augustus	130	133	120	160	104	185	161	116	113	205	110	70	117	79	59																							522
Glasgow	44	143	100	33	175	99	133	74	14	72	83	173	23	179	167	127																						396
Greenock	66	165	122	46	197	121	111	96	12	94	105	195	45	201	189	149	22																					418
Haddington	17	126	77	94	171	38	194	47	75	88	60	186	41	177	173	147	61	83																				375
Hamilton	37	146	97	38	186	92	134	58	23	61	80	184	22	190	178	138	11	33	54																			301
Inverary	104	169	125	93	207	159	73	108	46	132	108	173	83	182	162	103	60	38	121	71																		456
Inverness	157	104	153	195	75	212	208	136	148	228	136	41	146	50	29	32	162	184	174	173	135																	549
Jedburgh	47	156	107	98	201	33	222	77	103	73	90	216	71	207	203	177	89	111	46	78	149	204																354
John o' Groat's House	314	235	284	326	206	369	339	294	279	365	294	172	277	181	160	163	293	315	331	304	266	131	361															706
Kelso	43	152	103	120	212	23	220	73	101	83	86	212	67	203	199	173	87	109	36	80	147	200	10	357														364
Kirkcudbright	99	208	159	64	253	135	115	129	112	26	142	268	121	259	255	225	98	120	116	90	157	256	102	391	112													364
Lanark	31	140	91	51	185	86	158	61	39	58	74	199	32	191	187	152	25	47	48	14	85	187	64	318	62	82												375
Montrose	72	37	12	149	82	127	210	42	119	143	29	93	96	85	106	141	112	134	89	123	137	135	119	266	115	171	103											464
Paisley	52	151	103	34	183	107	127	82	9	80	91	181	31	187	175	135	8	16	69	19	54	170	97	301	95	106	33	120										407
Peebles	22	131	82	62	176	61	179	52	60	56	65	191	46	182	178	152	46	68	39	35	106	179	41	336	32	78	27	94	54									378
Perth	40	83	39	94	126	95	159	22	68	111	22	129	45	120	116	90	61	83	57	72	86	114	87	272	83	139	71	51	69	62								432
Port Patrick	133	242	193	56	264	188	60	163	103	78	172	262	112	268	256	216	89	111	150	92	149	251	135	382	126	55	95	201	90	135	150							421
St. Andrews	40	84	29	117	128	95	191	10	91	111	12	124	64	126	147	126	84	106	57	77	118	146	87	304	83	139	71	41	92	62	32	173						432
Stirling	35	116	73	60	148	90	153	47	34	99	56	146	11	152	140	109	27	49	52	38	80	135	88	266	78	125	37	85	35	57	34	116	57					427
Thurso	316	263	312	354	234	371	367	295	307	387	295	200	305	209	188	191	321	343	333	332	294	159	363	20	359	415	331	294	329	338	273	410	305	294				708
Wick	295	242	291	333	213	350	346	274	286	366	274	179	284	183	167	170	300	322	312	311	273	138	342	19	338	394	310	273	308	317	252	389	284	273	21			687
Wigton	105	214	165	50	258	106	93	135	97	55	148	256	121	262	250	210	83	95	122	84	143	245	128	404	138	31	70	176	83	85	144	37	145	110	403	383		395
Carlisle	92	201	151	92	246	88	180	122	109	37	135	261	116	252	248	222	95	117	109	84	155	249	53	388	63	63	74	164	106	77	132	120	132	110	408	387	94	301

☞ The names of the various towns are arranged at each end of the line of figures, and the angle where the perpendicular and horizontal lines meet, gives the distance of the respective towns from each other.

THE
PICTURESQUE TOURIST
OF
SCOTLAND.

ORIGIN OF THE NAME—EXTENT—GENERAL ASPECT—NATURAL DIVISIONS—MOUNTAINS—VALES—RIVERS—LAKES—MINERAL PRODUCE—CLIMATE—AGRICULTURE—ANIMAL KINGDOM—FISHERIES—MANUFACTURES—COMMERCE—REVENUE—CONSTITUTION—RELIGIOUS INSTITUTIONS—ADMINISTRATION OF JUSTICE—POPULATION.

SCOTLAND is the northern and smaller division of the island of Great Britain. The origin of the term is involved in much obscurity. That part of the country which lies beyond the Firths of Forth and Clyde received from the Romans the appellation of Caledonia, and its inhabitants were denominated Caledonians. They were afterwards known by the name of Picts, and from them the country was for some centuries called Pictland. The term Scotland began to come into use for the first time, in the 11th century, and this name is supposed to have been derived from a colony of Scots, who had previously left Ireland, and planted themselves in Argyleshire and the West-Highlands.

Extent.—The longest line that can be drawn in Scotland is, from its most southerly point, the Mull of Galloway, in lat. 54° 38′ N., long. 4° 50′ W., to Dunnet Head, its most northerly point, in lat. 58° 40′ 30″ N., long. 3° 29′ W., or about 285 miles; but the longest line that can be drawn in about the same parallel of longitude is, from the former point to Cape Wrath, in lat. 58° 36′ N., long. 4° 56′ W., a distance of 275 miles. The breadth is extremely various. From Buchanness point to the point of Ardnamurchan in Argyleshire, the distance is 160 miles; but from the bottom of Loch Broom to the Firth of Dornoch, it is only 24 miles. The whole coast is so much penetrated by arms of the sea; that there is only one spot throughout its whole circuit upwards of 40 miles from the shore. The area of the mainland is computed at 25,520 square miles of land, and 494 of fresh water lakes; the islands are supposed to contain about 4080 square miles of land, and about 144 of water.

General Aspect.—The surface of the country is distinguished for variety, and, compared with England, it is, generally speaking, rugged and mountainous. It is supposed, that estimating the whole extent of the country, exclusive of lakes, at 19,000,000 acres, scarcely so many as 6,000,000 are arable, that is less than one-third; whereas in England, the proportion of arable land to the entire extent of the country exceeds three-fourths. With the exception of a few tracts of rich alluvial land along the courses of the great rivers, Scotland has no extensive tracts of level ground, the surface of the country being generally varied with hill and dale.

Natural Divisions.—Scotland is naturally divided into Highlands and Lowlands. The former division comprehends, besides the Hebrides, the Orkney and Shetland islands, the counties of Argyle, Inverness, Aberdeen, Banff, Elgin, Nairn, Ross, Cromarty, Sutherland, and Caithness, with parts of Dumbarton, Stirling, Perth, Forfar, and Kincardine, with the exception, however, of the level ground on the eastern coast to the south of the Moray Firth. The Highlands, again, are divided into two unequal portions, by the chain of lakes occupying the Glenmore-nan-albin, or "Great glen of Caledonia," stretching north-east and south-east across the island, from Inverness to Fort William, now connected together, and forming the Caledonian Canal. The northern division of the Highlands is decidedly the most barren and unproductive of the two, though the other division contains the highest mountains. In the eastern parts of Ross and Cromarty there are level tracts of considerable fertility. The Lowland division of the kingdom, though comparatively flat, comprises also a great deal of mountainous country.

MOUNTAINS.—Of the Highland mountains, the most celebrated is the chain of the Grampians. It commences on the east side of Loch Etive in Argyleshire, and terminates between Stonehaven and the mouth of the Dee on the eastern coast. The most elevated part of this range lies at the head of the Dee. Ben Macdui, the highest mountain in Scotland, rises to the height of 4418 feet, and the adjoining mountains of Cairngorm, Cairntoul, and Ben Avon, are respectively 4050, 4245, and 3967 feet high. The other principal summits of the Grampian chain are, Schehallion, near the east end of Loch Rannoch, 3613 feet above the level of the sea; Ben Lawers on the north side of Loch Tay, 3945; Ben More at the head of Glendochart, 3818; Ben Lomond, on the side of Loch Lomond, 3191; and Ben Cruachan at the head of Loch Awe, 3390. Ben Nevis, till recently reputed the highest of the British mountains, lies immediately to the east of Fort William, being separated from the Grampians by the moor of Rannoch; it rises 4358 feet above the level of the sea, and its circumference at the base is supposed to exceed 24 miles. To the south of the Grampians, and running parallel to them across the island, there is a chain of hills divided by the valleys of the Tay and the Forth into three distinct portions, and bearing the names of the Sidlaw, Ochil, and Campsie hills. The low country between them and the Grampians is called the valley of Strathmore. In the Lowland division of the country, the highest mountains lie on the confines of the counties of Dumfries, Peebles, Lanark, and Selkirk; Broadlaw in the parish of Tweedsmuir, the most elevated mountain in the south of Scotland, is 2741 feet above the level of the sea; Hartfell contiguous to Broadlaw, is 2635 feet above the level of the sea, and several of the neighbouring hills rise to the height of about 2000 feet.

Vales.—The most important level tracts in Scotland are, the Carse of Stirling and Falkirk, which occupies the country on both sides the Forth, from Borrowstounness on the south, and Kincardine on the north, westward to Gartmore; the tract between Dundee and Perth, bounded by the Sidlaw hills on the north, and the Tay on the south, denominated the Carse of Gowrie; the Merse of Berwickshire, extending from the Leader water along the Tweed to Berwick; and the valley of Strathmore, which comprises the low country in Angus and Perthshire, stretching from Laurencekirk in the former, to Methven in the latter. Besides these there are several smaller straths, such as Teviotdale in Roxburghshire, Tynedale in East Lothian, and the *How of Fife*.

RIVERS.—The principal rivers of Scotland are, the Tweed, the Forth, the Tay, and the Clyde. The Tweed rises in Tweedsmuir about 6 miles from Moffat. It runs first north-east to Peebles, then east, with a little inclination to the south, to Melrose; it next passes Kelso and Coldstream, and pursuing a north-easterly direction, falls into the sea at Berwick. During the latter part of its course, the Tweed forms the boundary between England and Scotland. The descent from its source to Peebles is 1000 feet, and thence to Berwick about 500 feet more. Including windings, its length is reckoned at rather more than 100 miles. Its principal tributaries are, the Ettrick which it receives near Selkirk; the Gala a little above, and the Leader a little below Melrose; the Teviot at Kelso; the Till at Tillmouth; and the Adder near Berwick.

The Forth rises on the east side of Ben Lomond, and runs in an easterly direction, with many windings, till it unites with the Firth of Forth at Kincardine. Its most important tributary is the Teith, which it receives a short way above Stirling. The Tay conveys to the sea a greater quantity of water than any other river in Britain. It has its source in the western extremity of Perthshire, in the district of Breadalbane, on the frontiers of Lorn in Argyleshire. At first it receives the name of the Fillan. After a winding course of eight or nine miles it spreads itself out into Loch Dochart, and, under the appellation of the Dochart, flows in an easterly direction through the vale of Glendochart, at the eastern extremity of which, having previously received the waters of the

Lochy, it expands into the beautiful long narrow lake, called Loch Tay. Issuing thence, it speedily receives a great augmentation by the river Lyon, and running north and east at Logierait, about eight miles above Dunkeld, it is joined by the Tummel. It now takes a direction more towards the south, to Dunkeld, where, on its right bank, it receives the beautiful river Bran. On leaving Dunkeld, it runs east to Kinclaven, and after receiving a considerable augmentation to the volume of its waters by the accession of the Isla, the Shochie, and the Almond, it flows in a south-westerly course to Perth. A short way below Perth, it assumes the appearance of a firth or estuary. At the foot of the vale of Strathearn, it receives on its right bank its last great tributary, the Earn, and gradually expanding its waters, it flows in a north-easterly direction past Dundee, till it falls into the sea, between Tentsmoor Point and Buttonness.

The Spey is admitted to be the most rapid of the Scottish rivers. It has its source in Loch Spey, within about six miles of the head of Loch Lochy. It runs in a north-easterly direction through Badenoch and Strathspey, to Fochabers, below which, it falls into the Moray Frith, at Garmouth. During its course, it receives numerous mountain streams, but no important tributary. From its source to its mouth, the distance is about 75 miles; but following its windings, its course is about 96 miles. Owing to the origin and course of its tributary waters, the Spey is very liable to sudden and destructive inundations. It flows through the best wooded part of the Highlands, and affords a water carriage for the produce of the extensive woods of Glenmore and Strathspey, large quantities of which are floated down to the seaport of Garmouth.

The Clyde is, in a commercial point of view, the most important river of Scotland. It has its origin in the highest part of the southern mountain land, at no great distance from the sources of the Tweed and the Annan. It flows at first in a northerly direction, with a slight inclination, to the east, as far as Biggar. Being joined by the Douglas, near Harperfield, it takes a north-west course by Lanark, Hamilton, and Glasgow, falling into the Firth of Clyde, below Dumbarton. Following its windings, the course of the Clyde, from its source to Dumbarton, is about 73 miles, but the length of the river, in a direct line, is only about 52 miles. Its principal tributaries are, the Douglas, Nethan, Avon, Mouse, Kelvin, Cart, and Leven. Of the celebrated falls of the Clyde, two are above, and two below Lanark; the uppermost is Bonninton Linn, the height of which is about 30 feet; the second fall is Cora Linn, where the water dashes over the rock in three distinct leaps; Dundaff Fall is 10 feet high, and at Stonebyres there are three distinct falls, altogether measuring about 76 feet in height. The Clyde is navigable at high water, as far as Glasgow, and large sums of money have been expended, especially of late, in improving and deepening the channel. The Forth and Clyde Canal falls into the latter river, at Dunglass, a little above Dumbarton.

Lakes.—The chief lakes of Scotland are, Loch Lomond, lying between Dumbartonshire and Stirlingshire; Loch Ness, in Inverness-shire; Loch Maree, in Ross-shire; Loch Awe, in Argyleshire; Lochs Tay, Rannoch, and Ericht, in Perthshire, &c.

Mineral Produce.—The minerals of Scotland are numerous and valuable. The great coal-field of Scotland extends, with little interruption, from the eastern, to the western coast. The most valuable part of this field, is situated on the north and south sides of the Forth, about the average breadth of 10 or 12 miles on each side, and on the north and south sides of the Clyde, ranging through Renfrewshire, part of Lanarkshire, and the north of Ayrshire. Detached coal-fields have also been found in various other parts of Scotland. Lime is very generally diffused throughout the country. Iron abounds in many parts, particularly in the Coal-field. Lead-mines are wrought to a great extent, at Leadhills, and at Wanlockhead, in Dumfries-shire. In the soil which covers these fields, a considerable quantity of gold was formerly found; copper-ore is found at Blair Logie, Airthrie, and at Fetlar, in Orkney; antimony at Langholm; silver has been wrought at Alva, in Clackmannanshire, and at Leadhills, in Lanarkshire; there are extensive slate-quarries in Argyleshire, Perthshire, and Peebles-shire; marble is found in Argyleshire, Sutherland, and the Hebrides; sandstone abounds generally throughout the country; and granite, and other primitive rocks, within the limits of the Grampians.

Climate.—The climate of Scotland is extremely variable; owing to its insular situation, however, neither the cold in winter, nor the heat in summer, are so intense as in similar latitudes on the continent. The annual average temperature may be estimated at from 44° to 47° of Fahrenheit. The quantity of rain which falls on the east coast of Scotland, varies from 22 to 26 inches, while on the west coast, and in the Hebrides, it ranges from 35 to 46 inches. The average number of days, in which either rain or snow falls in parts situated on the west coast is about 200, on the east coast about 145. The winds are more variable than in England, and more violent, especially about the equinoxes. Westerly winds generally prevail, particularly during autumn, and the early part of winter, but north-east winds are prevalent and severe, during spring, and the early part of summer.

Agriculture.—There is very great variety in the nature of the soil in Scotland; but it is generally inferior to that of England. Many of the valleys, however, are highly productive, and in Berwickshire, the three Lothians, Clydesdale, Fifeshire, the Carses of Stirling, Falkirk, and Gowrie, Strathearn, Strathmore, Moray, &c., there are tracts of land not inferior to any in the empire.

The following tables exhibiting the proportion which the cultivated parts of the soil bear to the uncultivated, were digested by Sir John Sinclair from his Statistical Account:—

Proportion of Cultivated and Uncultivated Soil.

	Eng. Acres.
Number of acres fully or partially cultivated, .	5,043,450
Acres uncultivated, including woods and plantations,	13,900,550
Total extent of Scotland in English acres, . .	18,944,000

Extent of Woods and Plantations.

	Eng. Acres.
Extent of plantations, ...	412,226
Extent of natural woods, ...	501,469
Total,	913,695

Nature of the Productive Soils.

	Eng. Acres.
Sandy soils, ...	263,771
Gravel, ...	681,862
Improved mossy soils, ...	411,096
Cold, or inferior clays, ...	510,265
Rich clays, ...	987,070
Loams, ...	1,869,193
Alluvial haugh, or carse land, ...	320,193
	5,043,450

Since these tables were compiled, however, extensive tracts of waste lands, particularly in the interior, have been planted with wood, and immense improvements have taken place in every department of agriculture.

Animal Kingdom.—The domestic animals common to Scotland, are the same as those of England, with some varieties in the breeds. Among the wild animals, the roe, and the red-deer are most worthy of notice. The golden-eagle and other birds of prey, are found in the mountainous districts, and the country abounds with all kinds of moor-game, partridges, and water-fowl.

Fisheries.—There are many valuable fisheries in Scotland; the salmon fisheries, especially, produce a large revenue to their owners, but during late years, they have experienced an extraordinary decline.

The herring fishery is carried on to a considerable extent, on the east coast of Scotland, and there are most productive and valuable fisheries of ling and cod, in the neighbourhood of the Shetland and Orkney Islands.

Manufactures.—The manufactures of Scotland, especially those of linen and cotton, are extensive and flourishing. The making of steam engines, and every other sort of machinery, is carried on to a great extent, and vast quantities of cast-iron goods are produced, especially at Carron, in Stirlingshire.

Commerce.—The commerce of Scotland has increased with astonishing rapidity, especially within a comparatively recent period, and a vast trade is now carried on, particularly with America and the West Indies. It is supposed, that since 1814, the increase in the principal manufactures and trades carried on in the country, and in the number of individuals employed in them, amounts to at least 30, or 35 per cent.

Revenue.—The increase in the revenue has fully kept pace with the increasing prosperity of the country. At the period of the Union, the revenue amounted only to £110,696; in 1788, it was £1,099,148; in 1813, it amounted to £4,204,097; and in 1831, to £3,525,114.

Constitution.—Under the Reform-Act of 1832, Scotland returns 53 members to the Imperial Parliament, of whom, 30 are for the shires, and 23 for the cities, boroughs, and towns; 27 counties return one member each, and the counties of Elgin and Nairn, Ross and Cromarty, and Clackmannan and Kinross, are combined in pairs, each of which returns one member. Of the cities, boroughs, and towns—76 in number—Edinburgh and Glasgow return two members each; Aberdeen, Paisley, Dundee, Greenock, and Perth, one each; the remaining burghs and towns are combined into sets or districts, each set, jointly, sending one member. The county population is 1,500,107, and the number of electors 33,115, giving one elector in every forty-five persons, whilst in the boroughs the population being 865,007, and the electors 31,332, the proportion is one in every twenty-seven persons. The Scottish Peers choose 16 of their number to represent them in the House of Lords. The Peers, like the Commoners, hold their seats for only one parliament.

Religious Institutions.—Scotland is divided into 1023 parishes, (including parishes, *quoad sacra,*) each of which is provided with one minister, or, in a few instances in towns, with two. The number of parishes, *quoad sacra,* has been increasing of late, but down to January 1836, the number above mentioned was the total amount. The stipends of the endowed clergy, with the glebe and manse, probably average from £260, to £300 a year. The government of the Church is vested in kirk-sessions, presbyteries, synods, and the General

Assembly. The number of churches belonging to dissenters of all denominations, amounts to 800, besides a considerable number of missionary stations. The incomes of the dissenting clergy are wholly derived from their congregations; they average, probably, from £120, to £130, a year, including a house and garden. In many cases, however, the income is considerably larger. Scotland has four Universities, that of St. Andrews, founded by papal authority in 1413; that of Glasgow by the same authority in 1450; that of Aberdeen, also with the sanction of the Pope, in 1494, though education did not commence there till 1500; and that of Edinburgh, the only one instituted since the Reformation, in 1582. None of these colleges or universities can be said to be liberally endowed. St. Andrews has 11 professorships; Glasgow 19; King's College, Aberdeen, 9; Marischal College 12; and Edinburgh 30. The aggregate number of students in these universities is at present above 3550, of which Edinburgh has 1459. Of the remaining 2091 Glasgow has above two-thirds. The attendance at St. Andrews and Aberdeen, particularly the former, is comparatively small. In every parish there is at least one school, for teaching the ordinary branches of education. The emoluments of the schoolmaster are derived from a small annual salary, with a free house and garden, provided by the landed proprietors, and moderate school fees. Private schools, also, are very numerous, and it is supposed, on good authority, that the total number of schools of every kind in Scotland, amounts to about 5162.*

* From returns made to the House of Commons, it appears that the voluntary schools are to the established schools nearly as four to one, or about 4000 to 1162. The aggregate attendance is calculated to amount to about 230,600, and adding to this number the pupils instructed in female seminaries, private boarding schools for boys, &c., we shall find that about a ninth part of the total population is receiving the benefit of education.

ADMINISTRATION OF JUSTICE.—The supreme civil court of Scotland, is called the Court of Session. It holds in Edinburgh two sessions, annually. The number of judges was formerly 15, but is now 13; they are styled Lords of Session, and sit in two courts or chambers, called the first and second divisions, which form, in effect, two courts of equal and independent authority. The Court of Justiciary, the supreme criminal court of Scotland, consists at present of six judges, who are also judges of the Court of Session. The president of the Court is the Lord Justice Clerk. The Court holds sittings in Edinburgh during the recess of the Court of Session, and twice a year, in the spring and autumn vacations, the judges hold circuits in the chief provincial towns, two going each circuit. There was formerly a Court of Exchequer, for the trial of cases connected with the revenue, but it is now abolished as a separate establishment, and the duties are devolved on one of the judges of the Court of Session. There are also inferior courts of law, viz. the courts of the boroughs, of the justices of peace, and of the sheriffs.

POPULATION.—The population of Scotland at the period of the Union, in 1707, is supposed not to have exceeded 1,050,000. In 1755, it amounted to 1,265,380, and in 1831, it had increased to 2,365,114, of which, 1,114,816 were males, and 1,250,298 females. The average population of Scotland per square mile, is 70.7. During the ten years ending with 1820, the entire population of Scotland increased 16 per pent., and during the ten years ending with 1830, 13 per cent.; while the population of the great towns increased during the same periods, 26¼, and 26½ per cent. The population of Scotland has increased less rapidly than that of England,

and much less so than that of Ireland; and, in consequence, the Scotch have advanced more rapidly than the English or Irish, in wealth, and the command of the necessaries and conveniences of life. Their progress in this respect has indeed been quite astonishing. The habits, diet, dress, and other accommodations of the people have been signally improved. It is not too much to affirm, that the peasantry of the present day are better lodged, better clothed, and better fed than the middle class of landowners a century ago!

The approach to Scotland by Tourists from other countries, must, of course, be determined by the particular views and circumstances of individuals. Those who enter the kingdom by the western road may either proceed to Glasgow, and assume it as their starting point, or to Edinburgh, visiting, on the way, the classic banks of the Tweed, Teviotdale, the valleys of Ettrick and Yarrow, with Melrose, Dryburgh, and Abbotsford. The great majority of Tourists come at once to the metropolis, and to all who, for the first time, approach Scotland on the east coast, this plan possesses many advantages. Edinburgh is not only easily reached from London, Hull, and Newcastle, but is in itself, with its environs, an object of very great interest and curiosity, and is by the increased facilities of travelling, placed cheaply within from one to two days journey of the finest scenery of Perth, Stirling, Dumbarton, and Argyleshires; while the approach to all of these scenes lies through those lowland districts which abound the most in landscape beauty, and in historical and traditionary interest. We shall therefore assume Edinburgh as our first great starting point, and commence our descriptions with a notice of that city and its interesting environs.

EDINBURGH.

SITUATION—ARCHITECTURE—POPULATION—LEGAL PROFESSION—MANUFACTURES—LITERATURE.

THE metropolis of Scotland is situated in the northern part of the County of Mid-Lothian, and is about two miles distant from the Firth of Forth.* Its length and breadth are nearly equal, measuring about two miles in either direction. Its site is generally admitted to be unequalled in panoramic splendour by any capital in Europe, and the prospect from the elevated points of the city and neighbourhood is of singular beauty and grandeur. The noble estuary of the Forth expanding from river into ocean, and reflecting from its bosom the villages and scattered dwellings that smile along its shores; the solitary grandeur of Arthur's Seat, with its majestic crags, its pastoral slopes, and sequestered valleys; the fertile fields, and the varied park and woodland scenery which enrich the southward prospect; the undulating acclivities of the Pentland Hills brightly outlined upon the sky, and the more shadowy splendour of the Lammermoors, the Ochils, and the Grampians, blending with the horizon in the obscurity of distance; these are some of the features in a landscape combining in one noble expanse, the richest elements of the beautiful and the sublime.

"Traced like a map, the landscape lies
In cultured beauty stretching wide;

* The precise geographical position of the centre of the city, is 55° 57′ 58″ north latitude, and 3° 11′ 55″ west longitude.

There Pentland's green acclivities;
There Ocean, with its azure tide;
There Arthur's Seat; and, gleaming through
Thy southern wing, Dunedin blue!
While in the orient, Lammer's daughters,
A distant giant range, are seen,
North Berwick-Law, with cone of green,
And Bass amid the waters." *

The resemblance between Edinburgh and Athens has been remarked by most travellers who have been so fortunate as to have visited both capitals. Edinburgh has hence acquired the honorary title of "The Modern Athens." Stuart, the author of "The Antiquities of Athens," was the first to draw attention to the circumstance, and his opinion has been confirmed by the high testimony of Dr. Clarke, and of Mr. H. W. Williams. Dr. Clarke remarks, that the neighbourhood of Athens is just the Highlands of Scotland enriched with the splendid remains of Art, and Mr. Williams observes, that if the lakes of Scotland were plains, he knows no country so like illustrious Greece. The latter author also adds, "The distant view of Athens from the Ægean Sea, is extremely like that of Edinburgh from the Firth of Forth, *though certainly the latter is considerably superior*.†

* Delta.

† From Mr. Chambers' interesting volume entitled "Walks in Edinburgh," we quote the parallel drawn between Edinburgh and Athens, by the distinguished artist above mentioned: "The epithets Northern Athens and Modern Athens," says Mr. Williams, "have been so frequeytly applied to Edinburgh, that the mind unconsciously yields to the illusion awakened by these terms, and imagines that the resemblance between these cities must extend from the natural localities, and the public buildings, to the streets and private edifices. The very reverse of this is the case; for, setting aside her public structures, Athens, even in her best days, could not have coped with the capital of Scotland. The truth is, that the comforts of the Athenians were constantly sacrificed to the public benefit; and the ruins which still remain to attest the unrivalled magnificence of the temples of Athens, afford no criterion by which we may judge of the character of her private dwellings. Athens,—as it now exists, independent of its ruins, and deprived of the charm of associa-

The general architecture of the city is very imposing, whether we regard the picturesque confusion of the buildings in the Old Town, or the symmetrical proportions of the streets and squares in the New. Of the public buildings it may be observed, that, while the greater number are distinguished by chaste design and excellent masonry, there are none of those sumptuous structures, which, like St. Paul's or Westminster Abbey, York Minster, and some other of the English provincial Cathedrals, astonish the beholder alike by their magnitude and their architectural splendour. But in no city of the kingdom is the general standard of excellence so well maintained. If there be no edifice to overwhelm the imagination by its

tion,—is contemptible; its houses are mean, and its streets scarcely deserve the name. Still, however, "when distance lends enchantment to the view," even the mud-walls of Athens assume features of importance, and the modern city appears almost worthy of the Acropolis which ornaments it. It is when seen under this advantage, that the likeness of Edinburgh to Athens is most strikingly apparent.

There are several points of view, on the elevated grounds near Edinburgh, from which this resemblance is almost complete. From Tor-Phin, in particular, one of the low heads of the Pentlands, immediately above the village of Colinton, the landscape is exactly that of the vicinity of Athens, as viewed from the bottom of Mount Anchesmus. Close upon the right, Brilessus is represented by the mound of Braid; before us, in the abrupt and dark mass of the Castle, rises the Acropolis; the hill Lycabetus, joined to that of the Areopagus, appears in the Calton; in the Firth of Forth we behold the Ægean Sea; in Inch-Keith, Ægina; and the hills of the Peloponnesus are precisely those of the opposite coast of Fife. Nor is the resemblance less striking in the general characteristics of the scene; for, although we cannot exclaim, "these are the groves of the Academy, and that the Sacred Way!" yet, as on the Attic shore, we certainly here behold,—

> " ———————— A country rich and gay,
> Broke into hills with balmy odours crowned,
> And ———————————————— joyous vales,
> Mountains and streams, ——————————
> And clustering towns, and monuments of fame,
> And scenes of glorious deeds, in little bounds!"

It is, indeed, most remarkable and astonishing, that two cities, placed at such a distance from each other, and so different in every political and artificial circumstance, should *naturally* be so alike. Were the National Monument to be erected upon the site of the present Barracks in the Castle, an important additional feature of resemblance would be conferred upon the landscape; that being the corresponding position of the Parthenon in the Acropolis."

magnificence, there are comparatively few to offend taste by their deformity or meanness of design. Above all, Edinburgh is wholly exempt from such examples of ostentatious deformity as in London may be seen to mingle with some of the most graceful specimens of domestic architecture in the Regent Park.

Nor are the natural or artificial beauties of the place its only attractions, for many of its localities teem with the recollections of "the majestic past," and are associated with events of deep historical importance. Other of its localities have been invested with an interest no less engrossing by the transcendant genius of Sir Walter Scott, whose novels have not only refreshed and embellished the incidents of history, but have conferred on many a spot formerly unknown to fame, a reputation as enduring as the annals of history itself.

In literary eminence, also, Edinburgh claims a distinguished place. At the commencement of the present century, its University displayed an array of contemporaneous talent unequalled by any similar institution either before or since,* and many of the present professors honourably uphold its scientific and literary reputation.

By the last population returns, made in 1831, the inhabitants of Edinburgh, with Leith, its sea-port, amounted to 161,909. Of this number, a large proportion is engaged in literary and professional pursuits, a circumstance which gives an elevated tone to the general society of the place. Some idea may be formed of the large proportion which the professional and other liberally educated classes bear to the other orders of society, by

* We have only to remind our readers of the names of Robertson, Playfair, Black, Cullen, Robison, Blair, Dugald Stewart, Gregory, and Monro, to vindicate what might otherwise appear a sweeping assertion.

comparing the population returns of Edinburgh with those of five other of the large towns of the kingdom.

NAMES OF TOWNS AND THEIR SUBURBS.	TOTAL POPULATION.	MALES 20 YEARS OF AGE.					MALE SERVANTS.	FEMALE SERVANTS.
		Employed in Manufactures, or in making Manufacg. Machiny.	Employed in Retail or Handicraft Trades.	Capitalists, Bankers, Professional, and other liberally educated Men.	Labourers employed in Labour not Agricultural.	Other Males (except Servants.)		
EDINBURGH and Leith.	161,909	792	19,764	7463	4448	2296	1422	12,429
GLASGOW.	202,426	19,913	18,832	2723	574	4012	946	8006
LIVERPOOL and Toxteth Park.	189,242	359	21,208	5201	16,095	1214	363	9033
MANCHEST. and Salford.	182,812	15,342	17,931	2821	7629	1695	398	3985
BRISTOL and Barton-Regis.	103,886	415	11,270	2654	7312	1867	814	5702
BIRMINGHAM.	146,986	5028	19,469	2388	5292	1371	966	5233

This table, compiled from the Parliamentary Returns, not only demonstrates the large proportion borne by the educated ranks to the general mass of the population, but, from the number of male and female domestic servants, it is also obvious that the average number of families in comfortable circumstances must exceed that of any of the other large towns of the empire. It must not, however, be concluded that there are many of the inhabitants of Edinburgh in circumstances of great opulence; in this respect it cannot be compared with the other towns in the table, but competence is as generally possessed and comfort as widely diffused as in any other community of like magnitude.

The prosperity of the city essentially depends upon its College and Schools, and still more essentially upon the

Courts of Judicature. The former attract many strangers who desire to secure for their families a liberal education at a moderate expense; the latter afford employment for the gentlemen of the Legal Profession, whose number is so great that they may be said to form one-third of the population in the higher and middle ranks of society.*

As there are no very extensive manufactures, the city is exempt from those sudden mercantile convulsions productive of so much misery in many other of the great towns of the kingdom. Printing and publishing are car-

* The great family of Lawyers may be divided into the following classes. The first class consists of the Judges of the Court of Session. Their nomination is with the Crown: they are now invariably chosen from among the Advocates, and, before their appointment, they must have been practising at the bar for at least five years. Their number was formerly 15, but is now reduced to 13. The Advocates (*Anglice* Barristers) form the second class. They are united into a Society or Incorporation called the Faculty of Advocates, and possess the privilege of pleading before every Court in Scotland, and also before the House of Lords. The present number of the body is about 450, but there are not one-third of them in practice, and probably not one-fifth of them subsist solely by their professional gains. A considerable number of them are gentlemen wholly independent of their profession, but who have joined the body on account of the status which they acquire from the learning and accomplishment of its members. The next class consists of the Writers to the Signet, who also form an Incorporation. They were originally called Clerks to the Signet, from their having been employed in the Secretary of State's office in preparing summonses, and other writts which received the Royal Signet, and they have still the sole privilege of preparing such writts. They are in other respects similar to the English Attorneys or Solicitors, and they are the oldest, most numerous, and most wealthy body of Law Practitioners in Scotland. Before admission to the body an apprenticeship of five years is required, and an attendance of two Sessions at one of the Universities, independent of four courses of the Law Classes. The number of the Society is at present nearly 700, of whom about 450 are in practice. The Solicitors before the Supreme Court, and Advocates' First Clerks, form another section of this class, their duties being the same as the Writers to the Signet, with the exception of their not being entitled to sign writts passing the Signet. These three classes, along with certain functionaries connected with the Court, form the College of Justice, which possesses certain privileges, the members being exempted from most of the local taxes; among others, from poors'-rates, and the annuity levied for payment of the stipend of the Clergy of Edinburgh. They are not amenable to the jurisdiction of any inferior Court, excepting the small debt Court held by the Sheriff. The Solicitors at Law, (who practise before the inferior Courts), the Accountants, and others, who pass under the more general name of Writers, are also included in the great family of Lawyers, but their distinctive peculiarities we think it unnecessary to mention here.

ried on to a large extent. In this department of industry Edinburgh far surpasses all the towns of the kingdom, London only excepted; many of the most valuable and popular works of the age emanating from the Edinburgh press.* Shawls and ale are also among the celebrated productions of the place; and there has recently been established on the banks of the Union Canal, a very extensive manufactory for the spinning of silk. Printing papers are manufactured to a large extent in the neighbourhood, but none of the mills are in the immediate vicinity of the city. Although there are several other branches of manufacture, they are for the most part on an insignificant scale.

The most convenient mode of imparting information to strangers, is to select a particular district of the city to be perambulated, describing the objects of interest on the way. With this view, we shall visit all the more important public buildings and institutions in successive walks, adding in notes such collateral or subordinate information as may appear necessary to convey a more accurate idea of the city and its institutions, as well as other matter which may tend to enliven the dullness of dry topographical details.

* The Edinburgh Review, the Encyclopædia Britannica, Blackwood's Magazine, Tait's Magazine, the Medical Journal, the Journal of Agriculture, and the Philosophical Journal, are some of the more important periodical publications. In circulation it is worthy of remark, that both Blackwood's and Tait's Magazines far exceed any of their London contemporaries.

Chambers' Journal deserves especial notice as being the most successful attempt ever made to circulate, at so cheap a rate, informatlon at once interesting and instructive to the great mass of the people. There are ten newspapers, of which two are published thrice a-week, three twice a-week, and the rest weekly.

WALK FIRST.

REGISTER-HOUSE—THEATRE-ROYAL—STAMP OFFICE—POST OFFICE—PRISON—BRIDEWELL—CALTON HILL—STEWART'S MONUMENT—OBSERVATORY—PLAYFAIR'S MONUMENT—CAMERA OBSCURA—NELSON'S MONUMENT—NATIONAL MONUMENT—HIGH SCHOOL—BURNS'S MONUMENT—HOLYROOD PALACE—HOLYROOD ABBEY—ARTHUR'S SEAT—HOUSE OF JOHN KNOX—NORTH BRIDGE.

THE central situation of the building, and the large number of hotels in its neighbourhood points out

THE REGISTER HOUSE

as an appropriate starting point. This handsome edifice, designed by the celebrated Robert Adams, is the Depository of the Public Records.* It forms a square of 200

* This important establishment includes various offices, such as the offices of the clerks and extractors of the Court of Session, of the Jury Court, and of the Court of Justiciary, the office of the Great and Privy Seal, of the Chancery, the Lord Lyon's office, the Bill-Chamber, &c. But it is most celebrated for the different registers which are there kept, and from which it derives its name. The most important and useful of these are the Registers of Sasines, of Inhibitions, and of Adjudications.

When a party wishes either to dispose absolutely of a landed estate in Scotland, or to grant a security over it, (such as an heritable bond,) it is necessary for him not only to grant a conveyance of the property to the purchaser or creditor, as the case may be, but also to give him infeftment or sasine, which is a symbolical delivery of the lands. An instrument of sasine is then written out by a notary, which must be recorded within sixty days in the Register of Sasines. And in the case of a competition it is not the party whose conveyance or instrument of sasine is *first in date*, but the party whose sasine is *first recorded*, who is preferred to the property. The sasine may be recorded either in the General Register for all Scotland, which is kept in the Register-House at Edinburgh, or in the Particular Register for the County where the lands lie. These County Registers are transmitted at stated periods to the Keeper of the Records in Edinburgh.

This is the manner in which a party *voluntarily* divests himself of his lands; but there are also two kinds of diligence, inhibition and adjudication, by which an individual's heritable property may be affected without his consent. By the former a debtor is prohibited from conveying or burdening his property to the prejudice of the creditor using the inhibition; by the latter, he is divested of the property, which, by a decree of the court, is declared to belong to his creditor, in satisfaction of his debt, and inhibition must be recorded within forty

feet, surmounted by a dome of 50 feet diameter. It contains upwards of 100 apartments for the transaction of public business. Among these the great room, in which the older records are deposited, is distinguished for its handsome proportions. Admission can only be obtained by an introduction to some of the public officers.

Directly opposite the east end of the Register House, stands

THE THEATRE-ROYAL.

Its exterior is plain almost to meanness, but its internal accommodation is excellent. Its management is unexceptionable, the manager, Mr. W. H. Murray, being equally esteemed for his distinguished ability in his profession, and for the virtues and accomplishments of his private life.*

Proceeding due east we enter Waterloo Place, and on

days of its date, either in the General Register of Inhibitions at Edinburgh, or in the Particular Register for the County, which, like the County Registers of Sasines, are transmitted at stated periods to the Keeper of the Records at Edinburgh. An abbreviate of a decree of adjudication must be recorded within sixty days of its date, in a register kept in the Register-House for that purpose, called the Register of Abbreviates of Adjudications.

A party, therefore, who wishes either to purchase a property or make a loan over it, may, by a search of the Registers of Sasines, Inhibitions, and Adjudications, ascertain whether there has been any previous sale or conveyance of it by the proprietor or his predecessors—to what extent it may be burdened with heritable debts—whether the proprietor has been prohibited by inhibition from granting any voluntary conveyance—or whether there has been any judicial assignation of it by adjudication. It is a principle of the Scotch law, that no party who has possessed a property upon an heritable title for forty years, shall be disquieted in his possession thereafter; and, also, that any party who may have possessed a title to a property without insisting in or prosecuting it for a period of forty years, shall be held to have abandoned his right. A forty years' search of the records, showing no incumbrances, is therefore generally considered sufficient evidence that the property is not liable to any burden or ground of eviction, and that any one may with safety either purchase it or lend money on its security. No such assurance of the safety of a transaction, relative to landed property, can be obtained in England, nor probably in any other country in Europe.

* A smaller theatre, under the same management, is open during the summer months. It stands at the head of Leith Walk, but possesses no architectural attraction.

the right pass successively, the STAMP OFFICE, and the POST OFFICE. The lightness of the open colonnades on either side of the street are generally much admired by English Tourists. It was upon entering this street, and contemplating the Calton Hill before him, that George IV. exclaimed in royal rapture, "How superb!" Still advancing in the same direction we reach the stair leading to the Calton Hill, from the top of which may be seen, in the churchyard across the street, the circular tower erected as a monument to David Hume the Historian. THE PRISON is immediately to the east of the churchyard, and a little further along in the same direction is BRIDEWELL. To both of these institutions strangers are admitted by orders from any of the magistrates of the city, which there is no difficulty in procuring.

Upon the left hand, in ascending the second flight of steps to the hill, is the graceful MONUMENT to DUGALD STEWART, a reproduction, with some variations, of the Choragic monument of Lysicrates. For the design of this monument, Edinburgh is indebted to the classical taste of Mr. Playfair. Close by, are THE OBSERVATORY, and MONUMENT to PROFESSOR PLAYFAIR. In the OLD OBSERVATORY, an unshapely building, occupying a prominent position a little to the west, is a CAMERA OBSCURA accessible to strangers, by an order from any of the subscribers. Upon the summit of the hill stands NELSON'S MONUMENT, a structure more ponderous than elegant, "modelled exactly after a Dutch skipper's spy-glass, or a butter churn,* but which, from the grandeur of its site, and greatness of dimensions, must be admitted to possess those attributes of sublimity which are independent of grandeur of design. The prospect from the top of the

* The Modern Athens. By a Modern Greek, London, 1825.

monument is very fine; the admission fee is sixpence for each person. Near Nelson's Monument are the twelve columns of the NATIONAL MONUMENT. The object proposed by the erection of this structure, was the commemoration of the heroes who fell at Waterloo. The splendour of the intended building, (which was to be a literal restoration of the Parthenon,) was worthy of so patriotic a cause, but, unfortunately the architectural taste of the projectors was far in advance of the pecuniary means at their disposal; and the monument, we fear, is doomed to commemorate the inadequacy of metropolitan means to give effect to the designs of metropolitan taste. The columns are very fine examples of Scottish masonry.

On the southern slope of the hill, overlooking the buildings of the Old Town,

THE HIGH SCHOOL

occupies a site worthy of its architectural beauty. The business of the school is conducted by a Rector, four Classical Masters, a French Teacher, a Teacher of Writing, and a Teacher of Arithmetic and Mathematics. Of these, the first five have a small endowment from the city in addition to the Class-fees. Although essentially a classical seminary, due consideration is given to those collateral branches of learning which form a necessary part of a liberal education. The extent of the building affords ample accommodation for conducting the business of instruction upon the most approved principles; and the play-ground, extending to nearly two acres, commands a fine prospect of the Old Town, Arthur's Seat, and the adjacent country.* Opposite the High

* In 1823 the increasing population of the city appeared to demand the institution of another seminary for the same branches of learning as the High School. THE NEW ACADEMY was accordingly then founded in the northern suburbs of

School, close upon the road side, stands BURNS' MONUMENT, with a statue of the Poet by Flaxman.

From this point a descent may be made by a footpath to the North Back of the Canongate, at the lower end of which the stranger reaches

HOLYROOD PALACE.

This ancient residence of Scottish Royalty is a handsome building of a quadrangular form, with a central court 94 feet square. Its front is flanked with double castellated towers, imparting to the building that military character which the events of Scottish History have so often proved to have been requisite in her Royal residences.

The changes which from time to time the edifice has undergone, renders it a matter of difficulty to affix a precise date to any part of it. The towers of the north-west corner, built by James V. are understood to be the most ancient portion of the present building. In 1822, previous to the visit of George IV. some improvements were made in its internal accommodation, and since that time its walls have undergone a thorough repair at the expense of the Crown. The most interesting relic is the BED OF QUEEN MARY, which remains in the same state as when

the city, by an influential body of the inhabitants, and its situation renders it more convenient for those residing in that neighbourhood. In both institutions the instruction of the pupils is conducted with the utmost zeal and success, many of them, after completing their curriculum of study, carrying off the highest honours in the Universities of Oxford and Cambridge. Still more recently has been instituted THE SOUTHERN ACADEMY for the convenience of the inhabitants of that quarter of the city. Here also the instruction of the pupils is most judiciously superintended. To the admirable mental culture these institutions afford, may principally be imputed the advanced intelligence which distinguishes the great body of the inhabitants of the Scottish Metropolis, a great proportion of the children of the higher and middle classes receiving their education in one or other of these seminaries. Besides the public Institutions, there are many admirably conducted private schools. Those interested in the instruction of the humbler ranks would do well to visit the CITY FREE SCHOOL in Niddry Street, and MR. WOOD'S SCHOOL in Market Street.

last occupied by that unhappy Princess. The CLOSET where the murderers of Rizzio surprised their victim, is also an object of interest to visitors. This bloody tragedy was acted on the 9th of March, 1566. "The Queen was seated at supper in a small cabinet adjoining to her bed-room, with the Countess of Argyle, Rizzio, and one or two other persons. Darnley suddenly entered the apartment, and, without addressing or saluting the company, gazed on Rizzio with a sullen and vindictive look; after him followed Lord Ruthven, pale and ghastly, having risen from a bed of long sickness to be chief actor in this savage deed; other armed men appeared behind. Ruthven called upon Rizzio to come forth from a place which he was unworthy to hold. The miserable Italian, perceiving he was the destined victim of this violent intrusion, started up, and, seizing the Queen by the skirts of her gown, implored her protection. Mary was speedily forced by the king from his hold. George Douglas, a bastard of the Angus family, snatched the King's own dagger from his side, and struck Rizzio a blow; he was then dragged into the outer apartment, and slain with 56 wounds. The Queen exhausted herself in prayers and entreaties for the wretched man's life; but when she was at length told that her servant was slain, she said, "I will then dry my tears, and study revenge." During the perpetration of this murder, Morton, the chancellor of the kingdom, whose duty it was to enforce the laws of the realm, kept the doors of the Palace with one hundred and sixty armed men, to insure the perpetration of the murder."*

Stains are still shewn at the door of the apartment,

* Scott's Scotland, vol. ii. p. 105.

said to be produced by the blood of the murdered man.* The largest apartment in the Palace is the Picture Gallery, which measures 150 feet long, by 27 broad. Upon the walls of this room are suspended the portraits of 106

* A pleasant story, suggested by these reputed blood-marks, occurs in the introductory chapter to the Second Series of Chronicles of the Canongate. Our readers, we are assured, will thank us for enlivening our narrative by here introducing it.

"My long habitation in the neighbourhood," says Mr. Chrystal Croftangry, "and the quiet respectability of my habits, have given me a sort of intimacy with good Mrs. Policy, the housekeeper in that most interesting part of the old building, called Queen Mary's Apartments. But a circumstance which lately happened has conferred upon me greater privileges ; so that, indeed, I might, I believe, venture on the exploit of Chatelet, who was executed for being found secreted at midnight in the very bedchamber of Scotland's Mistress.

It chanced, that the good lady I have mentioned, was, in the discharge of her function, showing the apartments to a cockney from London ;—not one of your quiet, dull, commonplace visitors, who gape, yawn, and listen with an acquiescent *umph*, to the information doled out by the provincial cicerone. No such thing—this was the brisk, alert agent of a great house in the city, who missed no opportunity of doing business, as he termed it, that is, of putting off the goods of his employers, and improving his own account of commission. He had fidgeted through the suite of apartments, without finding the least opportunity to touch upon that which he considered as the principal end of his existence. Even the story of Rizzio's assassination presented no ideas to this emissary of commerce, until the housekeeper appealed, in support of her narrative, to the dusky stains of blood upon the floor.

"These are the stains," she said ; "nothing will remove them from the place —there they have been for two hundred and fifty years—and there they will remain while the floor is left standing—neither water nor any thing else will ever remove them from that spot."

Now, our Cockney, amongst other articles, sold Scouring Drops, as they are called, and a stain of two hundred and fifty years standing was interesting to him, not because it had been caused by the blood of a Queen's favourite, slain in her apartment, but because it offered so admirable an opportunity to prove the efficacy of his unequalled Detergent Elixir. Down on his knees went our friend, but neither in horror nor devotion.

"Two hundred and fifty years, ma'am, and nothing take it away? Why, if it had been five hundred, I have something in my pocket will fetch it out in five minutes. D'ye see this elixir, ma'am? I will show you the stain vanish in a moment."

Accordingly, wetting one end of his handkerchief with the all-deterging specific, he began to rub away on the planks, without heeding the remonstrances of Mrs. Policy. She, good soul, stood at first in astonishment, like the Abbess of St. Bridget's, when a profane visitant drank up the vial of brandy which had long passed muster among the relics of the cloister for the tears of the blessed saint. The venerable guardian of St. Bridget probably expected the interference of her patroness—She of Holy Rood might, perhaps, hope that David Rizzio's spectre would arise to prevent the profanation. But Mrs. Policy stood not long

Scottish Kings, in a style of art truly barbarous. They appear to be "mostly by the same hand, painted either from the imagination, or porters hired to sit for the purpose."* In the olden time many a scene of courtly gaiety has enlivened this gloomy hall; among the last were the balls given by Prince Charles Edward in 1745. The election of the representative Peers of Scotland is now the only ceremony performed within its walls. In the south side of the quadrangle is the Hall of State fitted up for the levees of George IV. in 1822; and in the eastern side is the suite of apartments occupied by Charles X. (of France) and his family in 1830-33. The Palace is shewn to strangers by the domestics of the Duke of Hamilton, hereditary keeper. Three different persons are employed to exhibit the Palace and Abbey.

in the silence of horror. She uplifted her voice, and screamed as loudly as Queen Mary herself, when the dreadful deed was in the act of perpetration—

"Harrow now out! and walawa!" she cried.

I happened to be taking my morning walk in the adjoining gallery, ponderin in my mind why the Kings of Scotland, who hung around me, should be each and every one painted with a nose like the knocker of a door, when lo! the walls once more re-echoed with such shrieks, as formerly were as often heard in the Scottish palaces as were sounds of revelry and music. Somewhat surprised at such an alarm in a place so solitary, I hastened to the spot, and found the well-meaning traveller scrubbing the floor like a housemaid, while Mrs. Policy, dragging him by the skirts of the coat, in vain endeavoured to divert him from his sacrilegious purpose. It cost me some trouble to explain to the zealous purifier of silk-stockings, embroidered waistcoats, broad-cloth, and deal planks, that there were such things in the world as stains which ought to remain indelible, on account of the associations with which they are connected. Our good friend viewed every thing of the kind only as the means of displaying the virtue of his vaunted commodity. He comprehended, however, that he would not be permitted to proceed to exemplify its powers on the present occasion, as two or three inhabitants appeared, who, like me, threatened to maintain the housekeeper's side of the question. He therefore took his leave, muttering that he had always heard the Scots were a nasty people, but had no idea they carried it so far as to choose to have the floors of their palaces blood-boltered, like Banquo's ghost, when to remove them would have cost but a hundred drops of the Infallible Detergent Elixir, prepared and sold by Messrs. Scrub and Rub, in five shilling and ten shilling bottles, each bottle being marked with the initials of the inventor, to counterfeit which would be to incur the pains of forgery."

* Humphrey Clinker.

There is no fixed fee, the gratuities being left to the discretion of visitors. Many remonstrances have been made by the public press that an unnecessary number of domestics are thus employed, and that there should be no regulated admission-fee ; but such complaints have led to no redress of the grievance.

On the north side of the Palace, are the ruins of the

ABBEY OF HOLYROODHOUSE.

This Abbey was founded in 1128, by David I., a prince whose prodigal liberality to the clergy drew from James VI. the pithy observation that he was "a sair sanct for the Crown."* Of this building nothing now remains but the mouldering ruins of the chapel, situated immediately behind the palace. "It was fitted up by Charles I. as a chapel royal, that it might serve as a model of the English form of worship, which he was anxious to introduce into Scotland. He was himself crowned in it in 1633. James II. (VII. of Scotland) afterwards rendered it into a model of Catholic worship to equally little purpose. Since the fall of the roof in 1768, it has been a ruin."† In the south-east corner are deposited the remains of David II., James II., James V., and Magdalen his Queen, Henry Lord Darnley, and other illustrious persons. The precincts of the Abbey, including Arthur's Seat and Salisbury Crags, are a sanctuary for insolvent debtors. The limit of the privileged territory, on the side next the town, is marked by a strand or gutter at

* Tradition gives the following account of the foundation of the Abbey :—The pious David having been out hunting, was placed in the utmost peril by the attack of a stag. When defending himself from his assailant, a cross miraculously slipped from heaven into his hand, upon seeing which the stag instantly fled. The sequel is more credible. In a dream which visited the slumbers of the monarch, he was commanded to erect an abbey on the spot of his remarkable preservation, and in obedience to the heavenly mandate, he founded the Abbey of Holyroodhouse.

† Chambers' Picture of Scotland.

the foot of the Canongate, about a hundred yards from the Palace.*

The immediate proximity of Arthur's Seat may induce many tourists to ascend the hill from this point, the most favourable which can be selected for the purpose. Its height is 822 feet above the level of the sea, and the ascent being neither difficult nor dangerous, the tourist is amply rewarded for his slight exertion, by the magnificent prospect from the summit. "A nobler contrast there can hardly exist than that of the huge city, dark with the smoke of ages, and groaning with the various sounds of active industry or idle revel, and the lofty and craggy hill, silent and solitary as the grave; one exhibiting the full tide of existence, pressing and precipitating itself forward with the force of an inundation; the other resembling some time-worn anchorite, whose life passes as silent and unobserved as the slender rill, which escapes unheard, and scarce seen, from the fountain of his patron saint. The city resembles the busy temple, where the modern Comus and Mammon held their court, and thousands sacrifice ease, independence, and virtue itself, at their shrine; the misty and lonely mountain seems as a throne to the majestic but terrible genius of feudal times, where the same divinities dispensed coronets and domains to those who had heads to devise, and arms to execute bold enterprises."† On the left of the footpath leading up the hill stand the ruins of St. Anthony's Chapel,‡ and upon the right is the semicircular ridge of

* In Croftangrie, a narrow lane close by the Abbey, is a house said to have been occupied by the Regent Murray.

† Sir Walter Scott—Introduction to the Chronicles of the Canongate.

‡ The spot where Jeanie Deans is represented as having met with the ruffian Robertson, may be seen in ascending the hill, although no remains of the cairn are now visible. "It was situated,' says the novelist, "in the depth of the valley behind Salisbury Crags, which has for a background the north-western

bold and precipitous rocks known by the name of Salisbury Crags. Those who are indisposed to ascend the hill, may either walk along the top of the Crags or along the promenade immediately below.* From this walk may be seen the site of the cottage of Davie Deans, and other objects rendered imperishably interesting by the novels of Sir Walter Scott.

shoulder of the mountain, called Arthur's Seat, on whose descent still remain the ruins of what was once a chapel, or hermitage, dedicated to Saint Anthony the Eremite. A better site for such a building could hardly have been selected; for the chapel, situated among the rude and pathless cliffs, lies in a desert, even in the immediate vicinity of a rich, populous, and tumultuous capital; and the hum of the city might mingle with the orisons of the recluses, conveying as little of worldly interest as if it had been the roar of the distant ocean. Beneath the steep ascent on which these ruins are still visible, was, and perhaps is still pointed out, the place where the wretch Nicol Muschat had closed a long scene of cruelty towards his unfortunate wife, by murdering her with circumstances of uncommon barbarity. The execration in which the man's crime was held, extended itself to the place where it was perpetrated, which was marked by a small *cairn* or heap of stones, composed of those which each passenger had thrown there in testimony of abhorrence, and on the principle, it would seem, of the ancient British malediction, 'May you have a cairn for your burial-place.'"—*Heart of Mid-Lothian.*

* "If I were to choose a spot from which the rising or setting sun could be seen to the greatest possible advantage, it would be that wild path winding around the foot of the high belt of semi-circular rocks, called Salisbury Crags, and marking the verge of the steep descent which slopes down into the glen on the south-eastern side of the City of Edinburgh. The prospect, in its general outline, commands a close-built, high-piled city, stretching itself out in a form which, to a romantic imagination, may be supposed to represent that of a dragon; now a noble arm of the sea, with its rocks, isles, distant shores, and boundary of mountains; and now, a fair and fertile champaign country, varied with hill, dale, and rock, and skirted by the picturesque ridge of the Pentland Mountains. But as the path gently circles around the base of the cliffs, the prospect, composed as it is of these enchanting and sublime objects, changes at every step, and presents them blended with, or divided from each other, in every possible variety which can gratify the eye and the imagination. When a piece of scenery so beautiful, yet so varied—so exciting by its intricacy, and yet so sublime—is lighted up by the tints of morning or of evening, and displays all that variety of shadowy depth, exchanged with partial brilliancy, which gives character even to the tamest of landscapes, the effect approaches near to enchantment. This path used to be my favourite evening and morning resort, when engaged with a favourite author, or new subject of study."—*Heart of Mid-Lothian.*

The solid and commodious pathway which has now superseded the winding footpath above described, was suggested by this glowing eulogy of the surrounding landscape.

Retracing our steps to Holyrood, and proceeding up the Canongate, we reach, upon the left, MORAY HOUSE, the ancient mansion of the Earls of Moray, erected in 1618. From the balcony in front of the building, the Marquis of Argyle and his family saw the Marquis of Montrose conducted to prison, from whence he was shortly afterwards led to execution. Still ascending the street, we pass, upon the right and left, Leith Wynd and St. Mary's Wynd, two narrow streets, the latter of which is the great emporium for the sale of old clothes. At the head of the Netherbow, where it expands into the High Street, stands the HOUSE OF JOHN KNOX. Over the door is an inscription, at present totally eclipsed by the numerous signboards of the inhabitants, but which if visible would run thus:

LUFE · GOD · ABOVE · AL · AND · YOUR · NICHBOUR · AS · YOUR · SELF.

Close beneath the window from which Knox is said to have preached to the populace, there has long existed a coarse effigy of the Reformer stuck upon the corner in the attitude of addressing the passers by.* After having

* "Of this no features were, for a long time, discernible, till Mr. Dryden * about three years ago, took shame to himself for the neglect it was experiencing, and got it daubed over in glaring oil-colours, at his own expense. Thus a red nose, and two intensely black eyes were brought strongly out upon the mass of the face; and a pair of white-iron Geneva bands, with a new black gown, completed the resuscitation. A large canopy of Chinese fashion, hung at the edges with tassels, was spread over the preacher's head, making him look much finer than he had ever done in his life-time, and a demure precentor was placed underneath his yellow pulpit, in order to prevent strangers from taking up an idea that our great Reformer, like the poor itinerant Methodists of modern times, had to direct the singing as well as the doctrine of his hearers. The precentor, however, was not very well used in his station, for, provoking only the laughter of the spectators, while the preacher excited their veneration, he was soon after taken down. There is a stone in the building, at a little distance

* An intelligent tonsor occupying the house at the time Mr. Chambers visited the premises. The house is now possessed by a member of the same family, who cherishes the effigy of the Reformer with similar affection, and displays a more classical taste in its colouring and decorations.

bestowed a becoming meed of admiration on this great effort of sculpture, the stranger will pursue his way up the High Street. The stupendous height of many of the houses will to some strangers be matter of surprise. From either side of the street descend numerous lanes or *closes,* of a width frequently limited to six feet, and so steep as to be of very laborious ascent. In these closes are the squalid abodes of some of the lowest of the population.

Upon reaching the North Bridge, our first walk will terminate by returning to the Register Office. If the stranger desires to prolong it, he will continue to ascend the High Street, commencing with the Tron Church. For the sake of arrangement, however, we must designate the next division of his progress the Second Walk.

WALK SECOND.

TRON CHURCH—ROYAL EXCHANGE—ST. GILES'S CATHEDRAL—PARLIAMENT HOUSE—ADVOCATES' LIBRARY—SIGNET LIBRARY—COUNTY HALL—BANK OF SCOTLAND—CASTLE—GEORGE IV. BRIDGE—HERIOT'S HOSPITAL.

PROCEEDING as before from the Register Office, the stranger will now walk along the North Bridge. From

from the diminutive pulpit, and pointed at by the preacher, bearing the name of the Deity in Greek, Latin, and English carved upon it, from which rays seem to diverge upon the side next the effigy, and clouds upon the side most remote from his irradiating finger. Some ingenuity seems to have been exercised here, in painting the radiance of a bright saffron, while the reprobate clouds are treated with a villanous dark green,—a distinction of wonderful delicacy, considering what the rays and the clouds are intended to emblematise. The modern possessor, to whom the general thanks of Scotland are due, takes care to paint the whole piously over every second of May."—TRADITIONS OF EDINBURGH, Vol. i. p. 243.

each side of the parapet is an extensive view of the city towards the east and the west. The fish and vegetable markets may be seen immediately below, upon the west side of the parapet. At the upper end of the North Bridge is the High Street, part of which the stranger traversed in the preceding walk. Its length from the Castle to Holyrood Palace is about a mile.* At the point where the High Street and the North and South Bridges cross each other, stands the Tron Church, an edifice of no architectural pretension. It derived its name from a *tron* or weighing beam in its immediate neighbourhood, to which in former times it was customary to nail false notaries and other malefactors by the ears. Its clock is provided with a dial plate of dimmed glass, which is lighted with gas from the inside after nightfall.

Ascending the High Street,

THE ROYAL EXCHANGE BUILDINGS

lie upon the right hand side of the way opposite St. Giles's Cathedral. The Council Chamber for the meetings of the Magistracy and various other apartments for the transaction of municipal business, occupy that side of the quadrangle opposite the entrance. Parties proposing to visit the Crown Room in the Castle, will here obtain orders of admission on the terms mentioned on page 48 of the present work. The spot where the city Cross formerly stood is now indicated by a radiated pavement about twenty-five yards from the entrance to the Exchange.

* Although we have here given the general designation of High Street to this imposing line of buildings, its various divisions, commencing at the Castle, are severally known by the names, Castle Hill—Lawnmarket—High Street—Netherbow and Canongate.

ST. GILES'S CATHEDRAL

is nearly opposite the Royal Exchange. It derives its name from its patron, St. Giles, abbot and confessor, and tutelar saint of Edinburgh.* The date of its foundation

* Mr. Stark, in his very accurate work, relates that the legend regarding St. Giles, describes him as "a native of Greece born in the sixth century. On the death of his parents, he gave all his estate to the poor, and travelled into France, where he retired into the deep recess of a wilderness, near the conflux of the Rhone with the sea, and continued there for three years, living upon the spontaneous produce of the earth and the milk of a doe. Having obtained the reputation of extraordinary sanctity, various miracles were attributed to him; and he founded a monastery in Languedoc, long after known by the name of St. Giles. In the reign of James II. Mr. Preston of Gourton, a gentleman whose descendants still possess an estate in the county of Edinburgh, procured a supposed arm bone of this holy man, which relic he most piously bequeathed to the Church of St. Giles in Edinburgh. In gratitude for this invaluable donation, the magistrates of the city, in 1454, considering that the said bone was 'freely left to oure moyer kirk of Saint Gele of Edinburgh, withoutyn ony condition makyn, granted a charter in favour of Mr. Preston's heirs, by which the nearest heir of the name of Preston was entitled to the honour of carrying it in all public processions. This honour the family of Preston continued to enjoy till the Reformation."—*Picture of Edinburgh*, p. 217.

is unknown. It is first mentioned in the year 1359, in a charter of David II. In 1466, it was made a collegiate church, and no fewer than forty altars were at this period supported within its walls. The Scottish poet, Gavin Douglas, (the translator of Virgil,) was for some time Dean of St. Giles. After the Reformation it was partitioned into four places of worship, and the sacred vessels and relics which it contained, including the arm-bone referred to in the preceding note, were seized by the magistrates of the city, and the proceeds of their sale applied to the repairing of the building. On the 13th October 1643, the Solemn League and Covenant was sworn to and subscribed within its walls by the Committee of Estates of Parliament, the Commission of the Church, and the English Commission. The Regent Murray and the Marquis of Montrose are interred near the centre of the south side of the church, and on the outside of its northern wall is the monument of Napier of Merchiston, the inventor of logarithms.

The cathedral is now divided into three places of worship, viz. the High Church, the Tolbooth Church, and a Hall, originally intended for the meetings of the General Assembly, but which, after its completion, was found to be unfit for the purpose. In the High Church the Magistrates of the City, the Judges of the Court of Session, and the Barons of Exchequer, attend divine service in their official robes. The patronage of these, as well as of all the other city churches, is vested in the Magistrates and Town Council. The remains of John Knox, the intrepid Ecclesiastical Reformer, were deposited in the cemetry of St. Giles, which formerly occupied the ground where the buildings of the Parliament Square now stand.

With the exception of the spire, the whole of the external walls of the Cathedral have in recent years been renovated—a circumstance which has materially impaired the venerable aspect of the building.

In the centre of the Parliament Square, of which the Cathedral just described may be said to form the northern side, stands The Equestrian Statue of Charles II., which, in vigour of design and general effect, still maintains its rank as the best specimen of bronze statuary which Edinburgh possesses.

The Chambers of the Court of Exchequer, the Parliament House, and the Libraries of the Faculty of Advocates and of the Writers to the Signet, form the eastern, western, and southern sides of the Square.

THE PARLIAMENT HOUSE

is situated in the south-west angle. The large hall, now known by the name of the *Outer-House,* is the place in which the Scottish Parliament met before the Union. This hall is 122 feet long by 49 broad. Its roof is of oak, arched and handsomely finished. It contains two statues, one of Henry Dundas, the first Lord Melville, and the other of that eminent lawyer, Lord President Blair, who died in 1811. At the south end of the Outer-House are four small chambers or Courts, in which the Lords Ordinary sit. Entering from the east side, are two larger Courts of modern and elegant structure, appropriated to the First and Second Divisions of the Court, before whom are tried those cases which are of unusual importance or difficulty, or where the judgment of a Lord Ordinary has been brought under review of the Court by a reclaimer or appeal. Adjoining to the Court-Rooms of the Divisions is another Court-Room of nearly similar appearance, in which sits the High Court of Justiciary, the supreme criminal tribunal of Scotland.

In session time, and during the hours of business, the Outer-House presents a very animated scene. As all the Courts open into it, it affords a very convenient promenade or lounging place for all those counsel or agents whose cases are not then actually going on in Court. The well-employed advocates may be seen flitting from bar to bar, or Court to Court, while agents whose causes have just been called may be observed pressing through the crowd, with anxious face and hurried step, looking out for the counsel, whose absence from the debate might be ruin to their clients. Occasionally may be seen some unfortunate litigant, receiving, with all reverence and humility, an opinion on the merits of his case from one of the fathers of the bar, his countenance unequivocally indicating whether he is saddened by the prospect of defeat or cheered with the hope of success. The less employed and unemployed counsel and agents, and a number of loungers who make this hall a place of resort, may be seen in groups conversing together, in every variety of tone and manner, from the gravity of consultation to the gaiety of uncontrolled merriment.

THE ADVOCATES' LIBRARY

adjoins the Parliament House, with which it has a communication. It contains the most valuable collection of books in Scotland, the printed works amounting to 150,000 volumes, and the manuscripts to 1700. The collection of Scottish poetry is exceedingly rare and curious. The volumes in this department amount to nearly 400, and the number is likely to be still further increased by the zeal and research of Dr. Irving, the present librarian, who devotes unremitting attention to augment its treasures. Of the manuscripts the most valuable are those relating to the civil and ecclesiastical history of Scotland. The funds of the Library are chiefly derived from the fees paid by each advocate upon his entering as a member of the Faculty. It is also one of the five libraries which receive from Stationers' Hall a copy of every new work published in Great Britain or Ireland. No public institution in Great Britain is conducted with greater liberality. Strangers are freely admitted without introduction; and no one who is at all known, is ever denied the privilege of resorting to, and of reading or writing in the Library. The members are entitled to borrow twenty-five volumes at one time, and to lend any of the books so borrowed to their friends. The literary wealth of the library is at present deposited in a suite of apartments neither spacious, elegant, nor commodious. It is proposed to build a new library in the neighbourhood for their reception. The office of principal librarian has been held by men eminently distinguished in the world of letters, Thomas Ruddiman, David Hume, and Adam Ferguson, having honoured the institution by filling this situation; and David Irving, LL.D., who at present holds the appointment, is an accomplished scholar, a learned civilian, and eminently skilled in ancient Scottish history, biography, and poetry.

THE SIGNET LIBRARY

is also immediately adjoining to the Parliament House. It possesses two handsome rooms, one of which was acquired a few years ago from the Advocates' Library. These rooms, more especially the upper one, are well worthy the attention of strangers. This Library is peculiarly rich in the department of history, more especially in British and Irish history. The total number of volumes it contains may be estimated at 50,000. It is supported exclusively by the contributions of the Writers to Her Majesty's Signet, and the same liberality which distinguishes the Advocates' Library, also prevails in the management of its affairs. The present librarian, Mr. David Laing, is distinguished by the extent and accuracy of his bibliographical knowledge. He also possesses that general acquaintance with literature which forms one of the most valuable qualifications for the office which he holds.

THE COUNTY HALL stands at the western termination of the Libraries above described. The general plan is taken from the Temple of Erectheus at Athens, and the principal entrance, from the Choragic Monument of Thrasyllus. The Hall is decorated with a Statue of Lord Chief Baron Dundas, by Chantry.

THE OLD TOLBOOTH, which the inhabitants sometimes quaintly called "The Heart of Mid-Lothian," and which under this name has become so renowned in the novel of Sir Walter Scott, formerly stood in the middle of the High Street, at the north-west corner of St. Giles's Church.* This gloomy looking building was built in 1561. From that period till the year 1640, it served for the accommodation of Parliament and the Courts of Justice, as well as for the confinement of prisoners; but after the erection of the present Parliament House, it was employed only as a prison. Its situation, jammed as it was into the middle of one of the chief thoroughfares of the city, was signally inconvenient, and in 1817, when the New Prison was prepared for the re-

* A ludicrous blunder was lately committed by one of those itinerant orators who constitute themselves the political instructors of the people. Conscious of the value of a striking exordium in rivetting the attention of his auditors, the orator opened his speech in these words, "Men of the Heart of Mid-Lothian!" The compliment was, of course, acknowledged by a unanimous burst of laughter.

ception of inmates, the ancient pile of the Tolbooth was demolished. The great entrance-door, with its ponderous padlock and key, were removed to Abbotsford, the seat of Sir Walter Scott, where they are now to be seen with the other curiosities of the place. Alluding to the removal of these relics, Sir Walter observes, "it is not without interest that we see the gateway through which so much of the stormy politics of a rude age, and the vice and misery of later times, had found their passage, now occupied in the service of rural economy. Last year, to complete the change, a tom-tit was pleased to build her nest within the lock of the Tolbooth—a strong temptation to have committed a sonnet, had the author, like Tony Lumpkin, been in a concatenation accordingly."

Proceeding up the High Street we pass, upon the left, George the Fourth's Bridge, and on the right, Bank Street, at the foot of which stands THE BANK OF SCOTLAND, an edifice of high architectural merit, erected at an expense of £75,000. At the head of the High Street, upon a precipitous rocky eminence, stands

THE CASTLE.

Edinburgh Castle is one of the four fortresses which, by the Articles of Union, are to be kept constantly fortified.* It consists of a series of irregular fortifications, and although, before the invention of gunpowder, it might be considered impregnable, it is now a place of more apparent than real strength. Its elevation is 383 feet above the level of the sea, and from various parts of the fortifications a magnificent view of the surrounding country may be obtained. It contains accommodation for 2000 soldiers, and its armoury affords space for 30,000 stand

* The other fortresses included in this provision are the Castles of Dumbarton, Blackness, and Stirling.

of arms. Facing the north-east is the principal or Half-Moon Battery, mounted with twelve, eighteen, and twenty-four pounders, the only use of which, in these piping times of peace, is to fire on holydays and occasions of public rejoicing. The architectural effect of the Castle has been much marred by a modern addition on its western side, designed in a style most uncongenial to the character of a fortress.

In the earlier periods of Scottish history this fortress experienced the vicissitudes common to the times, and was frequently taken and re-taken by various conflicting parties. In the present work we can only advert to one or two of the more striking events in its annals.

In 1296, during the contest for the crown between Bruce and Baliol, it was besieged and taken by the English. It still remained in their possession in 1313, at which time it was strongly garrisoned and commanded by Piers Leland, a Lombard. This governor having fallen under the suspicion of the garrison, was thrown into a dungeon, and another appointed to the command, in whose fidelity they had complete confidence. It has frequently been remarked that in capturing fortresses, those attacks are generally most successful which are made upon points where the attempt appears the most desperate. Such was the case in the example now to be narrated. Randolph Earl of Moray was one day surveying the gigantic rock, and probably contemplating the possibility of a successful assault upon the fortress, when "he was accosted by one of his men-at-arms with the question, 'Do you think it impracticable, my lord?' Randolph turned his eyes upon the querist, a man a little past the prime of life, but of a firm, well-knit figure, and bearing in his bright eye, and bold and open brow, indications of an intrepidity which had already made him remarkable in the Scottish army.

"Do you mean the rock, Francis?"* said the earl; "perhaps not, if we could borrow the wings of our gallant hawks."

"There are wings," replied Francis, with a thoughtful smile, "as strong, as buoyant, and as daring. My father was keeper of yonder fortress."

"What of that? you speak in riddles."

"I was then young, reckless, high-hearted; I was mewed up in that convent-like castle; my mistress was in the plain below—"

"Well, what then?"

"'Sdeath, my lord, can you not imagine that I speak of the wings of love? Every night I descended that steep at the witching hour, and every morning before the dawn, I crept back to my barracks. I constructed a light twelve-foot ladder, by means of which I was able to pass the places that are perpendicular; and so well, at length, did I become acquainted with the route, that in the darkest and stormiest night, I found my way as easily as when the moonlight enabled me to see my love in the distance, waiting for me at her cottage door."

"You are a daring, desperate, noble fellow, Francis! However, your motive is now gone; your mistress—"

"She is dead: say no more; but another has taken her place."

"Ay, ay, it is the soldier's way. Woman will die, or even grow old; and what are we to do? Come, who is your mistress now?"

"My Country. What I have done for love, I can

* The soldier's name was William Frank. Mr. Leitch Ritchie here uses the novelist's licence in dealing with the name, and in throwing the story into the form of a dialogue, but the events are faithfully narrated.

do again for honour; and what *I* can accomplish, you, noble Randolph, and many of our comrades, can do far better. Give me thirty picked men, and a twelve-foot ladder, and the fortress is our own!"

The Earl of Moray, whatever his real thoughts of the enterprise might have been, was not the man to refuse such a challenge. A ladder was provided, and thirty men chosen from the troops; and in the middle of a dark night, the party, commanded by Randolph himself, and guided by William Francis, set forth on their desperate enterprise.

By catching at crag after crag, and digging their fingers into the interstices of the rocks, they succeeded in mounting a considerable way; but the weather was now so thick, they could receive but little assistance from their eyes; and thus they continued to climb, almost in utter darkness, like men struggling up a precipice in the nightmare. They at length reached a shelving table of the cliff, above which the ascent, for ten or twelve feet, was perpendicular; and having fixed their ladder, the whole party lay down to recover breath.

From this place they could hear the tread and voices of the "check-watches" or patrol above; and surrounded by the perils of such a moment, it is not wonderful that some illusions may have mingled with their thoughts. They even imagined that they were seen from the battlements; although, being themselves unable to see the warders, this was highly improbable. It became evident, notwithstanding, from the words they caught here and there, in the pauses of the night-wind, that the conversation of the English soldiers above, related to a surprise of the castle; and at length, these appalling words broke like thunder on their ears: "Stand! I see you well!" A fragment of the rock was hurled down at the same instant; and, as rushing from crag to crag, it bounded over their heads, Randolph and his brave followers, in this wild, helpless, and extraordinary situation, felt the damp of mortal terror gathering upon their brow, as they clung, with a death-grip, to the precipice.

The startled echoes of the rock were at length silent, and so were the voices above. The adventurers paused, listening breathless; no sound was heard but the sighing of the wind, and the measured tread of the sentinel, who had resumed his walk. The men thought they were in a dream, and no wonder; for the incident just mentioned, which is related by Barbour, was one of the most singular coincidences that ever occurred. The shout of the sentinel, and the missile he had thrown, were merely a boyish freak; and while listening to the echoes of the rock, he had not the smallest idea that the sounds which gave pleasure to him, carried terror, and almost despair, into the hearts of the enemy.

The adventurers, half uncertain whether they were not the victims of some illusion, determined that it was as safe to go on as to turn back; and pursuing their laborious and dangerous path, they at length reached the bottom of the wall. This last barrier they scaled by means of their ladder; and leaping down among the astonished check-watches, they cried their war-cry, and in the midst of answering shouts of "treason! treason!" notwithstanding the desperate resistance of the garrison, captured the Castle of Edinburgh."*

Robert Bruce then entirely demolished its fortifications, that it might not again be occupied by a hostile power.

* Heath's Picturesque Annual. *Scott and Scotland*, pp. 174-7.

The wisdom of this policy was subsequently proved by the conduct of Edward III. who, on his return from Perth, caused it to be rebuilt and strongly garrisoned. But his possession of it was destined to be of short duration. One of those stratagems characteristic of the adventurous spirit of the times, was successfully resorted to for its deliverance. In 1341, Sir William Douglas, with three other gentlemen, waited upon the governor. One of them professing to be an English merchant, informed him that he had a vessel in the Forth richly laden with wine, beer, and biscuits exquisitely spiced, and produced at the same time samples of the cargo. The governor, pleased with their quality, agreed for the purchase of the whole, which the pretended captain requested permission to deliver early next day to avoid interruption from the Scots. He accordingly arrived at the time appointed, attended by a dozen of armed followers, disguised as seamen, and the gates being opened for the reception of the provisions, they contrived, just in the entrance, to overturn one of the carriages, thus effectually preventing the closing of the gates. The porter and guards were then put to the sword, and the assailants being re-inforced by Douglas and his party, who lay in ambush near the entrance, the English garrison was overpowered, and expelled from the castle.

During the reign of Queen Mary, when the country was distracted by intestine wars, this fortress was gallantly defended for the Queen by Kircaldy of Grange. The rest of Scotland had submitted to the authority of Morton the Regent, Kircaldy alone, with a few brave associates, remaining faithful to the cause of his Royal Mistress. Morton was unable, with the troops at his command, to reduce the garrison, but Elizabeth having sent Sir William Drury to his aid with 1500 foot, and a train of artillery, trenches were opened, and approaches regularly carried on against the castle. For three and thirty days Kircaldy gallantly resisted the combined forces of the Scots and English, nor did he demand a parley till the fortifications were battered down, and the wells were dried up, or choked with rubbish. Even then, with a heroism truly chivalrous, he determined rather to fall gloriously behind the ramparts, than surrender to his enemies. But his garrison were not animated with the same inflexible courage. Rising in a mutiny, they compelled him to capitulate. Drury, in the name of his mistress, engaged that he should be honourably treated; but Elizabeth, insensible alike to the claims of valour, and to the pledged honour of her own officer, surrendered Kircaldy to the Regent, who, *with her consent,* hanged the gallant soldier and his brother at the Cross, on the 3d of August 1573.

In 1650 the castle was besieged by the Parliamentary army, under Cromwell; and capitulated on honourable terms. In 1745, although Prince Charles Stuart held possession of the city, he did not attempt the reduction of the castle. In modern times, some of the prisoners during the French war, were confined within its walls. THE SCOTTISH REGALIA are exhibited in the Crown-Room every day from twelve till three o'clock. Visitors are gratuitously admitted by an order from the Lord Provost, which may be obtained by applying at the City Chambers between eleven and three o'clock. Persons procuring orders are required to sign their names and places of residence in a book kept in the City Chambers for this purpose, and the order is available only upon that day on which it is dated. These insignia of Scottish Royalty consist of a Crown, Sceptre, and Sword of State.* Along with them is also shewn the Lord Treasurer's Rod of Office, found deposited in the same strong oak chest in which the Regalia were discovered. The room where Queen Mary gave birth to James VI., in whom the crowns of England and Scotland were united, will be an object of interest to many strangers. The gigantic piece of artillery called MONS MEG, from being cast at Mons in Flanders, is mounted on an elegant carriage on the Bomb Battery. It was employed at the siege of Norham, and afterwards burst, when firing a salute to the Duke of York in 1682, since which time it has never been repaired.

In returning from the Castle, an opening upon the left, immediately upon leaving the esplanade, conducts to the house of Allan Ramsay, the author of "The Gentle Shep-

* "Taking these articles in connection with the great historical events and personages that enter into the composition of their present value, it is impossible to look upon them without emotions of singular interest, while, at the same time, their essential littleness excites wonder at the mighty circumstances and destinies which have been determined by the possession or the want of possession of what they emblematise and represent. *For* this diadem did Bruce liberate his country; *with* it, his son nearly occasioned its ruin. It purchased for Scotland the benefit of the mature sagacity of Robert II.—did not save Robert III. from a death of grief,—procured, perhaps, the assassination of James I. —instigated James IV. to successful rebellion against his father, whose violent death was expiated by his own. Its dignity was proudly encreased by James V. who was yet more unfortunate, perhaps, in his end, than a long list of unfortunate predecessors. It was worn by the devoted head of Mary, who found it the occasion of woes and calamities unnumbered and unexampled. It was placed upon the infant brow of her son, to the exclusion of herself from all its glories and advantages, but not to the conclusion of the distresses in which it had involved her. Her unfortunate grandson, for its sake, visited Scotland, and had it placed upon his head with magnificent ceremonies; but the nation whose sovereignty it gave him was the first to rebel against his authority, and work his destruction. The presbyterian solemnity with which it was given to Charles II. was only a preface to the disasters of Worcester; and afterwards, it was remembered by this monarch, little to the advantage of Scotland, that it had been placed upon his head with conditions and restrictions which wounded at once his pride and his conscience. It was worn by no other monarch, and the period of its disuse seems to have been the epoch from which we may reckon the happiness of our monarchs, and the revival of our national prosperity."—*Chambers' Walks in Edinburgh*, p. 49.

herd," a pastoral drama of charming simplicity, and still highly popular among the rural population of Scotland.

The stranger will now retrace his steps to

GEORGE IV. BRIDGE,

which spans the Cowgate, and forms an important feature in the modern improvements of the city. At its northern end is the WEST BOW, which before the erection of this bridge, presented an aspect highly interesting to the lover of antique buildings. Although now a place of small consideration, it is not 100 years since the Assembly Rooms of Edinburgh were situate within its precincts. Before the erection of the North and South Bridges, it was also the principal avenue by which wheel-carriages reached the more elevated streets of the city. It "has been ascended by Anne of Denmark, James I., and Charles I., by Oliver Cromwell, Charles II., and James II. How different the avenue by which George IV. entered the city!"* But the West Bow has also been the scene of many more mournful processions. Previous to the year 1785, criminals were conducted through the Bow to the place of execution in the Grassmarket, and the murderers of Porteous after securing their victim, hurried him down this street to meet the punishment they had destined for him.† At the head of this street also stood the HOUSE OF

* Chambers' Traditions of Edinburgh, vol. i. p. 140.

† The murder of Captain Porteous forms an event so memorable, not only in the annals of the city, but in what might be termed the philosophy of mobs, that it would be an unpardonable omission to pass it over unnoticed. We need hardly remind our readers that it forms one of the most striking incidents in the Heart of Mid-Lothian.

John Porteous was the son of a tailor in Edinburgh; his father intended to breed him up to his own trade, but the youthful profligacy of the son defeated the parent's prudent intention, and he enlisted into the Scotch corps at that time in the service of the States of Holland. Here he learned military discipline, and, upon returning to his own country in 1715, his services were engaged by the magistrates of Edinburgh to discipline the City Guard. For such a task

MAJOR WEIR the celebrated necromancer, who, along with his sister, suffered death for witchcraft in 1670.

he was eminently qualified, not only by his military education, but by his natural activity and resolution; and, in spite of the profligacy of his character, he received a captain's commission in the corps.

The duty of the Edinburgh City Guard was to preserve the public peace when any tumult was apprehended. They consisted principally of discharged veterans, who, when off duty, worked at their respective trades. To the rabble they were objects of mingled derision and dislike, and the numerous indignities they suffered rendered them somewhat morose and austere in temper. At public executions they generally surrounded the scaffold, and it was on an occasion of this kind that Porteous their captain committed the outrage for which he paid the penalty of his life.

The criminal, on the occasion in question, had excited the commiseration of the populace by the disinterested courage he displayed in securing the escape of his accomplice. At this time it was customary to conduct prisoners under sentence of death to attend divine service in the Tolbooth Church. Wilson, the criminal above alluded to, and Robertson, his companion in crime, had reached the church, guarded by four soldiers, when Wilson suddenly seized one of the guards in each hand, and a third with his teeth, and shouted to his accomplice to fly for his life. Robertson immediately fled, and effected his escape. This circumstance naturally excited a strong feeling of sympathy for Wilson, and the magistrates, fearing an attempt at rescue, had requested the presence of a detachment of infantry in a street adjoining to that where the execution was to take place, for the purpose of intimidating the populace. The introduction of another military force than his own into a quarter of the city where no drums but his own were ever beat, highly incensed Captain Porteous, and aggravated the ferocity of a temper naturally surly and brutal. Contrary to the apprehension of the authorities, the execution was allowed to pass undisturbed, but the dead body had hung only a short time upon the gibbet when a tumult arose among the multitude; stones and other missiles were thrown at Porteous and his men, and one of the populace, more adventurous than the rest, sprung upon the scaffold, and cut the rope by which the criminal was suspended.

Porteous was exasperated to frenzy by this outrage on his authority, and leaping from the scaffold, he seized the musket of one of the guards, gave the word to fire, and, discharging his piece, shot a man dead upon the spot. Several of his soldiers also, having obeyed his order to fire, six or seven persons were killed and many others wounded. The mob still continuing their attack, another volley was fired upon them, by which several others fell, and the scene of violence only closed when Porteous and his soldiers reached the guard house in the High Street. For his reckless and sanguinary conduct in this affair, Captain Porteous was arraigned before the High Court of Justiciary, and sentence of death was passed upon him. His execution was appointed to take place on the 8th of September, 1736.

The day of doom at length arrived, and the ample area of the Grassmarket was crowded in every part with a countless multitude, drawn together to gratify their revenge or satisfy their sense of justice by the spectacle of the execution. But their vengeance met with a temporary disappointment. The hour of execution was already past without the appearance of the criminal, and the expectant multitude began to interchange suspicions that a reprieve might have arrived.

The fate of Weir is chiefly remarkable from his being a man of some condition, (the son of a gentleman, and his

Deep and universal was the groan of indignation which arose from the crowd, when they learned that such was indeed the fact. The case having been represented to her Majesty Queen Caroline, she intimated her royal pleasure that the prisoner should be reprieved for six weeks. The shout of disappointed revenge was followed by suppressed mutterings and communings among the crowd, but no act of violence was committed; they saw the gallows taken down, and then gradually dispersed to their homes and occupations.

Night ushered in another scene;—a drum was heard beating to arms, and the populace promptly answered its summons by turning out into the streets. Their numbers rapidly increased, and, separating into different parties, they took possession of the city gates, posting sentinels for their security. They then disarmed the City Guard, and, having thus possessed themselves of weapons, they were the uncontrolled masters of the city. During the progress of the riot, various efforts were made to communicate with the Castle, but the vigilance of the insurgents defeated all such attempts. The Tolbooth was now invested, and a strong party of the rioters having surrounded it, another party proceeded to break up the doors. For a considerable time the great strength of the place rendered their efforts fruitless, but, having brought fire to their aid, they burned the door, and rushed into the prison.

Porteous, elated with his escape from the sentence he so richly merited, was regaling a party of his boon companions within the building, when the assault was made upon its gates. The wretched man well knew the hatred with which he was regarded by the populace, and was at no loss to comprehend the motive for their violence. Escape seemed impossible. The chimney was the only place of concealment that occurred to him, and, scrambling into it, he supported himself by laying hold of the bars of iron with which the chimnies of a prison-house are crossed to prevent the escape of criminals. But his enemies soon dragged him from his hiding place, and, hurrying him along the streets, they brought him to the very spot, where, that morning, he ought to have paid the forfeit of his life. The want of a rope was now the sole obstacle to the accomplishment of their purpose, and this want was soon supplied by breaking open a shop where the article was sold; a dyer's pole served in room of a gallows, and from it they suspended the unhappy man. Having thus propitiated the spirit of offended justice, they threw down the weapons of which they had possessed themselves, and quietly dispersed to their respective homes.

It has been justly observed that the murder of Porteous has more the character of a conspiracy than of a riot. The whole proceedings of the insurgents were marked by a cool and deliberate intrepidity, quite at variance with the accustomed conduct of rioters. No violence was perpetrated either upon person or property, save the single act of vengeance executed upon Porteous. So studious were the insurgents to avoid every appearance of prædial outrage, that a guinea was left upon the counter of the shop from which they took the rope to hang their victim. None of the offenders were ever discovered, although government made the most strenuous exertions, and offered large rewards for their apprehension. There can be little doubt, however, that many of the participators in that night's transactions were of a class unaccustomed to mingle in scenes of vulgar tumult.

mother a lady of family in Clydesdale,) which was rarely the case with those who were the victims of such accusations. Whether the crimes which he confessed were the offspring of an imagination labouring under temporary insanity, or whether he was in reality a man of atrociously depraved life, does not very clearly appear. After his condemnation he doggedly refused to have recourse to prayer, "arguing, that as he had no hope whatever of escaping Satan, there was no need of incensing him by vain efforts at repentance." * The modern improvements in this part of the city have now swept away all vestiges of the house, which ever after the death of Weir, enjoyed the reputation of being haunted. So general was the horror entertained for the crimes of the man and the terrors of his abode, that no family was ever found hardy enough to occupy the house as a residence.

In the Grassmarket—situated, as we have already mentioned, at the foot of the Bow—a weekly market is held on Wednesday for grain, horses, cattle, and sheep. At its south-west corner it is entered by the West Port, the scene of the appalling atrocities of the monster Burke. As the name of this wretched man is now generally employed to distinguish the crime for which he suffered, we need scarcely remind our readers that his victims were destroyed by strangulation, and that his object was not to possess himself of their property, for they were all of a humble rank in life, but to convert their bodies into a source of gain by selling them to the anatomist.

Proceeding along the Bridge, Heriot's Hospital will be seen occupying a fine situation on the right. Upon

* Sir Walter Scott's Letters on Demonology and Witchcraft, p. 330.

reaching the southern end of the Bridge, and proceeding a short way up the Candlemaker-Row, we reach upon the right the entrance to THE GREYFRIAR'S CHURCHYARD, in ancient times the garden belonging to the monastery of Greyfriars, which was situated in the Grassmarket. In this church-yard are interred George Buchanan the accomplished Latin poet, and preceptor of James VI., Allan Ramsay the Scottish poet, Principal Robertson the historian, Dr. Black the distinguished chemist, Dr. Hugh Blair, and Colin Maclaurin. There are two churches in the burying-ground, known by the name of Old Greyfriars, and New Greyfriars. Of the former, Principal Robertson was pastor for many years. Leaving the churchyard, and still ascending the Candlemaker-Row, the entrance to the CHARITY WORK HOUSE is the next opening upon the right. The grounds around the house are laid out as a kitchen garden for the establishment, and the inmates are frequently employed in its cultivation. The house itself is a large building of the plainest description. The funds by which the institution is supported are derived from an assessment on house property, collections at the church doors, and occasional donations and voluntary contributions from the citizens. The average number of inmates is about 750.*

Leaving the Work-house grounds by the entrance from Laurieston, a short walk conducts us to

HERIOT'S HOSPITAL.

This handsome edifice owes its foundation to George Heriot, jeweller to James VI., whose name will probably be more familiar to the ear of strangers as the "jingling

* Besides this institution, the parish of St. Cuthberts and the Canongate have each a house for the reception of paupers, with peculiar funds, and separate boards of management.

Geordie" of "The Fortunes of Nigel."* The design is attributed to Inigo Jones. The building was commenced in 1628 and completed in 1660, and the erection is said to have cost £27,000. It forms "a noble quadrangle of the Gothic order, as ornamental to the city as a building, as the manner in which the youths are provided for and educated, renders it useful as an institution." The chapel, occupying the south side of the quadrangle, a few years ago presented nothing but a clay floor and bare walls, round which a stone seat was carried, to accommodate the boys when assembled for morning and evening service. It is now fitted up in a very different style, and with its splendid pulpit, fine oaken carvings, and richly adorned ceiling, forms one of the principal attractions of the place. The object of this splendid institution is the maintenance and education of "poor and fatherless boys," or whose parents are in indigent circumstances, "freemen's sons of the town of Edinburgh," of whom 180 are accommodated within its walls. The course of instruction consists of English, Latin, Greek, French, Writing, Arithmetic, Book-keeping, Mathematics, and Geography. To these branches have recently been added Gymnastics, Drawing, and the Elements of Music. Boys are admitted between the age of seven and ten, and generally leave at fourteen, unless superior scholarship appears to fit them for prosecuting some of the learned professions, in which case the period of their stay is extended, with the view of preparing them for the studies of the University. All the boys upon leaving the hospital receive a bible, and two suits

* "For the wealth God has sent me, it shall not want inheritors while there are orphan lads in Auld Reekie." *Fortunes of Nigel, Chapter IV.*

A brief outline of the benevolent founder's history is given in the Note to Chapter II. of the same work.

of clothes of their own choice. Those going out as apprentices are allowed £10 annually for five years, and £5 at the termination of their apprenticeship. Those destined for any of the learned professions are sent to college for four years, during which period they receive £30 a-year, and have their class-fees paid by the hospital. In 1836, an act was obtained from Parliament, empowering the Governors to extend the benefits of the Institution, and employ their surplus funds in establishing Free Schools in the different parishes of the city. One of these has already been finished to the north of the hospital, in which 250 children, of both sexes, are instructed in the usual branches of a parochial education, the females being, in addition, taught sewing and knitting. On the Sunday evenings all in the district, who choose to avail themselves of the privilege, are admitted indiscriminately to the religious instructions. Several other schools are in a state of considerable forwardness, and when completed, will be conducted on the same general principles, with such modifications as experience may suggest. This great scheme of instruction, when in full operation, must prove of incalculable benefit to the community, as the advantages of a substantial education will be brought within the reach of the very humblest citizen. In addition to these liberal provisions for the instruction of youth, there are also ten bursaries, or exhibitions, open to the competition of boys not connected with the institution. The successful competitors for these bursaries receive £20 *per annum*, for four years. The management is vested in the Town Council and Clergy of the city, and visitors are admitted by an order from any of the magistrates.

Retracing our steps to the entrance to the Charity

Work House, the Meadow Walk will be seen exactly opposite. In a field, upon the right hand, a short way down the walk, stands

GEORGE WATSON'S HOSPITAL.

This hospital is for the benefit of the children and grandchildren of decayed merchants of the city of Edinburgh. The building is plain but commodious. Boys are received into this hospital between seven and ten, and remain till fifteen years of age. The number of boys amounts to about eighty, and the education they receive very much resembles that of Heriot's Hospital. Each boy, after leaving the hospital, receives £10 a-year for five years, and upon attaining the age of twenty-five, if unmarried, and well-conducted, he receives a further sum of £50. Those who prefer an academical education receive £20 a-year for five years. The management is vested in the Master, Assistants, and Treasurer of the Merchant Company of Edinburgh, the ministers of the Old Church, and five members of the Town Council. A little to the west of George Watson's Hospital stands the Merchant Maiden Hospital, but as it does not come within the scope of any of our walks, we think it better to include the description of it and of the other more important hospitals, which we do not pass in our progress, in a foot note.*

* *The Merchant Maiden Hospital* was founded in 1695, for the maintenance and education of the daughters of merchant burgesses in the city. Nearly 100 girls are maintained in this hospital. They are admitted between seven and eleven years of age, and leave at seventeen. The course of instruction includes English, Writing, Arithmetic, Geography, French, Music, Drawing, Dancing, and Needle-work. Upon leaving the hospital each girl receives £9, 6s. 8d. The original edifice stood in Bristo Street; the present building is agreeably situated in Laurieston, a little to the west of George Watson's Hospital.

The Trades Maiden Hospital stands on the south side of Argyll Square. The girls eligible for admission into this institution, are the daughters of decayed tradesmen. It supports about 50 girls, who are admitted at the same age, and

Immediately adjoining to the Meadows, on the south-west, are Bruntsfield Links, (*anglice* Downs,) where many of the inhabitants are accustomed to amuse themselves with the national game of golf. The game is played with a club and ball. The club is formed of ash, finely tapered, and highly flexible. The head is faced

instructed in the same branches as in the Merchant Maiden Hospital. They go out at the age of seventeen, each girl receiving £5, 11s. and a bible.

The Orphan Hospital maintains and educates about 150 children of both sexes. The old building, situated near Trinity College Church was abandoned as unhealthy, and a handsome new edifice was erected in 1833, on the property of Dean. The benefits of the institution are extended to the whole of Scotland.

John Watson's Institution is a spacious and showy edifice also situated on the property of Dean. The purpose of the endowment, is the maintenance and education of destitute children. About 120 children are maintained in it. They are admitted between the ages of five and eight, and leave at fourteen.

Cauvin's Hospital is pleasantly situated at Duddingston, a village about a mile and half to the east of Edinburgh. The children enjoying the benefit of this institution are, "the sons of respectable but poor teachers," and, "of poor but honest farmers; whom failing, the sons of respectable master-printers or booksellers," and, "of respectable servants in the agricultural line." Twenty boys are maintained in it. They are admissible from six to eight years of age, and are retained in the hospital for six years.

Trinity College Hospital, the oldest charitable institution in the city, stands at the foot of the lane called Leith Wynd. It was founded in 1461 by Mary of Gueldres. Its benefits are conferred on "burgesses, their wives or children not married, nor under the age of 50 years." Forty persons are maintained within the walls of the hospital, and about ninety out-pensioners receive £6 a-year.

Gillespie's Hospital enjoys a fine situation on the south-west confines of the city. The founder was a tobacconist in Edinburgh, who devoted the greater part of his property to endow an hospital for the maintenance of indigent old men and women, and for the elementary education of 100 poor boys. The number of the aged inmates is between thirty and forty. None are admitted under the age of fifty-five, a preference being given to servants of the founder or persons of his name.

Besides the endowments for the relief of the destitute, there are many other charitable associations maintained by private subscription. Among them may be mentioned The House of Refuge—The House of Industry—The Strangers' Friend Society—The Society for relief of the Destitute Sick—The Society for the relief of indigent Old Men, and two similar institutions for the relief of indigent Old Women—The Seamen's Friend Society—and The Society for clothing the Industrious Poor.

There are also many public Dispensaries and a Lying-in Hospital, where medicines and medical attendance are gratuitously afforded to the poor; but a further enumeration of such institutions does not appear to be required for the purposes of the present publication.

with horn and loaded with lead. The ball is about the size of a common tennis ball, made of feathers compressed into a very hard but slightly elastic leathern shell or cover. The game consists in striking the ball successively into a certain number of small holes, about a quarter of a mile apart, the player who does so in the smallest number of strokes being the victor. Each player carries an assortment of clubs, varying in elasticity, and thus adapted to the distance the ball is to be driven, the best club for a long stroke being laid aside for one less elastic when the distance becomes shortened. An expert player will strike a ball from 130 to 150 yards.

Returning from the Links to that point of the Meadows where the walks cross each other, the stranger will be in the immediate neighbourhood of

GEORGE'S SQUARE.

This is the only large square in the Old Town. Towards the close of the last century it was the principal place of residence of the higher ranks: The Duchess of Gordon, the Countess of Sutherland, the Countess of Glasgow, Viscount Duncan, the Hon. Henry Erskine, and many other persons of rank residing there. The house of Walter Scott, Esq. W.S., father of the novelist was on the west side of the Square.

Passing along Charles' Street, Bristo Street, Lothian Street, and South College Street, and then turning to the right, a short distance along Nicolson Street, the stranger will observe upon his left the fine portico of

THE ROYAL COLLEGE OF SURGEONS.

In classic elegance few buildings will be found to surpass this handsome structure, although its effect is much impaired by the uncongenial architecture of the surrounding houses. The principal portion of the building is occupied with an extensive museum of anatomical and surgical preparations. The arrangement is, in every respect, admirable, and a praiseworthy liberality is exhibited in the admission of strangers. Although by the strict letter of the regulations, a member's order is requisite, yet even this form is in most cases dispensed with. A little further south on the same side of the street is the Asylum for the Industrious Blind.

Returning northward, the next object of importance is

THE UNIVERSITY.

No regular University existed in Edinburgh till the year 1582, although long previous to this period teachers of philosophy and divinity had been established in the city. On the 24th of April of that year, King James VI. issued the charter for its foundation, and in the following year the course of instruction was commenced. By the liberality of James and private benefactions, the university rapidly advanced in importance, and as its revenues increased, its sphere of usefulness was extended by the addition of new professorships, till in the 18th century, it attained a celebrity unsurpassed by any academical institution in Europe.

The present structure is of modern erection. The old buildings were both unsightly and incommodious, and a subscription having been set on foot, the foundation of the present handsome and spacious edifice was laid in 1789. The local subscriptions however were insufficient to accomplish the object; and upon the case being brought before Parliament, an annual grant of £10,000 was obtained to complete the undertaking. The plan is by Mr. Robert Adam, with some subsequent modifications, principally in the internal arrangement, by Mr. W. H. Playfair. The buildings are of a quadrangular form, the sides measuring 358 by 255 feet, with a spacious court in the centre. The eastern front is adorned with a portico, supported by Doric columns, 26 feet in height, each formed of a single block of stone.

No test of any description is required from the students; they are not resident within the College, nor are they distinguished by any peculiarity of dress. In pursuing their studies they are at perfect liberty to select the classes they attend—a certain curriculum of study is however requisite in taking degrees in Medicine and Arts, those who intend to qualify for a degree in the latter being required to attend the Classes of Humanity, Greek, Logic, Rhetoric, Moral Philosophy, Natural Philosophy, and Mathematics. The number of students attending the University during the present session (1838-39,) is about 1400.

There are 34 foundations for bursaries, the benefit of which is extended to 80 students. The greater number of these bursaries do not exceed in value £10 per annum.

The Museum contains a large collection of specimens in the various departments of Natural History. The Ornithogical department is peculiarly valuable, both from its extent and admirable classification. Visitors are admitted upon payment of one shilling each. There is also an Anatomical Museum, where the professional visitor will be highly interested by the variety and beauty of the preparations.

The Library occupies the south side of the building. The principal apartment is equally distinguished by the symmetry of its proportions, the chasteness of its decorations, and its admirable adaptation to the purpose for which it is intended. It is incomparably the finest library-room in Scotland; measuring 187 feet in length, by 50 in breadth, with an arched roof from 50 to 58 feet high. A small collection of paintings, bequeathed to the University by Sir James Erskine of Torry, adorns the west end of the room.

Proceeding northward upon leaving the University,

THE ROYAL INFIRMARY

is situated in the first street upon the right. A detailed account of this institution does not appear to be necessary in the present work. The last annual report shows that no fewer than 4903 patients received the benefit of the institution within the year, of whom 2244 were fever patients. Besides the relief afforded to patients, clinical lectures, or discourses on the cases in the several wards, are delivered within the walls by the Professors of the University. The professor of clinical surgery also lectures upon the more important surgical cases in the wards under his inspection. Besides the professorial lectures, the ordinary physicians and surgeons of the institution deliver clinical discourses on the cases under their immediate care. Journals of the cases are regularly kept, recording the symptoms, progress, and termination of the disease, with the various remedies employed. To these journals the students have access.

The fees paid by students for the right to attend the medical and surgical practice in the Hospital, are five guineas for an annual, or twelve guineas for a perpetual ticket.

Proceeding along the South Bridge, an open railing, for a short distance on either side, affords a view of the Cowgate, with which the tourist will in all probability, have no wish to cultivate a closer acquaintance. The Register House will again come into view on reaching the Tron Church, thus terminating our Second Walk.

WALK THIRD.

ROYAL INSTITUTION—NEW CLUB—ST. JOHN'S CHAPEL—ST. CUTHBERT'S CHURCH—CHARLOTTE SQUARE—ST. GEORGE'S CHURCH—DEAN BRIDGE—AINSLIE PLACE—MORAY PLACE—HERIOT ROW—PITT MONUMENT—GEORGE FOURTH'S MONUMENT—ASSEMBLY ROOMS—PHYSICIAN'S HALL—ST. ANDREW'S SQUARE—MELVILLE MONUMENT—ROYAL BANK.

In this walk we shall conduct the stranger through the principal streets of the New Town, adverting to all the more striking objects in our progress.

Proceeding to the westward the buildings of the High Street will be seen upon the left, towering to the heavens like the habitations of a race of Titans. These buildings, standing upon a steep and lofty ridge, with tributary lanes or closes descending abruptly to the valley beneath, produce an effect highly picturesque and majestic. The inter-jacent valley extending westward to the end of Prince's Street, and now tastefully laid out in pleasure-grounds, was formerly a stagnant pond or marsh, known by the name of the Nor-Loch. The Earthen Mound, formed by the deposition of the rubbish accumulated in digging the foundations of the houses in the New Town, is a convenient avenue of communication between the New Town and the Old. Its southern end has for many years been disfigured by wooden structures of all shapes and sizes, erected for successive exhibitions of wild beasts, horsemanship, wax-works, and panoramas. At its northern extremity stands

THE ROYAL INSTITUTION,

One of the handsomest modern buildings of which Edinburgh can boast. The expense of driving the piles upon which this fine structure is built, exceeded £1600. The Royal Society, the Royal Institution for the Encouragement of the Fine Arts in Scotland, the Board of Trustees for the Improvement of Manufactures, and the Society of Antiquaries, have apartments in this building. To the Museum of the Antiquarian Society strangers are admitted by an order from any of the members. Among the reliques of antiquity preserved in this collection may be mentioned the colours carried by the Covenanters during the civil war; the stool which Jenny Geddes, in her zeal against Prelacy, launched at the head of the Bishop of Edinburgh in St. Giles's Church; and the *Maiden*, or Scottish guillotine, with which the Earl of Morton, the Marquis of Argyle, Sir Robert Spottiswood and many other distinguished persons were beheaded.* The paintings of the Scottish Artists are exhibited in the Institution during the spring months, and the native manufactures are also exhibited here for a short period during the same season. The Royal Society holds its meetings once a fortnight during the winter months, when papers connected with the varied departments of science and learning, falling within the scope of the Society's plan, are read by the several members.

Continuing our walk towards the west, we pass on the right THE NEW CLUB, an association of Noblemen and Gentlemen, partaking of the character of a joint-stock Hotel and Reading Room, for the exclusive accommodation of members. These are elected by ballot, the number being limited to 660. The entrance-money

* It is very generally believed that it was the Earl of Morton who introduced the Maiden into Scotland. This opinion, however, has been proved to be erroneous, entries in the Council Records shewing that it was in use long before his time.

is thirty five guineas, and the annual subscription five guineas.

The frowning grandeur of the Castle Rock now becomes very imposing, and presents a vivid contrast to the tranquil beauty of the green sward and shrubberies that adorn the valley beneath. These pleasure grounds, endowed with natural features of the most varied character, and improved by all the resources of modern Horticulture, form one of the chief ornaments of the City.

Upon reaching the west end of Prince's Street, ST. JOHN'S CHAPEL and ST. CUTHBERT'S CHURCH will be seen upon the left, the former an elegant structure of the florid Gothic Order, the latter in a style of architecture, which can be referred to no school, nor age, nor country. It has, however, the merit of being the largest church in Edinburgh, and is furnished with an upper and lower gallery. St. John's, is one of the places of worship belonging to the Scottish Episcopal Communion, and is embellished with all those graces of internal and external architecture, by which the English Church usually distinguishes the edifices dedicated to her religious service.*

Turning to the north, the stranger will now enter Charlotte Square, a spacious quadrangle of excellent houses. In the centre of its western side stands ST. GEORGE'S CHURCH, the handsomest place of worship in the Scotch Establishment. Its erection cost £33,000.

After passing along the narrow lane by the side of St. George's, and through Charlotte Place, turn to the

* The other Episcopal Chapels in Edinburgh are St. Paul's, York Place, a Gothic structure of singular elegance; St. George's, also in York Place, a small but commodious place of worship; St. James's, Broughton Place; St. Paul's, Carrubber's Close; St. Peter's, Roxburgh Place, and Trinity Chapel, near the Dean Bridge.

right and proceed by Melville Place, Randolph Crescent, and Lynedoch Place, through the Toll-Bar to

THE DEAN BRIDGE.

For this fine bridge Edinburgh is principally indebted to the enterprize of one individual, who contributed largely to the expense of its erection, for the improvement of his property on the northern side of the river. The road-way passes at the great height of 106 feet above the bed of the stream.* The arches are four in number, each 96 feet span, the breadth between the parapets being 39 feet, and the total length of the bridge 447 feet.

As no object of any interest occurs on the river side, the stranger may retrace his steps to Randolph Crescent, through which he will pass to Great Stuart Street, Ainslie Place, and

MORAY PLACE.

This is the quarter of the city most celebrated for the architectural magnificence of its buildings. The ground is the property of the Earl of Moray, and the various streets, squares and crescents erected upon it, are in accordance with a uniform plan designed by Mr. Gillespie Graham, architect. By some persons it has been objected that the severe simplicity of style and massive solidity of structure which particularly distinguish these buildings, impart an aspect of solemnity and gloom repugnant to the character of domestic architecture. Even the harmony of design and uniformity of plan have offended

* This is the stream which Richie Moniplies, in the Fortunes of Nigel, represents as a navigable river superior to the Thames. Strangers who have seen both will be enabled to estimate how far Richie's patriotism had obscured his power of memory.

"I suppose you will tell me next" (said Master Heriot) "that you have at Edinburgh as fine a navigable river as the Thames with all its shipping?"

"The Thames!" exclaimed Richie in a tone of ineffable contempt—"God bless your honour's judgment, we have at Edinburgh the Water of Leith and the Nor-Loch!"

some critics. "The New Town of Edinburgh," says Dr. James Johnson, in his work entitled 'The Recess'* "is beautifully monotonous, and magnificently dull." Until philosophers shall succeed in establishing a uniform standard of taste, it will be vain to contend with such cavillers. We therefore leave them in peaceful possession of their opinions, and shall only observe, that the massive dignity of the architecture in this quarter of the City, has called forth the admiration of the large majority of intelligent visitors. Nor is the substantial comfort of the dwellings to be overlooked. The walls are of the most solid and durable masonry; both the building materials and workmanship being of the best description.

The rent of the houses in Moray Place, varies from L.140 to L.160, and in Ainslie Place, from L.100 to L.130.

Leaving Moray Place by Darnaway Street, Heriot Row introduces us to another *suite* of those Pleasure-Grounds, which tend so much to beautify the city. Ascending the first opening on the right we reach Queen Street, which runs parallel with Heriot Row, and overlooks the interjacent Pleasure-Grounds. Through the openings formed by the streets running to the north, a noble prospect is obtained of the Firth of Forth, the shores of Fife, the Ochil Hills, and the more distant Grampians.

THE PITT STATUE

occupies the spot where George's Street is intersected by Frederick Street. It is executed by Chantrey, and

* "The learned SMELFUNGUS travelled from Boulogne to Paris—from Paris to Rome—and so on—but he set out with the spleen and jaundice, and every object he passed by was discoloured or distorted.—He wrote an account of them, but 'twas nothing but the account of his miserable feelings."—STERNE'S SENTIMENTAL JOURNEY.

possesses considerable dignity of expression. Proceeding eastward along George's Street, THE ASSEMBLY ROOMS will be seen upon the right. Their external appearance is plain and unpretending, the only approach to ornament being the four Doric columns, doing duty as a portico in the front of the building. In these Rooms are held the public Balls and Concerts, and other meetings of various kinds. The principal ball-room is 92 feet long, 42 feet wide, and 40 feet high. There are also various other apartments of smaller dimensions. A little to the east stands

GEORGE IV. STATUE.

It is also executed by Chantrey. The majesty of the monarch must be admitted to be somewhat transcendental. The figure is so far thrown back, as to give it the appearance of deriving a share of its support from the drapery behind, an expedient suggesting some particulars in the natural history of the kangaroo, which by no means contribute to sublimity of effect. It must, however, be granted, that by caricaturing the Monarch the artist has exalted the Minister, for the exaggerated pomp of the one, powerfully contrasts with the intellectual elevation of the other.

Continuing our progress eastward, ST. ANDREW'S CHURCH stands upon the left. It possesses a portico supported by four Corinthian columns, and a handsome spire, rising to the height of 168 feet. Among the numerous spires in Edinburgh, this is the only one at all remarkable for lightness of design, or elegance of proportion. Upon the opposite side of the street stands the PHYSICIAN'S HALL, with a portico in front, supported by four Corinthian columns.

THE MELVILLE MONUMENT,

which graces the centre of St Andrew's Square, was

erected to the memory of the late Lord Melville. Whatever difference of opinion may prevail as to the political views of this nobleman, it will be admitted by all parties, that, in the exercise of his patronage, the claims of his own countrymen were never overlooked. This handsome column records their gratitude for his services. It rises 136 feet high, to which the statue adds other 14 feet. The design is that of the Trajan column, the shaft being fluted instead of ornamented with sculpture. The only other deviation from the model, is in the pedestal of the statue, and when the reader is reminded, that in the Trajan pillar the pedestal is a perfect sphere, he will be enabled to determine whether the modern innovation is an improvement.

In the centre of the east side of the square, standing apart from the other buildings, is THE ROYAL BANK. In front of the bank, is an equestrian STATUE OF THE EARL OF HOPETOUN.

Passing through St. Andrew's Street, we again reach Princes Street, and terminate our Third Walk, by returning to the Register House.

WALK FOURTH.

ROYAL TERRACE—LEITH WALK—(LEITH—NEWHAVEN)—INVERLEITH ROW—EXPERIMENTAL GARDENS—BOTANIC GARDENS.

IN the three preceding walks, we have exhausted most of the objects of interest in the city, and if the stranger should with them close his perambulations, he sacrifices very little worthy of notice. But in order to render our

Handbook more complete, we find it necessary to give a short description of Leith, and a passing notice of Newhaven.* By omitting both of these places, the circuit

* As neither of these places presents any peculiar features of attraction, we shall embody in this note all the information regarding them, which can possess any interest for a stranger. To both places omnibuses ply several times a-day. The hours of starting may be ascertained at the Duty House, end of North Bridge.

Leith, the sea-port of Edinburgh, is distant about a mile and half from the centre of the metropolis. It was not only the first, but for several centuries the only port in Scotland, traces of its existence being found in documents of the 12th century. During its early history, few places have so often been the scene of military operations. "In 1313, all the vessels in the harbour were burned by the English, and, again, in 1410. In 1544 it was plundered and burned, its pier destroyed, and its shipping carried off, by the Earl of Hertford, to avenge the insult which Henry VIII. conceived the Scotch had offered him, by refusing to betroth their young queen, Mary, to his son Prince Edward. Three years subsequently to this, it was again plundered and burned by the English under Hertford, then Duke of Somerset, and its whole shipping, together with all that in the Forth, entirely annihilated by the English admiral, Lord Clinton. Four years after this, the town was fortified by Desse, a French general, who came over with 6000 men to assist the queen-regent in suppressing the Reformation. On the completion of these fortifications, which consisted in throwing a strong and high wall, with towers at intervals, around the town, the queen-regent took up her residence there, and, surrounded with her countrymen, hoped to be able to maintain her authority in the kingdom. These measures, however, had only the effect of widening the breach between her and her subjects, till they finally took up arms, and besieged her in her stronghold. In October 1559, the lords of the congregation invested Leith with an army, but after various ineffectual attempts to gain access to the town by scaling the walls, they were driven back with great slaughter by a desperate sally of the besieged.

In the month of April in the succeeding year, the forces of the congregation again invested the town, being now aided by an army of 6000 men under Lord Grey of Wilton, dispatched to their assistance by Elizabeth. On this occasion the contest was protracted and sanguinary. For two months, during which the town suffered dreadfully from famine, as well as from the more violent casualties of war, the struggle continued, without any decisive advantage being gained by either side. At the end of that period, both parties being heartily tired of the contest, a treaty was entered into, by which it was stipulated that the French should evacuate the kingdom, that they should be allowed to embark unmolested, and that the English army should, upon the same day, begin its march to England. Immediately after the conclusion of this treaty, the walls of Leith were demolished by order of the town-council of Edinburgh, and no vestige of them now remains."* In 1561, when Queen Mary came from France, to take possession of the throne of her ancestors, she landed upon the pier of Leith. Of this pier no vestiges now remain. In 1650 the town was

* Encyclopædia Britannica, Seventh Edition, Article Leith.

of the present walk is very materially abridged, without any corresponding diminution of its interest; we believe

occupied by Cromwell, who exacted an assessment from the inhabitants. In 1715 the citadel was taken by a party of the adherents of the Stuart family, but, upon being threatened by the Duke of Argyll, it was speedily evacuated. George IV. upon visiting Scotland in 1822, landed at a spot a little to the north of the New Drawbridge, where an inscribed plate has been inserted in the pavement to commemorate the event.

Leith presents few antiquities of any interest. Among those which remain, may be mentioned, the parish church of South Leith, a Gothic edifice built previous to the year 1496, and the old church of North Leith, founded in 1493. In the Links, upon the south-east side of the town, may be seen several mounds raised for the purpose of planting cannon by the besieging army in 1560.

The town "is for the most part irregularly and confusedly built, and a great portion of it is extremely filthy, crowded, and inelegant. Some parts of it, again, are the reverse of this, being spacious, cleanly, and handsome. Such are two or three of the modern streets, and various ranges of private dwellings erected of late years on the eastern and western skirts of the town.

"The modern public buildings worthy of remark are, the Exchange Buildings, a large and elegant structure in the Grecian style of architecture; containing a spacious and handsome assembly-room, a commodious hotel, and public reading room. The expense of the erection was £16,000. The Custom-house, situated in North Leith, is also a very splendid building; it was erected in 1812, at an expense of £12,000; the Leith Bank, a neat little edifice, erected in 1805–6: the new Court-house, by far the most elegant building in the town, and forming altogether, whether the chasteness of the design or the neatness of the workmanship be considered, a very favourable specimen of modern architecture on a small scale."* The parish church of North Leith is a handsome though unpretending structure, surmounted by a tasteful spire. The living is one of the best in the Church of Scotland.

The chief manufactures are, ropes and cordage, sail-cloth, bottles, soap, and candles. There are several breweries and a distillery, and shipbuilding is carried on to a considerable extent.

Leith is the most important naval station on the east coast of Scotland, and a considerable traffic is carried on at the port, the gross revenues of which average above £20,000 a-year; but "it is universally admitted that the harbour, in its present state, is very inadequate to the accommodation of the trade of Edinburgh and of the Firth of Forth, especially to the important branches of steam navigation and the ferry communication between the opposite shores of the Firth."† Large sums have been expended from time to time with the view of improving the harbour and docks, but they are still considered inadequate to the trade. Government, in the arrangement of the affairs of the City of Edinburgh, by an act passed in July 1838, made provision for making an extensive improvement in the harbour, which, it is hoped, will be ere long carried into effect.

Leith, with Musselburgh, Portobello, and Newhaven, returns a member to Parliament. The population, which we have included under that of Edinburgh, amounted in 1831 to 25,855.

---

* Encyclopædia Britannica.

† Parliamentary Report, July 1835.

therefore, that we shall consult the convenience of a very large majority of tourists, by excluding these places from our present line of progress.

Proceeding from the Register House down Greenside Street, nothing worthy of remark occurs till we reach the head of LEITH WALK, one of the most splendid roads in the kingdom. Turning to the right at this point, a noble range of buildings called the ROYAL TERRACE, will be seen occupying the northern side of the Calton Hill. These buildings command a magnificent prospect of the Firth of Forth, and the opposite shores, with all the interjacent country. Returning to the head of Broughton Street, the neat Gothic front of the ROMAN CATHOLIC CHAPEL will be observed on the west side of the street, close by the Adelphi Theatre. At the end of York Place, stands ST. PAUL'S CHAPEL, an elegant Gothic

NEWHAVEN is a small fishing village, with a stone and chain pier, situate about a mile farther up the Firth than Leith. Its chief importance is derived from the steamers which ply from its piers. Of these piers, however, neither the one nor the other has sufficient depth of water to admit of the approach of steamers of large size. The London boats, accordingly, now land and take on board their passengers at Granton, a little farther up the Firth, where a low-water pier has recently been constructed by the Duke of Buccleugh.

The inhabitants of Newhaven are a laborious and hardy race. They form a distinct community, rarely intermarrying with any other class. The male inhabitants are almost all fishermen, and the females are constantly occupied in vending the produce of their husbands' industry in the markets or streets of Edinburgh. When provoked, the *fishwives* as they are called, display resources of abuse quite equal to their Billingsgate contemporaries. They are also celebrated for the exorbitant prices they demand for their goods, very frequently asking three or four times the sum they finally consent to take. Other traders, when purchasers are cheapening their wares, or offering a price which they consider much below their value, are therefore in the habit of saying, "What! would you mak a fishwife o' me." Although a very hardworking people, they do not indulge in an excessive use of ardent spirits. The quantity they consume is indeed very considerable, but the prodigious loads with which they are burdened, may be allowed to form an apology for the occasional use of such a stimulus, and their constant exercise in the open air appears to prevent any injurious effects from following the indulgence. They are for the most part tidy in their habits, and, in these days, when one dull uniformity pervades the dress of all classes, it is refreshing to the lover of the picturesque to contemplate the gaudy garb of the rosy, hearty, mirth-making fishwife.

structure, one of the places of worship of the Episcopal communion. Continuing to proceed down Broughton Street, the stranger will next pass the chapel of the sect called Rowites, whose vagaries made so much noise in the religious world some years ago. Immediately contigous to this place of worship, is ALBANY STREET CHAPEL, belonging to the Independents, a body known in England as Congregationalists. At the corner of Broughton Place is ST. JAMES'S CHAPEL, an Episcopal place of worship, and at the east side of the same street is the principal Chapel of the Burghers, the most numerous Dissenting body in Scotland. Continuing to proceed northwards by Mansfield Place, and Bellevue Crescent, ST. MARY'S CHURCH will be seen terminating the northern extremity of the latter street. It is one of the neatest of the Edinburgh churches, possessing a portico and spire respectable in design and of excellent masonry.

The road now declines towards the village of Canonmills. After passing this squalid suburb,* the stranger crosses the Water of Leith by Canonmills Bridge. Upon his left he will observe some massive and singular looking buildings erected some years ago, by an Oil Gas Company. The speculation was soon abandoned as an unprofitable one, and the buildings are now occupied as Warehouses. At the further end of Howard Place are the Experimental Gardens, and upon the same side of the road, considerably further along, is the Botanic Garden. To the latter, strangers are freely admitted, but

* The general character of the place has one redeeming feature. Dr. Neill's pleasant suburban residence, "like a jewel of gold in a swine's snout," is situated on the confines of the village, his garden bordering on the loch, though separated from it by a wall. The proprietor is a distinguished botanist and naturalist, his gardens displaying a variety of botanical rarities, as well as many choice living specimens of interesting objects in the animal kingdom.

the hot-houses are open to the public only on Saturday, between the hours of 12 and 4.

The garden embraces an extent of 14½ English acres, and presents every facility for prosecuting the study of Botany. Immediately upon his entrance the stranger is struck with the luxuriance and vigour of the evergreens, to the cultivation of which, Mr. M'Nab, the able superintendant, has devoted much attention. On the southern side of the garden there is a large collection of hardy plants according to the Natural System of Jussieu, such as ferns, grasses, labiate, cruciform, and leguminous plants, &c. Close to this collection is a small pond containing rushes, water lilies, &c., and a ditch containing those plants which thrive best in such a situation. To the north of this arrangement is a collection of British plants, arranged according to the Linnæan or artificial system, with the name attached to each species. On the eastern side are the plants peculiar to Scotland, and on the west a few which are peculiar to England and Ireland. A little to the east of this British arrangement is a collection of roses. Proceeding northwards, we come to a general collection of hardy evergreens, to the east of which, is a small collection of Medical plants, with the names attached. We then reach the Greenhouses, which have of late been much increased by a liberal grant from government. These houses contain a large collection of exotics, which thrive admirably. The western division contains heaths, epacrideæ, dryandras, proteas, grevillias, diosmas, &c., while in the eastern division, we have a stove with a northern exposure, in which epiphytes and parasites, are cultivated with great success. The peculiar forms of these plants, and their remarkable mode of growth, attract the attention of all.

In the other greenhouses of the front range, there are many interesting plants; among these may be noticed Plantains, which bear fruit well, Papaw tree, Pitcher-plant, Papyrus, Indian rubber fig, cacti, cinnamon, tea plants, camphor tree, Astrapæa, some of the Fig tribe growing suspended in the air, amaryllides, arums, euphorbias, &c. In front of this range of houses is a piece of ground, on which many of the plants of warmer regions, such as palms, acacias, &c., are cultivated in the open air, being carefully protected during winter. Behind these houses is a smaller range in which numerous seedlings are cultivated, and a large Palm-house about 45 feet high, in which are found Plantains and Bananas, Sago Palms, Fan Palms, European Palms, Cabbage Palms, Date Palms, Cocoa Nut Trees, Sugar Cane, Bamboos, Screw Pine, Elephant's foot, &c. The houses are heated partly by hot water and partly by steam. From the top of the boiler-house there is a very fine view of Edinburgh. On the high northern wall of the garden, many valuable exotics are trained, as Magnolias, Myrtles, Eucalypti, &c.

The garden is surrounded by trees, on the west, south, and eastern sides, and among these there are some of considerable interest. Many of them were removed in their full grown state, from the former garden in Leith Walk, and, under the judicious management of Mr. M'Nab, they have all succeeded. To the west of the general European collection is an old Yew, which has been twice transplanted, having been transferred first, from the old Physic Gardens below the North Bridge, to the garden in Leith Walk, and afterwards removed to its present situation. Beside the British collection is a magnetic observatory, superintended by the Professor of Natural

Philosophy. The class-room of the Professor of Botany, and the house of the superintendant are situated on the right hand side of the entrance.

In returning, the stranger may vary his route by turning to the right, immediately after recrossing Canonmills Bridge, and proceeding by Brandon Street, Pitt Street, and Dundas Street, to George's Street, from which he may pursue the same line of progress to the Register House, as in the preceding walk.

The objects of interest in the City being now exhausted, we proceed to introduce the tourist to some spots in the vicinity more particularly worthy of notice. Among these we may observe, that Roslin is generally regarded as the most attractive, although we have commenced with Habbie's Howe, as the best geographical arrangement.

ENVIRONS OF EDINBURGH.

HABBIE'S HOWE.

A very delightful excursion may be made from Edinburgh to Newhall, distant about twelve miles, supposed, with great probability, to be the scene of Allan Ramsay's celebrated pastoral, "The Gentle Shepherd."

Leaving Edinburgh by Burntsfield Links, the tourist passes on the right MERCHISTON CASTLE, the birth-place of the celebrated Napier, the inventor of Logarithms. A little further on is the village of Morningside, and a number of villas and country boxes. Two miles from Edinburgh is the Hermitage of Braid, (J. Gordon, Esq. of Clunie,) situated at the bottom of a narrow and thickly wooded dell, through which a small rivulet, called the Braid Burn, strays. Braid once belonged to a family called Fairly, and the Laird of Baird, during the Reformation, was a personal friend and zealous defender of John Knox. The road now skirts the rocky eminences called the Hills of Braid, which command a most beautiful view of the Scottish metropolis, with the Firth of Forth, its islands, and the shores of Fife in the background. The more northern side, called Blackford Hill, the property of Richard Trotter, Esq. of Mortonhall, is the spot mentioned in "Marmion."

> "Still on the spot Lord Marmion stay'd,
> For fairer scene he ne'er survey'd, &c.

The space of ground which extends from the bottom

of Blackford Hill to the suburbs of Edinburgh, was formerly denominated the Borough Moor. We are informed by historians that it was studded with magnificent oaks at the time when James IV. arrayed his army upon it, previous to his departure for the fatal expedition which terminated in the Battle of Flodden. The HARE STONE, in which the Royal Standard was fixed, is still to be seen built into the wall, which runs along the side of the footpath at the place called Boroughmoor-head. At about half a mile's distance to the southward, there is another stone called the Buck Stone, upon which the proprietor of the barony of Pennycuik is bound, by his charter, to place himself and to wind three blasts of a horn when the king shall visit the Borough Moor. On the right, at some distance, is Dreghorn, (A. Trotter, Esq.) the village of Colinton, delightfully situated at the bottom of the Pentland Hills, and Colinton House, (Sir John Forbes, Bart.) About five miles from Edinburgh is WOODHOUSELEE, the seat of P. Fraser Tytler, Esq., on the southern slope of the Pentland Hills, surrounded by fine woods. The ancient house of the same name, once the property of Bothwellhaugh, the assassin of the Regent Murray, was four miles distant from the present site. Woodhouselee had been bestowed upon Sir James Ballenden, one of the Regent's favourites, who seized the house, and turned out Lady Bothwellhaugh naked, in a cold night, into the open fields, where, before next morning, she became furiously mad.* The ruins of the mansion are still to be seen in a hollow glen beside the river. Popular

* This event forms the subject of Sir Walter Scott's first ballad of "Cadyow Castle." Its length precludes our quoting it entire, but we give the following touching stanzas :—

"Few suns have set since Woodhouselee
Saw Bothwellhaugh's bright goblets foam,

report tenants them with the restless ghost of the lady. The road now passes the hamlet of Upper Howgate, and a little farther on Glencorse Church, embosomed in a wood. On the right is the vale of Glencorse, watered by a little rill, called Logan Water, or more commonly Glencorse Burn. The head of this valley is supposed by some to be the scene of Allan Ramsay's Pastoral Drama, "The Gentle Shepherd," but the appearance of the scenery, as well as the absence of all the localities noticed by Ramsay, render this opinion extremely improbable. The sequestered pastoral character of this valley, however, renders it well worthy of a visit. After crossing Glencorse Burn, the road passes House of Muir, in the neighbourhood of which is the place where the Covenanters were defeated 28th November 1666. The insurrection, which ended in this skirmish, began in Dumfries-shire, where Sir James Turner was employed to levy the arbitrary fines imposed for not attending the Episcopal churches. The people rose, seized his person, disarmed his soldiers, and, having continued together, resolved to march towards Edinburgh, expecting to be

---

When to his hearth, in social glee,
  The war-worn soldier turned him home.

"There, wan from her maternal throes,
  His Margaret, beautiful and mild,
Sate in her bower, a pallid rose,
  And peaceful nursed her new-born child.

"O, change accursed! past are those days;
  False Murray's ruthless spoilers came,
And for the hearth's domestic blaze,
  Ascends destruction's volumed flame.

"What sheeted phantom wanders wild,
  Where mountain Eske, through woodland flows,
Her arms enfold a shadowy child—
  Oh! is it she, the pallid rose?

joined by their friends in that quarter. In this they were disappointed, and being now diminished to half their numbers, they drew up on the Pentland Hills, at a place called Rullion Green. They were commanded by one Wallace, and here they awaited the approach of General Dalziel of Binns, who having marched by Calder to meet them on the Lanark road, and finding that, by passing through Colinton, they had got to the other side of the hills, cut through the mountains, and approached them. The Covenanters were drawn up in a very strong position, and withstood two charges of Dalziel's cavalry, but upon the third shock they were broken, and utterly dispersed. There were about fifty killed, and as many made prisoners. Passing through the village of Silver Burn, the road reaches

NEWHALL,

On the banks of the north Esk, about three miles from Pennycuick House, and twelve south-west from Edinburgh. Newhall is now the property of Robert Brown, Esq. At the era of Ramsay's drama, it belonged to Dr. Alexander Pennycuick, a poet and antiquary. In 1703 it passed into the hands of Sir David Forbes, a distinguished lawyer; and, in Ramsay's time, was the property of Mr. John Forbes, son to Sir David, and cousin-german to the celebrated President Forbes of Culloden. The scenery around Newhall answers most minutely to the description in the drama. Near the house, on the north side of the vale, there is a crag (called the Harbour Crag, from having afforded refuge to the Covenanters,) which corresponds exactly with the first scene of the first act:

> "Beneath the south side of a craggy bield,
> Where chrystal springs the halesome waters yield."

Farther up the vale, and behind the house, there is a

spot beside the burn, which corresponds to the description of the second scene:

"A flow'ry howm between twa verdant braes,
Where lasses used to wash and spread their claes;
A trottin' burnie wimplin through the ground,
Its channel pebbles shining smooth and sound."

A little farther up the vale there is a place called the Howe Burn, where the stream forms a small cascade, and where the scenery in every respect corresponds with the exquisite description of the spot called "Habbie's Howe,"

"Gae farer up the burn to Habbie's Howe,
Where a' the sweets o' spring and summer grow,
There 'tween twa birks, out ower a little linn,
The water fa's and mak's a singand din;
A pule breast deep, beneath as clear as glass,
Kisses wi' easy whirls the bordering grass."

Still farther up the vale, at a place called the Carlops,* a tall rock shoots up on each side, near an old withered solitary oak tree, is the site of Mause's cottage, described in the second scene of the second act:

"The open field, a cottage in the glen,
An auld wife spinnin' at the sunny end.
At a sma' distance, by a blasted tree,
Wi' faulded arms and half raised look ye see
Bauldy his lane."

PENNYCUIK HOUSE, the seat of Sir George Clerk, Bart. is well worthy of a visit. The neighbouring scenery is extremely beautiful, and the pleasure-grounds are highly ornamented. The house contains an excellent collection of paintings, with a number of Roman antiquities found

* A contraction of Carline's Loups, in consequence, it is said, of a witch or carline having been frequently observed to leap, by night, from the rock at one side over to that at the other.

in Britain, and, among other curiosities, the buff coat worn by Dundee at the battle of Killiecrankie. The principal apartment, called Ossian's Hall, has a ceiling beautifully decorated with paintings by Runciman.

ROSLIN.

Another interesting scene visited more frequently than any other by the inhabitants of Edinburgh, is ROSLIN CHAPEL, situated about seven miles from the city, on the banks of the North Esk. The vale of Roslin is one of those beautiful and sequestered dells which so often occur in Scotland, abounding with all the romantic varieties of cliff, and copsewood, and waterfall. Its beautiful Gothic chapel is one of the most entire and exquisitely decorated specimens of ecclesiastical architecture in Scotland. It is in the florid style of the fifteenth century, and displays a profusion of ornament executed in the most beautiful manner. The centre of the church is one continued arch, supported by clustered pillars eight feet high, adorned with foliage, and finely sculptured. The prentice's pillar in particular is a piece of exquisite workmanship. The chapel was founded in 1446 by William St. Clair, Earl of Orkney, and Lord of Roslin; at the Revolution of 1688 part of it was defaced by a mob from Edinburgh, but it was repaired in the following century by General St. Clair, and since that time has been partially renovated, without impairing its venerable character, by the late Earl of Rosslyn. Beneath this chapel lie the Barons of

Roslin, all of whom were, till the time of James VII. buried in armour.*

The mouldering ruin of ROSLIN CASTLE, with its tremendous triple tier of vaults, stands upon a peninsular rock, overhanging the picturesque glen of the Esk, and is accessible only by a bridge of great height thrown over a deep cut in the solid rock, which separates it from the

* This circumstance, as well as the superstitious belief that on the night before the death of any of these barons, the chapel appeared in flames, is beautifully described by Sir Walter Scott in his exquisite ballad of Rosabelle:—

O listen, listen, ladies gay!
  No haughty feat of arms I tell;
Soft is the note and sad the lay,
  That mourns the lovely Rosabellé.

"Moor, moor the barge, ye gallant crew!
  And, gentle ladye, deign to stay!
Rest thee in Castle Ravensheuch,
  Nor tempt the stormy firth to-day.

"The blackening wave is edged with white;
  To inch and rock the sea-mews fly;
The fishers have heard the Water-Sprite,
  Whose screams forbode that wreck is nigh.

Last night the gifted Seer did view
  A wet shroud swathed round ladye gay;
Then stay thee, Fair, in Ravensheuch:
  Why cross the gloomy firth to-day?"

"'Tis not because Lord Lindesay's heir
  To-night at Roslin leads the ball,
But that my ladye-mother there
  Sits lonely in her castle-hall.

"'Tis not because the ring they ride,
  And Lindesay at the ring rides well,
But that my sire the wine will chide,
  If 'tis not fill'd by Rosabellé."—

"O'er Roslin all that dreary night,
  A wondrous blaze was seen to gleam;
'Twas broader than the watch-fires light,
  And redder than the bright moon-beam.

It glared on Roslin's castled rock,
  It ruddied all the copse-wood glen;
'Twas seen from Dryden's groves of oak,
  And seen from cavern'd Hawthornden.

adjacent ground. This castle, the origin of which is involved in obscurity, was long the abode of the proud family of the St. Clairs, Earls of Caithness and Orkney. In 1544 it was burned down by the Earl of Hertford; and in 1650 it surrendered to General Monk. About sixty or seventy years ago the comparatively modern mansion which has been erected amidst the ruins of the old castle, was inhabited by a genuine Scottish laird of the old stamp, the lineal descendant of the high race who first founded the pile, and the last male of their long line. He was Captain of the Royal Company of Archers, and Hereditary Grand Master of the Scottish Masons. At his death the estate descended to Sir James Erskine St. Clair, father of the present Earl of Rosslyn, who now represents the family.

The neighbouring moor of Roslin was the scene of a celebrated battle, fought 24th February 1302, in which the Scots under Comyn, then guardian of the kingdom,

---

Seem'd all on fire that chapel proud,
  Where Roslin's chiefs uncoffin'd lie,
Each baron, for a sable shroud,
  Sheathed in his iron panoply.

Seem'd all on fire within, around,
  Deep sacristy and altar's pale;
Shone every pillar foliage-bound,
  And glimmer'd all the dead men's mail.

Blazed battlement and pinnet high,
  Blazed every rose-carved buttress fair—
So still they blaze, when fate is nigh
  The lordly line of high St. Clair.

There are twenty of Roslin's barons bold
  Lie buried within that proud chapelle;
Each one the holy vault doth hold—
  But the sea holds lovely Rosabellé!

And each St. Clair was buried there,
  With candle, with book, and with knell;
But the sea-caves rung, and the wild winds sung,
  The dirge of lovely Rosabellé.

and Simon Fraser, attacked and defeated three divisions of the English on the same day.

After leaving Roslin, we pass the caves of Gorton, situated in the front of a high cliff on the southern side of the stream. These caverns, during the reign of David II. while Scotland was overrun by the English, afforded shelter to the gallant Sir Alexander Ramsay of Dalwolsey, with a band of chosen patriots.

Passing through scenery of great natural beauty, the footpath down the river conducts the tourist to

HAWTHORNDEN,

the classical habitation of the poet Drummond, the friend of Shakspeare and Jonson; it is now the property of Sir Francis Walker Drummond. Being built with some view to defence, the house rises from the very edge of the grey cliff, which descends sheer down to the stream. An inscription on the front of the building testifies that it was repaired by the poet, 1638. It is well known that Ben Jonson walked from London on foot to visit Drummond, and lived several weeks with him at Hawthornden. Under the mansion are several subterraneous caves, hewn out of the solid rock with great labour, and connected with each other by long passages; in the court-yard there is a well of prodigious depth, which communicates with them. These caverns are supposed to have been constructed as places of refuge when the public calamities rendered the ordinary habitations unsafe. The walks around the house are peculiarly fine, but admission to them can only be obtained by an order from the proprietor.

Farther down the river is the pretty village of LASSWADE, the name of which is said to be derived from a young woman or *lass* who in former times waded across the stream, carrying upon her back those whose circumstances enabled them to purchase the luxury of such a conveyance. In a cottage in the vicinity, Sir Walter Scott spent some of the happiest years of his life. At a short distance is

MELVILLE CASTLE,

the seat of Viscount Melville. The building was erected by the celebrated Harry Dundas, first Viscount Melville. The park contains some fine wood. Two miles farther is the town of

DALKEITH, AND DALKEITH HOUSE.

a seat of the Duke of Buccleuch. It is situated on an overhanging bank of the North Esk, a little to the east of the town. It is a large but by no means elegant structure, situate on an overhanging bank of the North Esk, a little to the east of the town, and surrounded by an extensive park, through which the rivers of North and South Esk run, and unite their streams a short way below the house. The first proprietors of Dalkeith upon record are the Grahams; from them it passed, in the reign of David II. by a daughter, into the possession of Sir William Douglas, ancestor of the Earls of Morton. In the reign of Queen Mary, Dalkeith was the head quarters of the celebrated Regent Morton, and, after resigning his regency, he retired to this stronghold, which, from the general idea entertained of his character, acquired at that time the expressive name of the Lion's Den. In the year 1642, the estate was purchased from the Earl of Morton by Francis Earl of Buccleuch. Anne, Duchess of Buccleuch and Monmouth, after the execution of her unhappy husband, substituted the modern for the ancient mansion, and lived here in royal state, and for more than a century it has formed the residence of the Buccleuch family. Since the union of the crowns, Dalkeith House has twice been the temporary residence of royalty, namely, of King Charles in 1633, and of George IV. in 1822. It is worthy of notice, that Froissart, the historian of chivalry, visited the Earl of Douglas, and lived with him several weeks at the Castle of Dalkeith. There is a popular belief current that the treasure unrighteously amassed by the Regent Morton lies hidden somewhere among the vaults of the ancient building, but Godscroft assures us that it was expended by the Earl of Angus in supporting the companions of his exile in England, and that, when it was exhausted, the Earl generously exclaimed, "Is it, then, all gone? let it go, I never looked it should have done so much good!" The environs of Dalkeith are interesting, and the tourist may be conveyed thither from Edinburgh by the railroad, in a short space of time, and at a very low rate.*

* The beautiful scenes through which the North and South Esk flow, and the various seats that adorn the banks of these streams, are very happily described by Sir Walter Scott, in his ballad of the Grey Brother:—

Sweet are the paths,—O, passing sweet!
  By Esk's fair streams that run,
O'er airy steep, through copsewoods deep,
  Impervious to the sun.

There the rapt poet's step may rove,
  And yield the Muse the day,
There Beauty, led by timid Love,
  May shun the tell-tale ray.

From that fair dome where suit is paid,
  By blast of bugle free,†
To Auchendinny's hazel glade,
  And haunted Woodhouselee.

Who knows not Melville's beechy grove,
  And Roslin's rocky glen,
Dalkeith, which all the virtues love,
  And classic Hawthornden.

† Pennycuik. See ante, p. 78.

About a mile south-west from Dalkeith, on the northern bank of the South Esk, is

NEWBATTLE ABBEY,

a seat of the Marquis of Lothian. This mansion stands on the spot formerly occupied by the abbey of Newbattle, founded by David I. for a community of Cistercian monks. An ancestor of the present noble proprietor was the last abbot, and his son, Mark Ker, got the possessions of the Abbey erected into a temporal lordship in the year 1591. The house contains a number of fine paintings and curious manuscripts, and the land is interspersed with some straggling trees of great size.

Higher up the South Esk is

DALHOUSIE CASTLE,

a modernized building in the castellated form. The original structure was of vast antiquity and great strength. The present possessor, the Earl of Dalhousie, is the lineal descendant of the celebrated Sir Alexander Ramsay. The scenery around Dalhousie is romantic and beautiful.

Passing Arniston, the residence of the celebrated family of Dundas, the tourist, at the distance of about 11 miles from Edinburgh, comes in sight of BORTHWICK CASTLE, an ancient and stately tower rising out of the centre of a small but well-cultivated valley, watered by a stream called the Gore. This interesting fortress is in the form of a double tower, 74 feet in length, 68 in breadth, and in height 90 feet from the area to the battlements. It occupies a knoll or moat, surrounded by the small river, and is enclosed within an outer court, fortified by a strong outward wall, having flanking towers at the angles. The interior of the castle is exceedingly interesting. The hall is a stately and magnificent apartment, the ceiling of which consists of a smooth vault of ashler work. Three stairs, ascending at the angles of the building, gave access to the separate stories; one is quite ruinous, but the others are still tolerably entire. The licence for building Borthwick Castle was granted by James I. to Sir William Borthwick, 2d June, 1430. It was to Borthwick that Queen Mary retired with Bothwell, three weeks after her unfortunate marriage with that nobleman, and from which she was obliged, a few days afterwards, to flee to Dunbar in the disguise of a page. During the civil war, Borthwick held out gallantly against the victorious Cromwell, and surrendered, at last, upon honourable terms. The effect of Cromwell's battery still remains, his fire having destroyed a part of the freestone facing of the eastern side of the castle. Borthwick is now the property of John Borthwick, Esq. of Crookstone, a claimant of the ancient peerage of Borthwick, which has remained in abeyance since the death of the ninth Lord Borthwick in the reign of Charles II.

Two miles to the eastward of Borthwick Castle, and within sight of its battlements, stands CRICHTON CASTLE, on the banks of the Tyne, ten miles south from Edinburgh, and about two miles above the village of Pathhead on the Lauder road. Crichton Castle was built at different periods, and forms on the whole one large square pile enclosing an interior court-yard. A strong old tower, which forms the east side of the quadrangle, seems to have been the original part of the building. The northern quarter, which appears to be the most modern, is built in a style of remarkable elegance. The description of the castle given by Sir Walter Scott in his poem of Marmion, is so minutely accurate, that we transcribe it in preference to any remarks of our own.

That Castle rises on the steep
  Of the green vale of Tyne;

And, far beneath, where slow they creep
From pool to eddy, dark and deep,
Where alders moist, and willows weep,
You hear her streams repine.
The towers in different ages rose;
Their various architecture shows
The builders' various hands;
A mighty mass that could oppose,
When deadliest hatred fired its foes,
The vengeful Douglas bands.

Crichtoun! though now thy miry court
But pens the lazy steer and sheep,
Thy turrets rude, and tottered Keep
Have been the minstrel's loved resort.
Oft have I traced, within thy fort,
Of mouldering shields the mystic sense,
Scutcheons of honour, or pretence,
Quartered in old armorial sort,
Remains of rude magnificence.
Nor wholly yet hath time defaced
Thy lordly gallery fair;
Nor yet the stony cord unbraced,
Whose twisted knots with roses laced,
Adorn thy ruined stair.
Still rises unimpaired, below,
The court-yard's graceful portico;
Above its cornice, row and row
Of fair hewn facets richly show
Their pointed diamond form,
Though there but houseless cattle go,
To shield them from the storm.
And, shuddering, still may we explore,
Where oft whilom were captives pent,
The darkness of thy Massy More;*
Or, from thy grass-grown battlement,
May trace, in undulating line,
The sluggish mazes of the Tyne.

* The pit or prison-vault.

Crichton was the patrimonial estate and residence of the celebrated Sir William Crichton, Chancellor of Scotland, during the minority of James II., and whose influence contributed so much to destroy the formidable power of the Douglas family. On the forfeiture of William, third Lord Crichton, the castle and barony of Crichton was granted to Sir John Ramsay a favourite of James III. The defeat and death of James involved the ruin of Ramsay. He in his turn was proscribed, exiled, and his estate forfeited, and the castle and lordship of Crichton were granted anew to Patrick Hepburn, third Lord Hales, who was created Earl of Bothwell. He was ancestor of the infamous James Earl of Bothwell, who exercised such an unhappy influence over the fortunes of Queen Mary. On his outlawry, Crichton was conferred by James VI. on his kinsman Francis Stewart, Earl of Bothwell, so noted for the constant train of conspiracies and insurrections in which he was engaged. Since that period, Crichton has passed through the hands of about a dozen proprietors, and is now the property of William Burn Callander, Esq. The ancient church of Crichton still exists, at the distance of half a mile to the north of the castle. It is a small but venerable building in the shape of a cross with a low and truncated belfry. The west end has been left unfinished.

Returning to the road, about a mile from Pathhead, stands OXENFORD CASTLE, the residence of Sir John H. Dalrymple, Bart. It is situated on the north bank of the Tyne, in the midst of an extensive park.

About three miles south from Edinburgh are the ruins of CRAIGMILLAR CASTLE, situated on the top of a gentle eminence, and surrounded with some fine old trees. The date of the original erection is unknown, but the rampart wall which surrounds the castle appears from a date preserved on it to have been built in 1427. Craigmillar, with other fortresses in Mid-Lothian, was burned by the English after Pinkey fight in 1555, and Captain Grose surmises with great plausibility, that much of the building as it now appears was erected when the castle was repaired after that event.

In point of architecture and accommodation, Craigmillar surpasses the generality of Scottish castles. It consists of a strong tower, flanked with turrets, and connected with inferior buildings. There is an outer court in front, defended by the battlemented wall already mentioned, and beyond these there was an exterior wall, and in some places a deep ditch or moat.

Being so near Edinburgh, Craigmillar was often occupied as a royal residence. Here John, Earl of Mar, younger brother of James III. was imprisoned in 1477. James V. occupied it occasionally during his minority, and it was so often the residence of Queen Mary, that the adjacent village acquired the name of Little France; from her French guards being quartered there.

The castle and estate of Craigmillar was acquired by Sir Simon Preston in 1374, from one John de Capella, and they continued in the possession of the Preston family till about the Revolution, when they were purchased by Sir Thomas Gilmour the great lawyer, to whose descendant, Walter Little Gilmour, Esq. they still belong.

FIRST TOUR.

EDINBURGH TO PEEBLES—INNERLEITHEN—SELKIRK—(VALES OF ETTRICK AND YARROW)—MELROSE—KELSO—COLDSTREAM AND BERWICK.

LEAVING Edinburgh by Nicholson Street, the tourist sees on an eminence, a short distance to the left, the ruins of CRAIGMILLAR CASTLE, an interesting edifice in which Queen Mary often resided. A little farther on, and nearer the road, stand the village and church of Libberton, pleasantly situated on a rising ground, and commanding a splendid view of Edinburgh and the surrounding scenery. Passing on the right, Morton Hall, (Richard Trotter, Esq.,) and upon the left, Gracemount, (Mrs. Hay,) and St. Catherine's (Sir William Rae,) we reach the small village of Burdiehouse, a corruption of Bourdeaux House, the name conferred on it by a native of that part in France. A little farther on is the village of Straiton, near which was fought the second of three conflicts which took place in one day, in 1303, styled the battle of Roslin. Six miles from Edinburgh we pass Bilston toll-bar, where a road strikes off on the left to Roslin. About a mile farther the tourist passes Greenlaw, built as a depôt for French prisoners during the late war, and on the right, Glencorse House and church, and a little beyond, Auchindinny House, once the residence of Henry Mackenzie, author of the Man of Feeling, and Auchindinny paper mill, and at the distance of other two miles enters PENNYCUIK VILLAGE, ten miles distant from Edinburgh. In the immediate vicinity are the extensive paper mills of Messrs. Cowan and Sons. On the right stands Pennycuik House, the seat of Sir George Clerk, Bart., a fine specimen of modern architecture surrounded by beautiful woods. Three miles from Pennycuik the tourist enters Peebles-shire, where the direct road to Dumfries parts off on the right. The tract of country around is bleak and moorish. Three miles from Kingside Edge is The Cottage, (W. F. Mackenzie, Esq. of Portmore, M.P.,) and a mile beyond this, Eddlestone village. Passing in succession, Darnhall, (Lord Elibank,) Cringletie, (Murray, Esq.,) Winkstone, (M'Gowan, Esq.,) Rosetta, (Dr. Young,) Venelaw, (Erskine, Esq.,) and Tweedside House, (W. Allan, Esq. of Glen,) the tourist enters the royal burgh of

PEEBLES,

the county town, beautifully situated on the Tweed, twenty-two miles distant from Edinburgh. Peebles is a town of great antiquity, and must from a very early period have been a seat of population, as is indicated by its name, which in British signifies shielings or dwelling places; it is certain that at the end of the 11th century there were at this place, a village, a church, a mill, and a brewhouse. Owing to its situation in the midst of a fine hunting country, and on the direct road to the royal forest of Ettrick, it became at an early period the occasional residence of the kings of Scotland, and is the scene of the celebrated poem of James I., entitled, "*Peblis to the Play.*" On account of its sequestered situation this town figures little in Scottish history, and seems to have taken no part in any great historical event. It was, however, burnt and laid waste oftener than once during the invasions of the English. Peebles is divided into two districts, the old and new town. A bridge of great antiquity, consisting of five arches, connects the town with an extensive suburb on the opposite bank. The appearance of the whole is very pleasing, and the surrounding scenery is extremely beautiful. Peebles is a town possessed of very little commerce or manufacture. It has a weekly market, and seven annual fairs. At the end of the fifteenth century Peebles possessed no fewer than eleven places of worship, out of which the remains of only two are now visible. There is a large edifice of a castellated appearance still existing, known to have belonged to the Queensberry family, which is believed to be the scene of a highly romantic incident thus related by Sir Walter Scott. There is a tradition in Tweeddale, that when Neidpath Castle, near Peebles, was inhabited by the Earls of March, a mutual passion subsisted between a daughter of that noble family, and a son of the laird of Tushielaw, in Ettrick forest. As the alliance was thought unsuitable by her parents, the young man went abroad. During his absence the young lady fell into a consumption, and at length, as the only means of saving her life, her father consented that her lover should be recalled. On the day when he was expected to pass through Peebles, on the road to Tushielaw, the young lady, though much exhausted, caused herself to be carried to the balcony of a house in Peebles, belonging to the family, that she might see him as he rode past. Her anxiety and eagerness gave such force to her organs, that she is said to have distinguished his horse's footsteps at an incredible distance. But Tushielaw, unprepared for the change in her appearance, and not expecting to see her in that place, rode on without recognizing her, or even slackening his pace. The lady was unable to support the shock, and after a short struggle, died in the arms of her attendants.

The vale of the Tweed, both above and below Peebles, contained a chain of strong castles to serve as a defence against the incursions of English marauders. These castles were built in the shape of square towers, and usually consisted of three storeys—the lower one on the ground floor being vaulted and appropriated to the reception of horses and cattle in times of danger. They were built alternately on both sides of the river, and in a continued view of each other. A fire kindled on the top of these towers was the signal of an incursion, and, in this manner, a tract of country 70 miles long from Berwick to the Bield, and 50 broad, was alarmed in a few hours.* The strongest and the most entire of these fortresses is NEIDPATH CASTLE, situated about a mile west from the town of Peebles, on a rock projecting over the north bank of the Tweed, which here runs through a deep narrow glen, once well wooded on both sides. Neidpath was at one time the chief residence of the powerful family of the Frasers, from whom the families of Lovat and Salton in the north are descended. The last of the family in the male line was Sir Simon Fraser, who, in 1302, along with Comyn, then guardian of the kingdom, defeated three divisions of the English on the same day on Roslin Moor. Sir Simon left two daughters co-heiresses, one of whom married Hay of Yester, an ancester of the Marquis of Tweeddale. The second Earl of Tweeddale garrisoned Neidpath in 1636 for the ser-

* "——— A score of fires I ween,
From height, and hill, and cliff were seen,
Each with warlike tidings fraught,
Each from each the signal caught;
Each after each they glanced in sight,
As stars arise upon the night:
They gleamed on many a dusky tarn,
Haunted by the lonely earn,†
On many a cairn's grey pyramid,
Where urns of mighty chiefs lie hid."

† The Scottish Eagle.

vice of Charles II. and it held out longer against Cromwell than any place south of the Forth. The Tweeddale family were so much impoverished by their exertions in the royal cause, that they were obliged, before the end of the reign of Charles II., to dispose of their barony of Neidpath to William, first Duke of Queensberry, who purchased it for his son the first Earl of March. On the death of the last Duke of Queensberry, in 1810, the Earl of Wemyss, as heir of entail, succeeded to the Neidpath estate. The castle is now falling fast to decay. It was formerly approached by an avenue of fine trees, all of which were cut down by the late Duke of Queensberry to impoverish the estate before it descended to the heir of entail. The poet, Wordsworth, has spoken of this conduct with just indignation in the following sonnet:—

"Degenerate Douglas! oh, the unworthy Lord!
Whom mere despite of heart could so far please,
And love of havoc, (for with such disease
Fame taxes him,) that he could send forth word
To level with the dust a noble horde,
A brotherhood of venerable Trees,
Leaving an ancient dome, and towers like these,
Beggared and outraged!—Many hearts deplored
The fate of those old Trees; and oft with pain
The traveller, at this day, will stop and gaze
On wrongs, which Nature scarcely seems to heed:
For sheltered places, bosoms, nooks, and bays,
And the pure mountains, and the gentle Tweed,
And the green silent pastures, yet remain."

Leaving Peebles, the tourist proceeds along the northern bank of the Tweed, and passing in succession Kerfield (—— Ker, Esq.)—on the opposite bank of the river, King's Meadows and Hayston, (Sir Adam Hay,

Bart.)—the ruins of Horsburgh Castle, the property of the ancient family of the Horsburghs now resident at Pirn—Kailzie (—— Campbell, Esq.), Nether Horsburgh (Campbell, Esq.), Cardrona, the seat of the old family of Williamson, and Glen Ormiston House; six miles below Peebles reaches the village of

INNERLEITHEN,

situated about a quarter of a mile from the mouth of Leithen water. It occupies a pleasant situation at the bottom of a sequestered dell, environed on the east and west by high and partially wooded hills, and having the Tweed rolling in front. Till little more than 30 years ago, Innerleithen was one of the smallest and most primitive hamlets in this pastoral district. But, about the beginning of the present century, its mineral spring began to attract notice, and it has now become a favourite watering-place, much frequented in the summer and autumn by visitors from Edinburgh. The healthiness of the climate—the beauty of the situation—its proximity to St. Mary's Loch in Yarrow, and various trouting streams, as well as other advantages connected with its locality, render Innerleithen a very delightful residence. A handsome wooden bridge leads across the Tweed to the hamlet of Traquair and Traquair House, the seat of the Earl of Traquair. At a short distance, at the base of a hill overlooking the lawn, a few birch trees may be seen, the scanty remains of the famed "Bush aboon Traquair." A few years ago an association was instituted at Innerleithen called the St. Ronan's Border Club, consisting of a number of gentlemen connected with all parts of the country, who hold an annual festival for the performance of games and gymnastic exercises.

Leaving Innerleithen, at a short distance upon the right is Pirn; and three miles farther on, the road enters Selkirkshire, passing, on the left, Holylee (Ballantyne, Esq.) A mile beyond, on the opposite side of the river, are the ruins of Elibank Tower, from which Lord Elibank takes his title. Two miles farther on is Ashiesteel (Col. Russell), once the residence of Sir Walter Scott. A mile beyond this, the road crosses Caddon Burn, and, at the village of Clovenfords, joins the road from Edinburgh to Selkirk. Two miles beyond, it passes Fairnielie (Pringle of Clifton) and Yair, the seat of Alexander Pringle, Esq. of Whytbank, M.P., one of the loveliest spots in Scotland, closely surrounded by hills most luxuriantly wooded. The road then crosses the Tweed at Yair Bridge, and, two miles farther on, crosses the Ettrick and enters the royal burgh of

SELKIRK,

situated on a piece of high ground overhanging the Ettrick. Selkirk is a town of neat appearance, and the beautiful woods surrounding The Haining, the seat of Robert Pringle, Esq. of Clifton, form an excellent back ground to it. The population of the town and parish is 2883. It gives the title of Earl to a branch of the Douglas family.

A party of the citizens of Selkirk, under the command of their town-clerk, William Brydone, behaved with great gallantry at the battle of Flodden, when, in revenge for their brave conduct, the English entirely destroyed the town by fire. A pennon taken from an English leader by a person of the name of Fletcher, is still kept in Selkirk by the successive deacons of the weavers, and Brydone's sword is still in the possession of his lineal descendants. The well known and pathetic ballad of the "The Flowers of the Forest" was composed on the loss sustained by the inhabitants of Ettrick Forest at the fatal battle of Flodden. The principal trade carried on in Selkirk at the time of the battle, and for centuries afterwards, was the manufacture of thin or *single-soled* shoes.* Hence, to be made a sutor of Selkirk is the ordinary phrase for being created a burgess, and a *birse* or hog's bristle is always attached to the seal of the ticket.

[Those tourists whose time does not admit of their visiting the vales of Ettrick and Yarrow, may pass over the following chapter, which, forming a sort of episode in the tour, we have printed in a smaller type.]

ETTRICK AND YARROW.

Leaving Selkirk, the tourist will retrace his steps to the bridge over the Ettrick, and turn up the north bank. The large level plain on the northern side of the river is Philiphaugh, the scene of the defeat of Montrose by General Leslie, 13th September, 1645. Montrose himself had taken up his quarters with his cavalry in the town of Selkirk, while his infantry, amounting to about twelve or fifteen hundred men, were posted on Philiphaugh. Leslie arrived at Melrose the evening before the engagement, and next morning, favoured by a thick mist, he reached Montrose's encampment without being descried by a single scout. The surprisal was complete, and when the Marquis, who had been alarmed by the noise of the firing, reached the scene of the battle, he beheld his army dispersed in irretrievable rout. After a desperate but unavailing attempt to retrieve the fortune of the day, he cut his way through a body of Leslie's troopers, and fled up Yarrow and over Minchmoor towards Peebles. This defeat destroyed the fruit of Montrose's six splendid victories, and effectually ruined the royal cause in Scotland. The estate of Philiphaugh is the property of Colonel

* Up wi' the Souters o' Selkirk,
And down wi' the Earl o' Home;
And up wi' a' the braw lads
That sew the single-so'd shoon.

Murray, the descendant of the "Outlaw Murray," commemorated in the beautiful ballad of that name. At the head of Philiphaugh the Yarrow comes out from Newark's "birken bower" to join the Ettrick. At the confluence of these streams, about a mile above Selkirk, is Carterhaugh, the supposed scene of the fairy ballad of "Tamlane." The vale of Yarrow parts off from the head of Philiphaugh towards the right, that of Ettrick towards the left. The whole of this tract of country was, not many centuries ago, covered with wood, and its popular designation still is "the Forest." A native of Selkirk, who died about eighty years ago at an advanced age, used to tell that he had seen a person older than himself who said he had in his time walked from that town to Ettrick, a distance of eighteen miles, and never once all the way escaped from the shadow of trees; of this primeval forest no vestige is now to be seen.

> "The scenes are desert now and bare,
> Where flourished once a forest fair,
> Up pathless Ettrick and on Yarrow,
> Where erst the outlaw drew his arrow."
>
> SCOTT.

Turning up the vale of Ettrick, the first object of interest that occurs is Oakwood, the residence of the hero of the ballad called "The Dowie Dens of Yarrow," and, from time immemorial, the property of the Scotts of Harden; it is supposed, also, to have been the mansion of the famous wizard Michael Scott. Two or three miles farther up the glen is the village of Ettrick-brig-end, and, about six miles above, the remains of the tower of Tushielaw may be discerned upon the brae which rises from the north bank of the river. Tushielaw was the residence of the celebrated freebooter Adam Scott, called the King of the Border, who was hanged by James V. in the course of that memorable expedition in 1529 which proved fatal to Johnnie Armstrong, Cockburn of Henderland, and many other marauders; the elm tree on which he was hanged still exists among the ruins. Opposite to Tushielaw the Rankleburn joins the Ettrick. The vale of Rankleburn contains the lonely farm of Buccleuch, supposed to have been the original property of the noble family of that name. There are remains of a church and burial ground and of a kiln and mill in this district, but no traces of a baronial mansion. Farther up are the ruins of Thirlstane Castle, and, close by, the modern mansion of Thirlestane, the seat of the late Lord Napier, the lineal descendant of the old family of the Scotts of Thirlestane, as well as of the still more famous one of the Napiers of Merchiston. Sir John Scott of Thirlestane, his paternal ancestor, was the only chief willing to follow James V. in his invasion of England, when the rest of the Scottish nobles, encamped at Fala, obstinately refused to take part in the expedition. In memory of his fidelity, James granted to his family a charter of arms entitling them to bear a border of fleurs-de-luce similar to the tressure in the royal arms, with a bundle of spears for the crest, motto, "ready, aye ready."—See Lay of the Last Minstrel, canto iv. Thirlestane is surrounded with extensive plantations, and its late noble and benevolent owner employed for many years his whole time and talents in carrying on, at great expense, important improvements in this district. About a mile farther up stands the kirk and hamlet of Ettrick. A cottage near the sacred edifice is pointed out as the birth-place of the Ettrick Shepherd. The celebrated Thomas Boston was at one time minister of Ettrick, and, in the church-yard, a handsome monument has been erected to his memory since the commencement of the present century.

Crossing the hills which bound the vale of Ettrick on the right, the tourist descends into the celebrated vale of Yarrow. At the head of the vale is the beautiful sheet of water called St. Mary's Loch, four miles long, and nearly one broad.

—— "lone St. Mary's silent lake,
———— nor fen nor sedge,
Pollute the pure lake's crystal edge ·
Abrupt and sheer the mountains sink,
At once upon the level brink;
And just a trace of silver sand,
Marks where the water meets the land.
Far in the mirror bright and blue,
Each hill's huge outline you may view;
Shaggy with heath, but lonely bare,
Nor tree, nor bush, nor brake, is there,
Save where of land yon slender line,
Bears 'thwart the lake the scatter'd pine.
Yet even this nakedness has power,
And aids the feeling of the hour:
Nor thicket, dell, nor copse, you spy,
Where living thing concealed might lie;
There's nothing left to fancy's guess,
You see that all is loneliness;

And silence aids—though the steep hills
Send to the lake a thousand rills;
In summer tide, so soft they weep,
The sound but lulls the ear asleep;
Your horse's hoof-tread sounds too rude,
So stilly is the solitude."*

The river Yarrow flows from the east end, and a small stream connects the Loch of Lowes with its western extremity. In the winter it is still frequented by flights of wild swans; hence Wordsworth's lines:

"The swan on sweet St. Mary's lake,
Float double swan and shadow."

In the neighbourhood is the farm of Blackhouse, adjacent to which, are the remains of a very ancient tower in a wild and solitary glen, upon a torrent named Douglas Burn, which issues from the hills on the north, and joins the Yarrow, after passing a craggy rock, called the Douglas-craig. This wild scene, now a part of the Traquair estate, formed one of the most ancient possessions of the renowned family of Douglas, and is said by popular tradition, to be the scene of the fine old ballad of "The Douglas Tragedy." Near the eastern extremity of St. Mary's Loch are the ruins of Dryhope Tower, the birth-place of Mary Scott, famous by the traditional name of the "Flower of Yarrow," and a mile westward, is the ancient burying-ground of St. Mary's Kirk, but the Church has long ago disappeared.

—— "Though in feudal strife, a foe
Hath laid Our Lady's chapel low,
Yet still beneath the hallow'd soil,
The peasant rests him from his toil,
And, dying, bids his bones be laid,
Where erst his simple fathers pray'd."*

A funeral in a spot so very retired, has an uncommonly striking effect. At one corner of the burial-ground, but without its precincts, is a small mound, said by tradition to be the grave of Mass John Birnam, the former tenant of the chaplainry.

"That wizard priest, whose bones are thrust,
From company of holy dust."

* Marmion. Introduction to Canto II.

In the adjacent vale of Megget, is Henderland Castle, the residence of Cockburn, a border freebooter, who was hanged over the gate of his own tower by James V. Tradition says that Cockburn was surprised by the king while sitting at dinner. A mountain torrent called Henderland Burn, rushes impetuously from the hills through a rocky chasm, named the Dow-glen, and passes near the site of the tower. To the recesses of this glen, the wife of Cockburn is said to have retreated, during the execution of her husband, and a place called the *Lady's Seat*, is still shown, where she is said to have striven to drown amid the roar of a foaming cataract, the tumultuous noise which announced the close of his existence. The beautiful and pathetic balled, entitled "The Lament of the Border Widow," was composed on this event. On the north side of St. Mary's Loch is a hill called the Merecleuchhead, over which there is a scarcely visible track, termed the King's Road, which passes over the hills into Ettrick.* At the head of the Loch of the Lowes, on the east, is Kirkinhope, and on the west, Chapelhope, the scene of the tale of "The Brownie of Bodsbeck." A few miles farther on through the hills, is a small house called Birkhill, opposite the door of which, Claverhouse shot four Covenanters, whose grave-stones were discernible in Ettrick churchyard, a few years ago. Opposite the little inn at Birkhill, is a hill called the Watch Hill, from the circumstance of the Covenanters stationing one of their number there, to give notice of the approach of the soldiers; and a little below is a hideous gully, which contains a waterfall, called Dobbs Linn, and a cave which served as a place of retreat for the persecuted remnant. Near the head of Moffat water, is the "dark LOCH SKENE," a mountain lake of considerable size. The stream into which it discharges itself, after a short and precipitate course, falls from a cataract of immense height, and gloomy grandeur, called from its appearance THE GREY MARE'S TAIL. The water is precipitated over a dark rugged precipice, about 300 feet high. A little way from the foot of the cataract, is a sort of trench, called "The Giant's Grave," which has evidently

* An old song opens with this stanza:—

"The king rade round the Merecleuchhead,
Booted and spurred as we a' did see;
Syne dined wi' a lass at Mossfennan yett,
A little below the Logan Lee."

been a battery designed to command the pass. The character of the surrounding scenery is uncommonly savage and gloomy, and the earn or Scottish eagle, has for many ages built its nest yearly upon an islet in Loch Skene. This rude and savage scene is well described in the introduction to the second canto of Marmion.

> "There eagles scream from isle to shore;
> Down all the rocks the torrents roar;
> O'er the black waves incessant driven,
> Dark mists infect the summer heaven;
> Through the rude barriers of the lake
> Away its hurrying waters break
> Faster and whiter, dash and curl,
> Till down yon dark abyss they hurl.
> Rises the fog-smoke, white as snow
> Thunders the viewless stream below.
> * * *
> ——————— the bottom of the den,
> Where, deep deep down and far within,
> Toils with the rocks the roaring linn;
> Then issuing forth one foamy wave,
> And wheeling round the Giant's Grave,
> White as the snowy charger's tail,
> Drives down the pass of Moffatdale."

The Grey Mare's Tail is nearly ten miles north-east from the village of Moffat, noted for its mineral well.

Returning to the Vale of Yarrow, a short way below St. Mary's Loch, is MOUNT BENGER, at one time occupied by the Ettrick Shepherd; and a little farther on, Gordon's Inn, about thirteen miles from Selkirk, where a bridge over the Yarrow leads to ALTRIVE, where the poet died. The next object of interest that occurs is the Church of Yarrow, a neat little edifice, erected about the time of Cromwell. On the moor, a little way west from the kirk, two tall unhewn masses of stone about eighty yards distant from each other, mark the scene of the duel fought between John Scott of Tushielaw and his brother-in-law, Walter Scott, third son of Robert Scott of Thirlestane, in which the latter was slain. The alleged cause of malice was the lady's father having proposed to endow her with half his property, upon her marriage with a warrior of such renown. This incident has given rise, directly or indirectly, to ballads, songs, and poems innumerable. The most famous are the old ballad called "The Dowie Dens of Yarrow," and those composed by Hamilton of Bangour and Logan, and more recently the three charming poems of Wordsworth,—Yarrow Unvisited, Yarrow Visited, and Yarrow Revisited. A few verses of Yarrow Visited may here be quoted, as, in addition to the beauty of the poetry, they give an excellent description of the scenery.

"And is this—Yarrow?—This the stream
Of which my fancy cherished
So faithfully a waking dream?
An image that hath perished!
O that some minstrel's harp were near
To utter tones of gladness,
And chase this silence from the air
That fills my heart with sadness.

Yet why?—a silvery current flows
With uncontrolled meanderings;
Nor have these eyes, by greener hills,
Been soothed in all my wanderings.
And through her depths St. Mary's Lake
Is visibly delighted,
For not a feature of those hills
Is in the mirror slighted.

Where was it that the famous Flower
Of Yarrow Vale lay bleeding?
His bed, perchance, was yon smooth mound
On which the herd is feeding:
And haply from this crystal pool,
Now peaceful as the morning,
The water-wraith ascended thrice
And gave his doleful warning.

Delicious is the lay that sings
The haunts of happy lovers;
The path that leads them to the grove,
The leafy grove that covers:
And pity sanctifies the verse
That paints by strength of sorrow,
The unconquerable strength of love;
Bears witness, rueful Yarrow!

But thou that didst appear so fair
To fond imagination,
Dost rival in the light of day
Her delicate creation:
Meek loveliness is round thee spread,
A softness still and holy;
The grace of forest charms decayed,
And pastoral melâncholy.

That region left, the vale unfolds
Rich groves of lofty stature,
With Yarrow winding through the pomp
Of cultivated nature;
And, rising from these lofty groves,
Behold a ruin hoary!
The shattered front of Newark's Tower,
Renown'd in Border story."

Farther down the vale is the village of Yarrowford, near which are the remains of the strong and venerable Castle of Hangingshaw, one of the possessions of the Outlaw Murray, and, till within these few years, of his descendants. It stood in a romantic and solitary situation, and was the scene of the beautiful old ballad, called "The Sang of the Outlaw Murray."* When the mountains

* The scene is, by the common people, supposed to have been the Castle of Newark, but this is highly improbable, as Newark was always a royal fortress; and Mr. Plummer, who at one time held the office of sheriff-depute of Selkirkshire, assured Sir Walter Scott that he remembered the *insignia* of the unicorns, &c. so often mentioned in the ballad, in existence upon the old tower at Hangingshaw. The house was burnt down by accident about 70 or 80 years ago, to the great grief of the people, who loved the proprietor on account of his numerous virtues. As a trait of the hospitality practised at Hangingshaw, t is recorded by tradition, that whosoever called at the house was treated with a draught of stout ale from a capacious vessel called "the Hangingshaw Ladle."

around Hangingshaw were covered with the wild copse which constituted a Scottish forest, a more secure stronghold for an outlawed baron can hardly be imagined. A little beyond is the handsome modern mansion of Broadmeadows (—— Boyd, Esq.) commanding a delightful view; and a mile below are the romantic ruins of NEWARK CASTLE, standing on an eminence overhanging the Yarrow, with dark wooded hills rising closely around on both sides. It is scarcely necessary to remind the tourist that this is the mansion in which Anne Duchess of Buccleuch and Monmouth is made to listen to the "Lay of the Last Minstrel." At Newark, Leslie, after the battle of Philiphaugh, caused a number of his prisoners to be executed in cold blood. The spot where this atrocious deed was perpetrated is still called the "Slain-mens-lee." Opposite Newark is the farm of Foulshiels, where Mungo Park, the celebrated African traveller, was born. Farther down at the mouth of the vale on the right is Bowhill, a summer residence of the Duke of Buccleuch, standing on the face of an eminence, and embowered amidst its beautiful new woods; and on the left Philiphaugh House (Colonel Murray) situated on a hill overlooking Carterhaugh and the confluence of the Ettrick and Yarrow. The road now passes Philiphaugh and enters the town of Selkirk.

Leaving Selkirk for Melrose, the road leads along the south bank of the Ettrick, and at the distance of about a mile, enters Roxburghshire. Near this spot is the secluded burying-ground of Lindean, to which a church was formerly attached. Three miles from Selkirk, the Ettrick flows into the Tweed. At this spot bridges have lately been thrown over both rivers. Proceeding along the banks of the Tweed, the tourist, at the distance of a mile and a half, reaches

ABBOTSFORD,

the seat of Sir Walter Scott, Bart. situated on a bank overhanging the south side of the Tweed, which at this place makes a beautiful sweep around the declivity on which the house stands. It is surrounded by flourishing plantations, and commands an interesting though not ex-

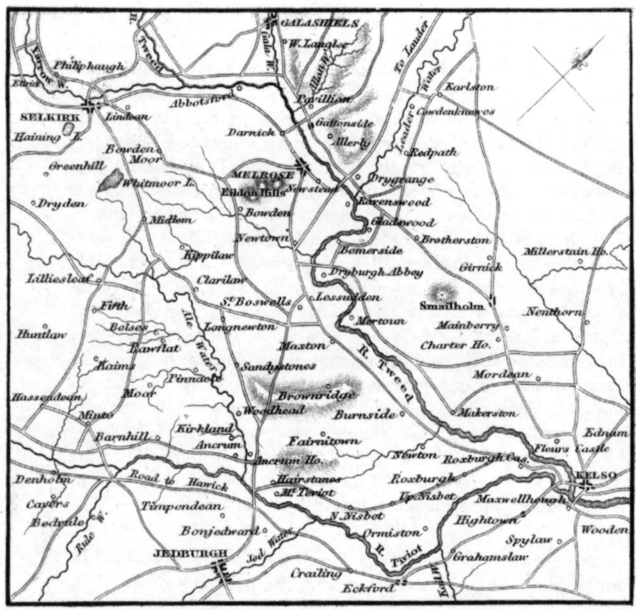

CHART OF THE VALES OF TEVIOT AND TWEED.

tensive view. The house is of very extraordinary proportions, and though irregular as a whole, produces a very striking effect. The entrance to the house is by a porchway, adorned with petrified stags' horns, into a hall, which is perhaps the most interesting of all the apartments. The walls are panelled with richly carved oak from the palace of Dunfermline, and the roof consists of painted arches of the same material. Round the cornice there is a line of coats armorial richly blazoned, belonging to the families who kept the borders,—as the Douglasses, Kers, Scotts, Turnbulls, Maxwells, Chisholms,

Elliots, Armstrongs, &c. The floor is of black and white marble from the Hebrides, and the walls are hung with ancient armour and various specimens of military implements. From the hall you proceed to the armoury, a narrow low-arched room which runs quite across the house, having a blazoned window at either extremity, and filled with smaller pieces of armour and weapons. This apartment communicates with the drawing-room on the one side and the dining-room on the other. The former is a large and lofty saloon with wood of cedar. Its antique ebony furniture, carved cabinets, &c. are all of beautiful workmanship. The dining-room is a very handsome apartment, with a roof of black oak richly carved. It contains a fine collection of pictures; the most interesting of which are the head of Queen Mary in a charger the day after she was beheaded, and a full length of Lord Essex on horseback, Oliver Cromwell, Claverhouse, Charles II., Charles XII. of Sweden, and, among several family pictures, one of Sir Walter's great grandfather, who allowed his beard to grow after the execution of Charles I. The breakfast parlour is a small handsome apartment, which overlooks the Tweed on the one side and the wild hills of Ettrick and Yarrow on the other. It contains a beautiful and valuable collection of water-colour drawings, chiefly by Turner and Thomson of Duddingston, the designs for the magnificent work entitled "Provincial Antiquities of Scotland." The library, which is the largest of all the apartments, is a magnificent room fifty feet by sixty. The roof is of carved oak, chiefly after models from Roslin. The collection of books in this room amounts to about 20,000 volumes, many of them extremely rare and valuable. From the library there is a communication with the study, a room of about twenty-five feet square by twenty feet high, containing of what is properly called furniture nothing but a small writing-table in the centre, a plain arm-chair covered with black leather, and a single chair besides. There are a few books chiefly for reference and a light gallery of tracery work runs round three sides of the room, which contains only one window, so that the place is rather sombre. From this room you enter a small closet, containing what must be viewed by all with the deepest interest—the body-clothes of Sir Walter worn by him previous to his decease. The external walls of the house, as well as those of the adjoining garden, are enriched with many old carved stones, which have originally figured in other and very different situations. The door of the old tolbooth of Edinburgh, the pulpit from which Ralph Erskine preached, and various other strange and interesting relics may also be seen. Through the whole extent of the surrounding forests there are a number of beautiful winding walks, and near the waterfalls in the deep ravines are benches or bowers commanding the most picturesque views. The mansion of Abbotsford and its woods have been entirely created by its late proprietor, who, when he purchased the ground about thirty years ago, found it occupied by a small onstead called "Cartley Hole." The first purchase was made from the late Dr. Douglas of Galashiels. It is said that the money was paid by instalments, and that the letter enclosing the last remittance contained these lines:

"Noo the gowd's thine,
And the land's mine."

Various other "pendicles" were purchased at different times from the neighbouring bonnet-lairds, at prices greatly above their real value. In December 1830, the library, museum, plate, and furniture of every description were presented to Sir Walter as a free gift by his creditors, and he afterwards bequeathed the same to his eldest son, burdened with a sum of L.5000 to be divided among his younger children. The proceeds of a subscription set on foot in London a considerable time ago, are to be applied to the payment of this debt, so as to enable the trustees to entail the library and museum as an heir-loom in the family, and it is expected that the mortgage on the lands will be liquidated by the profits of the new edition of Sir Walter's works, and thereby enable the executors to complete an entail of the entire property.

A little to the east of Abbotsford, and on the opposite bank of the river, the Allan water runs into the Tweed. There can be little doubt that the vale of the Allan is the true "Glendearg" of the Monastery.* The banks on each side are steep, and rise boldly over the eccentric stream which juts from rock to rock, rendering it absolutely necessary for the traveller to cross and recross it, as he pursues his way up the bottom of the narrow valley. "The hills also rise at some places abruptly over the little glen,

* "When we had ridden a little time on the moors, he said to me rather pointedly, 'I am going to show you something that I think will interest you;' and presently, in a wild corner of the hills, he halted us at a place where stood three small ancient towers, or castellated houses, in ruins at short distances from each other. It was plain, upon the slightest consideration of the topography, that one (perhaps any one) of these was the tower of Glendearg, where so many romantic and marvellous adventures happen in The Monastery. While we looked at this forlorn group, I said to Sir Walter that they were what Burns called 'ghaist-alluring edifices.' 'Yes,' he answered, carelessly, 'I dare say there are many stories about them.' As we returned, by a different route, he made me dismount and take a footpath through a part of Lord Somerville's grounds, where the Elland runs through a beautiful little valley, the stream winding between level borders of the brightest green sward, which narrow or widen as the steep sides of the glen advance or recede. The place is called the Fairy Dean, and it required no cicerone to tell that the glen was that in which Father Eustace, in The Monastery, is intercepted by the White Lady of Avenel." *Letter of Mr. Adolphus—Lockhart's Life of Scott*, vol. v.

displaying at intervals the grey rock overhung with wood, and farther up rises the mountain in purple majesty—the dark rich hue contrasting beautifully with the thickets of oak and birch, the mountain ashes and thorns, the alders and quivering aspens which chequered and varied the descent, and not less with the dark green velvet turf which composed the level part of the narrow glen." At a short distance from Abbotsford is the small village of Bridgend, which received its name from a bridge erected over the Tweed by David I., to afford a passage to the Abbey of Melrose. It consisted of four piers, upon which lay planks of wood; and in the middle pillar was a gateway large enough for a carriage to pass through, and over that a room in which the toll-keeper resided. It was at a ford below this bridge that the adventure with the White Lady of Avenel befel Father Philip, the sacristan of the Monastery (See Monastery, Vol. I.) From this bridge the Girthgate, a path to the sanctuary of Soutra, runs up the valley of Allan Water, and over the moors to Soutra Hill. Between Bridgend and Darnick is a place called Skinnersfield (a corruption for Skirmishfield), where a battle was fought in 1526 between the Earl of Angus and the Laird of Buccleuch, for possession of the person of James V., which terminated in favour of Angus.* The road now

* "The Earl of Angus, with his reluctant ward had slept at Melrose, and the clans of Home and Kerr, under the Lord Home, and the barons of Cessford and Fairnihirst had taken their leave of the king, when, in the grey of the morning, Buccleuch, and his band of cavalry, comprehending a large body of Elliots, Armstrongs, and other broken clans, were discovered, hanging like a thunder cloud upon the neighbouring hill of Haliden. The encounter was fierce and obstinate, but the Homes and Kerrs returning at the noise of the battle, bore down and dispersed the left wing of Buccleuch's little army. The hired banditti fled on all sides, but the chief himself, surrounded by his clan, fought desperately in the retreat. The laird of Cessford, chief of the Roxburgh Kerrs, pursued the chase fiercely, till, at the bottom of a steep path, Elliot of Stobs turned and slew him with a stroke of his lance. When Cessford fell the pursuit ceased, but his death, with those of Buccleuch's friends who fell in the

passes the village of Darnick, in which there is an ancient tower, built during the fifteenth century, and a little farther on reaches

MELROSE,

situated on the south side of the Tweed, near the base of the Eildon Hills. It is 36 miles from Edinburgh, 13 from Jedburgh, and 14 from Kelso. "The vale of the Tweed is everywhere fertile and beautiful, and here grandeur is combined with beauty and fertility. The eye is presented with a wide range of pleasing and impressive scenery—of villages and hamlets—the river winding rapidly among smiling fields and orchards, the town with its groves, and gardens, and neat rural church, wooded acclivities, and steep pastoral slopes crowned with the shapely summits of majestic hills, forming a richly diversified and striking panorama, not to speak of the elegant and graceful remains of the ancient Abbey, the sight of which conveys a deep interest to the mind, carries it back through ages and events long past, and leads to sober reflections on the vicissitude of human affairs, and the instability of human institutions."* Near the village are the remains of the famous Abbey, which afford the finest specimen of Gothic architecture and Gothic sculpture ever reared in this country. The stone of which it is built, though it has resisted the weather for so many ages, retains perfect sharpness, so that even the most minute ornaments seem as entire as when newly wrought. The other buildings being completely destroyed, the ruins of the church alone remain to indicate the ancient magnificence of this celebrated monastery. It is in the usual

action, to the number of eighty, occasioned a deadly feud betwixt the clans of Scott and Kerr, which cost much blood upon the marches."—*See Introduction to Minstrelsy of the Scottish Border, and Lay of the Last Minstrel.*

* Monastic Annals of Teviotdale, p. 196.

form of a Latin cross, with a square tower in the centre, eighty-four feet in height, of which only the west side is standing. The parts now remaining of this structure are the choir and transept—the west side, and part of the north and south walls of the great tower, part of the nave, nearly the whole of the southmost aisle, and part of the north aisle. The west gable being in ruins, the principal entrance is by a richly moulded Gothic portal in the south transept. Over this doorway is a magnificent window, twenty-four feet in height and sixteen in breadth, divided by four bars or mullions, which branch out or interlace each other at the top in a variety of graceful curves. The stone work of the whole window yet remains perfect. Over this window are nine niches, and two on each buttress, which formerly contained images of our Saviour and his apostles. Beneath the window is a statue of John Baptist, with his eye directed upward, as if looking upon the image of Christ above. The carving upon the pedestals and canopies of the niches exhibits quaint and curious figures and devices. The buttresses and pinnacles on the east and west sides of the same transept present a curious variety of sculptured forms of plants and animals. On the south-east side are a great many musicians admirably cut. In the south wall of the nave are eight beautiful windows, each sixteen feet in height and eight in breadth, having upright mullions of stone with rich tracery. These windows light eight small square chapels of uniform dimensions, which run along the south side of the nave, and are separated from each other by thin partition walls of stone. The west end of the nave and five of the chapels included in it are now roofless. The end next the central tower is arched over —the side aisles and chapels with their original Gothic roof, and the middle avenue with a plain vault thrown over it in 1618, when this part of the building was fitted up as a parish church. The choir or chancel, which is built in the form of half a Greek cross, displays the finest architectural taste. The eastern window in particular is uncommonly elegant and beautiful. Sir Walter Scott, in describing this part of the building, says—

> "The moon on the east oriel shone
> Through slender shafts of shapely stone
> By foliaged tracery combined:
> Thou would'st have thought some fairy's hand
> 'Twixt poplars straight the osier wand
> In many a freakish knot had twined:
> Then framed a spell when the work was done,
> And changed the willow wreaths to stone."

The original beautifully fretted and sculptured stone roof of the east end of the chancel is still standing, and rises high

> "On pillars lofty, and light, and small,
> The keystone that locked each ribbed aisle,
> Was a fleur-de-lys or a quatre-feuille:
> The corbells were carved grotesque and grim,
> And the pillars with clustered shafts so trim,
> With base and with capital flourished around,
> Seemed bundles of lances which garlands had bound."

The outside of the fabric is every where profusely embellished with niches having canopies of an elegant design exquisitely carved, and some of them still containing statues.

The cloisters formed a quadrangle on the north-west side of the church. The door of entrance from the cloisters to the church is on the north side, close by the west wall of the transept, and is exquisitely carved. The foliage upon the capitals of the pilasters on each side is so nicely chiselled that a straw can be made to penetrate through the interstices between the leaves and stalks. Through this door the "monk of St. Mary's aisle," in the Lay of the Last Minstrel, is said to have conducted William of Deloraine to the grave of Michael Scott, after conducting him through the cloister.

Within the Abbey lie the remains of many a gallant warrior and venerable priest. A large slab of polished marble, of a greenish black colour, with petrified shells imbedded in it, is believed to cover the dust of Alexander II. who was interred beside the high altar under the east window. Here also the heart of King Robert Bruce is supposed to have been deposited after Douglas had made an unsuccessful attempt to carry it to the Holy Land. Many of the powerful family of Douglas were interred in this church, among these were William Douglas, "the dark knight of Liddesdale," who tarnished his laurels by the barbarous murder of his companion in arms, the gallant Sir Alexander Ramsay, and was himself killed by his godson and chief, William Earl of Douglas, while hunting in Ettrick Forest; and James, second Earl of Douglas, who fell at the celebrated Battle of Otterburn. Their tombs, which occupied two crypts near the high altar, were defaced by the English under Sir Ralph Evers and Sir Brian Latoun, an insult which was signally avenged by their descendant, the Earl of Angus at the Battle of Ancrum Moor.

Melrose Abbey was founded by David I. by whom it was munificently endowed. It was destroyed by the English in their retreat under Edward II. in 1322, and four years after, Robert Bruce gave £2000 Sterling to rebuild it. In 1384 it was burnt by Richard II; in 1545 it was despoiled by Evers and Latoun, and again, in the same year, it was destroyed by the Earl of Hertford. At the period of the Reformation it suffered severely from the misdirected zeal of the Reformers. In 1609 the abbey and its possessions were erected into a temporal lordship for Sir John Ramsay, who had been created Viscount Haddington, for his service in preserving James VI. from the treasonable attempt of the Earl of Gowrie. At his death in 1625 without issue, these estates fell to the the Crown, and the greater part of them were granted to Sir Thomas Hamilton, ("Tam o' the Cowgate,") a celebrated lawyer who was created Earl of Melrose in 1619, and afterwards Earl of Haddington. Part of the lands were granted to Walter Scott, Earl of Buccleuch, and his descendants, about the beginning of the eighteenth century, acquired by purchase the remainder of the Abbey lands, included in the lordship of Melrose, which still form a part of the extensive possessions of the same noble family.

At the abolition of heritable jurisdictions in 1747, the Lady Isabella Scott was allowed the sum of £1200 sterling, as compensation for the regality of Melrose.

About the centre of the village stands a cross about twenty feet high, supposed to be coeval with the Abbey. There is a ridge in a field near the town called the Corse-rig, which the proprietor of the field holds upon the sole condition that he shall keep up the cross.

In the vicinity of Melrose are the Eildon Hills, the *Trimontium* of the Romans.* Opposite to the village, a wire bridge leads across the Tweed, to the scattered little village of Gattonside, with its numerous orchards. A short way farther down the river, on a peninsula formed

* It is said that Eildon hills were once a uniform cone, and that the summit was divided into the three picturesque peaks, which it now bears by a spirit, for whom Michael Scott was under the necessity of finding constant employment. See Lay of the Last Minstrel, Canto xi.-xiii.

by a remarkable sweep of the Tweed, stood the ancient Monastery of Old Melrose. The estate of Old Melrose was long possessed by a family of the name of Ormestoun. It is now the property of William Elliot Lockhart, Esq., who has a house there delightfully situated. Two miles below Melrose, the Leader pours its waters from the north, through a beautiful wooded vale to join the Tweed. In the immediate vicinity is Drygrange, (John Tod, Esq.,) beautifully situated. About a mile and a half from Drygrange is the house of Cowdenknows, (Dr. Home,) situated on the east bank of the Leader, at the foot of the hill of Cowdenknows, celebrated for its "bonny bonny broom." A mile farther up the Leader is the village of Earlstoun, where the famous Thomas Learmont, commonly called Thomas the Rhymer, resided. The remains of the Rhymer's Tower are still pointed out, in the midst of a beautiful haugh, on the east side of the Leader. About four miles from Melrose, on the north bank of the Tweed, within the county of Berwick, stand the picturesque ruins of

DRYBURGH ABBEY,

on a richly wooded haugh, round which, the river makes a fine circuitous sweep. The situation is eminently beautiful, and both the abbey, and the modern mansion-house of the proprietor, are completely embosomed in wood. Dryburgh Abbey was founded in the reign of David I., by Hugh de Moreville, constable of Scotland, upon a site which is supposed to have been originally a place of Druidical worship. The principal remains of the building are, the western gable of the nave of the church, the ends of the transept, part of the choir, and a portion of the domestic buildings. In St.

Mary's aisle, which is by far the most beautiful part of the ruin, Sir Walter Scott was buried, 26th September 1832, in the burying ground of his ancestors, the Haliburtons of Newmains, the ancient proprietors of the Abbey. Nature has been most profuse in her decorations around the Gothic walls which form the poet's grave. The chapter house is a spacious apartment, containing a great number of plaster of Paris figures, representing the most distinguished characters of ancient and modern times. The ruins of the Abbey are almost completely overgrown with foliage, and a number of fine trees have sprung up among the rubbish. In 1604, James VI. granted Dryburgh Abbey to John, Earl of Mar, and he afterwards erected it into a temporal lordship and peerage, with the title of Lord Cardross, to the same Earl, who made it over to his third son, Henry, ancestor of the Earl of Buchan. The Abbey was afterwards sold to the Haliburtons of Mertoun, from whom it was purchased by Colonel Tod, whose heirs sold it to the Earl of Buchan in 1786. The Earl at his death bequeathed it to his son, Sir David Erskine, at whose death, in 1837, it reverted to the Buchan family.

In the immediate vicinity of the Abbey is the neat mansion-house of Dryburgh, surrounded by stately trees. At a short distance is a chain suspension-bridge over the Tweed, erected in 1818, at the expense of the late Earl of Buchan; and on a rising ground at the end of the bridge is a circular temple dedicated to the Muses, surmounted by a bust of Thomson, the author of the "Seasons." Farther up, on a rocky eminence overlooking the river, is a colossal statue of the Scottish patriot Wallace. The whole prospect around is eminently beautiful, embracing both wood and water, mountain and rock scenery.*

On the opposite bank of the Tweed lies the village of St. Boswell's Green or Lessuden, formerly a place of some importance, for, when burned by the English in 1544, it contained sixteen strong towers. On the Green is held the fair of St. Boswell's, the principal market for sheep and lambs in the south of Scotland. Two miles from St. Boswell's is the village of Maxton, and on the opposite side of the river, in a delightful situation, is Mertoun House, the seat of Scott of Harden, who has lately established his claim to the title of Lord Polwarth. Near to Maxton, on a cliff on the south bank of the river, are the ruins of Littledean Tower, formerly a place of great note, and long the residence of the Kerrs of Littledean and Nenthorn, a branch of the Cessford family. It is now the property of Lord Polwarth. Six miles from St. Boswell's Green is Makerston, the lovely

* Connected with Dryburgh is the following story, told by Sir Walter Scott in his Border Minstrelsy:—" Soon after the Rebellion in 1745, an unfortunate female wanderer took up her residence in a dark vault among the ruins of Dryburgh Abbey, which, during the day, she never quitted. When night fell, she issued from this miserable habitation, and went to the house of Mr. Haliburton of Newmains, or to that of Mr. Erskine of Shielfield, two gentlemen of the neighbourhood. From their charity she obtained such necessaries as she could be prevailed on to accept. At twelve each night she lighted her candle and returned to her vault, assuring her neighbours that during her absence her habitation was arranged by a spirit, to whom she gave the uncouth appellation of Fatlips, and whom she described as a little man, wearing heavy iron shoes, with which he trampled the clay floor of the vault, to dispel the damps. This circumstance caused her to be regarded by the well-informed with compassion, as deranged in her understanding, and by the vulgar with some degree of terror The cause of her adopting this extraordinary mode of life she would never explain. It was, however, believed to have been occasioned by a vow, that during the absence of a man to whom she was attached, she would never look upon the sun. Her lover never returned. He fell during the civil war of 1745-46, and she never more would behold the light of day. The vault, or rather dungeon, in which this unfortunate woman lived and died, passes still by the name of the supernatural being with which its gloom was tenanted by her disturbed imagination.

residence of Sir Thomas Brisbane Makdougal, Bart., surrounded by luxuriant woods. To the north a view may be obtained of Smailholm Tower, the scene of Sir Walter Scott's admirable ballad of the "Eve of St. John." The poet resided for some time while a boy at the neighbouring farm-house of Sandyknowe, then inhabited by his paternal grandfather, and he has beautifully described the scenery in one of his preliminary epistles to Marmion. The Tower is a high square building, surrounded by an outer wall, now ruinous. The circuit of the outer court being defended on three sides by a precipice and morass, is accessible only from the west by a steep and rocky path. The apartments are placed one above another, and communicate by a narrow stair. From the elevated situation of Smailholm Tower, it is seen many miles in every direction. It formerly belonged to the Pringles of Whytbank, and is now the property of Lord Polwarth. Continuing along the road amidst the richest scenery, the tourist passes on the right the scanty remains of the famous Castle of Roxburgh, situated near the junction of the Tweed and Teviot, which here approach so close as to form a narrow isthmus, and part of the defences of the Castle was a deep moat, filled with water from the Teviot. Roxburgh Castle was formerly a fortress of great extent and importance; but having been dismantled about 400 years ago, a few fragments of walls are all that now remain to attest its former strength. In 1460, when in possession of the English, it was besieged by James II., and after his death taken by his army under the direction of his widow. The spot where James was killed by the bursting of a cannon is marked by a holly tree which grows upon the opposite bank of the Tweed. Nearly opposite to the ruins of the Castle, on the left bank of the river, is FLEURS CASTLE, the seat of the Duke of Roxburghe, commanding a fine view of the surrounding country. On the haugh on the south side of the river is held, on the 5th of August, St. James's Fair, the greatest fair, next to St. Boswell's, in the south of Scotland. Proceeding onward, the tourist crosses the Teviot, and shortly after the Tweed, and enters the town of

KELSO,

occupying a beautiful situation on the north margin of the Tweed. It consists of four streets and a spacious square or market-place, in which stands the town-hall, erected in 1816, and a number of well-built houses with elegant shops. Kelso is the residence of a great number of idle and affluent people, who live in a style of considerable elegance. It carries on a good inland trade, and has a weekly market, and four annual fairs. The most prominent object in Kelso is the venerable abbey, a noble specimen of the solid and majestic style of architecture called the Saxon or early Norman. It was founded by David I. in 1128, and reduced to its present ruinous state by the English under the Earl of Hertford, in 1545. The only parts now remaining are the walls of the transepts, the centre tower, and west end, and a small part of the choir. After the Reformation, a low gloomy vault was thrown over the transept to make it serve as a parish church, and it continued to be used for this purpose till 1771, when, one Sunday, during Divine service, the congregation were alarmed by the falling of a piece of plaster from the roof, and hurried out in terror, believing that the vault over their heads was giving way, and this, together with an ancient prophecy attributed to Thomas the Rhymer, "that the kirk should fall when at the fullest," has caused the old church to be deserted, and it has never since had an opportunity of tumbling on a full congregation. The ruins were disencumbered of the rude modern masonry, by the good taste of William Duke of Roxburghe and his successor Duke James, and in 1823, the decayed parts were strengthened and repaired by subscription. After the Reformation, the lands and possessions of Kelso abbey were conferred upon Sir Robert Kerr of Cessford, and they are still enjoyed by his descendant the Duke of Roxburghe.

The environs of Kelso are singularly beautiful. They are thus described by Leyden in his *Scenes of Infancy.*

> "Bosom'd in woods where mighty rivers run,
> Kelso's fair vale expands before the sun,
> Its rising downs in vernal beauty swell,
> And fringed with hazel winds each flowery dell,
> Green spangled plains to dimpling lawns succeed,
> And Tempe rises on the banks of Tweed,
> Blue o'er the river Kelso's shadow lies,
> And copse-clad isles amid the waters rise."

The most admired view is from the bridge looking up the river. In this view is comprehended the junction of the rivers—the ruins of Roxburgh castle; in front, the palace of Fleurs with its lawn sloping to the margin of the Tweed, and lofty trees behind. On the south bank of the river are the woods and mansion of Springwood Park, with the elegant bridge of the Teviot. On the right is the town, extended along the bank of the river; nearer is Ednam House, and beyond the lofty ruins of the Abbey. In the back ground are the hills of Stitchel and Mellerstain—the castle of Home—the picturesque summits of the Eildon Hills, Penielheugh, &c. An excellent view may also be obtained of the district around

Kelso, from the top of an eminence called Pinnaclehill on the south bank of the river.*

About two miles north from Kelso, on the banks of the Eden, is the village of EDNAM, the birth-place of the poet Thomson. A little to the west, is Newtondon, the splendid seat of Sir William Don, Bart. and two miles farther to the north is Stitchel, the fine mansion of Sir John Pringle, Bart. A short way beyond, on a considerable eminence commanding a view of the whole Merse and a great deal of Roxburghshire, is Home Castle, once the residence of the ancient and powerful family of that name. After the battle of Pinkie, in 1547, it was taken by the English under the Duke of Somerset, and again during the time of the Commonwealth it was besieged and taken by Oliver Cromwell. Three miles to the west is Mellerstain House, the seat of George Baillie, Esq. of Jerviswood, surrounded by extensive plantations.

Leaving Kelso, the road proceeds by Hendersyde Park, (Waldie, Esq.) along the north banks of the Tweed. At the distance of two miles is the village of Sprouston, on the south bank of the river. A mile beyond this the Eden joins the Tweed, and half a mile farther the tourist enters the Merse or Berwickshire. The Tweed now forms the boundary between England and Scotland. On its south bank is Carham Church, with Carham Hall. A mile and a half farther, on the same side, are the ruins of Wark Castle, celebrated in border history. A mile farther on the left is the Hirsel, the seat of the Earl of Home,—the park contains some

* From Kelso a road leads to Jedburgh by the villages of Maxwellhaugh and Heaton, the beautiful banks of the Kale Grahamslaw, where there are some remarkable caves, the villages of Eckford and Crailing, Crailing House, (J. Paton, Esq.) formerly the seat of the noble family of Paton, and Bonyward, (Jerdan Esq.)

fine preserves. The road now crosses the water of Leet, and nine miles from Kelso enters the thriving town of

COLDSTREAM,

occupying a level situation on the north bank of the Tweed, which is here crossed by a handsome bridge. The population of the town is about 3000. In consequence of its proximity to England, Coldstream, like Gretna Green, is celebrated for its irregular marriages. In the principal inn Lord Brougham was married. General Monk resided in Coldstream during the winter of 1659-60, before he marched into England to restore Charles II., and here he raised a horse regiment, which is still denominated the Coldstream Guards. On the bank of the Tweed, to the west of the town, is Lees, the beautiful seat of Sir William Marjoribanks, Bart. About a mile and a half to the east of the town are the ruins of the Church of Lennel, which was the name of the parish before Coldstream existed. Near it is Lennel House, (Earl of Haddington,) in which the venerable Patrick Brydone, author of "Travels in Sicily and Malta," spent the latter years of his long life.* Following the course of the river, we come to Tillmouth, where the Till a narrow, sullen, deep, dark, and slow stream, flows into the Tweed.† On its banks stands Twisel Castle, (Sir Francis Blake, Bart.) Beneath the Castle the ancient bridge is still standing by which the English crossed the

* There are two roads from Coldstream to Berwick, one along the north bank and one along the south bank of the Tweed. The latter is the more interesting, and is generally preferred.

† The different characteristics of the two rivers are distinctly pointed out in the following rhyme:—

Tweed said to Till,
"What gars ye rin sae still?"
Till said to Tweed,
"Though ye rin wi speed,
And I rin slaw,
Yet where ye drown ae man
I drown twa!"

Till before the battle of Flodden.* The glen is romantic and delightful, with steep banks on each side covered with copse. On the opposite bank of the Tweed is Milne-Graden, (Admiral Sir David Milne, Bart.) once the seat of the Kerrs of Graden, and at an earlier period the residence of the chief of a border clan, known by the name of Graden.† A little to the north-east is the village of Swinton. The estate of Swinton is remarkable as having been, with only two very brief interruptions, the property of one family, since the days of the Anglo-Saxon monarchy. The first of the Swintons acquired the name and the estate as a reward for the bravery which he displayed in clearing the country of the wild swine which then infested it. The family have produced many distinguished warriors. At the battle of Beaugé, in France, Thomas Duke of Clarence, brother to Henry V. was unhorsed by Sir John Swinton of Swinton, who distinguished him by a cornet of precious stones which he wore around his helmet.‡ The brave conduct of another of this warlike family, at the battle of Homildon Hill, in 1402, has been dramatised by Sir Walter Scott, whose grandmother was the daughter of Sir John Swinton of Swinton. Three miles eastward is Ladykirk, nine miles from Ber-

* "————————they crossed
The Till by Twisel Bridge.
High sight it is, and haughty, while
They dive into the deep defile;
Beneath the cavern'd cliff they fall,
Beneath the castle's airy wall.
By rock, by oak, by hawthorn tree,
Troop after troop are disappearing;
Troop after troop, their banners rearing,
Upon the eastern bank you see,
Still pouring down the rocky den,
Where flows the sullen Till,
And rising from the dim-wood glen,
Standards on standards, men on men,
In slow succession still,
And sweeping o'er the Gothic arch,
And pressing on, in ceaseless march,
To gain the opposing hill."
Marmion, c. VI.

† Sir Walter Scott's Border Antiquities, p. 152.

‡ "And Swinton laid the lance in rest
That tamed of yore the sparkling crest
Of Clarence's Plantagenet."—*Lay of Last Minstrel, c. V. s.* 4.

wick. The church of this parish is an ancient Gothic building, said to have been erected by James IV. in consequence of a vow made to the Virgin, when he found himself in great danger while crossing the Tweed by a ford in the neighbourhood. By this ford the English and Scottish armies made their mutual invasions before the bridge of Berwick was erected. The adjacent field, called Holywell Haugh, was the place where Edward I. met the Scottish nobility to settle the dispute between Bruce and Baliol, relative to the crown of Scotland. On the opposite bank of the Tweed, stands the celebrated Castle of Norham. The description of this ancient fortress in the poem of Marmion is too well known to require to be quoted here. About four miles from Berwick, is Paxton House, the seat of Forman Home, Esq. which contains a fine collection of pictures. In the immediate neighbourhood, the Tweed is crossed by the Union Wire Suspension Bridge, constructed in 1820, by Capt. Samuel Brown. Its length is 437 feet, width 18, height of piers above low water mark 69, and is one of the finest structures of that kind in this part of the island. Near Paxton, the Tweed is joined by the Whitadder, the principal river which flows through Berwickshire; on its banks, a few miles to the northwest, is Ninewells, the paternal seat of David Hume. Before entering Berwick, we pass Halidon Hill, the scene of a battle in 1333, between the English and the Scotch, in which the latter were defeated. The town of Berwick is more remarkable for its historical recollections than for its present importance. It is 23 miles distant from Kelso, and 58 from Edinburgh, and is a respectable looking town, containing about 9000 or 10,000 inhabitants. It is still surrounded by its ancient walls, which only of late years ceased to be regularly fortified.

SECOND TOUR.

EDINBURGH TO GALASHIELS—MELROSE—JEDBURGH AND HAWICK.

Leaving Edinburgh by the great south road through the centre of Newington, the tourist passes on the right, Grange House, (Sir T. Dick Lauder, Bart.) Three miles from the city, the road passes the Village and Kirk of Libberton, and a mile farther, the village of Gilmerton. Six miles from Edinburgh, is the pretty village of Lasswade, beautifully situated on the banks of the north Esk. On the right above Lasswade are, Mavis Bank, (Mercer, Esq.,) Polton House, and Paper Mill, and the mansion of Hawthornden, and on the left Melville Castle, (Lord Melville.) After crossing the Esk, the tourist passes on the left Eldin, (Clerk, Esq.,) formerly the residence of Mr. John Clerk, author of the well known treatise on Naval Tactics, and father of the late Lord Eldin. Passing in succession Newbattle Abbey, (Marquis of Lothian,) Dalhousie Castle, (Earl of Dalhousie), Cockpen Kirk, and Arniston, (Dundas, Esq.,) the tourist reaches Fushie Bridge Inn, eleven miles distant from Edinburgh. On the left are the oldest powder mills in Scotland. Immediately after passing Fushie Bridge, a view is obtained of Borthwick Castle, and Borthwick Kirk, standing in the midst of a valley on the left. The father of Dr. Robertson, the historian, was minister of Borthwick, and a room in the manse is still shewn as the place where that distinguished writer was born. Passing Middleton Inn, the road now crosses a bleak upland, called Heriot Muir, and a few miles farther on, descends into the vale of Gala. Sixteen miles from Edinburgh, is Heriot House, and on the right at the distance of a mile, Heriot Kirk. Three miles beyond, on the left, is Crookston, (Borthwick, Esq.) A little farther on Pirntaiton, (Miss Innes,) on the right, Burn House, (Thomson Esq.,) Pirn, (Tait, Esq.,) and Torquhan, (Colvin, Esq.) on the left. On the right, the comfortable Inn of Torsonce, and a short way beyond, the irregular and ancient village of Stow, situated in the middle of a district, which formerly bore the name of We-dale, (the vale of Woe.) The whole of this territory, belonged at one time, to the Bishops of St. Andrew's, and many of their charters are dated from We-dale. Proceeding onwards, with the Gala on the right, the tourist reaches Crosslee, on the confines of the county of Roxburgh. The river now forms the boundary between the counties of Roxburgh and Selkirk, and the alder, birch, and hazle, are found in abundance on its banks. The "braw lads of Gala water," are celebrated in Burns' well known beautiful lyric of that name. A short way farther on is Torwoodlee, the fine mansion of Pringle of Torwoodlee, situated in the midst of stately trees, upon a fine terrace overhanging the Gala. A few hundred yards from the modern mansion, are the ruins of the old house, jutting out from the side of a hill. At a little distance to the west of the ruin, lies the family burying ground, embowered in the midst of a dark grove. The Pringles of Torwoodlee are a very old family, and celebrated in Border story. Their representative in the reign of Charles II. was peculiarly obnoxious to government, on account of his exertions in the cause of the covenant, and his concern in Argyle's rebellion. Within a mile of his house, on different sides of the vale of Gala, were two old towers called Buckholm, and Blindlee, occupied by two of his inveterate enemies, who are said to have kept continual watch over his motions, in order to find occasion to accuse him to government. A short way beyond, at the distance of 30½ miles from Edinburgh, the tourist reaches

GALASHIELS,

a thriving town, finely situated on the banks of the Gala, which joins the Tweed about a mile below. It contains about 2000 inhabitants, principally engaged in the production of woollen cloths, scarcely inferior in texture to the finest manufactured in England. The inhabitants are remarkable for their steady industry and ingenuity, combined with a strictness of morality very uncommon in manufacturing towns. The old village of Galashiels, of which hardly a vestige now remains, lay upon an eminence, a little way to the south of the present town, which was erected only about fifty or sixty years ago. Galashiels is a burgh of barony, under Scott of Gala, whose family came in place of the ancient Pringles of Gala, in the year 1623. In 1813, Mr. Richard Lees, manufacturer, assisted by a blacksmith, constructed a wire bridge over the Gala, being the first specimen of this American invention erected in the old world.

Leaving Galashiels, a fine view is obtained of the vale of the Tweed, and a passing glance of the towers of Abbotsford on the right, overtopping the surrounding trees. On the left is Langlee, (Bruce, Esq.) Farther on is Allan Water, (see ante p. 111,) and soon after, the road crosses the Tweed, passes the village of Darnick, and two miles beyond it, reaches

MELROSE,

with the ruins of the Abbey, for a full description of which, see ante p. 113. Two miles from Melrose is Newton-Dryburgh. From the road, a beautiful view is obtained of Dryburgh Abbey, and the course of the Tweed. A few miles farther on, the road passes ANCRUM MOOR, where the Earl of Angus routed the English, in 1545. Lord Evers and Sir Brian Latoun, during the year 1544, committed the most dreadful ravages upon the Scottish frontiers. As a reward for their services, the English monarch promised to the two barons a feudal grant of the country which they had thus reduced to a desert; upon hearing which, Archibald Douglas, the seventh Earl of Angus, is said to have sworn to write the deed of investiture upon their skins, with sharp pens, and bloody ink, in resentment for their having defaced the tombs of his ancestors at Melrose. In 1545, Lord Evers and Latoun again entered Scotland, with an army of upwards of 5000 men, and even exceeded their former cruelty. As they returned towards Jedburgh, they were overtaken by Angus at the head of 1000 horse, who was shortly after joined by the famous Norman Lesley with a body of Fife-men. While the Scottish general was hesitating whether to advance or retire, Sir Walter Scott of Buccleuch came up at full speed, with a small, but chosen body of his retainers, and, by his advice, an immediate attack was made. The battle was commenced upon a piece of low flat ground, called Peniel-heugh, and, just as it began, a heron, roused from the marshes by the tumult, soared away betwixt the encountering armies. "O!" exclaimed Angus, "that I had here my white gosshawk, that we might all yoke at once." The Scots obtained a complete victory, and Lord Evers, and his son, together with Sir Brian Latoun, and 800 Englishmen, many of whom were persons of rank, fell in the engagement. A mile beyond this, the road passes Ancrum House, (Sir William Scott, Bart.) on the right, and on the opposite bank of the Ale, is the village of Ancrum.* At the manse of Ancrum, Thomson the poet spent much of his time, with Mr. Cranston, the clergyman of the parish. A short way beyond, at some distance on the left, is Mount Teviot, a seat of the Marquis of Lothian, whose second title is Earl of Ancrum. On the right, is Chesters, (W. Ogilvie, Esq.) The tourist now crosses the Teviot by Ancrum Bridge. A short way beyond, on the right, is Tympandean, and a mile farther on the left, is Bonjedward,† (Jerdan, Esq.,) and, at the distance of another mile, the tourist enters the royal burgh of

JEDBURGH,‡

standing in a picturesque and romantic situation, on the banks of the sylvan Jed, and surrounded by beautiful gardens and woods. Jedburgh is a royal burgh of very ancient erection; and appears from a statute of William the Lion, to have been a place of note previous to the year 1165. It was one of the chief Border towns, and a place of considerable importance before the Union. After that period, it retrograded in prosperity for a

* Ancrum is situated near a bend of the Ale; and derives its name (Alncrum) from that circumstance.

† "Beanjeddard, Hundlie, and Hunthill,
Three, on they laid weel at the last."
Raid of Reidswire.

‡ Jedburgh is vulgarly called Jethart, a corruption of its former name Jedworth; from Jed, and the Saxon "*weorth,*" a hamlet.

century and a half, but its trade has now greatly revived. It is the county town, the seat of a circuit, and of a presbytery, and contains about 5000 inhabitants. The remains of the Abbey form the principal object of curiosity in Jedburgh. It was founded by David I. either in 1118, or in 1147, and, after various dilapidations in the course of the Border wars, was burnt by the Earl of Hertford in 1545. At the Reformation, the lands of the Abbey were converted into a temporal lordship, with the title of Lord Jedburgh, in favour of Sir Andrew Kerr of Ferniehirst, and they are now possessed by his descendants. It is a magnificent ruin, and is considered the most perfect and beautiful specimen of the Saxon and early Gothic in Scotland. The principal parts now remaining are, the nave, nearly the whole of the choir, with the south aisle, the centre tower, and the north transept. In the western gable is a door of exceedingly beautiful workmanship. The west end is fitted up as a parish church, in a most barbarous and unseemly style. It is to be hoped that this huge mis-shapen mass will, ere long, be removed. Some public spirited individuals have lately expended a considerable sum in repairing the decayed parts of the building, so as to prevent farther dilapidation.

The best view of the Abbey is obtained from the banks of the river. Near the Abbey formerly stood the cross, and there also, were the court-house and jail. The castle of Jedburgh, situated on an eminence at the town head, was a fortress of such strength, that when the Scottish government determined to destroy it, it was meditated to impose a tax of two pennies on every hearth in Scotland, as the only means of accomplishing so arduous an undertaking. The site of this ancient fortress is now occupied by a new jail. In Jedburgh may yet be seen, the old mansion in which Queen Mary lodged, after her visit to Bothwell, at Hermitage.

The inhabitants of Jedburgh, in ancient times, were a warlike race, and were celebrated for their dexterity in handling a particular sort of partisan; which, therefore, got the name of the "Jethart staff." Their timely aid is said to have turned the fortune of the day, at the skirmish of Reidswire. Their proud war-cry was, "Jethart's here."* The ordinary proverb of Jedburgh justice, where men were said to be hanged first, and tried afterwards, appears to have taken its rise from some instances of summary justice executed on the Border marauders.†

The environs of Jedburgh abound in rich woodland scenes, and the walk through the picturesque grove which adorns the left bank of the Jed, is especially delightful. A short distance from the town, the half ruinous castle of Ferniehirst, the ancient seat of the Kerrs, occupies a romantic situation on the right bank of the river. It was built by Sir Thomas Kerr in 1490, and was taken by the English in 1523, and, again, after the battle of Pinkie. Near the castle grows a large oak tree, called on account of its prodigious size, "the king of the wood," and at the foot of the bank, stands another, equally large, called, "the capon tree." Both trees are noticed in Gilpin's Forest Scenery.

From Jedburgh to Hawick there is a fine walk of about

* Then raise the slogan with ane shout,
"Fy, Tindaill to it! Jebrugh's here."
Raid of Reidswire.

† There is a similar English proverb concerning Lydford:
"I oft have heard of Lydford law,
Where in the morn men hang and draw,
And sit in judgement after."
Brown's Poems.

ten miles along the bank of the Teviot. The vale of the Rule intervenes, as also the chief hills of Teviotdale, the Dunian, and Ruberslaw. The whole course of the Teviot between these towns is studded on each side with cottages and mansions, the most distinguished of which is Minto House, the residence of the Earl of Minto. The grounds are ample and varied. In the immediate vicinity of the house are Minto Crags, a romantic assemblage of cliffs which rise suddenly above the vale of Teviot. A small platform on a projecting crag commanding a most beautiful prospect, is termed *Barnhill's Bed.* This Barnhill is said to have been a robber or outlaw. There are remains of a strong tower beneath the rocks where he is supposed to have dwelt, and from which he derived his name. On the summit of the crags are the fragments of another ancient tower in a picturesque situation.* Nearly opposite to Minto House lies the pleasant village of Denholm, the birthplace of the late Dr. John Leyden.

HAWICK

is a thriving town, situated upon a haugh at the junction of the Slitterick and Teviot. It is a burgh of regality, and is of considerable antiquity. Its inhabitants are principally engaged in manufactures, and are remarkable for their industry and intelligence. Hawick has made a con-

* "On Minto crags the moon beams glint,
Where Barnhill hewed his bed of flint,
Who flung his outlawed limbs to rest,
Where falcons hang their giddy nest,
'Mid cliffs from whence his eagle eye
For many a league his prey could spy,
Cliffs, doubling, on their echoes borne,
The terrors of the robbers horn;
Cliffs which for many a later year
The warbling Doric reed shall hear,
When some sad swain shall teach the grove
Ambition is no cure for love."†

† Sir Gilbert Elliot, grandfather to the present Lord Minto, was the author of the beautiful pastoral song, beginning "My sheep I neglected," &c.

siderable figure in Border history, and from its propinquity to the Border has frequently suffered severely from the inroads of the English. The Slitterick is crossed by a bridge of a peculiarly antique construction, and at the head of the town is a moat-hill, where the brave Sir Alexander Ramsay was acting in his capacity of Sheriff of Teviotdale, when he was seized by Sir William Douglas, the "dark knight of Liddisdale," and plunged into one of the dungeons of Hermitage Castle, where he perished of hunger. Hawick is noted among topers for its "gill." A *Hawick gill*, is well known in Scotland to be half a mutchkin, equal to two gills.* On the right bank of the Teviot, about two miles above Hawick, stands the ancient tower of Goldielands, one of the most entire now extant upon the Border. The proprietors of this tower belonged to the clan of Scott, the last of them is said to have been hanged over his own gate, for march treason. About a mile farther up the river on the opposite bank, stands the celebrated tower of Branxholm, the principal scene of the "Lay of the Last Minstrel," and during the 15th and 16th centuries the residence of the Buccleuch family. Branxholm was famous of yore for the charms of a *bonnie lass*, whose beauty has been celebrated by Ramsay in a ballad beginning

"As I came in by Teviot side,
And by the braes o' Branksome,
There first I saw my bloomin' bride,
Young, smiling, sweet and handsome." †

* "Weel she loo'ed a Hawick gill,
And leuch to see a tappit hen."
Andrew and his Cuttie Gun.
[A tappit hen is a frothing measure of claret.]

† The bonnie lass, was daughter to a woman nicknamed Jean the Ranter, who kept an ale house at the hamlet, near Branxholm Castle. A young officer named Maitland, who happened to be quartered somewhere in the neighbourhood, saw, loved, and married her. So strange was such an alliance deemed in those days, that it was imputed to the influence of witchcraft.

Nearly opposite Goldielands tower the Teviot is joined by the Borthwick water. In a narrow valley formed by this stream, stands Harden Castle, an interesting specimen of an ancient Border fortress. The carved stucco work upon the ceiling of the old hall is well worth attention. The lobby is paved with marble; and the mantel-piece of one of the rooms is surmounted with an earl's coronet and the letters W. E. T. wreathed together, signifying "Walter Earl of Tarras," a title borne in former times by the house of Harden. In front of the house there is a dark precipitous dell covered on both sides with beautiful trees; in the recesses of which, the freebooting lairds of former times were said to have kept their spoil.*

* "Where Bortho hoarse that loads the meads with sand,
Rolls her red tide to Teviot's western strand,
Through slaty hills, whose sides are shagged with thorn,
Where springs in scattered tufts the dark green corn,
Towers wood girt Harden, far above the vale,
And clouds of ravens o'er the turrets sail;
A hardy race who never shrunk from war,
The *Scott* to rival realms a mighty bar,
Here fixed his mountain home,—a wide domain,
And rich the soil had purple heath been grain;
But what the niggard ground of wealth denied
From fields more blessed his fearless arm supplied."

LEYDEN'S *Scenes of Infancy.*

"Wide lay his lands round Oakwood tower,
And wide round haunted Castle Ower;
High over Borthwick's mountain flood,
His wood embosomed mansion stood,
In the dark glen so deep below,
The herds of plundered England low."

Lay of Last Minstrel. C. III.

THIRD TOUR.

EDINBURGH—HADDINGTON—DUNBAR—BERWICK.

LEAVING Edinburgh by the Waterloo Bridge, and the south side of the Calton Hill, the tourist obtains a fine view of Salisbury Crags, Arthur Seat, and St. Anthony's Chapel. Passing Jock's Lodge and Piershill Barracks, the road enters

PORTOBELLO,

a favourite summer residence of the citizens of Edinburgh. Tradition asserts that the first house in this village was built by a retired sailor, who had been with Admiral Vernon in his celebrated South American expedition of 1739, and therefore named it "Portobello," in commemoration of the capture of that town. A great number of elegant new streets have been built in the village, and hot and cold baths were erected in 1807. About two miles further, the road enters Fisherrow, and on the opposite bank of the Esk, the town of

MUSSELBURGH,

connected with Fisherrow by three bridges, the oldest of which is supposed to have been built by the Romans. Musselburgh, including Fisherrow, is a very ancient burgh of regality,* and unites with Portobello, Leith, and New-

* "Musselburgh was a burgh
When Edinburgh was nane,
And Musselburgh 'ill be a burgh
When Edinburgh 's gane."—*Old Rhyme.*

haven in returning a member to Parliament. The population of the town and parish is about 8691. The lordship and regality of Musselburgh were granted by James VI. to his chancellor Lord Thirlstane, an ancestor of the Earls of Lauderdale. From them it was purchased in 1709 by Anne, Duchess of Buccleuch and Monmouth, and it still continues in the family of Buccleuch, along with the superiority of the burgh. The great Randolph, Earl of Moray, the nephew of Bruce, and regent of the kingdom, died of the stone, in Musselburgh, in 1332. On Musselburgh links, an extensive plain between the town and the sea, the Edinburgh races, formerly held at Leith, are run. On this plain, in 1638, the Marquis of Hamilton, representing Charles, met the Covenanting party; and here Oliver Cromwell, in 1650, quartered his infantry, while the cavalry were lodged in the town. In a garden, at the east end of Musselburgh, is a small cell, covered by a mound, which is the only remains of a religious establishment, called the Chapel of Loretto. After the Reformation, the materials of the ruined chapel were employed in building the present jail. For this sacrilegious act, it is said the inhabitants of Musselburgh were annually excommunicated at Rome till the end of the last century. At the east end of Musselburgh is Pinkie House, the seat of Sir John Hope, Bart., interesting for its many historical associations. It was originally a country mansion of the Abbot of Dunfermline, but was converted into its present shape at the beginning of the seventeenth century by Alexander Seton, Earl of Dunfermline. About half a mile southward of Pinkie House, on the east side of the Esk, is the spot where, in 1547, the battle of Pinkie was fought, in which the Scottish army was defeated by the English, commanded by the Duke of Somerset. Southward of Inveresk is Carbery Hill, where, in 1567, Queen Mary surrendered to the insurgent nobles.*

Leaving Musselburgh, the road passes Drummore, (W. Aitchison, Esq.) on the left, and St. Clements Wells Distillery, and Wallyford, (— Aitchison, Esq.) on the right. A short way beyond, on the left, is Preston Grange, (Sir J. G. Suttie, Bart.) and Dolphinton village, with its castle, in ruins.

A little farther on upon the left is Preston Tower, formerly the residence of the Hamiltons of Preston. On the coast is the large village of Prestonpans. In this neighbourhood, 21st September 1745, was fought the memorable battle between the royal forces under Sir John Cope and the Highland army under Prince Charles Stuart. Near Tranent is Bankton House, (— M'-Dowal, Esq.) which belonged to Colonel Gardiner, who fell nobly fighting for his country close beside the wall of the park attached to his own residence. Tranent is a very ancient village, chiefly inhabited by colliers. It is mentioned in a charter of the 12th century under the name of Travernent. A short way farther on to the left is Seton House, which stands on the site of the once

* In the year 1728, a woman named Maggy Dickson, resident in Inveresk, was tried and condemned for child murder, and duly (as was thought) executed in the Grassmarket of Edinburgh. When the dreadful ceremony was over, poor Maggy's friends put her body into a chest, and drove it away in a cart to Musselburgh. When about two miles from town, the cart was stopped at a place called Peffermill, and the relations adjourned to a tavern for refreshment. On coming out of the house, what was their astonishment to see Maggy sitting up in the chest, having been restored to life by the motion of the cart. They took her home to Musselburgh, and she was soon entirely recovered. Sir Walter Scott, in the "Heart of Mid Lothian," makes Madge Wildfire speak of "half-hangit Maggie Dickson, that cried saut mony a day after she had been hangit; her voice was roupit and hoarse, and her neck was a wee agee, or ye wad hae kend nae odds on her frae ony ither saut-wife."—*Waverley Novels*, vol. xiii. p. 28.

princely palace of Seton, for many centuries the seat of the Setons Earls of Winton.* The last Earl was attainted on account of his concern in the rebellion of 1715. After his attainder the furniture of the palace was sold by the Commissioners of Enquiry, and the building itself was removed about forty years since, and

* The Setons were one of the most distinguished Scottish families, whether in respect of wealth, antiquity of descent, or splendour of alliance. They took their original name from their habitation, Seaton, " the dwelling by the sea," where, it is said, their founder was settled by King David I. About the middle of the 14th century, the estate descended to Margaret Seton, who married Allan de Wyntoun, a neighbouring baron. This match was so displeasing to her own relations that it occasioned a deadly feud, in consequence of which, we are assured by Fordun, no fewer than a hundred ploughs were put off work. George Lord Seton, who lived in the time of Queen Mary, was one of her most attached friends, and it was to his Castle of Niddry that she repaired after her escape from Lochleven. He was grand-master of the household, in which capacity he had a picture painted of himself with his official baton, and the following motto,—

In adversitate patiens:
In prosperitate benevolus.
Hazard yet forward.

He declined to be promoted to an earldom which Queen Mary offered him. On his refusing this honour, Mary wrote, or caused to be written the following lines :—

Sunt comites, ducesque, alii sunt denique reges ;
Sethoni dominum sit satis esse mihi.

Which may be thus, rendered—

Earl, duke, or king be thou that list to be ;
Seton, thy lordship is enough for me.

After the Battle of Langside, Lord Seton was obliged to retire abroad for safety, and was an exile for two years, during which he was reduced to the necessity of driving a waggon in Flanders for his subsistence. His picture in this occupation, and the garb belonging to it, was painted at the lower end of the gallery in the ancient palace of Seton. In the time of James VI. the Seton family attained the dignity of Earl of Winton, and continued to flourish until the time of George, the fifth and last who enjoyed that dignity and the large fortune which was annexed to it. In 1715, this unfortunate nobleman entered into the rebellion and joined the Viscount of Kenmore with a fine troop of horse. He behaved with spirit and gallantry in the affair of the barricades at Preston ; and afterwards, when waiting his fate in the Tower, made his escape by sawing through with great ingenuity the bars of the windows. He ended his motley life at Rome in 1749, and with him closed the long and illustrious line of Seton, whose male descendants have by intermarriage come to represent the great houses of Gordon, Aboyne, and Eglinton. Their estate was forfeited, and has since passed through several hands.—*Provincial Antiquities, by Sir Walter Scott*, p. 97. See also *Abbot*, vol. i. p. 277.

the present mansion erected on its site. At a little distance from the house stands the Collegiate Church of Seton, which is now all that remains to attest the splendour of the family. It is a handsome little Gothic edifice, and is still nearly entire. There are still visible some monuments of the ancient lords of Seton fast mouldering into decay. Near Seton is Long Niddry, (Lady John Campbell,) the laird of which was a zealous reformer, and had John Knox for the tutor of his children. The ruins of the family chapel, in which John preached, are still pointed out. Northward, near the coast, is Gosford House, a splendid mansion belonging to the Earl of Wemyss. About three miles from Tranent the road passes Gladsmuir, noted as the birth-place of George Heriot, founder of the Hospital at Edinburgh. Dr. Robertson was clergyman of this parish, and here he composed his History of Scotland. Passing successively on the left, Elvingston, (— Law, Esq.) ; Huntingdon, (— Ainslie, Esq.) ; and Alderston, (— Steuart, Esq.) and, on the right, Letham, (Sir J. B. Hepburn, Bart.) and Clerkington, (— Houston, Esq.) the tourist reaches

HADDINGTON,

the county town of East Lothian, distant nearly 17 miles from Edinburgh. It occupies an agreeable situation on the north bank of the Tyne, and contains about 6000 inhabitants. The precise period at which Haddington became a royal burgh is unknown, its ancient records being lost, but it is known to be of very great antiquity, and is supposed to have received its name from Ada Countess of Northumberland, who founded a nunnery here in 1178. It has been several times burnt by the English or by accident, and has twice suffered greatly from an inundation of the Tyne. On the south side of the town is the Franciscan Church, a noble old Gothic building, partly in ruins. Fordun says, that on account of its splendour it was called the "Lamp of Lothian." The great tower and choir are roofless and fast going to ruin, but the chancel is still in repair as a parish church. The celebrated John Knox was born in a house about a hundred feet to the east of the church. Haddington is chiefly remarkable in the present day for its grain market, which is accounted the most extensive in Scotland. About a mile to the south of Haddington is Lennoxlove or Lethington, a seat of Lord Blantyre. It consists of a massive old tower erected by the Giffords, with a modern addition, and is surrounded by a grove of lofty aged trees. Lethington came by purchase into the possession of the Lauderdale family about the middle of the 14th century, and was for some time the chief residence of that family. It was there that the celebrated Secretary Lethington lived, and one of its alleys is still called the Politician's Walk, from having been used by him.* Within sight of Lethington stands the mansion-house of Coalstoun, a seat of the Earl of Dalhousie, whose mother was the heiress of the ancient family of Broun of Coalstoun.†

* Lethington contains several fine portraits, particularly a full-length, by Lely, of Frances Theresa Stuart, Duchess of Lennox, the most admired beauty of the court of Charles II. She was a daughter of Walter Stuart, M.D., a son of the first Lord Blantyre, and Lethington got the additional name of Lennoxlove, from being a compliment to her from her husband. It is reported by Grammont that the King caused this lady to be represented as the emblematical figure *Britannia* on the coin of the realm.

† One of the Brouns of Coalstoun, about 300 years ago, married a daughter of John, third Lord Yester, with whom he obtained in dowry a pear, with the assurance that as long as the pear was preserved, the family would be attended with unfailing prosperity. This celebrated pear is still preserved in a silver box. At no great distance, in the neighbourhood of Gifford, is Yester House, the elegant seat of the Marquis of Tweeddale, the descendant of the wizard

To the north of Haddington lies the little village of Athelstaneford, which in the early part of the last century had for its ministers successively two poets,—Robert Blair, author of "The Grave," and John Home, the author of "Douglas."

Resuming from Haddington the eastward course of the London Road, and passing on the right Amisfield, (Earl of Wemyss,) and Stevenston House, (Sir J. G. Sinclair, Bart.,) and on the left Beenston, (Earl of Wemyss,) the tourist perceives the ruins of Hailes Castle overhanging the south bank of the Tyne. It formerly belonged to the Hepburns, and was the chief residence of Queen Mary during her union with Bothwell. A mile to the south rises Traprain Law, a rocky hill anciently called Dunpender Law. The road now passes Hailes Castle, (Miss Dalrymple,) and Upper Hailes, and a short way farther on crosses the Tyne by Linton Bridge. Beyond the populous village of Linton, on the left, are seen Preston Kirk and village, and Smeaton, the seat of Sir T. B. Hepburn, Bart. Half a mile farther, the road passes Fantassie, (— Rennie, Esq.) on the left, and about a mile beyond, Nineware, (— Bell, Esq.) on the right. Tyningham House, the noble mansion of the Earl of Haddington, with its fine woods, is situated at some distance on the left, on the estuary of the river Tyne.* To the south of the Lon-

Lord who enchanted the Coalstoun Pear. The ancient Castle of Yester stood nearer the Lammermuir Hills, and the remains of it are still to be seen on a peninsula formed by two streams. It contained a capacious cavern, called in the country Bo' Hall, *i. e.* Hobgoblin Hall, supposed to have been formed by magical art. The reader will not need to be reminded of the use made of the Goblin Hall and the wizard Lord in the poem of "Marmion," Canto III.

* In the Tyningham grounds is a most magnificent series of holly hedges. "One of these hedges," says Mr. Miller in his "Popular Philosophy," "is no less than 25 feet high and 18 broad; and the length of what is denominated the Holly Walks, lying chiefly between two hedges of 15 feet high and 11 broad, is no less than 35 chains 80 links, English measure."

don Road is Biel, (Mrs. Ferguson,) with its extensive plantations and charming walks. A beautiful sheet of water called Presmennan Lake has recently been formed in the grounds, by throwing an artificial mound across a small rivulet which runs down from the Lammermuir Hills. The privilege of perambulating the grounds has been granted by the kindness of the proprietrix, who also allows the use of a boat upon the lake to the numerous summer parties who visit it. Beyond, on the right, is Belton Place (— Hay, Esq.,) and on the left Symfield, (Miss Newton,) and Hedderwick House, (Gen. Hardyman.) A short way farther on is the village of Beltonford, a mile farther West Barns, and half a mile beyond it the small village of Belhaven, from which Lord Belhaven takes his title. The road now passes Winterfield, (— Anderson, Esq.,) and on the right Lochend House, (Sir George Warrender, Bart.,) and shortly after enters

DUNBAR,

a royal burgh and thriving sea-port, twenty-eight miles distant from Edinburgh, and eleven from Haddington. The only public building worthy of notice is the church erected in 1819. It contains a most splendid marble monument to Sir George Home, created Earl of Dunbar and March by James VI. The coast in the neighbourhood of Dunbar is remarkably perilous, and the entrance to the harbour is rocky and difficult. Oliver Cromwell contributed three hundred pounds towards the erection of the eastern pier; another pier on the west has been lately built, and a dry dock has also been constructed. Dunbar House, the residence of the Earl of Lauderdale, stands in the immediate vicinity of the town. About two hundred yards west from the town stands the celebrated Castle of Dunbar. Its antiquity is unknown, but so early as 1070 it was given, with the adjacent manor, by Malcolm Canmore, to Patrick Earl of Northumberland, a princely noble, who fled from England at the Conquest, and became the progenitor of the family of Cospatricks, Earls of Dunbar and March. This once formidable fortress has passed through many varieties of fortune, but the most memorable incident in its history was the gallant and successful defence made by *Black Agnes*, Countess of March, against an English army under the Earl of Salisbury. When the battering engines of the besiegers flung massive stones on the battlements, she caused her maidens, as if in scorn, to wipe away the dust with their handkerchiefs, and when the earl of Salisbury commanded a huge military engine, called a sow, to be advanced to the foot of the walls, she, in a scoffing rhyme, advised him to take good care of his sow, for she would make her farrow her pigs. She then ordered an enormous rock to be discharged on the engine, which crushed it to pieces.* After a successful defence, which lasted six weeks, the siege was abandoned by the English troops. George, tenth Earl of Dunbar and March, on a quarrel with Alexander, Duke of Albany, brother of James III., re-

* A similar story is told of Judge Bank's lady, while holding out Corffe Castle against the Parliament forces. The incident is thus alluded to by Mr. W. Stewart Rose in his poem addressed to Corffe Castle,—

"'Twas when you reared mid sap and siege
The banner of your rightful liege
At your she captain's call;
Who, miracle of womankind!
Lent mettle to the meanest hind
That mann'd her castle wall.
What time the banded zealots swore,
Long foil'd thy banner'd towers before
Their fearful entrance made,
To raise thy walls with plough and harrow
Yet oft the wild sow cast her farrow,
And well the boar was bay'd."

treated into England, and his large estate was forfeited, and, with Dunbar Castle, passed into the hands of the Duke of Albany, to whom, on his memorable escape from Edinburgh Castle, it afforded shelter till he departed for France. In the year 1567, Queen Mary conferred the keeping of this important stronghold on the infamous Bothwell; and here she twice found shelter,—once, after the murder of Rizzio, and a second time, when she made her escape from Borthwick Castle, in the disguise of a page. After her surrender at Carberry Hill, Dunbar was taken, and completely destroyed by the Regent Murray.

Near the town of Dunbar were fought two battles, in both of which the Scots were defeated,—one in 1296, when Baliol was defeated by the forces of Edward I., the other in 1650, when the Scottish army, under General Leslie, was routed with great slaughter by Cromwell. This battle is still remembered by the people of Scotland under the opprobrious epithet of "the race of Dunbar," or "the Tyesday's chase;" the engagement having taken place on a Tuesday.*

* About seven miles northwest of Dunbar, and two and a half eastward from North Berwick, are the ruins of the famous Castle of Tantallon. From the land side they are scarcely visible, till the visitor, surmounting a height which conceals them, finds himself close under the external walls. The description of this Castle given in the poem of Marmion, renders any account of our own unnecessary.

——————— "Tantallon vast,
Broad, massive, high, and stretching far,
And held impregnable in war.
On a projecting rock it rose,
And round three sides the ocean flows,
The fourth did battled walls enclose
And double mound and fosse ;
By narrow drawbridge, outworks strong,
Through studded gates, an entrance long,
To the main court they cross.

Leaving Dunbar, the tourist passes on the left, Broxmouth, a large mansion of the Duke of Roxburghe, and crosses the stream of Broxburn. A mile and a half farther on the right, is Barnyhill, (Sandilands, Esq.,) and

It was a wide and stately square,
Around were lodgings fit and fair,
And towers of various form,
Which on the court projected far,
And broke its lines quadrangular;
Here was square keep, there turret high,
Or pinnacle that sought the sky,
Whence oft the warder could descry
The gathering ocean storm."

c. v. st. 33.

Tantallon was a principal stronghold of the Douglas family, and when the Earl of Angus was banished in 1527, it continued to hold out against James V. The king went in person against it, and, for its reduction, borrowed from the Castle of Dunbar, then belonging to the Duke of Albany, two great cannons, whose names, Pitscottie informs us, were "Thrawn-mouth'd Mow and her Marrow;" also "two great bocards, and two moyan, two double falcons, and four quarter-falcons," for the safe guiding and re-delivery of which three lords were laid in pawn at Dunbar. Yet, notwithstanding all this apparatus, James was forced to raise the siege, and only afterwards obtained possession of Tantallon by treaty with the governor, Simon Panango. Tantallon was at length "dung down" by the Covenanters; its lord, the Marquis of Douglas, being a favourer of the royal cause. About the beginning of the eighteenth century, the Marquis, afterwards Duke of Douglas, sold the estate of North Berwick, with the Castle of Tantallon to Sir Hew Dalrymple, President of the Court of Session, and they now remain in the possession of his descendant Sir. Hew H. Dalrymple, Bart. of Bargeny and North Berwick.

Two miles north from Tantallon lies the Bass Island or rather Rock, rising 400 feet sheer out of the sea. The Bass is about a mile in circumference, and is conical on the one side, presenting on the other an abrupt and overhanging precipice. It is remarkable for its immense quantities of sea fowl, chiefly solan geese. Upon the top of the rock gushes out a spring of clear water, and there is verdure enough to support a few sheep. The Bass was long the stronghold of a family of the name of Lauder, one of whom distinguished himself as a compatriot of Wallace. The Castle, situated on the south side of the island, is now ruinous. In 1671, it was sold by the Lauder family, for £4000, to Charles II., by whom it was converted into a royal fortress and state prison. Many of the most eminent of the Covenanters were confined here. At the Revolution, it was the last stronghold in Great Britain that held out for James VII. But, after a resistance of several months, the garrison were at last comcompelled to surrender by the failure of their supplies of provisions. The Bass is now the property of Sir Hew Hamilton Dalrymple, Bart. This remarkable rock is visited in summer by numerous pleasure parties. In order to perform the visit, it is necessary to apply for a boat either at North Berwick, or at Canty Bay near Tantallon.

the village of East Barns. A mile farther on, is Thurston, (Hunter, Esq.) A short way beyond on the right, are the ruins of Innerwick Castle, situated on the edge of a precipitous glen. On the opposite side of the glen stands Thornton Tower. Innerwick was burnt by the English, and Thornton blown up with gunpowder during Somerset's expedition. A mile farther on, is Thrieplandhill House, and a mile beyond this, on the right, is Dunglas House, the elegant mansion of Sir J. Hall, Bart., situated amidst beautiful plantations.* The road now crosses Dunglas Burn and enters Berwickshire. A mile farther on, is the village of Cockburnspath, (a corruption of Colbrandspath.) A mile beyond the village is the ancient tower of Cockburnspath, now the property of Sir J. Hall of Dunglas. The tract of country through which the road now passes is high and flat, but broken at little distances by numerous deep and narrow ravines, each of which has a small stream at the bottom running towards the sea. The most remarkable of these ravines, is that denominated the Peaths, over which, the celebrated Peaths or Pease bridge was thrown in 1786. This singular structure is 123 feet in height, 300 feet in length, and 15 feet wide. The road now crosses the glen, about a quarter of a mile above the bridge. In former times, the Peaths was a most important pass, and Oliver Cromwell describes it in his dispatch to the parliament after the battle of Dunbar, as a place "where one man to hinder, is better than twelve to make way." The road now passes in succession,

* Dunglas House stands on the site of the old Castle, which was originally a fortress of the Earls of Home, and still gives their second title to that family. After the attainder of the Earl of Home in 1516, it passed into the hands of the Douglasses. It was destroyed by Somerset in 1548, but was again rebuilt and enlarged. It was finally destroyed in 1640, on which occasion the Earl of Haddington, and a number of other persons of distinction, were killed by the blowing up of the powder magazine.

Grant's Inn, Renton Inn, Houndwood Inn, and Houndwood House, (Mrs. Coulson.) Two miles farther, the tourist passes on the right, the village of Reston, and a road turns off on the left to the beautiful village of Coldingham, distant about three miles.* Proceeding along

* Coldingham is situated upon a small eminence in the centre of a fine valley, at a short distance from the sea. It is remarkable for the ruins of its priory, so celebrated in Border history. The monastery was established by St. Abb, in the seventh century, and is said to have been the first in Scotland. The buildings were once of great magnificence and extent, but of late years they have been greatly dilapidated by the rapacious license of the people in taking away stones for the purpose of building their own houses, so that only a few detached fragments now remain. About fifty years ago, in taking down a tower at the southwest corner, the skeleton of a nun was found standing upright in a hollow of the wall, no doubt a victim to a breach of her vows.

Northeast of Coldingham about two miles is the celebrated promontory called St. Abb's Head. It consists of two tall hills, the western of which is occupied by an observatory; the eastern, called the Kirkhill, still exhibits the remains of a monastery and a church. The savage and dreary character of the scenery is exceedingly striking. The neighbouring promontory of Fast Castle derives its name from an ancient baronial fortress built upon the very point of the precipitous headland. Fast Castle is the Wolf's Crag of the "Bride of Lammermuir," and is thus described in that tragic tale. "The roar of the sea had long announced their approach to the cliffs, on the summit of which, like the nest of some sea-eagle, the founder of the fortalice had perched his eyry. The pale moon, which had hitherto been contending with flitting clouds, now shone out, and gave them a view of the solitary and naked tower, situated on a projecting cliff that beetled on the German Ocean. On three sides the rock was precipitous; on the fourth, which was that towards the land, it had been originally fenced by an artificial ditch and drawbridge, but the latter was broken down and ruinous, and the former had been in part filled up, so as to allow passage for a horseman into the narrow court-yard, encircled on two sides with low offices and stables, partly ruinous, and closed on the landward front by a low embattled wall, while the remaining side of the quadrangle was occupied by the tower itself, which, tall and narrow, and built of a greyish stone, stood glimmering in the moonlight, like the sheeted spectre of some huge giant. A wilder, or more disconsolate dwelling, it was perhaps difficult to conceive. The sombrous and heavy sound of the billows, successively dashing against the rocky beach, at a profound distance beneath, was to the ear what the landscape was to the eye,—a symbol of unvaried and monotonous melancholy, not unmingled with horror." That Castle was in former days a place of retreat of the great Earls of Home. Nothwithstanding its strength, it was repeatedly taken and recaptured during the Border wars. About the close of the sixteenth century it became the stronghold of the celebrated Logan of Restalrig, so famous for his share in the Gowrie Conspiracy; and it was to this place that the conspirators intended to convey the king after getting possession of his person. There is a contract existing in the charter-chest of Lord Napier, betwixt this Logan and the celebrated Napier of Merchiston, setting forth that, as Fast

the banks of the Eye, the tourist reaches the small village of Ayton, pleasantly situated on its northern bank. Ayton House, (Fordyce, Esq.) stands to the east of the village. The banks of the Eye afford some fine scenery. At its confluence with the sea, stands the sea-port and fishing village of Eyemouth. This village was formerly notorious for the smuggling carried on by its inhabitants, but, of late years, the contraband trade has been entirely destroyed.* Four miles from Ayton, the tourist passes the ruins of Lamerton Kirk, where, in 1503, Margaret, daughter of Henry VII., was married by proxy to James IV; a marriage which ultimately led to the union of the crowns. Lamerton is now the property of Colonel Renton. At Lamerton toll-bar, run-away lovers from England are frequently united in the bands of matrimony. At a distance of three miles, the road enters the town of

BERWICK,

situated upon a gentle declivity close by the German ocean, on the north side of the mouth of the river Tweed. It is a well built town, with spacious streets, and is sur-

Castle was supposed to contain a quantity of hidden treasure, Napier was to make search for the same by divination, and for his reward was to have the third of what was found, and to have his expenses paid in whatever event. Fast Castle now belongs to Sir J. Hall of Dunglass. The precipitous rocks on this coast are inhabited by an immense number of sea fowl, and a number of young men in the neighbourhood occasionally scale these dreadful and dizzy heights, in order to steal the eggs of the birds. Strange to say, an accident does not occur among them perhaps once in a century.

* "I stood upon Eyemouth fort,
And guess ye what I saw?
Fairnieside and Flemington,
Newhouses and Cocklaw,
The fairy fouk o' Fosterland,
The witches o' Edincraw,
The rye rigs o' Reston,
And Dunse dings a'."

Old Rhyme.

rounded by walls in a regular style of fortification. The population amounts to about 10,000. It is governed by a mayor, recorder, and justices, and sends two members to Parliament. The trade of the port is considerable. Berwick occupies a prominent place in the history of the Border wars, and has been often taken and retaken both by the Scots and English. It was finally ceded to the English in 1482, and since then, has remained subject to the laws of England, though forming, politically, a distinct territory. Its castle, so celebrated in the early history of these kingdoms, is now a shapeless ruin.

FOURTH TOUR.

EDINBURGH—LINLITHGOW—FALKIRK—STIRLING.

Leaving Edinburgh by Princes Street, the tourist passes along the side of Corstorphine Hill, richly wooded and studded with villas, and four miles from Edinburgh reaches the village of Corstorphine. At the seventh milestone the road crosses Almond water, and enters Linlithgowshire. A short way farther on is the village of Kirkliston. Near the village is Newliston, (Hog, Esq.) formerly the seat of the great Earl of Stair, who caused the woods around the house, it is said, to be planted so as to resemble the position of the troops at the battle of Dettingen, where he commanded under George II.* A short distance beyond, to the left, are

* During the rebellion of 1745, the route of the Highland army having brought them near Newliston, an alarm arose in the councils of Prince Charles lest the MacDonalds of Glencoe should seize the opportunity of marking their recollection of the massacre of Glencoe, by burning or plundering the house of the descendant of their persecutor; and it was agreed that a guard should be posted to protect the house of Lord Stair. MacDonald of Glencoe heard the resolution, and deemed his honour and that of his clan concerned. He demanded an audience of Charles Edward, and, admitting the propriety of placing a guard on a house so obnoxious to the feelings of the Highland army, and to those of his own clan in particular, he demanded as a matter of right rather than of favour, that the protecting guard should be supplied by the MacDonalds of Glencoe. The request of the high spirited chieftain was granted, and the MacDonalds guarded from the slightest injury the house of the cruel and crafty statesman who had devised and directed the massacre of their ancestors."—*Tales of a Grandfather*, vol. iv. p. 23.

It was in the family of the first Lord Stair that the tragic incident occurred which forms the groundwork of Sir Walter Scott's tale of the "Bride of Lammermuir."

the ruins of Niddry Castle, where Queen Mary passed the first night after her escape from Lochleven. It was at that time the property of the Earl of Seton,—it now belongs to the Earl of Hopetoun. The road now passes through the village of Winchburgh, where Edward II. first halted in his flight from the battle of Bannockburn. About the sixteenth milestone, the road crosses the Union Canal, under an aqueduct bridge, and a short way farther on enters

LINLITHGOW,*

an ancient royal burgh, and the county town of Linlithgowshire, situated in a hollow, along the borders of a beautiful lake. So early as the beginning of the 12th century, Linlithgow was one of the principal burghs in the kingdom. It contains a considerable number of old fashioned houses, many of which belonged of old to the knights of St. John, who had their preceptory at Torphichen, in this county.

The most interesting object in Linlithgow is the Palace, a massive quadrangular edifice, situated upon an eminence which advances a little way into the lake. It occupies about an acre of ground, and, though in ruins, is still a picturesque and beautiful object.† The inter-

* Popularly denominated "the faithful town of Linlithgow."

† "Of all the palaces so fair
Built for the royal dwelling,
In Scotland far beyond compare
Linlithgow is excelling.
And in its park in genial June
How sweet the merry linnet's tune,
How blythe the blackbird's lay!
The wild buck *bells* from thorny brake,
The coot dives merry on the lake,—
The saddest heart might pleasure take
To see a scene so gay."

Marmion, c. iv. *st.* 15.

nal architecture is extremely elegant, but the exterior has a heavy appearance from the want of windows. Over the interior of the grand gate is a niche which was formerly filled by a statue of Pope Julius II., who presented James V. with the sword of state, which still forms part of the regalia. It was destroyed during the last century by a blacksmith who had heard popery inveighed against in the neighbouring church. Above this entrance was the Parliament Hall,—once a splendid apartment, with a beautifully ornamented chimney at one end, and underneath it has been a magnificent piazza. This part of the palace is understood to have been begun by James IV. and finished and ornamented by his successor. The west side of the palace is the most ancient, and it contains the room where the unfortunate Queen Mary was born.*

In one of the vaults below James III. found shelter when he was in danger of assassination from some of his rebellious subjects. The north side of the quadrangle is the most modern, having been built by James VI. shortly after his visit to Scotland in 1617. In the centre of the court are the ruins of the Palace Well, a once beautiful and ingenious work, erected by James V. It was destroyed by the royal army in 1746.

The nucleus of the Palace seems to have been a tower or fort, first built by Edward I., who inhabited it in person a whole winter. It was taken and demolished by

* Her father, who then lay on his deathbed at Falkland, on being told of her birth, replied, "Is it so?' reflecting on the alliance which had placed the Stewart family on the throne, "then God's will be done. It came with a lass, and it will go with a lass." With these words he turned his face to the wall, and died of a broken heart.

Bruce in 1307.* It appears, however, to have been rebuilt by the English during the minority of David II., but was again burnt down in 1424. The Palace was finally reduced to its present ruinous condition by Hawley's dragoons, who were quartered in it on the night of the 31st of January, 1746. In the morning, when they were preparing to depart, the dastardly scoundrels were observed deliberately throwing the ashes of the fires into the straw on which they had lain. The whole Palace

* It was taken in the following remarkable way:—The garrison was supplied with hay by a neighbouring rustic, of the name of Binnock or Binning, who favoured the interest of Bruce. "Binnock had been ordered by the English governor to furnish some cart-loads of hay, of which they were in want. He promised to bring it accordingly; but the night before he drove the hay to the castle, he stationed a party of his friends, as well armed as possible, near the entrance, where they could not be seen by the garrison, and gave them directions that they should come to his assistance as soon as they should hear him cry a signal, which was to be,—'Call all, call all!' Then he loaded a great waggon with hay. But in the waggon he placed eight strong men, well armed, lying flat on their breasts, and covered over with hay, so that they could not be seen. He himself walked carelessly beside the waggon; and he chose the stoutest and bravest of his servants to be the driver, who carried at his belt a strong axe or hatchet. In this way Binnock approached the castle early in the morning; and the watchman, who only saw two men, Binnock being one of them, with a cart of hay, which they expected, opened the gates, and raised up the portcullis, to permit them to enter the castle. But as soon as the cart had gotten under the gateway, Binnock made a sign to his servant, who with his axe suddenly cut asunder the *soam*, that is, the yoke which fastens the horses to the cart, and the horses, finding themselves free, naturally started forward, the cart remaining behind under the arch of the gate. At the same moment, Binnock cried as loud as he could, 'Call all, call all!' and drawing the sword, which he had under his country habit, he killed the porter. The armed men then jumped up from under the hay where they lay concealed, and rushed on the English guard. The Englishmen tried to shut the gates, but they could not, because the cart of hay remained in the gateway, and prevented the folding doors from being closed. The portcullis was also let fall, but the grating was caught on the cart, and so could not drop to the ground. The men who were in ambush near the gate, hearing the cry, 'Call all, call all!' ran to assist those who had leaped out from amongst the hay; the castle was taken, and all the Englishmen killed or made prisoners. King Robert rewarded Binnock by bestowing on him an estate, which his posterity long afterwards enjoyed." The Binnings of Wallyford, descended from that person, still bear in their coat-armorial a wain loaded with hay, with the motto "Virtute doloque."

Tales of a Grandfather, vol. i. p. 139.

was speedily in a blaze, and it has ever since remained an empty and blackened ruin.*

The Church, a venerable and impressive structure, stands between the Palace and the town, and may be regarded as one of the finest and most entire specimens of Gothic architecture in Scotland. It was dedicated to the archangel Michael, who was also considered the patron saint of the town. The Church was founded by David I., but was ornamented chiefly by George Crichton, bishop of Dunkeld. It is now divided by a partition-wall, and the eastern half alone is used as a place of worship. It was in an aisle in this Church, according to tradition, that James IV. was sitting when he saw the strange apparition which warned him against his fatal expedition to England.† In front of the Town-

* "They halted at Linlithgow, distinguished by its ancient palace, which sixty years since was entire and habitable, and whose venerable ruins, *not quite sixty years since*, very narrowly escaped the unworthy fate of being converted into a barrack for French prisoners. May repose and blessings attend the ashes of the patriotic statesman (President Blair) who, amongst his last services to Scotland, interposed to prevent this profanation."—*Waverley*, vol. i. p. 92.

† The story is told by Pitscottie, with characteristic simplicity.—"The king came to Lithgow, where he happened to be for the time at the Council, very sad and dolorous, making his devotion to God, to send him good chance and fortune in his voyage. In this mean time, there came a man clad in a blue gown in at the kirk-door, and belted about him in a roll of linen-cloth; a pair of brotikings (buskins) on his feet, to the great of his legs; with all other hose and clothes conformed thereto; but he had nothing on his head, but syde (long) red yellow hair behind, and on his haffets (cheeks) which wan down to his shoulders; but his forehead was bald and bare. He seemed to be a man of two-and-fifty years, with a great pike-staff in his hand, and came first forward among the lords, crying and speiring (asking) for the king, saying, he desired to speak with him. While, at the last, he came where the king was sitting in the desk at his prayers: but when he saw the king, he made him little reverence or salutation, but leaned down grofling on the desk before him, and said to him in this manner, as after follows: 'Sir king, my mother hath sent me to you, desiring you not to pass, at this time, where thou art purposed; for if thou does, thou wilt not fare well in thy journey, nor none that passeth with thee. Further, she bade thee mell (meddle) with no woman, nor use their counsel, nor let them touch thy body, nor thou theirs; for if thou do it, thou wilt be confounded and brought to shame.'

"By this man had spoken thir words unto the king's grace, the evening song

house stands the Cross Well, a very curious and elegant erection. The present edifice was erected in 1805, but it is said to be an exact facsimile of the original, which was built in 1620. The sculpture is amazingly intricate, and the water is made to pour in great profusion from the mouths of a multitude of grotesque figures. The vast copiousness of water at Linlithgow is alluded to in the following well known rhyme,—

"Glasgow for bells,
Lithgow for wells,
Fa'kirk for beans and peas,
Peebles for clashes and lees."

It was in Linlithgow that David Hamilton of Bothwellhaugh, on the 23d of January, 1570, shot the Regent Murray, when passing through the town, in revenge for a private injury. The house from which the shot was fired belonged to the Archbishop of St. Andrews. It was taken down a number of years ago, and replaced by a modern edifice.

During the plague of 1645, Linlithgow happening to be comparatively free of the infection, the Palace and Church were used by the Courts of Justice and the members of the University of Edinburgh, as their meeting places. At the Restoration, the inhabitants of Linlith-

was near done, and the king paused on thir words, studying to give him an answer; but, in the mean time, before the king's eyes, and in the presence of all the lords that were about him for the time, this man vanished away, and could no wise be seen or comprehended, but vanished away as he had been a blink of the sun, or a whip of the whirlwind, and could no more be seen. I heard say, Sir David Lindesay, lyon-herauld, and John Inglis the marshal, who were, at that time, young men, and special servants to the King's grace, were standing presently beside the King, who thought to have laid hands on this man, that they might have speired further tidings at him; but all for nought; they could not touch him; for he vanished away betwixt them, and was no more seen." There can be little doubt that the supposed apparition was a contrivance of the queen to deter James from his impolitic warfare.

gow burned the Solemn League and Covenant amidst great rejoicing. The ringleader in this affair was one Ramsay, the minister of the parish, who had formerly been a zealous supporter of the Covenant. In Linlithgow is still kept up the old custom of riding the marches. The town has derived considerable advantage from the Union Canal, which passes along the high grounds immediately to the south. Leather is the staple commodity of the place, linen and woollen manufactures are also carried on to a considerable extent. The population of the burgh and parish in 1831 was 4874.

Proceeding westward from Linlithgow, the road crosses the Avon at Linlithgow Bridge, and enters Stirlingshire. After this nothing interesting occurs for some miles, till the tourist passes on the left Callander House (W. Forbes, Esq.), formerly the seat of the Earls of Callander and Linlithgow, and a short way farther on enters the town of

FALKIRK,

delightfully situated on the face of an eminence overlooking the wide extent of country called the Carse of Falkirk. It was a town of some note in the early part of the 11th century. The old church which was demolished about thirty years ago, was erected in 1057. The original name of the town was *Eglishbreckk,* signifying "the speckled church," in allusion, it is supposed, to the colour of the stones. In the churchyard are shown the graves of two celebrated Scottish heroes—Sir John Graham, the friend of Wallace, and Sir John Stewart of Bonkill, both of whom fell fighting bravely against the English at the battle of Falkirk. Over the former a monument was erected with an inscription, which has been renewed from time to time. It at present stands thus:—

> Mente manuque potens et Vallae fidus Achates,
> Conditur hic Gramus bello interfectus ab Anglis.

TRANSLATION.

> Here lyes Sir John Grame, baith wight and wise,
> Ane of the chiefs who rescewit Scotland thrice,
> Ane better knight not to the world was lent,
> Nor was gude Grame of truth and hardiment.

In the churchyard is also to be seen the monument of two brave officers, Sir Robert Munro of Foulis, and his brother Dr. Munro, who were killed in the second battle of Falkirk, January 17, 1746. Falkirk is noted for its great cattle markets or *trysts*, held thrice a-year, to which a vast number of black cattle are brought from the Highlands and Islands.

About two miles north of the town are the celebrated Carron Iron Works, the largest manufactory of the kind in the world.

A short way from Falkirk is the village of Grahamston, near which, in 1298, was fought a battle between the forces of Edward I. and the Scots, under Wallace and Sir John Graham, in which the latter were defeated. The battle of Falkirk-muir, between the Royal forces under General Hawley and the Highlanders, in which the latter gained a complete victory, was fought on the high ground lying to the south-west of the town. Hawley had suffered himself to be detained at Callander House by the wit and gaiety of the Countess of Kilmarnock (whose husband was with the Prince's army), until the Highlanders had taken up an advantageous position, and were ready to attack his army. The consequence of his incapacity and negligence was, that his troops were thrown into confusion and completely routed.*

The view from the eminence on which the battle was fought is remarkably extensive, varied, and beautiful.

Proceeding westward, the tourist, a short way from Falkirk, passes the village of Camelon, said to have been the situation of a Roman city built by Vespasian. A mile farther on, the road crosses the Carron. Near to this are the church and village of Larbert, and Larbert House, the seat of Sir Gilbert Stirling. In Larbert Kirk, Bruce, the famous Abyssinian traveller, lies interred. Kinnaird, his patrimonial estate, is at no great distance. A mile and a half farther on, the road passes through the remains of the Torwood Forest, where Sir William

* "Hawley had not a better head, and certainly a much worse heart than Sir John Cope, who was a humane, good-tempered man. The new general ridiculed severely the conduct of his predecessor, and remembering that he had seen, in 1715, the left wing of the Highlanders broken by a charge of the Duke of Argyle's horse, which came upon them across a morass, he resolved to manœuvre in the same manner. He forgot, however, a material circumstance—that the morass at Sheriffmuir was hard frozen, which made some difference in favour of the cavalry. Hawley's manœuvre, as commanded and executed, plunged a great part of his dragoons up to the saddle-laps in a bog, where the Highlanders cut them to pieces with so little trouble, that, as one of the performers assured us, the feat was as easy as slicing *bacon*. The gallantry of some of the English regiments beat off the Highland charge on another point, and, amid a tempest of wind and rain which has been seldom equalled, the field presented the singular prospect of two armies flying different ways at the same moment. The king's troops, however, ran fastest and farthest, and were the last to recover their courage; indeed, they retreated that night to Falkirk, leaving their guns, burning their tents, and striking a new panic into the British nation, which was but just recovering from the flutter excited by what, in olden times, would have been called the Raid of Derby. In the drawing-room which took place at Saint James's on the day the news arrived, all countenances were marked with doubt and apprehension, excepting those of George the Second, the Earl of Stair, and Sir John Cope, who was radiant with joy at Hawley's discomfiture. Indeed, the idea of the two generals was so closely connected, that a noble peer of Scotland, upon the same day, addressed Sir John Cope by the title of General Hawley, to the no small amusement of those who heard the *quia pro quo*."

SIR WALTER SCOTT'S *Prose Works*, vol. xix. p. 303.

Wallace is said to have found shelter in a tree when pursued by his enemies. At Torwood-head, Mr. Cargill, in 1680, excommunicated Charles II., the Duke of York, and the Ministry. About four miles farther on is the village of *Bannockburn,* remarkable for its manufactories of tartan and carpets. To the left of the road between Bannockburn and St. Ninians is the scene of the famous battle, fought June 24th, 1314, between the English army of 100,000 men, under Edward II., and the Scottish army of 30,000, commanded by Robert Bruce, in which the former were signally defeated, with the loss of 30,000 men and 700 barons and knights. The Scottish army extended in a north-easterly direction from the brook of Bannock, which was so rugged and broken as to cover the right flank effectually, to the village of St. Ninians, probably in the line of the present road from Stirling to Kilsyth. The royal standard was pitched, according to tradition, in a stone having a round hole for its reception, and thence called the Bore-stone. It is still shewn on the top of a small eminence called Brocks Brae, to the south-west of St. Ninians. To the northward, Bruce fortified his position against cavalry by digging a number of pits so close together as to resemble the cells in a honeycomb. They were slightly covered with brushwood and green sods, so as not to be obvious to an impetuous enemy.* Two large stones, erected in

* On the evening before the battle a personal encounter took place between Bruce and Sir Henry De Bohun, a gallant English knight, the issue of which had a great effect upon the spirits of both armies. It is thus recorded by Sir Walter Scott in "The Lord of the Isles."

"Dash'd from the ranks Sir Henry Boune,—
He spurr'd his steed, he couch'd his lance,
And darted on the Bruce at once.—

the lower extremity of a lawn which fronts a villa near the village of Newhouse, about a quarter of a mile from the south part of Stirling, mark the spot where a skirmish took place between Randolph Earl of Moray, and a party of English commanded by Sir Robert Clifford.* The place is still popularly called Randals-field.

As motionless as rocks that bide
The wrath of the advancing tide,
The Bruce stood fast. Each heart beat high,
And dazzl'd was each gazing eye.—
The heart had hardly time to think,
The eye-lid scarcely time to wink,
While on the King, like flash of flame,
Spurr'd to full speed the war-horse came!—
The partridge may the falcon mock,
If that slight palfrey stand the shock.—
But swerving from the knight's career,
Just as they met Bruce shunn'd the spear;
Onward the baffl'd warrior bore
His course—but soon his course was o'er—
High in his stirrups stood the king,
And gave his battle-axe the swing;
Right on De Boune, the whiles he pass'd,
Fell that stern blow—the first—the last!—
Such strength upon the blow was put,
The helmet crash'd like hazel-nut,
The axe-shaft with its brazen clasp
Was shiver'd to the gauntlet grasp;
Springs from the blow the startled horse;
Drops to the plain the lifeless corse.
First of that fatal field, how soon,
How sudden fell the fierce De Boune."

The Scottish leaders remonstrated with the king upon his temerity; he only answered, "I have broken my good battle-axe." The English vanguard retreated after witnessing this single combat.

* Bruce had enjoined Randolph, who commanded the left wing of his army, to be vigilant in preventing any advanced parties of the English from throwing succours into the Castle of Stirling. Eight hundred horsemen commanded by Sir Robert Clifford were detached from the English army; they made a circuit by the low grounds to the east, and approached the Castle. The king perceived their motion, and coming up to Randolph, angrily exclaimed, "Thoughtless man! you have suffered the enemy to pass." Randolph hastened to repair his fault or perish. As he advanced, the English cavalry wheeled to attack him. Randolph drew up his troops in a circular form, with their spears resting on the ground and protended on every side. At the first onset, Sir William Daynecourt, an English commander of distinguished note, was slain. The enemy, far superior in numbers to Randolph, environed him and pressed hard on his little band, Douglas saw his jeopardy, and requested the king's permission to go and succour him. "You shall not move from your ground,"

About a mile from the field of battle, in another direction, is a place called the Bloody Folds, where the Earl of Gloucester is said to have made a stand and died gallantly at the head of his own military tenants and vassals. There is also a place in this neighbourhood called Ingram's Crook, which is supposed to have derived its name from Sir Ingram Umfraville, one of the English commanders. In the rear of the Scottish army is the Gillies' Hill, which derived its name from the following circumstance: In a valley westward of this hill, Bruce stationed his baggage, under the charge of the gillies or servants and retainers of the camp. At the critical moment when the English line was wavering, these gillies, prompted either by the enthusiasm of the moment, or the desire of plunder, assumed, in a tumultuary manner, such arms as they found nearest, and shewed themselves on the hill like a new army advancing to battle. The English, taking these for a fresh body of troops, were seized with a panic, and fled in every direction.

About a mile westward from the field of Bannockburn, was fought in 1488, the battle of Sauchieburn, in which James III. was defeated and slain. The Barons of Scotland being dissatisfied with the government of the king, rose in rebellion against him, and drew into their party the king's eldest son, afterwards James IV. When the king saw his own banner displayed against him, and his son in the faction of his enemies, he lost the little courage

cried the king, "let Randolph extricate himself as he best may, I will not alter my order of battle and lose the advantage of my position." "In truth," replied Douglas, "I cannot stand by and see Randolph perish, and, therefore, with your leave, I must aid him." The king unwillingly consented, and Douglas flew to the assistance of his friend. While approaching, he perceived that the English were falling into disorder, and that the perseverance of Randolph had prevailed over their impetuous courage. "Halt," cried Douglas, "those brave men have repulsed the enemy, let us not diminish their glory by sharing it."—*Dalrymple's Annals of Scotland.*

he ever possessed, fled out of the field, and fell from his horse as it started at a woman and water-pitcher near the village of Millton. He was carried into the mill in a state of insensibility by the miller and his wife without being recognized. On recovering his senses he asked for a priest, to whom he might make confession. One of his pursuers coming up, exclaimed, " I am a priest," and, approaching the unfortunate monarch, who was lying in a corner of the mill, stabbed him several times to the heart. James IV. was seized with deep remorse for his conduct in this affair, which manifested itself in severe acts of penance,—among others,in wearing a heavy iron belt, to the weight of which he added certain ounces as long as he lived.

St. Ninians, or as it commonly called St. Ringans, is a thriving village a short way south from Stirling. Its steeple stands separate from the church which is in its immediate vicinity. The old church being used as a powder magazine by the Highlanders in 1746, was accidentally blown up, but though the church was completely destroyed, the steeple remained uninjured. A mile farther on, the tourist enters the royal burgh of

STIRLING,

delightfully situated on an eminence near the river Forth, and bearing in its external appearance a considerable resemblance to Edinburgh, though on a smaller scale. The most interesting and conspicuous object in Stirling is the Castle, the first foundation of which is lost in the darkness of antiquity. It was frequently taken and retaken after protracted sieges, during the wars which were carried on for the independence of Scotland. It became a royal residence about the time of the accession of the house of Stuart, and was long the favourite abode of the Scottish monarchs. It was the birthplace of James II. and James V.; and James VI. and his eldest son Prince Henry were baptized in it. The palace, which was built by James V., is in the form of a quadrangle, and occupies the south-east part of the fortress. The buildings on the south side of the square are the oldest part of the castle. One of the apartments is still called Douglas's Room, in consequence of the assassination of William Earl of Douglas by James II. after he had granted him a safe-conduct.*

On the west side of the square is a long low building, which was originally a chapel, and is now used as a store-room and armoury. This building was erected by James VI., and was the scene of the baptism of his son Prince Henry. Underneath the exterior wall on the west, a narrow road leads from the town, and descends the precipice behind the Castle. This is called Ballangeich, a Gaelic word signifying "windy pass," which is remarkable as having furnished the fictitious name adopted by James V. in the various disguises which he was in the habit of assuming, for the purpose of seeing that justice was regularly administered, and frequently also from the less justifiable motive of gallantry.† To the north of the

* "Ye towers! within whose circuit dread
A Douglas by his sovereign bled."
Lady of the Lake.

† The two excellent comic songs, entitled "The Gaberlunzie man," and "We'll gae nae mair a roving," are said to have been founded on the success of this monarch's amorous adventures when travelling in the disguise of a beggar. The following anecdotes respecting this frolicsome Prince are given by Sir Walter Scott:—

"Another adventure, which had nearly cost James his life, is said to have taken place at the village of Cramond, near Edinburgh, where he had rendered his addresses acceptable to a pretty girl of the lower rank. Four or five persons, whether relations or lovers of his mistress is uncertain, beset the disguised monarch, as he returned from his rendezvous. Naturally gallant, and an admirable master of his weapon, the king took post on the high and narrow bridge over the Almond river, and defended himself bravely with his sword. A peasant, who was threshing in a neighbouring barn, came out upon

Castle is a small mount on which executions commonly

the noise, and, whether moved by compassion or by natural gallantry, took the weaker side, and laid about with his flail so effectually, as to disperse the assailants, well threshed, even according to the letter. He then conducted the king into his barn, where his guest requested a bason and towel, to remove the stains of the broil. This being procured with difficulty, James employed himself in learning what was the summit of his deliverer's earthly wishes, and found that they were bounded by the desire of possessing, in property, the farm of Braehead, upon which he laboured as a bondsman. The lands chanced to belong to the crown; and James directed him to come to the palace of Holy-Rood, and inquire for the Guidman (*i. e.* farmer) of Ballangeich, a name by which he was known in his excursions, and which answered to *Il Bondocani* of Haroun Alraschid. He presented himself accordingly, and found, with due astonishment, that he had saved his monarch's life, and that he was to be gratified with a crown-charter of the lands of Braehead, under the service of presenting an ewer, bason, and towel, for the king to wash his hands, when he shall happen to pass the Bridge of Cramond. In 1822, when George IV. came to Scotland, the descendant of this John Howison of Braehead, who still possesses the estate which was given to his ancestor, appeared at a solemn festival, and offered his Majesty water from a silver ewer.

"Another of James' frolics is thus narrated by Mr. Campbell, from the Statistical Account. 'Being once benighted when out a hunting, and separated from his attendants, he happened to enter a cottage in the midst of a moor, at the foot of the Ochil hills, near Alloa, where, unknown, he was kindly received. In order to regale their unexpected guest, the *gude-man* (*i. e.* landlord, farmer) desired the *gude-wife* to fetch the hen that roosted nearest the cock, which is always the plumpest, for the stranger's supper. The king, highly pleased with his night's lodging and hospitable entertainment, told mine host, at parting, that he should be glad to return his civility, and requested that the first time he came to Stirling he would call at the castle, and inquire for the *gude-man of Ballangeich.* Donaldson, the landlord, did not fail to call on the *gude-man of Ballangeich,* when his astonishment at finding that the king had been his guest afforded no small amusement to the merry monarch and his courtiers; and, to carry on the pleasantry, he was thenceforth designated by James with the title of King of the Moors, which name and designation have descended from father to son ever since, and they have continued in possession of the identical spot, the property of Mr. Erskine of Mar, till very lately, when this gentleman, with reluctance, turned out the descendant and representative of the King of the Moors, on account of his majesty's invincible indolence, and great dislike to reform or innovation of any kind, although, from the spirited example of his neighbour tenants on the same estate, he is convinced similar exertion would promote his advantage.

The following anecdote is extracted from the genealogical work of Buchanan of Auchmar, upon Scottish surnames.

"'This John Buchanan of Auchmar and Arnpryor was afterwards termed King of Kippen,* upon the following account. King James V., a very sociable, debonair prince, residing at Stirling, in Buchanan of Arnpryor's time, carriers were very frequently passing along the common road, being near Arnpryor's

* A small district of Perthshire.

took place.* On this eminence, and within sight of their Castle of Doune and their extensive possessions, Murdoch Duke of Albany, Duncan Earl of Lennox, his father-in-law, and his two sons, Walter and Alexander Stuart, were beheaded in 1425. The execution of Walter Stuart is supposed, with great probability, to be the groundwork of the beautiful and pathetic ballad of "Young Waters." This "heading-hill" now bears commonly the name of Hurley-Hacket, from its being the scene of an amusement practised by James V. when a boy, and his courtiers, which consisted in sliding in some sort of chair from top to bottom of the bank. On the south side of the Castle Hill is a small piece of ground called the Valley, with a rock on the south side deno-

house, with necessaries for the use of the king's family, and he having some extraordinary occasion, ordered one of these carriers to leave his load at his house, and he would pay him for it; which the carrier refused to do, telling him he was the king's carrier, and his load for his majesty's use; to which Arnpryor seemed to have small regard, compelling the carrier, in the end, to leave his load; telling him, if King James was king of Scotland, he was king of Kippen, so that it was reasonable he should share with his neighbour king in some of these loads, so frequently carried that road. The carrier representing this usage, and telling the story, as Arnpryor spoke it, to some of the king's servants, it came at length to his majesty's ears, who, shortly thereafter, with a few attendants, came to visit his neighbour king, who was in the mean time at dinner. King James having sent a servant to demand access, was denied the same by a tall fellow with a battle-axe, who stood porter at the gate, telling, there could be no access till dinner was over. This answer not satisfying the king, he sent to demand access a second time; upon which he was desired by the porter to desist, otherwise he would find cause to repent his rudeness. His majesty finding this method would not do, desired the porter to tell his master that the good-man of Ballangeich desired to speak with the king of Kippen. The porter telling Arnpryor so much, he, in all humble manner, came and received the king, and having entertained him with much sumptuousness and jollity, became so agreeable to King James, that he allowed him to take so much of any provision he found carrying that road as he had occasion for; and, seeing he made the first visit, desired Arnpryor in a few days to return him a second at Stirling, which he performed, and continued in very much favour with the king, always thereafter being termed King of Kippen while he lived."'

* "Thou, O sad and fatal mound,
That oft has heard the death-axe sound."

Lady of the Lake.

minated the Ladies' Rock. On this spot tournaments used to be held. The view from the Castle Hill is remarkably magnificent. To the north and east are the Ochil Hills, and the windings of the Forth through the Carse of Stirling, with its fertile fields, luxuriant woods, and stately mansions. On the west lies the vale of Menteith, bounded by the Highland mountains. The Campsie hills close the horizon to the south, and in the foreground on the east are the town, the Abbey Craig, and the ruins of Cambuskenneth Abbey, and, in a clear day, the Castle of Edinburgh and Arthur's Seat are seen. Stirling Castle is one of the four fortresses of Scotland which, by the articles of the Union, are always to be kept in repair. It is now used as a barrack. Southwest of the Castle lies the King's Park, and to the east of it are the King's Gardens, which though now unenclosed and reduced to the condition of a marshy pasture, still retain the fantastic forms into which they had been thrown by the gardeners of ancient times.

The Greyfriars or Franciscan church of Stirling was erected in 1494 by James IV., and some additions were made to it by Cardinal Beaton. It is a handsome Gothic building, and, since the Reformation, has been divided into two places of worship, called the East and West Churches. In this church the Earl of Arran, Regent of the kingdom, abjured Romanism in 1543; it was also the scene of the coronation of James VI., 29th July 1597, when John Knox preached the coronation sermon. The celebrated Ebenezer Erskine, founder of the Secession Church, was one of the ministers of the West Church.

To the north of the Church stand the ruins of a haggard looking building called Mar's Work. It was built by the Earl of Mar out of the ruins of Cambuskenneth Abbey. This conduct excited a great deal of popular dissatisfaction, in allusion to which the Earl caused several inscriptions to be affixed to his house.

In the immediate neighbourhood of this building is a spacious edifice called Argyle's Lodging, which was built by Sir William Alexander, the poet, created Earl of Stirling. It afterwards passed into the hands of the Argyle family, and is now used as a military hospital.

Stirling has long been celebrated for its schools, and also for the number of its hospitals or residences for decayed persons. By an act of the Scottish Parliament in 1437, Stirling was appointed to be the place for keeping the Jug, or standard of dry measure, from which all others throughout the country were appointed to be taken, while the Firlot was given to Linlithgow, the Ell to Edinburgh, the Reel to Perth, and the Pound to Lanark. The Stirling Jug is still preserved with great care. In 1831 the population of the town and parish was 8340. Stirling Bridge was long a structure of great importance, having been, till lately, almost the only access into the northern part of Scotland for wheeled carriages. At a very early period there was a wooden bridge over the Forth about half a mile above the present structure, which was the scene of one of the most gallant achievements of Sir William Wallace, on the 13th of September 1297. An English army of 50,000 foot and 1000 horse, commanded by Cressingham, advanced towards Stirling in quest of Wallace, who, on his part, having collected an army of 40,000 men, marched southward to dispute the passage of the Forth. He posted his army near Cambuskenneth, allowing only a part of them to be seen. The English hurried across the river, to attack the Scots. After a considerable number of them had thus passed over, and the bridge was crowded with those who were following, Wallace charged those who had crossed with his whole strength, slew a very great number, and drove the rest into the river Forth, where the greater part were drowned. The remainder of the English army who were left on the southern bank of the river, fled in great confusion, having first set fire to the wooden bridge, that the Scots might not pursue them. Cressingham himself was among the slain, and his rapine and oppression had rendered him so detestable to the Scots, that they flayed off his skin, and cut it in pieces to make girths for their horses.

The view of Stirling Castle, with which our text is illustrated, represents the scene in Waverley, where the party of Balmawhapple, upon passing the fortress, are saluted by a bullet from its walls. The artist has selected the moment when the valorous laird is returning the compliment, by discharging his pistol at the inhospitable rock.

FIFTH TOUR.

FROM EDINBURGH TO STIRLING, BY STEAM BOAT.*

LOOKING straight across the Firth, upon leaving the Chain Pier, the burgh of Burntisland may be observed directly opposite. On the same side as the Chain Pier, the Duke of Buccleuch has lately built a low-water pier for the better accommodation of steam boats. After passing Granton, may be seen Lauriston Castle, the residence of John Law, the projector of the Mississippi scheme. On the north shore is the town of Aberdour, and near it the seat of the Earl of Morton, who is known here by the title of "the Gudeman of Aberdour." North of the Castle is the mansion house of Hillside, and a little farther on is Dalgetty Church. Near this point is the island of Inch Colm, with the remains of a monastery founded in 1123 by Alexander I. On the south shore, at the mouth of the river Almond, stand the village of Cramond, and Cramond House, (Lady Torphichen,) and a little farther west is Dalmeny Park, the seat of the Earl of Rosebery. Near it are the ruins of Barnbougle Castle, an ancient seat of the family of the Moubrays, now extinct. Directly opposite is Donnibrissal, a seat of the Earl of Moray, the scene of the atrocious murder, by the Earl of Huntly, of the youthful Earl of Moray, son-in-law of the celebrated Regent Murray.† A short way to

* Steam-boats sail for Alloa and Stirling every day from Trinity Chain Pier. Coaches to the boat run from the Duty House, end of North Bridge, where correct information as to the hours of sailing may be obtained.

† "The Earl of Huntly, head of the powerful family of Gordon, had chanced to have some feudal differences with the Earl of Murray, in the course of which

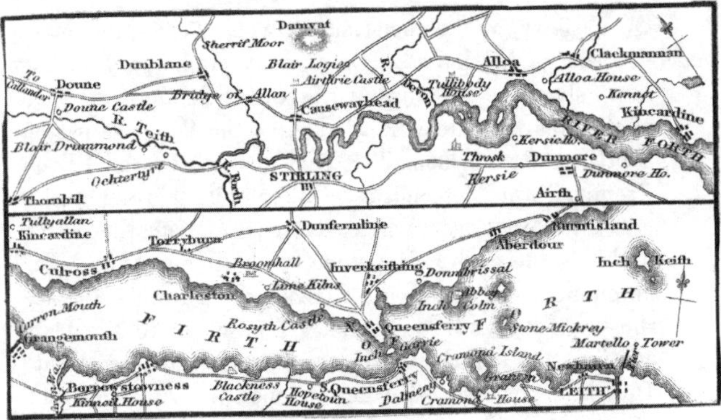

the westward lies the ancient burgh of Inverkeithing. On the two coasts are the towns of North and South

John Gordon, a brother of Gordon of Cluny, was killed by a shot from Murray's castle of Darnaway. This was enough to make the two families irreconcilable enemies, even if they had been otherwise on friendly terms. About 1591-2, an accusation was brought against Murray for having given some countenance, or assistance, to Stewart, Earl of Bothwell, in a recent treasonable exploit. King James, without recollecting, perhaps, the hostility between the two Earls, sent Huntly with a commission to bring the Earl of Murray to his presence. Huntly probably rejoiced in the errand, as giving him an opportunity of revenging himself on his feudal enemy. He beset the house of Dunnibrissle, on the northern shore of the Forth, and summoned Murray to surrender. In reply, a gun was fired, which mortally wounded one of the Gordons. The assailants proceeded to set fire to the house; when Dunbar, sheriff of the county of Moray, said to the Earl, 'Let us not stay to be burned in the flaming house: I will go out foremost, and the Gordons, taking me for your Lordship, will kill me, while you escape in the confusion.' They rushed out among their enemies accordingly, and Dunbar was slain. But his death did not save his friend, as he had generously intended. Murray, indeed, escaped for the moment, but as he fled towards the rocks of the sea-shore, he was traced by the silken tassels attached to his head-piece, which had taken fire as he broke out among the flames. By this means his pursuers followed him down amongst the cliffs near the sea; and Gordon of Buckie, who is said to have been the first that overtook him, wounded him mortally. As Murray was gasping in the last agony, Huntly came up; and it is alleged by tradition, that Gordon pointed his dirk against the person of his chief, saying, 'By heaven, my Lord, you shall be as deep in as I,' and so he compelled him to wound Murray whilst he was dying. Huntly, with a wavering hand, struck the expiring Earl in the face. Thinking of his superior beauty, even in that moment of parting life, Murray stammered out the dying words, 'You have spoiled a better face than your own.'

"After this deed of violence, Huntly did not choose to return to Edinburgh,

Queensferry, and in the straits between them is the fortified islet of Inchgarvie. On a rocky promontory on the north shore are the ruins of Rosyth Castle, once the seat of the Stuarts of Rosyth, a branch of the Royal House of Scotland, from whom it is said the mother of Oliver Cromwell was descended. Half a mile beyond Inchgarvie is Port Edgar, where George IV. embarked after a visit to the Earl of Hopetoun, 29th August 1822. On an eminence beyond South Queensferry is Dundas Castle, the original seat of the Dundas family before the 11th century, and still the residence of their lineal descendant, Dundas of that ilk. Farther on, upon the same side and about a mile from the shore, is Hopetoun House, the splendid mansion of the Earl of Hopetoun; and on a peninsula to the westward stands Blackness Castle, one

---

but departed for the north. He took refuge, for the moment, in the castle of Ravenscraig, belonging to the Lord Sinclair, who told him, with a mixture of Scottish caution and hospitality, that he was welcome to come in, but would have been twice as welcome to have passed by. Gordon, when a long period had passed by, avowed his contrition for the guilt he had incurred."—*Tales of a Grandfather*, vol. ii. p. 191.

Upon this tragical circumstance the following beautiful ballad is founded:—

" Ye Highlands, and ye Lawlands,
Oh, where have ye been?
They hae slain the Earl o' Murray,
And lain him on the green.

' Now wae be to you, Huntly!
And wherefore did ye sae?
I bade you bring him wi' you,
But forbade you him to slay.'

He was a braw gallant,
And he rade at the ring;
And the bonnie Earl o' Murray,
Oh! he micht ha' been a king.

He was a braw gallant,
And he rade at the gluve;
And the bonnie Earl o' Murray,
Oh! he was the Queen's luve!

Oh! lang will his lady
Look ower the Castle Doune,
Ere she see the Earl of Murray
Come sounding through the toun."

of the four fortresses which, by the articles of the Union, are to be kept constantly garrisoned. Close by the village of Charleston, on the north side of the Forth, stands Broomhall, the seat of the Earl of Elgin. Farther on is Crombie Point and Crombie House, then the village of Torryburn, next Torry House (Captain Erskine Wemyss of Wemyss Castle) and Newmills village. Returning to the south coast and proceeding westward, may be seen in succession Carriden House (James Hope, Esq.) Kirkgrange Salt Pans, Borrowstounness, Kinneil House, the property of the Duke of Hamilton, for some time the residence of the late Professor Dugald Stewart; and Grangemouth, situated at the mouth of Carron Water. On the north side is Valleyfield (Lady Baird Preston), and near it the ancient and decayed burgh of Culross (pronounced Cooross). The inhabitants are a remarkably primitive set of people. Immediately behind it are the ruins of a Cistertian Abbey, founded in 1217 by Malcolm Earl of Fife. At the Reformation, its possessions were conferred upon Sir James Colville, who was created Lord Colville of Culross. From the family of Colville it passed to the Earls of Dundonald, who sold it to the late Sir Robert Preston, Bart.* A little farther

* Culross was famous for the manufacture of *girdles,* the round iron plates on which the people of Scotland bake their barley and oaten bread. "The hammermen of Edinburgh are no' that bad at girdles for carcakes neither, though the Cu'ross hammermen have the gree for that."—*Heart of Mid Lothian,* Vol. II. 254.

Culross was also celebrated for its salt-pans and coal-mines. In the reign of James VI. the coal-mines were worked a great way under the bed of the Forth, and the coals were shipped at a mound which defended from the water the mouth of a subterraneous communication with the coal-pit. James VI. when on a visit to the proprietor, Sir George Bruce, being conducted by his own desire into the coal-pit, was led to ascend from it by the mound, when it was high tide. Seeing himself surrounded on all sides by water, he apprehended a plot and bawled out "Treason," but Sir George soon dispelled his Majesty's fears, by handing him into an elegant pinnace that was lying alongside.

on is Blair Castle (Dundas, Esq.) and about a mile beyond this is Sands House (Johnstone, Esq.) After which the tourist reaches the town and shipping port of Kincardine. Near it stand the ruins of the ancient castle of Tulliallan, formerly the property of the knights of Blackadder, and Tulliallan Castle, the splendid residence of Baroness Keith and Count Flahault, built by the late Admiral Lord Keith, the father of the present proprietrix, who is also the lineal representative of one of the most ancient families of Scotland—the Mercers of Aldie. On the opposite side is Higgin's Nook (J. Burn Murdoch, Esq.), and beyond it upon a height, Airth Castle, (Graham, Esq.), and about a mile to the west Dunmore House, the residence of the Earl of Dunmore. Nearly opposite, upon the right, is Kennet House, the seat of Robert Bruce, Esq. of Kennet. Farther on upon the same side is Clackmannan, the capital of the small county of that name; delightfully situated on an eminence, and to the west of the town is Clackmannan Tower, said to have been built by Robert Bruce. It is now the property of the Earl of Zetland. Close beside the tower once stood the palace of Robert Bruce, and family house of Bruce of Clackmannan now demolished. This was the residence of the old Jacobite lady, Mrs. Bruce of Clackmannan, who is mentioned in Currie's Life of Burns as having knighted that poet with a sword which belonged to Bruce. The sword and a helmet which had also belonged to the hero, are now in the possession of Lord Elgin, who represents the family of Bruce, and are to be seen at Broomhall near Dunfermline. About a mile beyond Clackmannan, is the flourishing town of Alloa, in the neighbourhood of extensive collieries and distilleries. Near the town and in the midst of a fine park, stands Alloa House, the ancient seat of the family of Erskine Earls of Mar, and the subject of a fine Scottish air. The principal part of the building was destroyed by fire about twenty years ago, but there is still standing the original tower, an erection of the thirteenth century. It is ninety feet high, and the walls are eleven feet thick. At Alloa commence those remarkable windings called the "Links of Forth." These windings of the river form a great number of beautiful peninsulas, which, being of a very luxuriant and fertile soil, gave rise to the old rhyme,—

"The lairdship o' the bonnie Links o' Forth
Is better than an earldom o' the North."

The distance by land from Alloa to Stirling Bridge is only six miles, while by water it is sixteen. On the same side as Alloa, and a little to the westward, is Tullibody House, a residence of the Abercromby family. The Ochil-hills, from their proximity, now assume an air of imposing grandeur, and Stirling Castle forms a magnificent feature in the landscape. Beyond Tullibody, on the same side, is Cambus village, at the mouth of the Devon. The vale of the Devon is famed for its romantic beauty, and for the striking cascades formed by the river. Nearly opposite Cambus is Polmaise, (Murray, Esq.) Farther on, upon the right, are the ruins of Cambuskenneth Abbey, situated on one of the peninsular plains formed by the windings of the river. It was founded by David I., in 1147, for canons regular of the order of St. Augustine. It was one of the richest and most extensive abbeys in Scotland. At the Reformation, its possessions were bestowed by James VI. on the Earl of

Mar, but about the year 1737 it was purchased by the Town Council of Stirling, for the benefit of Cowan's Hospital. Of the once extensive fabric of the Abbey nothing now exists except a few broken walls and a tower, which was the belfry. On the right is seen the Abbey Craig, and soon after the tourist reaches Stirling.

From Stirling a pleasant episodical tour may be made to Castle Campbell, the Rumbling Brig, and the Devil's Caldron.

Leaving Stirling, the tourist has on his left the soft green pastoral yet lofty hills of the Ochil range, with their magnificent wooded glades and warm sunward slopes, consisting of intermingling copse, cornfields, and meadows, while on the right is a rich and level country, bounded by the Forth, now untwining its silver links and spreading into a noble estuary. The most southerly of the Ochil-hills is Damyat, famous for the extensive and splendid view obtained from its summit. In its neighbourhood is Bencleuch, which shoots up into a tall rocky point, called Craigleith, remarkable in ancient times for the production of falcons. In a hollow near this the snow often lies far into the summer. The people give it the picturesque name of Lady Alva's Web. Three miles from Stirling the tourist reaches the beautiful village of Blairlogie, and four miles beyond it the village of Alva, which was formerly remarkable for its silver mines. Alva House, the residence of Johnstone of Alva, stands on an eminence projecting from the base of the Woodhill.* Three miles from Alva is Tillicoultry, and at the distance of other three miles is the village of Dollar, about thirteen miles from Stirling and seven from Alva. At Dollar there is an extensive academy, founded by a person of the name of MacNab, a native of the parish, who had realized a large fortune in London. It is a handsome Grecian building, and is furnished with good masters for the various branches of education. In the neighbour-

* "Oh, Alva woods are bonnie,
Tillicoultry hills are fair,
But when I think o' the bonnie Braes o' Menstrie
It maks my heart aye sair."

Fairy Rhyme.

The village of Menstrie lies two miles west of Alva. Menstrie House was the seat of the Earl of Stirling.

hood is the remarkable ruin of Castle Campbell, occupying a wild and romantic situation on the top of a high and almost insulated rock. The only access to the castle is by an isthmus connecting the mount with the hill behind. The mount on which it is situated is nearly encompassed on all sides by thick bosky woods, and mountain rivulets descending on either side unite at the base. Immediately behind rises a vast amphitheatre of wooded hills. Castle Campbell is a place of great antiquity. The precise period at which it came into the possession of the Argyle family is not certainly known. In 1493 an act of Parliament was passed for changing the name of "the castle called the Gloume,"* to Castle Campbell, and it continued to be the lowland residence of the great clan family of Argyle, till about thirty years ago, upon the death of the late Duke, it was sold to Mr. Tait of Harvieston. It is said that John Knox resided in Castle Campbell, under the protection of Archibald, the fourth Earl, who was the first of the Scottish nobility that publicly embraced the Protestant religion. Castle Campbell was destroyed in 1645. "The feudal hatred of Montrose and of the clans composing the strength of his army, the vindictive resentment also of the Ogilvies for the destruction of "the bonnie House of Airlie," and that of the Stirlingshire cavaliers for that of Menstrie, doomed this magnificent pile to flames and ruin. The destruction of many a meaner habitation by the same unscrupulous and unsparing spirit of vengeance has been long forgotten, but the majestic remains of Castle Campbell, still excite a sigh in those that view them, over the miseries of civil war."† About two miles above Dollar is an interesting spot where the Devon forms a series of cascades one of which is called the Caldron Linn.‡ The river

* The ancient name of the Castle, it is often said, was the Castle of Gloom. The mountain streams that flow on the different sides are still called the one the Water of Care, the other the Burn of Sorrow, and after the junction in front of the Castle, they traverse the valley of Dollar or Dolour. The proper etymologists, however, tell a different tale. The old Gaelic name of the stronghold was *Cock Leum*, or Mad Leap. The glen of Care, was the glen of *Caer* or castle, a British word; and Dollar is simply *Dalor*, the high field.—*Chambers's Gazetteer*, vol. i. 191.

† Tales of a Grandfather, vol. iii. p. 12.

‡ Instead of the usual route, pedestrians in coming from Dollar, should strike off the high road soon after they get above *Vicars Bridge*, and take along a path to the right, leading to *Cowden* and *Muckart Mill*, and from thence, by the *Blair Hill*, to the Caldron Linn. This is a short *cut*, which keeps near the river by a far more romantic line than the turnpike road.

here suddenly enters a deep gulf, where, finding itself confined, it has, by continual efforts against the sides, worked out a cavity resembling a large caldron. From this gulf the water finds its way through an aperture beneath the surface into a lower cavity, where it is covered with a constant foam. The water then works its way into a third caldron, out of which it is precipitated by a sheer fall of forty-four feet. The best view of this magnificent scene is from the bottom of the fall. About a mile farther up the vale, the rocks on each side rise to the height of eighty-six feet, and the banks of the stream are contracted in such a manner, that a bridge of twenty-five feet span connects them. A handsome new bridge has lately been erected above the old one, and a hundred and twenty feet from the bed of the stream. On account of the rocky nature of the channel, the river here makes a violent noise, hence the name of the Rumbling Bridge.* A few hundred yards farther up, there is another cascade, called the Devil's Mill, where the water vibrating from one side to another of the pool, and constantly beating against the sides of the rock, produces an intermittent noise like that of a mill in motion. The whole of the scenes around these remarkable cascades are of the most romantic kind, and strikingly different from all other Scottish scenery. "The clear, winding Devon," as almost every reader will recollect, has been celebrated by Burns in his beautiful lyric, "The banks of the Devon." Miss Charlotte Hamilton, (afterwards Mrs. Adair,) the lady on whom this song was composed, was at that time residing at Harvieston, near Dollar.

The tourist may, if he choose, proceed by the Crook of Devon to Kinross, and thence to Edinburgh,—a route which he will find described in the tour from Edinburgh to Perth, or he may proceed to Dunfermline, and thence to North Queensferry by a route much more agreeable and only two miles longer.

---

* A short distance from the Rumbling Bridge is Aldie Castle, the ancient seat of the Mercers of Aldie, now represented by Baroness Keith. At Aldie, a man, on being hanged for the slight offence of stealing a *caup fu' o' corn,* is said to have uttered a malediction upon the family, to the effect that the estate of Aldie should never be inherited by a male heir for nineteen generations. It is a somewhat singular coincidence that this has already so far taken effect,—Lady Keith being the daughter of an heiress who was the grand-daughter and successor of another heiress, and being herself the mother of an only daughter. The slogan or war cry of the Mercers of Aldie was "The grit pule."

A short but pleasant excursion may also be made from Stirling to Dunblane, distant six miles, and to the Roman Camp at Ardoch, twelve miles distant.

Leaving Stirling, the tourist crosses the Forth by Stirling Bridge. A short way farther up the river is the Old Bridge, a very antique structure, narrow and high in the centre. General Blakeney, the governor of the Castle, in 1745, caused the south arch to be destroyed, to interrupt the march of the Highlanders. On this bridge Archbishop Hamilton of St. Andrews, the last Roman Catholic Archbishop of Scotland, was hanged, in 1571, in full pontificals, for his alleged accession to the assassination of Regent Murray. The tourist now passes, on the right, Airthrey Castle, (Lord Abercromby,) and afterwards the pretty little village of the Bridge of Allan, much resorted to in summer on account of a mineral well in the neighbourhood. In the vicinity is Keir, the seat of Archibald Stirling, Esq. and a mile and a half beyond it, the road passes Kippenross, the seat of Stirling of Kippendavie. In the lawn there is a remarkable planetree, supposed to be the largest in the kingdom. It is twenty-seven feet in circumference at the ground, and thirty where the branches shoot out. A little beyond Kippenross is

DUNBLANE,*

an ancient cathedral city, situated on the banks of the beautiful little river Allan. The cathedral, which was founded in 1142, and richly endowed by David I. is still tolerably entire. The east end is fitted up in an elegant style, as a parish church. The prebendal stalls of richly carved dark oak, have fortunately been preserved. Several of the Bishops of Dunblane were distinguished persons, but the most celebrated of them was the good Bishop Leighton, afterwards Archbishop of Glasgow, who founded a library here, which has been greatly increased by subsequent literary donations. The mineral spring at Cromlix, in the vicinity of Dunblane, is greatly frequented.

About two miles east by north of Dunblane is Sheriffmuir, the scene of the battle which was fought in 1715 between the Earl of Mar and the Royal forces under the Duke of Argyle. In this engagement the left wing of both armies was defeated, and the right of both was victorious, but the fruits of the victory remained with

* Popularly characterized as "drucken Dumblane."

the Duke of Argyle.* Near the western extremity of the muir is Kippendavie, (— Stirling, Esq.) and four miles beyond is Greenloaning. A mile and a half farther on, the tourist reaches Ardoch House, the seat of Major William Moray Stirling. Within his parks is the celebrated Roman Camp of Ardoch, esteemed the most entire in the kingdom. General Wade's military road passes over one of its sides. The measure of the whole area is 1060 feet by 900, and it is calculated to have contained no fewer than 20,000 men. There appear to have been three or four ditches, and as many rampart walls surrounding the camp. The praetorium, which rises above the level of the camp, but is not precisely in the centre, forms a regular square, each side being exactly twenty yards. The camp is defended on the south-east side by a deep morass, and on the west side by the banks of the water of Knaick, which rises perpendicularly to the height of about fifty feet. In the immediate vicinity there are two other encampments more slightly fortified.

The tourist may proceed from Greenloaning to Perth, by Blackford, Auchterarder, and Dalraich Bridge, passing on the road Braco Castle, Orchill, Gleneagles, Kincardine Castle, Strathallan Castle, Gask, and Dupplin Castle.

---

* Some person having remarked to the Duke of Argyle that the rebels would probably claim the victory, his Grace replied,

"If it wasna weel bobbit, weel bobbit, weel bobbit,
If it wasna weel bobbit, we'll bobb it again ;"

alluding to the well known old song called "The Bob of Dunblane."

A number of noblemen and gentlemen on both sides were slain in this engagement, among others the Earls of Forfar and Strathmore, the chieftain of clan Ranald, &c. The body of the gallant young Earl of Strathmore was found on the field watched by a faithful old domestic, who, being asked the name of the person whose body he waited upon with so much care, made this striking reply, "He was a man yesterday." "There was mair *tint* (lost) at Sheriffmuir," is a common proverb in Scotland. It is told that a Highlander lamented that, at the battle of Sheriffmuir, he had "lost his father and his mother, and a gude buff belt weel worth them baith." Burns has made this battle the subject of a song replete with humour.

SIXTH TOUR

STIRLING—DOUNE—CALLANDER—THE TROSACHS—LOCH KATRINE LOCH LOMOND.

THERE are two roads which lead from Stirling to Doune, the first stage in the way to Loch Katrine; one crosses the Forth by Stirling Bridge, and proceeds along the east bank of the Teith, passing in succession the beautiful village of Bridge of Allan and the neat parish church of Lecropt, built in the Gothic style; the other, proceeding up the valley of the Forth, passes the House of Craigforth, (Callander, Esq.) and, two miles from Stirling, crosses the river at the Bridge of Drip. At the distance of about four miles from Stirling, the road passes Ochtertyre, (Dundas, Esq.) once the residence of Mr. J. Ramsay, the friend of Blacklock, of Burns, and of Scott; a mile and a half farther on the road passes the mansion of Blair Drummond, (Home Drummond, Esq.) embosomed in fine woods and plantations. About 60 or 70 years ago, the late Lord Kames became proprietor of this estate, and commenced that series of operations by which what was once a bleak marsh has been turned into rich corn fields. The road now crosses the Teith by a fine old bridge built by Robert Spittal, tailor to Queen Margaret, widow of James IV., and about nine miles from Stirling enters the village of

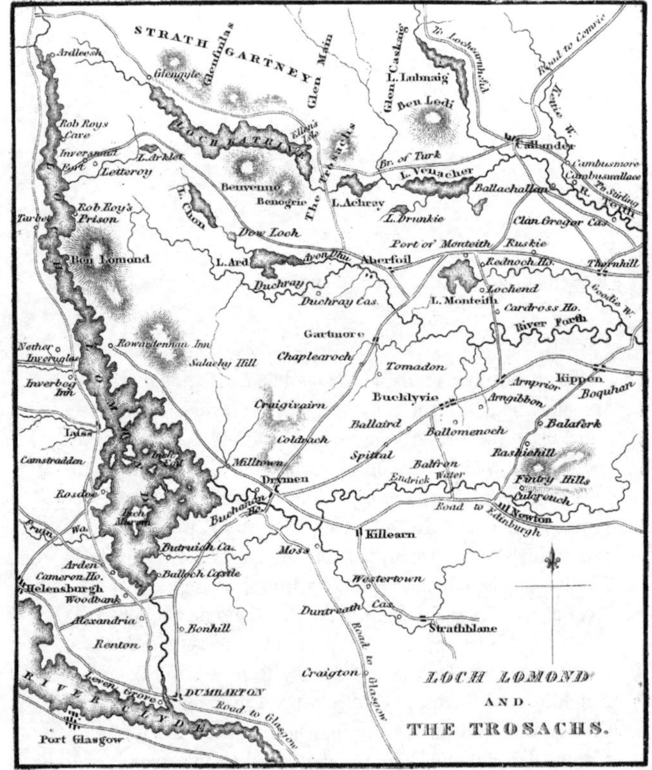

DOUNE.

Just before crossing the bridge, and on the left hand, are Deanston Works, one of the most extensive cotton factories in Scotland. The village of Doune was in former times celebrated for the manufacture of Highland pistols. The ruins of Doune Castle, a massive and extensive fortress, supposed to have been built about the fourteenth century, are situated on the point of a steep and narrow green bank, washed on one side by the Teith, and on the other by the Ardoch. It was anciently the seat of the Earls of Menteith, but about the beginning of the fifteenth century it was forfeited to the Crown, and became the favourite residence of the two successive Dukes of Albany, who governed Scotland during the captivity of James I.; Queen Margaret, and the unfortunate Queen Mary, are also said frequently to have resided in this fortress. It was held for Prince Charles during the rebellion of 1745, and here he disposed his prisoners taken at Falkirk, and among the rest the author of the tragedy of Douglas.* Doune Castle has long been the property of the Earls of Moray, who derive from it their second title of Lord

* "This noble ruin," says Sir Walter Scott, "holds a commanding station on the banks of the river Teith, and has been one of the largest castles in Scotland. Murdock, Duke of Albany, the founder of this stately pile, was beheaded on the Castlehill of Stirling, from which he might see the towers of Doune, the monument of his fallen greatness. In 1745-6, a garrison on the part of the Chevalier was put into the castle, then less ruinous than at present. It was commanded by Mr. Stewart of Balloch, as governor for Prince Charles; he was a man of property near Callander. This castle became at that time the actual scene of a romantic escape made by John Home, the author of Douglas, and some other prisoners, who, having been taken at the battle of Falkirk, were confined there by the insurgents. The poet, who had in his own mind a large stock of that romantic and enthusiastic spirit of adventure, which he has described as animating the youthful hero of his drama, devised and undertook the perilous enterprise of escaping from his prison. He inspired his companions with his sentiments, and when every attempt at open force was deemed hopeless, they resolved to twist their bed-clothes into ropes, and thus to descend. Four persons, with Home himself, reached the ground in safety. But the rope broke with the fifth, who was a tall lusty man. The sixth was Thomas Barrow, a brave young Englishman, a particular friend of Home's. Determined to take the risk, even in such unfavourable circumstances, Barrow committed himself to the broken rope, slid down on it as far as it could assist him, and then let himself drop. His friends beneath succeeded in breaking his fall. Nevertheless, he dislocated his ankle, and had several of his ribs broken. His companions, however, were able to bear him off in safety. The Highlanders next morning sought for their prisoners, with great activity. An old gentleman told the author, he remembered seeing the commander Stewart,

'Bloody with spurring, fiery red with haste,'

riding furiously through the country in quest of the fugitives."—*Note, Waverley*, vol. ii. pp. 81, 82.

Doune. About a mile to the north-west the Earl of Moray has a mansion named Doune Lodge, formerly designated Cambus-Wallace, when it was the property of the Edmonstones. At the distance of three miles from Doune, on the opposite side of the river, is Lanrick Castle, the seat of Sir Evan Murray M'Gregor, chieftain of Clan-Gregor, and three miles farther on Cambusmore, (A. Buchannan, Esq.) where Sir Walter Scott in his juvenile days spent some months for several summers.* The village of

CALLANDER,

sixteen miles from Stirling, is situated at the foot of the chain of mountains which form the Highland boundary. It is a neat and regular modern village, with a remarkably good inn. Behind are high bluff cliffs, the wild copse and rocks intermingled, and the scenery around the village is uncommonly beautiful. To the westward two

* He has given a striking sketch of the most interesting objects on this route in his description of Fitz-James' ride after the combat with Roderick Dhu:—

"They dash'd that rapid torrent through,
And up Carhonie's hill they flew;
Still at the gallop prick'd the Knight,
His merry-men follow'd as they might.
Along thy banks, swift Teith! they ride,
And in the race they mock thy tide;
Torry and Lendrick now are past,
And Deanstown lies behind them cast;
They rise, the banner'd towers of Doune,
They sink in distant woodland soon;
Blair-Drummond sees the hoofs strike fire,
They sweep like breeze through Ochtertyre;
They mark just glance and disappear
The lofty brow of ancient Kier;
They bathe their coursers' sweltering sides,
Dark Forth! amid thy sluggish tides,
And on the opposing shore take ground,
With plash, with scramble, and with bound.
Right-hand they leave thy cliffs, Craig-Forth!
And soon the bulwark of the North,
Grey Stirling, with her towers and town,
Upon their fleet career look'd down."

Lady of the Lake, c. v. st. 18

little rivers, issuing respectively from Loch Lubnaig and Loch Venachar, unite and form the Teith. At the east end of the village there is a neat villa, the property of Lady Willoughby D'Eresby. The Falls of Bracklinn, about a mile to the north of the village, form one of the most attractive objects in this vicinity. They consist in a series of short falls, shelving rapids, and dark linns, formed by the Keltie Burn. Above a chasm where the brook precipitates itself from a height of at least fifty feet, there is thrown a rustic foot-bridge of about three feet in breadth, which is scarcely to be crossed by a stranger without awe and apprehension. The magnificent mountain of Benledi, 3000 feet in height, which closes the prospect towards the west, forms the most striking feature of the scenery in this neighbourhood.* There are two roads which lead from Callander to the Trosachs, the north and south roads; the former is the most picturesque. Passing the valley of Bochastle, the House of Leny, (Hamilton Buchannan, Esq.) and the waterfalls of Carchonzie, the tourist reaches "Coilantogle Ford," about two and a half miles from Callander. This is the scene of the combat between Fitz-James and Roderick Dhu. Loch Venachar is four miles long, Loch Achray a mile and

* At Callander a road, much frequented by tourists, leads in a northerly direction to Loch-Earn-head (14 miles), by the beautiful Pass of Leny, Loch Lubnaig, and Balquidder. The Pass of Leny is thus described in the opening scene of the Legend of Montrose. "Their course had been for some time along the banks of a lake, whose deep waters reflected the crimson beams of the western sun. The broken path, which they pursued with some difficulty, was in some places shaded by ancient birches and oak-trees, and in others overhung by fragments of huge rock. Elsewhere the hill which formed the northern side of this beautiful sheet of water, arose in steep but less precipitous acclivity and was arrayed in heath of the darkest purple." By the side of Lubnaig is Ardhullary, a house built for a Highland retreat by Bruce the Abyssinian traveller, in which it is said he finished his work. In the churchyard of Balquidder, Rob Roy was interred beneath a stone, marked only with a fir-tree crossed by a sword, supporting a crown. "The braes o' Balquither" have been celebrated in song.

a half, the space between the lochs about half a mile, and from the western extremity of the latter to Loch Katrine one mile, making the whole distance between Callander and Loch Katrine from nine to ten miles. Laurick Mead, the mustering place of Clan Alpin, lies on the north side of Loch Venachar. Soon after the tourist passes the hamlet of Duncraggan, the huts of which

> "Peep like mossgrown rocks half seen,
> Half hidden in the copse so green."

The Bridge of Turk* crosses the water, which descending from Glenfinlas, joins the Teith between Lochs Venachar and Achray; and a mile and a half farther on, is the inn of Ardcheanochrochan, beautifully situated on the side of Loch Achray.† The tourist is now in the Trosachs, (etymologically, bristled territory,) the road which traverses them is rather more than a mile in length. The opening into the pass is flanked on the left by Ben Venue, 2800 feet high, and on the right by Ben-an. In the defile of Beal-an-Duine, (where Fitz-James lost his "gallant grey,") we are in the heart of

* Here a road strikes off on the right to Glenfinlas, once a royal hunting forest; it is now the property of the Earl of Moray, and is inhabited by a primitive race of small farmers, all Stewarts. In times of yore, it was chiefly inhabited by the Macgregors. Glenfinlas is the scene of Sir Walter Scott's ballad, entitled "Glenfinlas, or Lord Ronald's Coronach."

† The crowds of tourists visiting the Trosachs during the summer months make it a matter of great uncertainty whether accommodation can be obtained at the inn. The usual effects of monopoly will also be experienced, and the civilities are nicely proportioned to the means the tourist is supposed to possess for compensating them. The boats upon Loch Katrine belong to the inn, and after paying the regular fare (2s. 6d.), the boatmen proceed to extort gratuities from the passengers, which they state (with what truth we know not,) to be the only remuneration they receive for their services. The charge of these Highland gillies for conveying luggage from the inn to the loch is also most extravagant. The distance is about a mile, and three shillings have been occasionally extorted for carrying a small parcel this trifling distance. These practices, it must be admitted, are calculated in a high degree to uphold the ancient reputation of Loch Katrine, or, with more correctness of etymology, Loch Kateran, which being interpreted signifieth *The Loch of the Robbers*.

the great gorge.* Then appears a narrow inlet, and a moment afterwards, Loch Katrine itself bursts upon our

* "A skirmish actually took place at a pass thus called in the Trosachs, and closed with the remarkable incident mentioned in the "Lady of the Lake." It was greatly posterior in date to the reign of James V.

"In this roughly-wooded island,* the country people secreted their wives and children and their most valuable effects, from the rapacity of Cromwell's soldiers, during their inroad into this country, in the time of the republic. These invaders, not venturing to ascend by the ladders, along the side of the lake, took a more circuitous road, through the heart of the Trosachs, the most frequented path at that time, which penetrated the wilderness about half-way between Binean and the lake, by a tract called Yea-chailleach, or the Old Wife's Bog.

"In one of the defiles of this by-road, the men of the country at that time hung upon the rear of the invading enemy, and shot one of Cromwell's men, whose grave marks the scene of action, and gives name to that pass.† In revenge of this insult, the soldiers resolved to plunder the island, to violate the women, and put the children to death. With this brutal intention, one of the party, more expert than the rest, swam towards the island, to fetch the boat to his comrades, which had carried the women to their asylum, and lay moored in one of the creeks. His companions stood on the shore of the main land, in full view of all that was to pass, waiting anxiously for his return with the boat. But, just as the swimmer had got to the nearest point of the island, and was laying hold of a black rock, to get on shore, a heroine, who stood on the very point where he meant to land, hastily snatching a dagger from below her apron, with one stroke severed his head from the body. His party seeing this disaster, and relinquishing all future hope of revenge or conquest, made the best of their way out of their perilous situation. This Amazon's great-grandson lives at Bridge of Turk, who, besides others, attests the anecdote.'—*Sketch of the Scenery near Callander*. Stirling, 1806, p. 20. I have only to add to this account, that the heroine's name was Helen Stuart.—*Notes to the Lady of the Lake*, p 53.

The following striking description of the Trosachs is given by Sir Walter Scott in the Lady of the Lake;—

"The western waves of ebbing day
Roll'd o'er the glen their level way;
Each purple peak, each flinty spire,
Was bathed in floods of living fire.
But not a setting beam could glow
Within the dark ravine below,
Where twined the path, in shadow hid,
Round many a rocky pyramid,
Shooting abruptly from the dell
Its thunder-splinter'd pinnacle;
Round many an insulated mass,
The native bulwarks of the pass,
Huge as the tower which builders vain
Presumptuous piled on Shinar's plain.

* That at the eastern extremity of Loch-Katrine, called "Ellen's Isle."

† Beallach an duine.

view, the Alps of Arroquhar towering in the distance. Loch Katrine is of a serpentine form, encircled by lofty mountains, and is ten miles in length, attaining in some places a breadth of two miles. The scenery which fringes it at its eastern extremity is precisely of the same wild character with the Trosachs. Near the eastern shore there is an island exactly similar to that described in the poem as the residence of Douglas. A cottage was

The rocky summits, split and rent,
Form'd turret, dome, or battlement,
Or seem'd fantastically set
With cupola or minaret,
Wild crests as pagod ever deck'd,
Or mosque of Eastern architect.
Nor were these earth-born castles bare,
Nor lack'd they many a banner fair;
For, from their shiver'd brows display'd,
Far o'er the unfathomable glade,
All twinkling with the dew-drops sheen,
The briar-rose fell in streamers green,
And creeping shrubs, of thousand dyes,
Waved in the west-wind's summer sighs.

"Boon nature scatter'd, free and wild,
Each plant or flower, the mountain's child.
Here eglantine embalm'd the air,
Hawthorn and hazel mingled there;
The primrose pale, and violet flower,
Found in each cliff a narrow bower;
Foxglove and nightshade, side by side,
Emblems of punishment and pride,
Group'd their dark hues with every stain
The weather-beaten crags retain.
With boughs that quaked at every breath,
Grey birch and aspen wept beneath;
Aloft, the ash and warrior oak
Cast anchor in the rifted rock;
And, higher yet, the pine-tree hung
His shatter'd trunk, and frequent flung,
Where seem'd the cliffs to meet on high,
His boughs athwart the narrow'd sky.
Highest of all, where white peaks glanced,
Where glist'ning streamers waved and danced,
The wanderer's eye could barely view
The summer heaven's delicious blue;
So wondrous wild, the whole might seem
The scenery of a fairy dream."

erected upon it by Lady Willoughby D'Eresby, which, a few years ago, was accidentally burnt down. Coir-nan-Uriskin, "the Den of the Ghost," is marked by a deep vertical gash in the face of one of the extensive ramifications of Ben Venue, overhanging the lake. It is surrounded with stupendous rocks, and overshaded by birch trees, mingled with oaks, the spontaneous production of the mountain, even where its cliffs appear denuded of soil. Above the eastern hollow, is the pass of Beal-ach-nam-Bo, a magnificent glade overhung with birch trees; by this pass, in the days of blackmail and reivers, cattle were driven across the shoulder of the hill.

The district of Menteith, only a few miles to the south of the Trosachs, comprehends a range of scenery little inferior in beauty. It contains the Lake of Menteith, Aberfoyle, Loch Ard, and Loch Chon, and is approached from Stirling by Ochtertyre, Kincardine, and Ruskie. The Lake of Menteith is a beautiful circular sheet of water, about five miles in circumference, and adorned with ancient woods. There are two small islands in the centre, called Inchmachome and Talla. The former, which is the larger and more easterly island, consists of about five acres, and contains the ruins of a Priory, founded by Edgar, King of Scotland, where Queen Mary resided during the invasion of the English in 1547, before she was removed to France. The smaller island contains the remains of the Castle of the Grahams, Earls of Menteith, a race long extinct.*

* "The Earls of Monteith, you must know, had a castle situated upon an island in the lake, or loch, as it is called, of the same name. But though this residence, which occupied almost the whole of the islet upon which its ruins still exist, was a strong and safe place of abode, and adapted accordingly to such perilous times, it had this inconvenience, that the stables and other domestic offices were constructed on the banks of the lake, and were, therefore, in some sort defenceless.

"It happened upon a time that there was to be a great entertainment in the castle, and a number of the Grahams were assembled. The occasion, it is said, was a marriage in the family. To prepare for this feast, much provision was got ready, and, in particular, a great deal of poultry had been collected. While the feast was preparing, an unhappy chance brought Donald of the Hammer to the side of the lake, returning at the head of a band of hungry followers, whom he was conducting homewards to the West Highlands, after some of his

They had their garden on the isle of the Priory, and their pleasure-grounds on the neighbouring shore. Gartmore House (Graham, Esq.) lies to the west, and Rednock House, the seat of General Graham Stirling, to the east of the lake. Callander is distant seven miles. Proceeding westward, at the distance of four miles, the traveller reaches Aberfoyle, the scene of so many of the incidents in the novel of Rob Roy.* At the Clachan of Aberfoyle is the junction of the Duchray and Forth, here called Avondhu, or the Black River. Under the rocky precipice on the north, lies the pass of Aberfoyle, the scene of the defeat of a party of Cromwell's troops, by Graham of Duchray.† Loch Ard is a small lake, or rather two

usual excursions into Stirlingshire. Seeing so much good victuals ready, and being possessed of an excellent appetite, the Western Highlanders neither asked questions, nor waited for an invitation, but devoured all the provisions that had been prepared for the Grahams, and then went on their way rejoicing, through the difficult and dangerous path which leads from the banks of the Loch of Monteith, through the mountains, to the side of Loch Katrine.

"The Grahams were filled with the highest indignation. The company who were assembled at the castle of Monteith, headed by the earl himself, hastily took to their boats, and, disembarking on the northern side of the lake, pursued with all speed the marauders and their leader. They came up with Donald's party in the gorge of a pass, near a rock, called Craig-Vad, or the Wolf's Cliff. The battle then began, and was continued with much fury till night. The Earl of Monteith and many of his noble kinsmen fell, while Donald, favoured by darkness, escaped with a single attendant. The Grahams obtained, from the cause of the quarrel, the nickname of Gramoch an Garrigh, or Grahams of the Hens."—*Tales of a Grandfather*, vol. ii. p. 317—19.

* "To the left lay the valley, down which the Forth wandered on its easterly course, surrounding the beautiful detached hill, with all its garland of woods. On the right, amid a profusion of thickets, knolls, and crags, lay the bed of a broad mountain lake, lightly curled into tiny waves by the breath of the morning breeze, each glittering in its course under the influence of the sunbeams. High hills, rocks, and banks, waving with natural forests of birch and oak, formed the borders of this enchanting sheet of water; and, as their leaves rustled to the wind and twinkled in the sun, gave to the depth of solitude a sort of life and vivacity."—*Rob Roy*, vol. ii. p. 202.

† "Our route, though leading towards the lake, had hitherto been so much shaded by wood, that we only from time to time obtained a glimpse of that beautiful sheet of water. But the road now suddenly emerged from the forest ground, and, winding close by the margin of the loch, afforded us a full view of its spacious mirror, which now, the breeze having totally subsided, reflected in still magnificence the high, dark, heathy mountains, huge grey rocks, and shaggy banks, by which it is encircled. The hills now sunk on its margin so closely, and were so broken and precipitous, as to afford no passage except just upon the narrow line of the track which we occupied, and which was overhung with rocks, from which we might have been destroyed merely by rolling down stones, without much possibility of offering resistance."—*Ibid*, p. 208. An excellent road has now been formed along the northern margin of the lake.

lakes, connected by a stream of 200 yards in length, beautifully situated amid a fertile valley. A delightful view of the upper loch is obtained from a rising ground near its lower extremity. Looking westward, Ben Lomond is seen in the back-ground. On the right is the lofty mountain of Benoghrie. In the fore-ground is Loch Ard itself, three miles in length, and one and one-eight miles in breadth. The traveller passes along the verge of the lake, under a ledge of rock from thirty to fifty feet high. If a person standing immediately under this rock, towards its western extremity, pronounces with a firm voice a line of ten syllables, it is returned first from the opposite side of the lake, and then with equal distinctness from the wood on the east. But the day must be perfectly calm, and the lake as smooth as glass. In the upper loch is a rocky islet, on which are the mouldering ruins of a stronghold of Murdoch's, Duke of Albany. Near the head of the lake, on the northern side, behind the house of Ledeard, is the romantic waterfall, thus described in Waverley, vol. i., p. 234:—"It was not so remarkable either for great height or quantity of water, as for the beautiful accompaniments which made the spot interesting. After a broken cataract of about twenty feet, the stream was received in a large natural basin filled to the brim with water, which, where the bubbles of the fall subsided, was so exquisitely clear, that although it was of great depth, the eye could discern each pebble at the bottom. Eddying round this reservoir, the brook found its way as if over a broken part of the ledge, and formed a second fall, which seemed to seek the very abyss; then, wheeling out beneath from among the smooth dark rocks, which it had polished for ages, it wandered murmuring down the glen, forming the stream up which Waverley had just ascended."—A footpath strikes off towards Ben Lomond, by which the tourist may cross the hill and reach Rowardennan, on the banks of Loch Lomond; or he may proceed from Aberfoyle Inn, by Gartmore and Drymen, to Dumbarton, a distance of twenty-two miles. Loch Chon is a secluded sheet of water, three miles in length. The scenery around these lakes is eminently beautiful; but it is customary for travellers, after visiting only the first of the two, to cross over the hill from Aberfoyle to the Trosachs, a distance of only five miles.

During the summer and autumn, a boat sails every

forenoon from the east to the west end of Loch Katrine, pausing at all the places in which strangers are supposed to take an interest.

"In sailing along you discover many arms of the lake—here a bold headland, where black rocks dip in unfathomable water—there the white sand in the bottom of a bay, bleached for ages by the waves. In walking on the north side, the road is sometimes cut through the face of the solid rock, which rises upwards of 200 feet perpendicular above the lake, which, before the rock was cut, had to be mounted by a kind of natural ladder. Every rock has its echo, every grove is vocal with the harmony of birds, or by the airs of women and children gathering nuts in their season. Down the side of the opposite mountain, after a shower of rain, flow an hundred white streams, which rush with incredible noise and velocity into the lake. On one side, the water-eagle sits in majesty, undisturbed on his well known rock, in sight of his nest on the top of Ben Venue, the heron stalks among the reeds in search of his prey, and the sportive ducks gambol in the waters or dive below. On the other, the wild goats climb where they have scarce room for the soles of their feet, and the wild birds perched on exalted trees and pinnacles, look down with composed indifference on man. The scene is closed by a west view of the lake, which is ten miles long, having its sides lined with alternate clumps of wood and ample fields, and the smoke rising in spiral columns through the air from farm houses, which are concealed by intervening woods, and the prospect is bounded by the towering Alps of Arrochar." *

Those conversant with the writings of Sir Walter Scott,

* Statistical Account of Scotland.

will remember the spirited song sung by the retainers of Roderick Dhu while rowing down Loch Katrine :—

"Hail to the Chief, who in triumph advances!
Honour'd and bless'd be the ever-green Pine!
Long may the Tree, in his banner that glances,
Flourish, the shelter and grace of our line!
Heaven send it happy dew,
Earth lend it sap anew,
Gaily to bourgeon, and broadly to grow,
While every Highland glen
Sends our shout back agen,
'Roderigh Vich Alpine dhu, ho! ieroe!'

"Ours is no sapling, chance-sown by the fountain,
Blooming at Beltane, in winter to fade:
When the whirlwind has stripp'd every leaf on the mountain,
The more shall Clan-Alpine exult in her shade.
Moor'd in the rifted rock,
Proof to the tempest's shock,
Firmer he roots him the ruder it blow;
Menteith and Breadalbane, then,
Echo his praise agen,
'Roderigh Vich Alpine dhu, ho! ieroe!'

"Proudly our pibroch has thrill'd in Glen Fruin,
And Bannochar's groans to our slogan replied;
Glen Luss and Ross-dhu, they are smoking in ruin,
And the best of Loch-Lomond lie dead on her side.
Widow and Saxon maid
Long shall lament our raid,
Think of Clan-Alpine with fear and with woe;
Lennox and Leven-glen
Shake when they hear agen,
'Roderigh Vich Alpine dhu, ho! ieroe!'

"Row, vassals, row, for the pride of the Highlands,
Stretch to your oars, for the ever-green Pine!
O! that the rose-bud that graces yon islands
Were wreathed in a garland around him to twine!
O that some seedling gem,
Worthy such noble stem,
Honour'd and bless'd in their shadow might grow!
Loud should Clan-Alpine then
Ring from her deepmost glen,
'Roderigh Vich Alpine dhu, ho! ieroe!'"

From the west end of the lake, a wild valley, traversed by a pathway about five miles long, affords a communication with Loch Lomond, upon which it opens at Inversnaid Mill, where the steam-boat which every day plies along

Loch Lomond takes in the Loch Katrine tourists. The small lake, Arklet, lies in the hollow near this pathway. In one of the smoky huts in the valley between Loch Katrine and Loch Lomond may be seen a long Spanish musket, once the property of Rob Roy, whose original residence was in this lone vale. Beside the way are the ruins of Inversnaid Fort, erected in 1713 to check the MacGregors.* It is said that General Wolfe once resided in it. At Inversnaid Mill there is a little rivulet and a cataract, the scene of Wordsworth's beautiful poem to the "Highland Girl."

Loch Lomond,† ("the lake full of islands,") is unquestionably the pride of Scottish lakes. "This noble lake, boasting innumerable beautiful islands of every varying form and outline which fancy can frame,—its northern extremity narrowing until it is lost among dusky and retreating mountains, while, gradually widening as it extends to the southward it spreads its base

* The perusal of Sir Walter Scott's splendid lyric, "The Gathering of Clan-Gregor," may be gratifying to the tourist while he is in the midst of the country of the MacGregors.

"The moon's on the lake, and the mist's on the brae,
And the clan has a name that is nameless by day—
Then gather, gather, gather Gregalich!

Our signal for fight, which from monarchs we drew,
Must be heard but by night in our vengeful haloo—
Then haloo, haloo, haloo, Gregalich!

Glenorchy's proud mountains, Calchuirn and her towers,
Glenstrae and Glenlyon no longer are ours—
We're landless, landless, landless, Gregalich!

If they rob us of name, and pursue us with beagles,
Give their roof to the flame, and their flesh to the eagles—
Come then, Gregalich, come then!

While there's leaves on the forest or foam on the river,
Macgregor, despite them, shall flourish for ever—
Then gather, gather, gather Gregalich!"

† The tourist may proceed from the head of Loch Lomond, by Glenfalloch, Crianlaroch, Tyndrum, and Glencoe, to Fort William, (See Itinerary,) or by Arroquhar, Glencroe, and Cairndow, to Inverary.

around the indentures and promontories of a fair and fertile land, affords one of the most surprising, beautiful, and sublime spectacles in nature."* Its length is about 23 miles, its breadth, where greatest, at the southern extremity, is five miles, from which it gradually grows narrower, till it terminates in a narrow prolonged stripe of water. The depth varies considerably; south of Luss it is rarely more than 20 fathoms, in the northern part it ranges from 60 to 100, and in the places where deepest, never freezes. The total superficies of the lake is about 20,000 acres. About two-thirds of the loch and most of the islands are in the county of Dumbarton, the rest, with the right bank, are in the county of Stirling. After taking on board the tourists from Loch Katrine, the steam-boat visits the upper part of the lake, which is there narrowed and hemmed in by the neighbouring mountains. At the northern extremity of the lake is a wide elevated valley called Glenfalloch. Sailing southwards, three miles from the upper end is a small wooded island called Eilan Vhou, and two miles farther, another called Inveruglas, on each of which are the ruins of a stronghold of the family of Macfarlane; the slogan of this clan was "Loch Sloy," a small lake between Loch Long and Loch Lomond. At the distance of other three miles, Tarbet Inn is passed on the right, where there is a ferry by which Ben Lomond may be approached. Farther south, a projecting headland is seen on the right, where is the ferry of Inveruglas to Rowardennan Inn, the usual starting point for those who desire to ascend to the top of Ben Lomond. This mountain is 3210 feet above the level of the lake, which is 32 feet above the

* Rob Roy, vol. ii. p. 317.

level of the sea. The distance from the inn to the top of the mountain is six miles of continued ascent. The view from the summit is varied and most extensive, comprehending the counties of Lanark, Renfrew, and Ayr, the Firth of Clyde, and the islands of Arran and Bute to the south, and the counties of Stirling and the Lothians, with the windings of the Forth, and the Castles of Stirling and Edinburgh to the east. About 3½ miles from Inveruglas, is Luss, a delightful little village on a promontory which juts into the lake. One of the finest points for enjoying the scenery of Loch Lomond and the environs of Luss, is Stonehill, to the north of the village. Near Luss is Rossdow, the splendid residence of Sir James Colquhoun, Bart. In the vicinity of the mansion is a tower of the ancient castle of the family of Luss, the last heiress of which married Colquhoun of Colquhoun. A short way farther on are the ruins of the Castle of Banachra, overhanging the entrance to Glen Fruin.* This castle was anciently the residence of the Colquhouns, and here the chief of that clan was basely murdered, in 1640, by one of the M'Farlanes. Near it is the lofty hill of Dunfion, or the hill of Fingal, according to tradition one of the hunting seats of that hero. From Luss southward, the breadth

* It was in Glen Fruin, or the Glen of Sorrow, that the celebrated battle took place between the Macgregors and Colquhouns, fraught with such fatal consequences to both parties. There had been a long and deadly feud between the Macgregors and the Laird of Luss, head of the family of Colquhoun. At length the parties met in the vale of Glen Fruin. The battle was obstinately contested, but in the end the Macgregors came off victorious, slaying two hundred of the Colquhouns and making many prisoners. It is said that after the battle the Macgregors murdered about eighty youths who had been led by curiosity to view the fight. A partial representation of these transactions having been made to James VI. letters of fire and sword were issued against the clan Gregor. Their lands were confiscated, their very name proscribed, and, being driven to such extremity, they became notorious for acts of daring reprisal. Their legal rights were restored to them in 1755.

of the lake expands rapidly, and the surface of the water is studded with islands of many sizes and various aspects. The islands of Loch Lomond are about thirty in number, and ten of these are of considerable size.

> " All the fairy crowds
> Of islands, which together lie
> As quietly as the spots of sky
> Among the evening clouds."

After leaving Luss, the boat passes, in succession, Inch-bruin or the Round Island, (formerly used as a retreat for lunatics,) Inch Moan or the Peat Island, and Inch Fad, and, on the right, Inch Tavanagh, (to the south of which the ruins of Galbraith Castle start up from the water,) Inch Lonaig, (used as a deer-park by the family of Luss,) Inch Carachan, Buck Inch, and Inch Cardach. The steamer now skirts Inch Cailliach, the Island of Women, so called from its having been the site of a nunnery. Inch Cailliach formerly gave name to the parish of Buchannan. The church belonging to the nunnery was long used as the place of worship for the parish of Buchannan, but scarcely any vestiges of it now remain ; the burial ground continues to be used, and contains the family places of sepulture of several neighbouring clans ; the monuments of the Lairds of Macgregor, and of other families claiming a descent from the old Scottish King Alpine, are most remarkable.

> " The shafts and limbs were rods of yew,
> Whose parents, in Inch Cailliach, wave
> Their shadows o'er Clan Alpine's grave,
> And, answering Lomond's breezes deep,
> Soothe many a chieftain's endless sleep."
>
> LADY OF THE LAKE, c. iii. *and notes.*

At the north-east corner of Inch Cailliach, passengers are often landed at Bealmacha, a celebrated Highland pass. (See Lady of the Lake, Canto iv. st. 4.) Here some tourists choose to land to pursue their journey through the pass and along the banks of the loch to Rowardennan. The steam-boat next approaches the little island of Clar Inch, from which the Buchannans took their slogan or war-cry. The last island is a long narrow one, named Inch Murrin, the largest island in Loch Lomond. It is finely clothed with wood, and is employed as a deer-park by the Duke of Montrose. At its southern extremity there is an old ruined fortalice, called Lennox Castle, formerly a residence of the Earls of Lennox. On the east side of the lake are the ruins of Butruich Castle, farther south is Balloch Castle, (Buchannan, Esq.) and near it, on the margin of the lake, stood the ancient castle of Balloch, a strong-hold of the once powerful family of Lennox; its site and moat are still visible. The steam-boat now returns to Balloch, where a coach is waiting to convey the passengers to Dumbarton, and from thence a steam-boat lands them in Glasgow the same evening.

GLASGOW.

SITUATION—HISTORICAL NOTICES—GENERAL STATISTICS OF POPULATION—COMMERCE AND MANUFACTURES—EDUCATION AND LITERATURE—CHARITABLE AND RELIGIOUS INSTITUTIONS, &c.

Glasgow, the commercial metropolis of Scotland, and the third city in the United Kingdom, in wealth, population, and manufacturing and commercial importance, is situated in Lanarkshire, in the lower part of the basin of the Clyde; about twenty miles from the Atlantic Ocean, and nearly double that distance from the German Sea. The fine range of the Campsie and Kilpatrick hills, forms a screen around it, from north-east to north-west, at the distance of eight to ten miles, and the uplands of Lanarkshire and Renfrewshire, swell beautifully up on the east, south, and south west. The climate is temperate, but from its vicinity to the sea, and the high grounds in the neighbourhood, it is much subject to humidity. St. Mungo, or, as he has also been styled, St. Kentigern, is the reputed founder of the city. Somewhere about the year 560, he is supposed to have founded the bishoprick of Glasgow, where the older and upper part of the town still remains. In those rude times, the vicinity of churches and churchmen was eagerly desired, from the comparative security they afforded; and thus, the nascent elements of the future city, under the pastoral protection of the good saint and his pious successors, had leisure afforded them to extend and mature their natural capacities for improvement. The annals of Glasgow, from the period above mentioned, to the early part of the twelfth century, are involved in the obscurity which overshadows nearly the whole contemporary history of those rude ages, a fact we are disposed to acquiesce in rather cheerfully, as, where little is known, little probably exists that it would be useful to know. The first fact of any importance which emerges from the clouds of its earlier history, is the erection of its noble Cathedral, which, for so many centuries, has witnessed the growing prosperity and enlargement of the city, forming a fine link between the past and the present, and throwing the shadow of its venerable magnificence upon scenes memorable in Scottish history, but upon which modern civilization has impressed an entirely new character. This fine old Minster* was

* This venerable building contained formerly three churches, one of which, the Old Barony, was situated in a vault,† but now there is only one, a new church having recently been erected in place of the second, the space occupied by which has been thrown into the choir or central part of the fabric. Having fallen of late years much into decay, the Government, the custodiers of the cathedral, have agreed to repair and renew certain parts of the building, and plans for its renovation having been prepared by an eminent architect, the Corporation of Glasgow has granted a thousand pounds towards the object; other public bodies are expected also to contribute, and a private subscription is in flourishing progress, whilst we write, for the same laudable purpose. The revenues of the See of Glasgow were at one time very considerable, as, besides the royalty and baronies of Glasgow, eighteen baronies of land in various parts of the kingdom belonged to it, besides a large estate in Cumberland, denominated the spiritual dukedom. Part of these revenues have fallen into the University of Glasgow, and part to the Crown.

† "Conceive, an extensive range of lowbrowed, dark, and twilight vaults, such as are used for sepulchres in other countries, and had long been dedicated to the same purpose in this, a portion of which was seated with pews, and used as a church. The part of the vaults thus occupied, though capable of containing a congregation of many hundreds, bore a small proportion to the darker and more extensive caverns which yawned around what may be termed the inhabited space. In those waste regions of oblivion, dusky banners and tattered escutcheons indicated the graves of those who were once, doubtless, "princes in Israel." Inscriptions, which could only be read by the painful antiquary, in language as obsolete as the act of devotional charity which they implored, invited the passengers to pray for the souls of those whose bodies rested beneath."—*Rob Roy*, vol. ii. p. 267.

erected by John Achaius, Bishop of Glasgow, in 1133, or, according to M'Ure, in 1136, in the reign of David the First, whose pious largesses to the clergy obtained for him the name and honours of a saint, but drew from one of his impoverished successors, the splenetic remark, that "he had been a sair saunt for the crown."

About forty years after the building of the Cathedral, William the Lion granted a charter to the Bishop to hold "a weekly mercat" in Glasgow, and a few years after, another was obtained for an annual fair. In these concessions of a despotic Sovereign, we behold the rude and early germs of the future wealth and commercial greatness of Glasgow. The same indulgent Sovereign completed the emancipation of the city, by erecting it into a burgh of regality, and thus placing its rights of independent traffic upon a broad and liberal basis.* The new burgh was, however, unfortunately situated betwixt the more ancient royal burghs of Rutherglen and Renfrew, who beheld with a jealous eye its growing prosperity; and their rival exactions, and prescriptive immunities, for a time impeded the progress of the infant community, until the city obtained a charter of relief and independence in 1242, from Alexander the Second.

Some of the details of the early history of Glasgow, after it had fairly started on its career as an independent community, are not a little curious and instructive, from their graphic simplicity and statistical interest, but there is little to interest the general reader, till we turn the

*It is not a little curious to contemplate the "revenges which the restless whirligig of time" is sure to bring about.—Whilst Glasgow has shot up into the third city of the British Empire, Rutherglen and Renfrew, whose ancient importance is only to be traced in a few pages of Scottish history, have dwindled into absolute insignificance under the overshadowing influence of their ancient rival, whose commercial relations are now commensurate with the limits of civilisation and commerce.

corner of the seventeenth century. It was ravaged by the plague no less than four times during the fourteenth, and five times during the seventeenth century. The loathsome disease of leprosy prevailed also for a long time, and as late as 1589, some lepers were confined in a house in the suburbs of Gorbals. It is no wonder, indeed; for whatever might be the virtues of the citizens of Glasgow in these primitive times, cleanliness certainly was not one of them, as appears from sundry curious enough enactments by the city authorities. Previous to the seventeenth century, the principal part of the houses were built of wood, and the inhabitants lived chiefly in narrow lanes or closes leading from the main streets. The population in 1651 was about 14,000; in 1831 when the last census was taken, it amounted to 202,426; and at present it is considered to be somewhere about 270,000.

Previous to 1775, the mercantile capital and enterprize of Glasgow were almost wholly employed in the tobacco trade. Large fortunes were made, and the city still exhibits evidences of the wealth and social importance of the "Tobacco Lords," as they were termed, some of the finest private dwellings in the city, and several elegant streets, being the splendid relics of their former civic grandeur and importance. The interruption which the war of the American Revolution gave to this traffic turned the attention* of the citizens to the manufacture of cot-

* For more than forty years, however, previous to this period, there existed in Glasgow a considerable manufacture of linen lawns, and cambrics, which ultimately merged in the cotton manufacture. Its progress was not very rapid till towards the close of the last century, when the wars which sprung out of the French Revolution, by suspending and limiting for a time the manufactures of the continental nations, gave a new impetus to this manufacture in Great Britain, in which impetus Glasgow largely partook. Of the extent of that branch of the cotton manufacture in which hand-loom weavers are employed,

ton goods, then feebly developing its latent energies in Lancashire, and to this branch of manufacture Glasgow

it is impossible to form any thing like an accurate estimate, from the absence of any ascertained data. It is supposed, but the calculation is necessarily loose and imperfect, that 40,000 hand-loom weavers are employed by Glasgow manufacturers, the produce of whose labour, including the additional value appended to it before it is brought to market, has been assumed to be about three millions sterling.

Power-loom weaving was introduced into Glasgow as far back as 1792, but, until 1801, it may be considered as having been merely experimental. At present there are from sixteen to seventeen thousand steam-looms set in motion by Glasgow capital. Each loom, on an average of the different kinds of work, produces about 21 yards daily, or 336,000 yards in all, and, in a year of 300 working days, 100,800,000 yards. Assuming sixpence per yard as the average value, this branch of the cotton manufacture in Glasgow amounts to £2,520,000, a stupendous result, when it is considered that it is not quite forty years since its introduction.

The spinning of cotton yarn was begun in Glasgow in 1792, and has gradually, and, of late years, rapidly increased. The total number of spindles in motion in Glasgow, and belonging to Glasgow capitalists, has been calculated, by experienced persons, to be about 1100,000 at present. Of the value of the products no estimate can be attempted with any certainty, but from three to four millions sterling has been assumed as the probable amount. In 1818, only 46,565 bales of cotton were consumed, and in 1834 the consumption was 95,603 bales, since which it has considerably increased. Besides the spinning and weaving of cotton, the staple manufactures of Glasgow, silk has also become an extensive article of commerce and manufacture. This article, with various rich foreign wools, are now woven into cotton fabrics with the most brilliant success. Calico printing is also carried on to a vast extent, especially since the abolition of the duty on printed goods. It was first attempted, in 1742, on a small scale, at Pollockshaws, in the neighbourhood of Glasgow, and now there are few streams, in a vicinity of ten miles round the city, the waters of which do not carry abundant evidence of the printing establishments on their banks. The works of Henry Monteith and Co. at Barrowfield, those on the Leven lately the property of Messrs. Kibble, and of Messrs. Crum at Thornly Bank, are amongst the most noted and extensive. The establishment of the first mentioned house, from the perfection of their machinery and its close vicinity to Glasgow, has long been a point of interest to intelligent strangers.

Glasgow is the seat of various other extensive trades and manufactures, such as dying, bleaching, calendering, &c. The smelting of iron is also carried on to a vast extent in its neighbourhood, owing, in a great degree, to the adoption of the hot blast, an improvement, which, with less than one-half of fuel, produces one-third more of iron. In 1834, the whole produce of the iron-works of Scotland, (of which at least from two-thirds to three-fourths are carried on by Glasgow capital,) was 110,240 tons; and, although no accurate data are to be obtained as to the present amount of production, it cannot be far short of 150,000 tons. The coal trade is carried on to an enormous extent in the neighbourhood of Glasgow, chiefly for home consumption, though a considerable exportation takes place. In 1831, 561,049 tons passed into and through the city, of which 124,000 were exported, principally coastwise, since which a very large

chiefly owes her pre-eminence as a commercial and manufacturing city.

In 1451 application was made to the Pope for a bull to establish a university, and eight years afterwards a member of the illustrious house of Hamilton bequeathed four acres of ground, with a tenement of houses, for the same purpose. And thus this noble educational institution was established, and after encountering many difficulties, arising from the unsettled character of the times, from its origin to near the end of the seventeenth century, rose into fame, importance, and utility. It is unnecessary here to state the many eminent names which adorn its annals, and which have shed a lustre over the literary and civil history of Scotland. It is a corporate body, and is governed by a chancellor, rector, and dean. The number of students is seldom less than 1000, and generally considerably more. The Hunterian Museum, attached to the College, is one of the chastest buildings in Scotland, and is rich in various departments of natural history, particularly in anatomical preparations, and in coins and medals. The whole has been valued at L.70,000. The Grammar or High School, for elementary classical education, is supported by the Corporation, on whom its su-

increase has taken place. The manufacture of machinery employs also a large capital and numerous work people, especially the making of marine steam engines. Ship-building has been recently established in the vicinity, on the banks of the river Clyde, and is reported to be in a highly flourishing state, especially the building of steam vessels, for which Glasgow and Greenock are celebrated all over the kingdom; as the deepening and improvement of the river and harbour proceed, the two latter branches of trade may be expected largely to increase. In this rough outline of the trade and manufactures of Glasgow, it would be unpardonable to omit the extensive chemical manufactory of Messrs. Charles Tennant and Co. at St. Rollox near Glasgow, considered to be the largest in Europe, and containing four acres under roof. As the situation is high, on the north side of the city, the numerous chimnies form a prominent feature in the general view of Glasgow. The bleaching powder, sulphuric acid, and other chemical compounds are manufactured to a large extent, and of the best quality, besides there being an extensive manufactory of soap.

perintendance devolves. It costs the city about L.1000 per annum. Of late years the range of elementary instruction has been extended, and various modern languages, besides drawing and mathematics, are taught. The number of scholars is considerable.

Anderson's University was founded about the middle of last century by Professor Anderson, chiefly for the promotion of physical science; its lectures, particularly on medical and anatomical subjects, are well attended, and its professors are considered highly respectable. Its winter soirées have attracted much attention. There is an excellent museum attached to this institution. In Hanover Street, running from George's Square to the north, stands the Mechanics' Institution, the lectures of which are numerously attended; attached to it is an excellent library, with a valuable scientific apparatus; and they have, together with the Mechanics' class in Anderson's University, perhaps the most beautiful and extensive series of models of steam engines and machinery of various kinds to be found in any similar institution in the country. Besides these principal educational establishments, there are several others of an inferior, but respectable description in the suburbs, which are well attended. Lectures upon a variety of important subjects, scientific, educational, and economical, are also delivered by various scientific and philanthrophic individuals, at which great numbers attend. There is a Philosophical Society, two Statistical Societies, a Literary and Commercial Society, and various other societies for mutual instruction, indicating the intelligent activity of mind and thirst for knowledge of the good citizens of Glasgow. The elementary schools are numerous, and are attended by great numbers of children, but no certain data exist from which to estimate the entire number of scholars. Nearly

L.30,000 sterling have been mortified by various worthy individuals at different times for educational purposes in Glasgow. A normal seminary, the first of the kind in Scotland, and a handsome building, has recently been erected to the north of the city, and is reported to be in a flourishing condition. So that, on the whole, either in the amount or quality of its educational means, Glasgow is behind no city in the kingdom. In 1763 the illustrious James Watt began that memorable series of experiments in mechanical science which issued in the successful application of steam as a great motive power, and about fifty years after, Mr. Henry Bell launched on the Clyde the first steam vessel ever seen in this country. To the labours and discoveries of these eminent men, Glasgow may be said to owe her present prominent position as a manufacturing and commercial community. Monuments, to perpetuate their memory, have been erected by their grateful fellow-citizens. That of the former is placed in George's Square, in the centre of the city, and the latter at Dunglass, on the Clyde, eleven miles below the town, in a fine commanding situation.

Glasgow is also rich in religious, charitable, and philanthrophic institutions of every variety of description, which are supported by annual donations to the extent of L.50,000. To particularise these, would occupy far too much space, but two of the most recent establishments deserve especial notice, the Asylum for the Houseless Poor, and the House of Refuge for Indigent and Orphan Boys. A similar institution to the latter, for the reception of Destitute Young Females is also soon to be erected. The former of these affords shelter during the night to about a hundred houseless creatures, who must otherwise lie in the streets, and the latter has from one hundred and thirty to one hundred and forty boys within its walls, learning some trade, and receiving the elements of a useful education. It is a fine building, in a prominent situation to the north-east of the city.

In a commercial community like that of Glasgow, where the learned professions bear a small proportion to those engaged in the pursuits of trade and commerce, comparatively few individuals, not professional, are to be found of a purely literary character. Yet no city in the kingdom, the society of which is composed of similar elements, can exhibit a larger number of enlightened and well-educated mercantile men ; and it may be said generally, that whilst the chief springs of action are to be found in the stimulants of commercial and manufacturing enterprize, the general character of the population is that of intellectual activity, and eagerness for the acquisition of general and available knowledge.

WALK FIRST.

GEORGE'S SQUARE—STATUES OF SIR JOHN MOORE, JAMES WATT—MONUMENT TO SIR WALTER SCOTT—ROYAL EXCHANGE—ROYAL BANK—QUEEN STREET—ARGYLE STREET—ARCADE—DUNLOP STREET—THEATRE ROYAL—MILLER STREET—GLASFORD STREET STOCKWELL—HUTCHESON'S HOSPITAL—CANDLERIGGS, AND BAZAAR—TRON STEEPLE—CROSS—TONTINE BUILDINGS—EQUESTRIAN STATUE OF WILLIAM THE THIRD—TOWN HALL—CROSS STEEPLE—SALTMARKET—ST. ANDREW'S SQUARE, AND CHURCH—BRIDGEGATE—COURT-HOUSES, AND JAIL—HUTCHESON'S BRIDGE—GREEN—NELSON'S MONUMENT—LONDON STREET—HIGH STREET—COLLEGE BUILDINGS—BRIDEWELL—BELL OF THE BRAE—INFIRMARY—CATHEDRAL—NECROPOLIS—ASYLUM FOR THE BLIND—GEORGE'S STREET.

GLASGOW is far inferior in point of picturesque situation to Edinburgh. Whilst the latter stands upon a succession of bold ridges, sloping finely down to the Firth of Forth; with the rich indented coast of Fife, and the noble range of the Ochils in the distance, to the north, and on the south and west, the green swelling outlines of the Pentlands—Glasgow is situated in the valley of the Clyde, and chiefly on the levels along its banks, although some portions of the city are located on acclivities to the north, which, by their commanding position, vary and enliven the monotony of an otherwise nearly unbroken level. Neither can Glasgow exhibit the same rich and picturesque variety of surface within its limits proper, which Edinburgh presents. There is no Castle-hill, with its summit bristling with the rude fortifications of the middle ages, and an abrupt and lofty mass of rock, sinking suddenly down into the bed of an ancient lake, now transformed into pleasure gardens; or a Calton-hill, rising boldly in the centre of the city, gorgeous with splendid mansions, noble public buildings, and monuments to the illustrious dead; nor has it the bold and rough ridge of Salisbury Crags, diversifying the landscape, and carrying the mind of the spectator away from the busy hum and haunts of man, to the more still retreats, and the solitary grandeur of nature. So far therefore, Glasgow must suffer in the eye of the tourist, on a comparison of its natural advantages with those of Edinburgh, and not less so, perhaps, when the general character and appearance of the two cities are compared. Edinburgh, with its Old Town, still exhibiting in whole streets and divisions, the irregular but striking style of architecture patronized by our fathers, and teeming at every step with ancient buildings, associated with numberless historical reminiscences; and opposite to this, her New Town, with its splendid architectural vistas, and the chaste elegance of its general exterior. Glasgow has no such glowing and startling contrasts to present; yet, if the tourist will put himself under our guidance for a short time, we promise to shew him one of the finest cities in the British dominions, and even in a mere landscape point of view, presenting a series of pictures of equal beauty and interest. We shall adopt the same method we have found so convenient in perambulating Edinburgh, and conduct the stranger in a succession of walks through the busy city.

Suppose the tourist then snugly deposited in one of the excellent hotels in George's Square, one of the most central places in the city, and from which, as from a common centre, we shall commence our examination of the memorabilia of this great commercial emporium of the west.

Sallying from any of the various respectable hotels* in this spacious and handsome square, which of itself, from the elegance and agreeable bustle of its area, attracts attention from a stranger, the first object which strikes the eye, is the monument recently erected to Sir Walter Scott. It is in the form of a fluted Doric column, about eighty feet in height, with a colossal statue of the great Minstrel on the top. The figure is half enveloped in a shepherd's plaid,† and the expression of the countenance is characterised by that air of *bonhommie* and shrewd sense which distinguished that illustrious individual. Directly in front of Sir Walter's pillar, there is a fine pedestrian statue, in bronze, by Flaxman, of the lamented Sir John Moore, who was a native of Glasgow. To the right of

* There are four excellent hotels in George's Square, the George Hotel, Comrie's, Grimshaw's, and the Royal Hotel, at any of which the stranger is sure of the best entertainment, as the old sign hath it, for "Man and Horse."

† It is somewhat unfortunate that the plaid is placed on the wrong arm.

Sir John Moore's statue, in the south-west angle of the square, there is also a noble figure of James Watt, in bronze, and of a colossal magnitude. It is intended, as opportunity offers, to place the statues and monuments of other eminent men around the inclosed area of this handsome square, which is ornamented with shrubberies and walks, so that in process of time, it will become a sort of open Pantheon, dedicated to the illustrious dead. Standing on the north side of the square, the spectator has before him some of the finest architectural vistas in the city. On the right the bold spire of St. George's Church, 162 feet in height, catches the eye, surmounting a building, obviously too small for such a vast superstructure. An elegant building somewhat newer, and of a Grecian chasteness of conception somewhat nearer, is the Dissenting Chapel, in which the celebrated Dr. Wardlaw officiates. To the right and left a noble street, George Street, extends for about half-a-mile, without presenting any other objects of especial interest. Looking to the south, the lofty colonnade of the Royal Exchange * appears, towards which imposing mass of building we shall now conduct the tourist. It stands in Queen Street, at the termination of Ingram Street, one of the finest openings in the city. This splendid fabric is built in the florid Corinthian style of architecture, and is surmounted by a lantern, which forms one of the most conspicuous objects in the city. The News Room is one of the most striking apartments in the kingdom, about 100 feet long, by 40 broad, with a richly ornamented

* The colonnade of the Royal Exchange is one of the boldest and most imposing architectural objects in the kingdom; and consists of a double range of fluted Corinthian pillars of great height. As a whole, the Royal Exchange of Glasgow is one of the most striking edifices in the empire, the general effect of which is grand and impressive, though some of the details may be liable to the objections of a refined criticism.

oval roof, supported by fluted Corinthian columns. The Royal Exchange is placed in the centre of a noble area, two sides of which are lined with splendid and uniform ranges of buildings, but simpler in design than the Exchange, and occupied as warehouses, shops, and counting houses. Behind it is the Royal Bank, which is much admired by good judges, for the elegant simplicity and chasteness of its design. It is built after the model of a celebrated Greek temple. On each side of the Bank, two superb Doric arches, of bold and imposing character, afford access to Buchanan Street, also one of the principal streets of the city, in fact, the Regent Street of Glasgow.

Proceeding down Queen Street, one of the great thoroughfares and most animated avenues in the city, at the northern extremity of which, in the north west corner of George's Square, the terminus of the Edinburgh and Glasgow Railway is to be placed, the stranger emerges into the principal street, the main artery of Glasgow, here called Argyle Street, but which bears the names of the Trongate and Gallowgate, towards its eastern extremities. Taking in the whole extent of this noble avenue, from east to west, it exhibits a continuation of street of at least three miles in length.

Turning towards the east, the stranger finds himself involved in the bustle and animation of one of the most crowded thoroughfares in Europe, through which the stream of human existence flows at all hours of the day, and in all seasons, with undiminished volume and velocity. The general character of the buildings is plain, and there is no attempt at plan or uniformity of arrangement. An ancient tenement or two, with its narrow pointed gables and steep roofs occasionally attracts the eye, and forms a fine contrast to the modern elegance of the shops below. On the left, a handsome entrance gives access to a covered arcade, extending from this point to Buchanan Street, and containing numerous handsome shops, with a gay crowd of pedestrians at all hours. On the right, the first opening is Dunlop Street, containing the Royal Theatre, a building of no architectural pretensions whatever. A new Theatre is likely, it is understood, soon to be erected, more creditable in everyway to the city. There was formerly a handsome Theatre in Queen Street, which was destroyed by fire, about ten years ago. Opposite is Miller Street, in which were formerly the stately mansions of the old Virginian merchants, but which are now occupied as places of business. On the left, the next opening of any importance is Glasford Street, broad, and handsome in the style of its buildings, especially an edifice lately occupied as the Ship Bank. Here the new Post Office is to be placed, an accommodation much wanted, as at present that important establishment is situated in a narrow obscure street, near the cross, called Nelson Street, and is mean and vulgar to a degree in its appearance. Opposite Glasford Street, and running to the right towards the river, is the Stockwell, one of the oldest streets in the city. A few old tenements still shew their venerable fronts here, but the remorseless march of improvement has recently swept away some of the finest. Sixty years ago, this was one of the chief avenues of the city, and the principal approach from the south, being opposite to the old bridge of Glasgow. Passing several other streets of no great importance, with the exception of Hutcheson Street, with its fine hospital of that name, at the upper end, surmounted by an elegant tapering spire,* and Candleriggs Street, terminated by St. David's Church and tower, and containing the Bazaar, a large general market, and also the corn Exchange, covered in, and containing extensive accommodation, the stranger will observe on the right a rather puny but venerable looking spire, which is the Tron Steeple, and which finely breaks the monotony of the long line of street which he has just traversed. On the right side opposite the Candleriggs, is King Street, an old and well-frequented opening, containing the public markets for beef, mutton, fish, and vegetables. It terminates in the Bridgegate, a fine old street, irregular in its appearance, and of considerable breadth in some parts. An old steeple of remarkably good proportions rises up behind it, which anciently formed part of the building used as a hall for the merchants of Glasgow, but which has long ago been pulled down. Seventy years ago this street was inhabited by the most respectable classes of citizens, and contained many handsome buildings. Many lanes or closes run off from it on either side, inhabited by a numerous and rather turbulent population, of the poorest classes. Some very old buildings are still to be found in these closes, whose appearance tells a tale of other times, but the dun and squalid character of its present occupants does not invite to a lengthened examination of these remnants of antiquity.

* This building is erected on the site of the old hospital, founded by two brothers, whose statues are placed in the front of the edifice, and who left considerable property for its support, chiefly in ground on the south side of the river, and on which the extensive suburb of Hutchesontown is built. A number of poor boys receive a gratis education from its funds, besides being supported otherwise. In Candleriggs Street are situated also the extensive wholesale and retail warehouses of the Messrs. Campbells, said to be one of the largest commercial establishments in the kingdom, and worthy of a visit, from the excellence of its interior arrangements.

Returning to the Trongate, a little further on is the Cross of Glasgow, forming a centre, and termination to the Trongate, the Gallowgate (a continuation of this street), the High Street, and the Saltmarket. There is an equestrian statue of William the Third placed here, of no great merit as a work of art. A noble range of building, with a superb piazza under it, extends in front, denominated the Tontine, from having been built upon that principle. There is a fine large News Room here, which was formerly known by the appellation of the Coffee Room, and, until the New Exchange was erected, was the great focus of business and politics. The ancient jail of the burgh stood exactly at the corner of the High Street and Trongate. Criminals were executed formerly in front of this building. On its site a heavy tasteless pile of building has been erected, occupied by shops and warehouses. The old Court-houses also stood here, but they have been removed to the New Jail buildings at the foot of the Saltmarket. The Town Hall, however, still remains, a fine apartment containing portraits of some of the Scottish and English sovereigns, besides a very fine marble statue of William Pitt, by Chantrey. The Cross Steeple, too, survives still, a relic of the ancient civic splendour of this part of the city, and in itself an interesting object. Leaving the ancient Cross of Glasgow, we next enter the Saltmarket, not now, alas! as in the palmy days of Bailie Nicol Jarvie, the domicile of bailies, and other civic dignitaries, but occupied with a busy population of inferior shopkeepers, and trades people. The lower part, and some portions of the neighbourhood, form the Monmouth Street and Rag Fair of Glasgow, being chiefly occupied with furniture brokers and old clothes dealers. On the left is St.

Andrew's Square, the buildings of which are characterized by an elegant simplicity and chaste regularity of architecture. The greater part of the area of this square is occupied with St. Andrew's Church, the largest, and, in many respects, the first church in the city, the portico of which, for lightness and elevation, is much admired. On the right is the Bridgegate, of which notice has already been taken. Here stood anciently several fine old buildings of some historical note,—in one of which Cromwell is said to have lodged when in Glasgow,—but, with many other ancient tenements in this street, they have long since fallen victims to the progress of time and improvement. The stranger now emerges into a fine broad esplanade, with the Public Park or Green stretching away to the left, and the imposing pile of buildings forming the Court-houses and Jail, on the right. These elegant buildings are in the Grecian style of architecture. The front is chaste and simple, but thought to be rather low for its length. From the vast increase of the city and its population, these buildings are now found to be deficient in accommodation, and it is probable new Court-houses will soon be erected, and the whole of the present edifice used as a prison. An act for this purpose was obtained two years ago, but, from some unfortunate mistakes and local jarrings, has never been acted upon. On the right of the Court-houses is the river Clyde, crossed at this point by Hutcheson's Bridge, a recently built, but heavy and tasteless erection. A carriage drive extends around the Green, which is about two miles and a quarter in circumference. Passing up the green, on the left, is the fine obelisk erected to the memory of Nelson, 143 feet in height, and an exact resemblance of Trajan's Pillar at Rome. When the tide is at the full, the brimming waters of the Clyde appear at this point to great advantage, and there is a fine landscape view down the river, with the four bridges in the distance, and the variety of buildings, public and private, on the opposite banks. On the south side, vast ranges of chimneys appear, indicating the *locale* of some of the largest spinning and weaving factories in the city. The same appearances are beheld to the north-east, whilst, on the south and south-east appear, at a few miles distance, the beautiful slopes of the Cathkin Braes, adorned with fine plantations and gentlemen's seats. The Green is diversified with walks, some of which are shaded by noble rows of trees, and there are several fountains of fine spring water, round which abundance of damsels may be seen clustering with their *boynes* and pitchers,—the Green being the common property of the inhabitants, and much used for the washing and bleaching of clothes. The north side of this fine pleasure ground rises a little, and is termed the Calton Green, and has a handsome row of dwelling houses lining one side of it, called Monteith Row, which, from their elevation, and beauty of situation, are amongst the pleasantest in the city. Leaving the Green by the North-west Gate, (on the west and north it is surrounded for most of its length by an iron railing,) and crossing Charlotte Street, a quiet, dull-looking street, with some fine old mansions in it, we enter London Street, a broad and handsome avenue, but sorely bungled, and in a half built and disgraceful state of dilapidation, considering its immediate vicinity to the Cross, the centre of the city. Arrived again at the Cross, let us take a passing glance at the Gallowgate, the name of the eastern section of the main street of the city, and which begins at this point. It is irregular, both in the appearance of its buildings and in its width, sometimes steep and narrow, then broad and winding. It contains large barracks for foot soldiers, and, near its easterly extremity, the Cattle Market, one of the most interesting sights of Glasgow. It occupies 30,000 square yards, and is admirably, and even elegantly, laid out for its especial objects. The tower of St. John's Church is the most prominent feature in this part of the city, which, exhibiting no other objects of peculiar interest to a stranger, we shall return from this hasty sally, and proceed due north, up the High Street, which ancient avenue may be considered as the backbone of the skeleton of the old city.

The buildings in this fine old street are many of them venerable from their antiquity; but the presence of new ones on every side indicates the rapid disappearance of the ancient characteristics of this part of the city. On every side numerous *closes*, or narrow lanes, appear, teeming with population and alive with the hum and stir of active life. They are inhabited chiefly by the lower classes, and in many of them, as well as in those in the Saltmarket and Bridgegate, the inmates are so densely wedged together, that this, co-operating with other fatal causes, has tended to foster the elements of contagious diseases, and greatly to lower the average duration of life in the city. Proceeding up the street, and passing one or two inferior streets, on the right is a long range of venerable monastic-looking buildings, with a fine stone balcony in the front. These are the buildings of the University, the external aspect of which harmonizes well with the grave purposes to which they are devoted. There are three inner courts, and in the first there is a fine old staircase much admired for its stately elegance. The buildings are old, and imposing in their appearance, but some of the older portions having been taken down a few years ago, have been replaced by others of a character wholly foreign to the original style, thus marring the harmony and disturbing the uniformity and propriety of the structure. Behind is the Hunterian Museum, a splendid edifice of the Grecian character.

A little above the College is Duke Street, a fine opening to the east, and containing the City and County Bridewell, a large and striking mass of buildings in the old Saxon style of architecture.* The High Street becomes here rather steep and narrow, with a considerable curve, and is called the Bell of the Brae. Here, in the year 1300, a severe action took place betwixt the English and Scots; the former commanded by Percy and Bishop Beik, and the latter by the Scottish champion—Wallace. The English were defeated with the loss of their commander.—Within these twenty-five years, this part of the High Street contained the oldest and most curious-looking buildings in the city, but almost the whole of these ancient tenements have been pulled down, and replaced by others of the most ordinary character. At the top of this ascent, on the right, is the Drygate, and on the left the Rottenrow; both of them very old streets, and still exhibiting sundry venerable-looking buildings, the relics of their ancient grandeur and importance. A few yards further we reach a large open space, containing in front the Infirmary, a large and elegant building of a composite character of architecture, and light and airy in appearance; and a little to the right, the huge mass of

* This establishment is justly celebrated for the superior excellence and economy of its arrangements and management. It contains ample accommodation and means of classification for nearly 300 prisoners, by whose labour its expenses are almost wholly defrayed. Each prisoner, it is calculated, costs the community no more than £1, 10s. per annum, so judicious is the system pursued

the Cathedral at once arrests and detains the eye of the stranger. Having already, in the historical and introductory matter, briefly noticed this noble relic of antiquity, we shall merely further observe, that it is surrounded by a vast churchyard, in which the bones of many generations rest from their labours; besides which, it contains a great many rich and ancient monumental tombs of the worthies of the old city, and the grave dignities of church and state in the days of other times.—The Glasgow Infirmary is a very large building, including those recent additions made to it for a Fever Hospital. The extent of its accommodations may be inferred from the fact, that 6272 patients were admitted during the year 1837–1838. It bears a high character, not merely for the matured excellence of its arrangements, but the superior character of its medical school.* A building in the worst possible taste, stands a little to the right of these two fine specimens of ancient and modern architecture, which is the Barony Church. Betwixt this eye-sore to the public, and the wall of the Cathedral burying-ground, a narrow path conducts to the Bridge of Sighs, so called from its spanning the brawling waters of a rivulet termed the Molendinar Burn, and which, after being collected into a small lake or dam, dash briskly over an artificial cascade, down the steep ravine which separates the Cathedral grounds from the old Fir Park, anciently, as it is believed, a sacred retreat of the Druids, and now the superb Necropolis of Glasgow. This bold and rocky eminence shoots suddenly up to the height of from 200 to 300 feet, forming, with its fine shrubberies, a noble back-ground to the Cathedral. A

* Its affairs are managed by twenty-five Directors, ten of whom are elected by the subscribers of two guineas a-year, the others are elected by the various public bodies of the city; the Members for the city are also *ex officiis* Directors.

splendid gateway, in the Italian style, appears in front, and the entire surface of the rock is divided into walks, and bristling with columns and every variety of monumental erection, many of them peculiarly happy and chaste in style. The fine statue of Knox on the summit, and one erected to the memory of Mr. William M'Gavin, with the cenotaph to the late Rev. Dr. Dick of Glasgow, are particularly conspicuous, and will instantly attract the eye of the stranger. It is proposed to carry a tunnel through the hill from south to north, and to form galleries and chambers in the solid rock, so as to form a vast crypt in addition to the cemetery above. From the summit, 250 feet above the level of the Clyde, the Great Reformer just mentioned looks grimly down on one of the most striking scenes that can well be imagined. The huge mass of the venerable Cathedral, surrounded by the crumbling remains and memorials of two hundred and fifty generations, stands still and solemn at your feet, like the awful Genius of the Past; the vast city stretches away in long lines and perspectives before you in every direction, intersected by the broad and brimming Clyde, while the uplands of Lanarkshire and Renfrewshire, with the Dumbartonshire and Argyleshire hills, form a noble frame to the picture.* Descending from this elevated site, we shall retrace our steps down the High Street, and, striking to the right, enter George Street, a broad and handsome opening, but, with the exception of the buildings of Anderson's University, which are respectable

* A little to the west of the Cathedral is the asylum for the blind, (an establishment of great merit in its arrangements), the appearance of which is rather quaint, but in very good taste. The inmates are employed in various ways, and manufacture articles of use or ornament to a considerable extent, which are disposed of for the benefit of the institution. The new method of printing for the blind has been carried here to great perfection. Generally speaking, any respectable inn-keeper knows how to procure an order of admission for this and any other public institution in Glasgow.

but plain in appearance, and the New High School behind them, a large building and equally devoid of architectural attraction, it offers no particular inducement to the tourist to linger on its pavements, and he now finds himself again in George's Square, ready, after a brief repose, for

WALK SECOND.

BUCHANAN STREET—VIEW FROM THE TOP OF ST. VINCENT STREET—WEST GEORGE'S STREET—REGENT STREET—BATH STREET—CLELAND TESTIMONIAL—LUNATIC ASYLUM—SAUCHIEHALL ROAD—GARNET HILL—FINE VIEW FROM THE TOP—WOODSIDE CRESCENT—BOTANIC GARDEN—ELMBANK CRESCENT—INDIA STREET—ST. VINCENT STREET—BLYTHSWOOD SQUARE.

TURNING to the right, and still continuing in George's Street, now called West George's Street, and which, after passing round St. George's Church, continues its course for nearly half a mile further, till it is lost in Blythswood Square, the tourist enters Buchanan Street. Here it may be proper to observe, that four great lines of street run west from Buchanan Street, parallel to each other, two of them for nearly a mile in length,—Vincent Street, West George's Street, Regent Street, and Bath Street. The first and last named are the longest and finest. Turning north, we shall follow the easy ascent of Buchanan Street, and when at the top, we recommend a brief pause, to take a hasty look behind. The eye courses down the long vista of a spacious street, lined with handsome buildings, and in the lower half crowded with a gay population, for we have already mentioned that this is the Regent Street (London) of Glasgow. It is finely terminated by St. Enoch's

Church, standing in the Square of that name; and beyond, in the distance, the green slopes of the Renfrewshire uplands appear above the houses, giving a rich and half rural character to the view. A few yards farther on, we reach Sauchiehall Street or Road, at the corner of which stands a handsome pile of buildings, denominated the Cleland Testimonial, from having been built and presented to the eminent statist of that name, by his friends in Glasgow, on his retirement from the public service of the city, after having been for many years superintendant of public works. From this point, the lofty dome of the Lunatic Asylum meets the eye. This is one of the largest and finest buildings belonging to the city of Glasgow. From an octagonal centre four wings diverge, of three storeys in height, and the style of the whole building is impressive and striking. Its accommodation is very extensive, and the grounds contain about four acres. As a medical and restorative establishment, it ranks very high for the excellence of its management and arrangements. Sauchiehall Road is lined with handsome rows of houses, and is very broad the first half of its length. As the tourist proceeds, he finds on the left various handsome streets, opening into it from the south, forming part of the new town, and chiefly occupied by the wealthier classes. On the right, an elevated ridge accompanies him, containing many handsome villas, and intersected with streets. This is called Garnet Hill, and should be specially visited by the picturesque tourist, as it commands a noble view from its summit. To the north and north-west, bold ranges of hills appear at a few miles distance; and faintly looming on the horizon, the lofty peaks of the Argyleshire and Perthshire mountains are seen; nearer, the masts of vessels on the Forth and Clyde Canal appear in the basin at Port Dundas, and a rich undulating surface, crowded with villas, private dwellings, and the tall chimneys of numerous public works. Returning to Sauchiehall Street, the tourist arrives at Woodside Crescent, and is struck with surprise at the number and elegance of the fine streets, rows, and terraces, intermixed with ornamental shrubberies, which attract his eye. This part of the suburbs is the most recently built and is at present the most fashionable quarter for what are called self-contained houses. A quarter of a mile farther on, is the Botanic Garden, which, under the able superintendence of Sir William Hooker and Mr. Murray the curator, has obtained an extensive celebrity. Lectures are delivered here during the summer by the first named gentleman, professor of botany in the University, and strangers obtain admission to the garden on payment of a shilling. The collection of foreign plants is considered to be very complete, and in some departments unrivalled, and the plan of the garden is good. It is soon to be removed however, to a site a mile more to the north, on the fine slope of a gentle elevation, which will add to the general effect very considerably.

Retracing our steps, we shall strike down the first opening on the right into Elmbank Crescent, a very handsome row of houses, but only half built. Passing through a new street just begun, and containing a few very handsome buildings in the stately but somewhat stiff style of Louis the Fourteenth's time, and called India Street, the stranger finds himself at the western extremity of St. Vincent Street, here called Greenhill Place. Proceeding citywards, along this noble street, and ascending gradually, on the right is Blythswood Square, the buildings of which, from their lofty position, and elegant exterior, form one of the finest and most prominent objects to the stranger approaching Glasgow from the west. The view from this square to the south and west is very fine, but on the north it is intercepted by the more commanding ridge of Garnet Hill. Returning to St. Vincent Street, the stranger finds himself descending gradually, with elegant masses of building on each side, and a noble and lengthy street vista before him. On the left is a handsome building recently fitted up as a club-house, but there being no particular object to detain the eye, we shall suppose the tourist once more deposited in George's Square, in the north-west angle of which this noble opening has its termination.

WALK THIRD.

INGRAM STREET—ASSEMBLY ROOMS—OLD BRIDGE OF GLASGOW—POORS' HOUSE—CATHOLIC CHAPEL—CUSTOM HOUSE—GORBALS CHURCH—CARLTON PLACE—WOODEN OR SERVICE BRIDGE—GLASGOW BRIDGE—VIEW FROM—BROOMIELAW—HARBOUR—SHIPPING—STEAM VESSELS, &C.—SUBURBS OF LAURISTON, TRADESTON, AND HUTCHESONTOWN—BARONY OF GORBALS—PAISLEY CANAL.

Leaving George's Square again, and proceeding down Queen Street on the left, the eye glancing along Ingram Street, rests on the fine portico of the Assembly Rooms,* standing boldly forward, and the grave old College steeple in the distance, looking demurely down on the bustle and animation of this great business thorough-

* The Assembly Rooms is one of the finest edifices in the city, taken in connection with the buildings on each side, which are built on a plan connected with it. The principal room is 80 feet long, 35 feet wide, and 27 in height, with a tastefully painted ceiling.

fare. Entering Argyle Street once more, and threading our way eastward through its busy crowd to the Stockwell, we request the stranger to dash with us down this avenue towards the river, and there being no objects of any note on the route but those which have been already seen and commented on, we find ourselves on the Old Bridge of Glasgow. This bridge was built in 1345, and is the first stone bridge erected in Glasgow. It has been twice widened, and the last time in a very elegant and ingenious manner, by adding footpaths, supported by cast-iron frames of a tasteful character, from a design by the late Mr. Telford. Looking up the stream, the back and one side of the jail buildings are seen on the left, with the Green sloping beautifully down to the river. The view downwards is still finer; two bridges—the nearest a very fine and perfectly level one of wood—span the glittering waters of the river. On the right is a plain respectable looking building, the Poors' House. Next to it, the Catholic Chapel, one of the most striking modern buildings in the Gothic style of architecture in the kingdom. It is very large, and elegantly fitted up, and is officiated in by Bishop Murdoch, and several Catholic clergymen. Beyond it a little way is the New Custom House, a handsome-looking edifice, and nearly completed. On the left bank of the river, the spire of the Gorbals Church breaks the uniformity of the outline in a pleasing manner, and two fine masses of buildings, East and West Carlton Place, from their simplicity, good taste, and happy elevation, confer a peculiar dignity upon this part of the river vista. Proceeding along this noble street, Glasgow or Broomielaw Bridge next demands the attention of the tasteful stranger. It is one of the finest bridges in Europe—500 feet in length, and 60 feet wide, being seven feet wider than London Bridge. It is cased with Aberdeen granite, and consists of seven arches, whilst the curve is so slight as scarcely to be observed. It forms a superb entrance to the city from the south, and from it one of the finest river harbour views in the United Kingdom may be obtained. To the south, a fine broad avenue stretches away till it is lost in the country. On the right, the Broomielaw Street extends for nearly a mile, with a fine ample margin to the river, and long ranges of covered sheds and other harbour appurtenances. A noble basin, from three to four hundred feet wide, and about three quarters of a mile in length, with its range of quays, is before the eye, crowded with vessels of every description, from four hundred tons burden to the smallest coasting craft, whilst steam vessels are perpetually sending up clouds of smoke or steam, and dashing in or out with a startling velocity and noise.*

Crossing the river, the stranger will admire the spacious

* There are always several steam-vessels of the largest class lying in the river to get in their machinery, and there is a powerful crane, capable of raising thirty tons, for lifting the heavy boilers, &c. on board; a much larger one is preparing, expected to be the most powerful in Britain. Glasgow has attained great celebrity as a manufactory of marine steam engines, and, indeed, of machinery of every description. The depth of water at the Broomielaw at spring tides is now from 14 to 16 feet, and it is proposed by the Trustees of the harbour and river to deepen to the extent of 20 feet at neap tides, no obstacles existing, according to the report of the engineer, to prevent such a result being obtained. It is also intended to widen the river, for ten or twelve miles down, to from 300 to 400 feet wide, the width to increase downwards; to bevel off the banks on either side, and to remove every other obstacle to the freedom of the navigation; so that in a few years, with wet docks, for which a large space of ground on the south side, immediately below the suburb of Tradeston, has recently been purchased, Glasgow will possess one of the most spacious and convenient harbours in the kingdom. From July 1837 to July 1838, 4600 sailing vessels of every description arrived and departed from the harbour, with a tonnage of 214,471 tons; and the steam tonnage on the river during the same period was 731,028 tons; these latter vessels made 7850 trips in the same time. The revenue from the harbour and river last year was nearly £40,000, and it is expected to realise this amount during the current year. Customs levied in 1836, £314,701, 10s. 8d., and Post Office revenue, above £40,000.

and elegant streets, which, as he walks along, strike his eye. Portland Street is nearly a mile in length, very broad, and lined with handsome buildings. The population on this side of the river is understood to be about 60,000, located in Lauriston, Tradeston, and Hutchesontown, all in the Barony of Gorbals, which is a dependency of Glasgow.* The parliamentary constituency elect their own magistrates by poll election, who must however be approved of by the Town Council of Glasgow. The terminus of the Ayr, Paisley, and Greenock Railway, is on this side, close to Glasgow Bridge, and half a mile to the south is the basin of the Johnston and Paisley Canal, to which places light and swift passage-boats depart almost every hour during the summer. Arrived at the Old Bridge of Glasgow again, the stranger, before crossing, will probably cast one lingering look on the river, and noble view on either side, after which, retracing his steps up Stockwell Street, he may if he pleases, return to George's Square, by Glasford Street, Ingram Street, and the Royal Exchange, thus passing through the most crowded and interesting business thoroughfares of the city.

* The entire population of Glasgow and the suburbs may now be estimated at 250,000 souls.

SEVENTH TOUR.

GLASGOW — DUMBARTON — HELENSBURGH — GREENOCK — LARGS — DUNOON—ROTHSAY.

STARTING from Broomielaw in one of the steam-boats which ply on the river, a few minutes' sail brings the passengers to the mouth of the Kelvin, a stream celebrated in Scottish song. The village on the left is Govan. On both sides of the river there is a series of pleasant suburban villas. About two miles below Govan, on the same side of the river, is Shieldhall, A. Johnston, Esq. On the right, Jordanhill, James Smith, Esq. A little farther down the river, and on the same side, is Scotstoun, the seat of Miss Oswald. On the left is Elderslie House, the seat of Alexander Speirs, Esq.; and about a mile farther down is Blythswood House, the seat of Archibald Campbell, Esq. Between the two last mentioned places is Renfrew Ferry, where a near view may be obtained of the ancient burgh of Renfrew. The appearance of the town is mean and antiquated. In the neighbourhood, Somerled, Thane of Argyle and Lord of the Isles, who had rebelled against Malcolm IV., was defeated and slain in the year 1164. The barony of Renfrew was the first possession of the Stuart family in Scotland. It gives the title of Baron to the Prince of Wales. The collected waters of the two Carts and the Gryfe flow into the

Clyde at Inchinnan, about a mile below Renfrew. Near Inchinnan Bridge, the Earl of Argyle was taken prisoner in 1685. On the left, and a little above Erskine Ferry stands Northbarr, a plain and now dilapidated mansion, formerly the seat of Lord Sempill. Near the river, on the left, is the old mansion-house of Erskine, anciently the seat of the Earls of Mar, and latterly of the Blantyre family. Robert, eleventh Lord Blantyre, who perished accidentally in the commotions at Brussels, in 1830, erected the new princely mansion which crowns the rising ground a little farther down. The tourist is now half-way between Glasgow and Greenock. The river has expanded greatly, and assumed the appearance of a lake, apparently closed in front. The lofty heights on the right are the Kilpatrick Hills, and the village in the narrow plain between them and the river is Kilpatrick, supposed to have been the birth-place of St. Patrick, the tutelar saint of Ireland. The little bay in front of Kilpatrick is Bowling Bay. Opposite Bowling Inn may be perceived the mouth of the Great Junction Canal, which unites the east and west coasts of Scotland, by means of the Firths of Forth and Clyde. At a short distance below, on the right, is the little promontory of Dunglass Point, the western termination of Antoninus' Wall or Graham's Dyke, with the ruins of Dunglass Castle, formerly the property of the Colquhouns of Luss, but now belonging to Buchanan of Auchintorlie. On this spot a statue has lately been erected of the late Henry Bell, the first person who applied the steam-engine to river navigation. On the left, in the distance, are seen the church and manse of Erskine; Bishopton House (Lord Blantyre); Drums (Captain Darroch.) On the opposite side are Milton Island, Milton House, and Printworks, (Mitchell, Esq.); Dumbuck House

(Col. Geils); at the foot of Dumbuck Hill (*Hill of Roes*); Garshake (Dixon, Esq.); Chapel Green and Silverton Hill. But by far the most prominent object is the rock of Dumbarton, which rises suddenly from the point of junction of the Leven and Clyde, to the height of 560 feet, measuring a mile in circumference, terminating in two sharp points, one higher than the other, and studded over with houses and batteries. Previous to his being sent to England, Wallace was confined for some time in this castle, the governor of which was the infamous Sir John Menteith, who betrayed him. The highest peak of the rock is still denominated "Wallace's Seat," and a part of the castle "Wallace's Tower." In one of the apartments, a huge two-handed sword, said to have belonged to that hero, is still shown. At the union of Scotland with England, this was one of the four fortresses stipulated to be kept up; and, accordingly, it is still in repair, and occupied by a garrison.* Opposite to Dum-

* During the wars which desolated Scotland in the reign of Queen Mary, this formidable fortress was taken in the following remarkable way, by Captain Crawford of Jordanhill, a distinguished adherent of the King's party:—"He took advantage of a misty and moonless night to bring to the foot of the castle-rock the scaling-ladders which he had provided, choosing for his terrible experiment the place where the rock was highest, and where, of course, less pains were taken to keep a regular guard. This choice was fortunate; for the first ladder broke with the weight of the men who attempted to mount, and the noise of the fall must havé betrayed them, had there been any sentinel within hearing. Crawford, assisted by a soldier who had deserted from the castle, and was acting as his guide, renewed the attempt in person, and having scrambled up to a projecting ledge of rock where there was some footing, contrived to make fast the ladder, by tying it to the roots of a tree, which grew about mid-way up the rock. Here they found a small flat surface, sufficient, however, to afford footing to the whole party, which was, of course, very few in number. In scaling the second precipice, another accident took place:—One of the party, subject to epileptic fits, was seized by one of these attacks, brought on perhaps by terror, while he was in the act of climbing up the ladder. His illness made it impossible for him either to ascend or descend. To have slain the man would have been a cruel expedient, besides that the fall of his body from the ladder might have alarmed the garrison. Crawford caused him, therefore, to be tied to the ladder; then all the rest descending, they turned the ladder, and thus mounted with ease over the belly of the epileptic person. When the party

barton Castle, on the left, is West Sea Bank; and beyond the Leven, on the right, is Leven Grove, the seat of the Dixons of Dumbarton. Two miles farther, on the left, is Finlayston, formerly the family mansion of the Earls of Glencairn, now the seat of Graham of Gartmore; on the right are Clyde Bank and Clyde Cottage. Approaching Port-Glasgow, we reach the Castle of Newark, which, after having belonged, in succession, to a branch of the Maxwells and to the Belhaven family, is now the property of Lady Shaw Stewart. Port-Glasgow was founded, in 1668, by the merchants of Glasgow, for the embarkation and disembarkation of goods. Since the river was deepened, Port-Glasgow has lost much of the consequence which it originally possessed. On the opposite shore of the Clyde are the remains of an ancient castle, believed to have been that of Cardross, in which Robert Bruce breathed his last. For several miles the shore is thickly studded with villas, among which are Ardarden House, Ardmore House, Cames-Eskan, Kilmahew Castle, and Drumfork House, all on the right side of the Firth. Three and a half miles from Dumbarton is the Kirk of Cardross, with its little attendant village. Five miles further along the shore, the beautiful sea-bathing village of Helensburgh occupies a sheltered situation at the opening of the Gare Loch. It was founded about fifty years ago by Sir James Colquhoun. A mile to the westward is the pleasant inn of Ardincaple; and a mile and a half further are the village and kirk of Row, which is the parish church of Helensburgh. The promontory opposite to Helensburgh, between the Gare

gained the summit, they slew the sentinel, ere he had time to give the alarm, and easily surprised the slumbering garrison, who had trusted too much to the security of their castle to keep good watch. This exploit of Crawford may compare with any thing of the kind which we read of in history."

Loch and Loch Long, is occupied by the mansion and beautiful grounds of Roseneath, a seat of the Argyle family. This palace, built in the Italian style, occupies the site of a fine old castle, which was burnt down in 1802. After a sail from Glasgow of about two hours and a half, the steamer reaches the large and populous sea-port of Greenock, which occupies part of a narrow stripe of level ground stretching along the shore. Close upon the quay stands the Custom-house, the finest public building in Greenock. It is a remarkable proof of the opulence of the inhabitants, that the sum of L.10,000, required for the erection of this building, was subscribed in two days. This town was the birth-place of Watt. The situation of Greenock, with the mountains of Argyleshire and Dumbartonshire rising on the opposite side, is very fine. The view from the quay is perhaps the finest commanded by any sea-port in the kingdom. Leaving Greenock, the steamer makes direct for Kempock Point. The principal villas on the shore, to the left, are Rosebank, Seabank, Glenpark, Finnart, Ladyburn House, and Bridgend. About three miles below Greenock, at the bottom of a little bay, is situated the pretty village of Gourock. It commands a noble sea-view, and the walks along the shore towards the Cloch are very beautiful. About a quarter of a mile off Kempock Point, a promontory which forms the western boundary of Gourock Bay, the Comet steamboat was run down by the Ayr steam-packet, October 21, 1825, when upwards of fifty individuals found a watery grave. A mile further along this coast, is the old ruin of Laven Tower, crowning a fine eminence. About three miles below Gourock, the coast bends to the south at the Cloch Light-house, one of the most important beacons on the Clyde. A little below stands Ardgovan, the seat of Sir R. M. Shaw Stewart, Bart. A short way farther on, at the bottom of a small bay, is the little sequestered village of Innerkip, one of the most delightful watering-places on the west coast. In the neighbourhood is Kelly House, the seat of Robert Wallace, Esq. M.P. The counties of Renfrew and Ayr are here divided by Kellyburn. The next promontory is Knock Point, on rounding which we come in sight of the beautifully picturesque village of Largs. The battle of Largs, between the Scottish army and that of Haco, King of Norway, in which the latter was defeated with great slaughter, took place in 1623, on a large plain upon the sea-shore to the south of the village.

Returning to Cloch Point, straight opposite on the coast of Argyle, stands Dunoon, a sea-bathing village, which commands several fine and diversified sea-ward views. The Castle of Dunoon is an interesting relic of antiquity. It was once a royal residence, and a strong fortress. The hereditary keepership of this castle was conferred by Robert Bruce on the family of Sir Colin Campbell of Loch Awe, an ancestor of the Duke of Argyle. It was the residence of the Argyle family in 1673, but from the commencement of the eighteenth century was allowed to fall into a state of ruin. At a short distance from Dunoon, is the Holy Loch, surrounded by steep and picturesque hills. On its eastern shore is situated the little village of Kilmun, where may be still seen the ruins of the Collegiate Church, founded, in 1442, by Sir Duncan Campbell of Loch Awe, ancestor of the Argyle family. Here the Argyle family have their burying-place. On leaving Dunoon, the steamer skirts along Bawkie Bay. The peninsula of Cowal ends a few miles lower at Toward Point, where there is a light-house, besides a large modern edifice, Toward Castle, the seat of Kirkman Finlay, Esq. On the neighbouring height, on the right, are seen the venerable ruins of Toward Castle, the ancient seat of the Lamonts. Turning Toward Point, we enter the Kyles of Bute, the crooked strait which divides Argyleshire from Bute, and in a short time reach the pleasant town of Rothsay. The town consists of several neat streets, and the views to be obtained of the neighbouring coasts, from various elevated points around it, are extremely beautiful. The ancient royal castle of Rothsay, the favourite residence of Robert III., is one of the finest ruins in Scotland. It was burned down by the Earl of Argyle, in 1685. The closet in which Robert III. died is still pointed out. Rothsay gave the title of Duke to the eldest son of the Scottish kings, as it still does to the heir-apparent of the British crown. The western side of the Bay of Rothsay commands a noble view of the entrance to the Kyles, and the mouth of Loch Strevin, with the shores of Cowal. About two miles from Rothsay, the steamboat passes Port Bannatyne, a beautiful village encircling the bottom of Kames Bay. In the immediate vicinity stands Kames Castle, an old fortified mansion still inhabited. Between Rothsay and Kilchattan Bay stands Mount Stewart, the seat of the Marquis of Bute, surrounded by fine woods. EtterickBay, on the west side of the island, is often visited on account of its picturesque scenery. After passing the mouth of Loch Strevan, the channel rapidly narrows. Between the ferry and the entrance of Loch Ridden, it is contracted by four islands. The passage, though narrow and intricate, is exceedingly interesting. Leaving the entrance to Loch Ridden on the right, the steamer emerges into the open space between Ard, Lamont

Point, on the mainland, and Etterick Bay, in Bute. The heights of Arran are seen here to great advantage. On rounding, the steamer enters Loch Fyne. On the left is the islet of Inchmarnock, with the ruins of a chapel, and soon after we pass another islet, called Slate Island. On the left is the wild and rugged coast of Kintyre. The harbour of East Tarbert, however, into which the steamer now enters, is remarkably secure. East Tarbert is a picturesque fishing village, situated upon a very narrow isthmus, uniting Kintyre to Knapdale. In the immediate vicinity is the Castle of Tarbert, now in ruins. Here the Earl of Argyle kept his troops previous to his unsuccessful descent upon the Lowlands in 1685. Leaving Tarbert, and pursuing our course northward, we pass Barmere Island, and shortly after come in sight of the village of Lochgilphead, and the extremity of the Crinan Canal. This canal, which was formed to save doubling the Mull of Kintyre, is only nine miles in length, but has no fewer than fifteen locks. On entering the canal a good view is obtained of Lochgilphead and Kilmery, the seat of Sir John Ord. Two miles from the sea lock, on the left, is Oakfield. The canal here passes through an extensive tract of marshy uninteresting country. Passing the village of Bellanach, we enter the Bay of Crinan. Upon the right is the modernized Castle of Duntroon (Malcolm, Esq.), and northward, on the same side, Loch Craignish, a fine arm of the sea intersected by a chain of beautiful little islands, covered with ancient oak trees. The steamboat proceeds through the Dorishmere, or Great Gate, between the point of Craignish and one of the chain of islets just mentioned. Iona and Isla are now in sight. On the south are the shores of Knapdale, and to the north the islands of Shuna and Luing, with

Loch Melfort opening to the right. Two miles from the Point of Luing is Blackmill Bay, opposite to which is the Island of Lunga. Three miles farther north is the slate islet of Balnahuay, and farther to the west the Garveloch Isles. The Sound of Cuan runs between the northern extremity of Luing and the island of Seil. The length of this beautiful and diversified passage is about three miles. On the west side of Seil is the circular islet of Easdale, celebrated for its slate quarries. After passing Easdale and the Point of Ardincaple, Loch Feochan opens on the right, and a distinct view of the broad-shouldered and double-peaked Ben Cruachan is obtained. To the north is the Island of Kerrera, with the ruins of Gylen Castle occupying its southern point. This island forms a natural breakwater to the Bay of Oban. At the head of this bay is situated the pleasant and thriving village of Oban. The high cliffs on the north side of the bay command one of the finest views in Scotland. They terminate in a rocky promontory, surmounted by Dunolly Castle, an ivy-clad square keep, the ancient seat of the M'Dougals of Lorn, whose representative resides here in Dunolly House. A little to the north of Dunolly stands the Castle of Dunstaffnage, which is ranked as one of the royal palaces of Scotland, in consequence of its having been occasionally possessed by the early Scottish kings. From this ancient seat of royalty, it is said, the coronation stone, now in Westminster Abbey, was transferred by Kenneth II. to Scone.

EIGHTH TOUR.

GLASGOW—INVERARY—LOCH AWE—DALMELLY—TAYNUILT—OBAN.

THE tourist has his choice of several different routes to Inverary. He may proceed by Loch Lomond, or by Loch Long, to Arroquhar, and thence, by Cairndow, to Inverary,—or by Loch Goil and St. Catharine's,—or by the Holy Loch, Loch Eck, and Strachur,—or by Rothsay, Tarbert, and Lochgilphead.

Supposing him to take the first route, he proceeds by steamboat to Dumbarton, and thence, to the foot of Loch Lomond, where he embarks in a steamboat and sails fourteen miles northward, to Tarbet, on its west side. From this point to Arroquhar, on the shores of Loch Long, is a delightful walk of about half an hour, across the isthmus which lies between Loch Lomond and Loch Long. The inn of Arroquhar is twenty-two miles from Dumbarton. Loch Long is an arm of the sea about twenty-four miles in length. In 1263, the Norwegians, who invaded Scotland, and were ultimately defeated at Largs, sailed up this loch with a fleet of sixty vessels, ravaging the country on all sides, and, on reaching the head of the loch, they drew their boats across the isthmus into Loch Lomond, and committed the same depredations on its shores. Near the head of Loch Long is a fantastic peak, called Ben Arthur or the Cobbler, from its grotesque resemblance to a shoemaker at work. Arroquhar was formerly the seat of the chief of the clan Macfarlane,—it is now the property of Sir James Colquhoun of Luss. Starting from the inn at this spot, the tourist winds round the head of Loch Long, and crossing the water of Taing, enters Argyleshire. The road now skirts the western shore of Loch Long, till, within a few yards of Ardgarten House, (Campbell, Esq.) where it turns to the right, and enters the vale of Glencoe,—a desolate but magnificent glen about six miles in length, guarded on the right by the bold and fantastic peak of Ben Arthur. A steep path conducts the traveller to the summit of the pass, where there is a stone seat, with the inscription, "Rest and be thankful."* The road now gradually descends, passing, on the left, a small sheet of water, called Loch Restal, and enters the lonely valley of Glenkinglas. Passing through this solitary vale, at the distance of about three miles, the tourist is gladdened with a view of Loch Fyne. The road now passes, on the right, the farm house of Strowan, and, on the left, Ardkinglas, (Campbell, Bart.) and shortly after reaches the inn of Cairndow, (thirty-six miles from Dumbarton,) where there is a ferry across Loch Fyne to Inverary; or, if the tourist should prefer another route, there is a road of nine and a half miles round the head of the loch.

* On this Wordsworth has composed the following Sonnet:—

"Doubling and doubling with laborious walk,
Who, that has gained at length the wished-for Height,
This brief, this simple way-side Call can slight,
And rest not thankful? Whether cheered by talk
With some loved friend, or by the unseen hawk
Whistling to clouds and sky-born streams, that shine
At the sun's outbreak, as with light divine,
Ere they descend to nourish root and stalk
Of valley flowers. Nor, while the limbs repose,
Will we forget that, as the fowl can keep
Absolute stillness, poised aloft in air,
And fishes front, unmoved, the torrent's sweep,—
So may the Soul, through powers that Faith bestows,
Win rest, and ease, and peace, with bliss that Angels share."

The second route to Inverary leads the tourist up Loch Goil, which branches off from Loch Long. The peninsular group of rugged mountains which separate them is called Argyle's Bowling Green. The shores are bold and magnificent. Near Loch Goil are the ruins of Carrick Castle, an ancient seat of the Dunmore family, situated on a high and nearly insulated rock. From Loch Goil head an excellent road leads through a wild valley, called Hell's Glen, to St. Catharine's, a distance of seven miles, whence the tourist may proceed across Loch Fyne (four miles) to Inverary.

By the third route, the tourist sails from Glasgow up the small arm of the sea called the Holy Loch, and disembarks at Kilmun; from thence he may walk, or take a coach provided for the purpose, through a wild vale of four or five miles in length, to Loch Eck, where he embarks on board a steamboat by which he is carried to the head of that beautiful lake. Loch Eck is about six miles long and only half a mile broad. It occupies the centre of the peninsula formed by the approach of Loch Long and Loch Fyne to each other. The scenery around the lake is very fine. At its southern extremity it discharges its waters by the river Eachaig, which, after a course of about two miles, falls into the Holy Loch. At the head of Loch Eck a coach is provided which carries the tourist a distance of seven miles to the village of Strachur, on the banks of Loch Fyne, where a steamboat carries him across that loch to Inverary.

By the fourth, and much the longest route, the tourist proceeds to Rothsay, then through the Kyles of Bute, and into the long arm of the sea called Loch Fyne.

INVERARY,

the county town of Argyleshire, stands at the lower end

of a small bay, where the river Aray falls into Loch Fyne. It was erected into a royal burgh in 1648 by Charles I. while he was a prisoner in Carisbrook Castle. An obelisk has been erected in a garden beside the church to commemorate the execution of several gentlemen of the name of Campbell, who suffered here in 1615, for their opposition to Popery. The population of Inverary is about 1000 or 1100. Its staple trade is the herring fishery,—the herrings of Loch Fyne being celebrated for their superior excellence. Large sums of money have been laid out by the Dukes of Argyle in improving and adorning the town and neighbourhood. Inverary unites with Oban, Campbelton, Irvine, and Ayr in electing a member of Parliament.

The most interesting object in this vicinity is Inverary Castle, the seat of the Duke of Argyle. Both the inter-

INVERARY CASTLE.

nal decorations and the scenery around the mansion, are remarkably splendid. The Castle was begun by Duke Archibald in 1748, after a plan by Adam. It is built of blue granite, and consists of two storeys and a sunk floor, flanked with round overtopping towers, and surmounted with a square-winged pavilion. There is an interesting collection of old Highland armour in the saloon. The view from the hill of Duniquoich is very fine, and the rides and the walks through the grounds are remarkably extensive and picturesque.*

From Inverary a road leads through Glen Aray, to Loch Awe, distant about twelve miles. After leaving the pleasure grounds round Inverary Castle, the tourist will find little to attract his attention till he reaches the head of the glen and begins to descend towards Cladich, when the beautiful expanse of Loch Awe breaks upon his view. Loch Awe is about twenty-four miles in length, and varies from one and a half to two and a half in breadth. The mingled grandeur and beauty of the scenery are scarcely equalled in Britain.

Loch Awe is surrounded by lofty mountains of a rude and savage aspect, the highest of which (Ben Cruachan) rises to the height of 3400 feet, while its base, which reaches to Loch Etive, occupies an area of twenty square miles. Its towering proportions give a striking character to the scenery at the eastern extremity of Loch Awe. The sloping banks of the lake are well cultivated and wooded. The river Awe flows from its northern side, and pours its waters into Loch Etive at Bunawe. The gully or hollow through which the river flows is of the most frightful description. There are about twenty-four

* "Embarked on the bosom of Loch Fyne, Captain Dalgetty might have admired one of the grandest scenes which nature affords. He might have noticed the rival rivers Aray and Shiray, which pay tribute to the lake, each issuing from its own dark and wooded retreat. He might have marked, on the soft and gentle slope that ascends from the shores, the noble old Gothic castle, with its varied outline, embattled walls, towers, and outer and inner courts, which, so far as the picturesque is concerned, presented an aspect much more striking than the present massive and uniform mansion. He might have admired those dark woods, which for many a mile surrounded this strong and princely dwelling, and his eye might have dwelt on the picturesque peak of Duniquoich, starting abruptly from the lake, and raising its scathed brow into the mists of middle sky, while a solitary watch-tower, perched on its top like an eagle's nest, gave dignity to the scene by awakening a sense of possible danger."—*Legend of Montrose.*

little islands in Loch Awe, some of them beautifully crowned with trees. On one of these islets, (Inishiel, or the Beautiful Isle,) are the ruins of a small nunnery of the Cistertian order. The old churchyard in this island contains a number of ancient tomb-stones, curiously carved. On Innes Fraoch, or the Heather Isle, are the ruins of an ancient castle of the chief of the MacNaughtons. The island of Fraoch, with the contiguous lands, were granted in 1267 to Gilbert MacNaughton by Alexander III. The MacNaughtons formed part of the force of MacDougal, Lord of Lorn, when he attacked Robert Bruce at Dalry, near Tyndrum. It is stated by Barbour that MacNaughton pointed out to the Lord of Lorn the deeds of valour which Bruce performed in this memorable retreat, with the highest expressions of admiration. "It seems to give thee pleasure," said Lorn, "that he makes such havoc among our friends."—"Not so, by my faith," replied MacNaughton; "but be he friend or foe who achieves high deeds of chivalry, men should bear faithful witness to his valour; and never have I heard of one, who, by his knightly feats, has extricated himself from such dangers as have this day surrounded Bruce."

At the eastern extremity of Loch Awe, at the base of Ben Cruachan, the conjoined waters of two rivers, the Strae and the Orchy, descend from their respective glens and empty themselves into the lake. On a rocky elevation at the head of the lake, where the Orchy flows into it, stand the ruins of the celebrated castle of Kilchurn, or more properly Coalchuirn. The great tower is said to have been erected, in 1440, by the lady of Sir Colin Campbell, the Black Knight of Rhodes, second son of Sir Duncan Campbell of Loch Awe, ancestor of the Argyle family. Sir Colin acquired by marriage a considerable portion of the estates of the family of Lorn, and was the founder of the powerful family of Breadalbane. Sir Colin was absent on a crusade when his lady erected this noble pile, which (says Maculloch), "in the Western Highlands at least, claims the pre-eminence, no less from its magnitude and the integrity of its ruins, than from the very picturesque arrangements of the building." So late as 1745, Kilchurn was garrisoned by the King's troops, and all the exterior and greater part of the interior walls are still entire.*

There is a good inn at Dalmally, near the head of the

* Our space will not admit of our quoting the whole of Wordsworth's fine Address to Kilchurn Castle, but we give the introductory part of the Poem and the prose extract with which it is prefaced.

" From the top of the hill a most impressive scene opened upon our view, —a ruined castle on an Island (for an Island the flood had made it) at some distance from the shore, backed by a cove of the mountain Cruachan, down which came a foaming stream. The Castle occupied every foot of the Island that was visible to us, appearing to rise out of the water,—mists rested upon the mountain side, with spots of sunshine; there was a mild desolation in the low grounds, a solemn grandeur in the mountains, and the Castle was wild, yet stately—not dismantled of turrets—nor the walls broken down, though obviously a ruin."—*Extract from the Journal of my Companion.*

" Child of loud-throated War! the mountain stream
Roars in thy hearing; but thy hour of rest
Is come, and thou art silent in thy age;
Save when the wind sweeps by and sounds are caught
Ambiguous, neither wholly thine nor theirs.
Oh! there is life that breathes not; powers there are
That touch each other to the quick in modes
Which the gross world no sense hath to perceive,
No soul to dream of. What art thou, from care
Cast off—abandoned by thy rugged Sire,
Nor by soft Peace adopted; though, in place
And in dimension, such that thou might'st seem
But a mere footstool to yon sovereign Lord,
Huge Cruachan, (a thing that meaner hills
Might crush, nor know that it had suffered harm;)
Yet he, not loth, in favour of thy claims
To reverence, suspends his own; submitting
All that the God of Nature hath conferred,
All that he holds in common with the stars,
To the memorial majesty of Time
Impersonated in thy calm decay!

lake, and from it there is a beautiful view of the vale of Glenorchy. The old church of Glenorchy is of great antiquity, and the churchyard contains many ancient gravestones. The road from Dalmally to Taynuilt passes the new church of Glenorchy, and makes a long circuit round the head of the lake. Two miles from Dalmally, we cross the river Strae which descends from Glenstrae on the right. The whole of this district was at one time possessed by the Clan-Gregor, but they have long ago been deprived of all their possessions around Loch Awe, and may now say in the words of the poet—

"Glenorchy's proud mountains, Coalchuirn and her towers,
Glenstrae and Glenlyon no longer are ours,
We're landless, landless, Gregalich."*

In later times, this district fell into the hands of the Campbells, and often afforded them shelter in times of danger. "It's a far cry to Lochow," was the slogan of the clan, indicating the impossibility of reaching them in these remote fastnesses. Passing the farm-house of Corry, the road now skirts the tremendous base of Ben Cruachan, and leaving behind the majestic lake, descends the course of the foaming and rapid river Awe. The rocks and precipices which stoop down perpendicularly on the

* "In the early part of the 17th century, a young man, of the name of Lamont, travelling from Cowal, in Argyleshire, to Fort-William, fell in with the son of a chieftain of the clan Macgregor, resident in Glenstrae, while on a shooting excursion. Having adjourned to a public-house, a dispute arose, which terminated in a scuffle, in which Macgregor was mortally stabbed. Lamont instantly escaping, was closely pursued. Descrying a house, he sped thither for shelter; unquestioned, the host assured him of protection. Those in pursuit coming up, communicated the startling intelligence that the fugitive was the murderer of the eldest son of the family. Macgregor, however, faithful to his word, conducted the young man to Loch Fyne, and saw him safe across. His clemency and magnanimity were not without their recompense. Not long after, the clan Gregor were proscribed; when Lamont received the aged chieftain to his house, and, by every act of kindness to him and his relatives, sought to supply the place of him of whose support he had been the means of bereaving them."—*Anderson's Guide to the Highlands*.

path, exhibit some remains of the wood which once clothed them, but which has in later times been felled to supply the iron foundries at Bunawe. The whole of this pass is singularly wild, particularly near the bridge which has been thrown across the impetuous river. Here was fought the celebrated battle between Robert Bruce and John of Lorn, chief of the MacDougals, in which that warlike clan were almost destroyed. The Bridge of Awe is the scene of Sir Walter Scott's beautiful tale of the Highland Widow.* Proceeding onwards about two miles, a view is obtained of Loch Etive, and the little village of Bunawe. Crossing an old bridge, and passing the church on the right, the tourist reaches the Inn of Taynuilt, on the south side of Loch Etive, twelve miles distant from Dalmally. About a mile to the north is the village of Bunawe, where there is a ferry across Loch Etive, and an extensive iron furnace, which has been wrought since the middle of last century by a Lancashire company. The portion of Loch Etive above Bunawe possesses a high degree of simple and sequestered grandeur. Bunawe is the point from which the ascent of Ben Cruachan can be best effected. The prospect from the top of the mountain is remarkably extensive and interesting. Leaving Taynuilt, the road, at the distance of four miles, descends to the shore of Loch

* "The following beautiful description is given of the spot where her cottage stood:—" We fixed our eyes with interest on one large oak, which grew on the left hand towards the river. It seemed a tree of extraordinary magnitude and picturesque beauty, and stood just where there appeared to be a few roods of open ground lying among huge stones, which had rolled down from the mountain. To add to the romance of the situation, the spot of clear ground extended round the foot of a proud-browed rock, from the summit of which leaped a mountain stream in a fall of sixty feet, in which it was dissolved into foam and dew. At the bottom of the fall, the rivulet with difficulty collected, like a routed general, its dispersed forces, and, as if tamed by its descent, found a noiseless passage through the heath to join the Awe."

Etive, beautifully fringed with wood. On the north side of the loch, about three miles from Taynuilt, are seen the ruins of Ardchattan Priory and Ardchattan House, covered with luxuriant ivy, and o'ercanopied by trees. The Priory was built by John Macdougal in the 13th century, and burnt by Colkitto during Montrose's wars. Robert Bruce held a Parliament here. In the distance are seen the dark mountains of Mull and Morven, and the green island of Lismore. Three miles farther is Connel Ferry, where, from the narrowness of the passage and a reef of sunken rocks, a very turbulent rapid is occasioned at particular states of the tide. In the immediate vicinity, antiquaries have placed the Pictish capital of Beregonium. There is also a vitrified fort. Three miles beyond Connel Ferry, are the ruins of Dunstaffnage Castle, at the entrance of Loch Etive. They occupy the summit of a perpendicular rock near the extremity of a low peninsular flat projection from the southern shore. Dunstaffnage was inhabited by the MacDougals till 1448, when it was taken by Bruce after his victory at the Pass of Awe. It is now a royal castle, the Duke of Argyle being hereditary keeper. From Dunstaffnage, the celebrated stone on which our Scottish monarchs used to be crowned, was transported to Scone, whence it was removed to England by Edward I., and it is now deposited beneath the coronation chair in the chapel of Edward the Confessor in Westminster Abbey. At a little distance from the castle is a small roofless chapel, where one of the Scottish kings is said to have been buried. Three miles from Dunstaffnage is the pleasant thriving village of Oban, situated at the head of a fine bay. The scenery in its neighbourhood is very romantic. In the vicinity is Dunolly Castle, the ancient fortress of the MacDougals of Lorn, situated on the point of a rocky promontory. Near it is Dunolly House, inhabited by the representative of that once powerful family.*

* Nothing can be more wildly beautiful than the situation of Dunolly. The ruins are situated upon a bold and precipitous promontory overhanging Loch Etive, and distant about a mile from the village and port of Oban. The principal part which remains is the donjon or keep; but fragments of other buildings, overgrown with ivy, attest that it had been once a place of importance, as large apparently as Artornish or Dunstaffnage. These fragments enclose a court-yard, of which the keep probably formed one side; the entrance being by a steep ascent from the neck of the isthmus, formerly cut across by a moat, and defended, doubtless, by outworks and a drawbridge. Beneath the castle stands the present mansion of the family, having on the one hand Loch Etive, with its islands and mountains, on the other two romantic eminences tufted with copsewood. There are other accompaniments suited to the scene; in particular, a huge upright pillar, or detached fragment of that sort of rock called plum-pudding stone, upon the shore, about a quarter of a mile from the castle. It is called *Clachna-cau*, or the Dog's Pillar, because Fingal is said to have used it as a stake to which he bound his celebrated dog, Bran. Others say, that when the Lord of the Isles came upon a visit to the Lord of Lorn, the dogs brought for his sport were kept beside this pillar. Upon the whole, a more delightful and romantic spot can scarce be conceived; and it receives a moral interest from the considerations attached to the residence of a family once powerful enough to confront aud defeat Robert Bruce, and now sunk into the shade of private life. It is at present possessed by Patrick MacDougal, Esq., the lineal and undisputed representative of the ancient Lords of Lorn. The heir of Dunolly fell in Spain, fighting under the Duke of Wellington,—a death well becoming his ancestry.

NINTH TOUR.

GLASGOW TO INVERNESS BY THE CALEDONIAN CANAL.

Tourists generally proceed to Oban by Lochgilphead and the Crinan Canal. There are two routes by land from Oban to Fort-William; the coast line by Connel Ferry and Appin, which is the shorter of the two, and the other by Taynuilt, Dalmally, and Glencoe. Loch Linnhe, bounded on the one hand by the craggy knolls of Appin, and on the other by the purple hills of Morven, is the commencement of that chain of salt and fresh water lakes formed into the Caledonian Canal, and presents on both sides scenery of a most romantic character. Opposite to the upper extremity of the island of Lismore, Loch Creran branches off into Lorn. The first mansion to the north of this loch is Airds, the seat of Sir John Campbell; next is the ruin of Castle Stalker, Appin House, (Downie of Appin,) next occurs, and after that, at the mouth of Loch Leven, Ardshiel, (Stewart, Esq.) From Ballachulish Ferry on Loch Leven, noted for its slate quarry, the West Highland road penetrates the savage vale of Glencoe. Coran Ferry, nine miles from Fort-William, divides Loch Linnhe from Loch Eil. Fort-William and the contiguous village of Maryburgh, stand on a bend of Loch Eil, near the confluence of the river Lochy. The fort was erected in the reign of William III. It is provided with a bomb-proof magazine, and its barracks accommodate about 100 men. Maryburgh

is a village of about 1500 inhabitants, and contains two respectable inns. Ben Nevis, which till lately was considered the highest mountain in Scotland, is one of the most striking features of this neighbourhood. It rises 4358 feet above the level of the sea, and its circumference at the base, which, upon one side, is almost washed by the sea, is supposed to exceed 24 miles. "Its northern front consists of two grand distinct ascents or terraces, the level top of the lowest of which, at an elevation of about 1700 feet, contains a wild tarn or mountain lake. The outer acclivities of this the lower part of the mountain are very steep, although covered with a short grassy sward, intermixed with heath; but at the lake this general vegetable clothing ceases. Here a strange scene of desolation presents itself. The upper and higher portion seems to meet us, as a new mountain, shooting up its black porphyritic rocks through the granitic masses, along which we have hitherto made our way, and, where not absolutely precipitous, its surface is strewed with angular fragments of stone of various sizes, wedged together, and forming a singularly rugged covering, among which we look in vain for any symptoms of vegetable life, except where round some pellucid spring the rare little Alpine plants, such as Epilobium alpinum, Silene acaulis, Saxifraga stellaris and nivalis, which live only in such deserts wild, are to be found putting forth their modest blossoms, amid the encircling moss. The eagle sallying from his eyry may greet the approach of the wanderer, or the mournful plover with plaintive note salute his ear; but for those birds of the mountain, the rocky wilderness were lifeless and silent as the grave; its only tenants the lightnings and the mists of heaven, and its language the voice of the storm."* A terrific precipice on the north-eastern side makes a sheer descent from the snow-capt summit of not less than 1500 feet. The tourist who is so fortunate as to ascend the mountain in a favourable state of the atmosphere, is rewarded with a prospect of remarkable extent and grandeur. Ben Lomond, Ben Cruachan, Ben More, Ben Lawers, Schehallion, and Cairngorm, rear their gigantic heads around, while other peaks, scarcely less aspiring, extend in countless number and infinite variety of form and character, to the extreme verge of the horizon.† Two miles from Fort-William stands the old Castle of In-

* Guide to the Highlands and Islands of Scotland, by George Anderson and Peter Anderson, Esquires. London, 1834.

† "The ascent of Ben Nevis usually occupies three hours and a half from the base of the mountain, and the descent rather more than half that time. Some travellers go up at night, that they may enjoy the sunrise: by doing so, they run a great risk of being disappointed, as in the morning the view is generally obscured by mists, and only occasional glimpses can be caught of the glorious prospect, which is generally clearest from mid-day to six o'clock in the evening. It is imprudent for a stranger to undertake the ascent without a guide, and one can always be procured about Fort-William for seven or eight shillings. The inexperienced traveller, also, may be the better of being reminded to carry with him some wine or spirits (which, however, should be used with caution), wherewith to qualify the spring water, which is, fortunately, abundant, and to which he will be fain to have frequent recourse, ere he attain the object of his labours. It is customary to ascend the hill on the northern side. By making a circuit to the eastward beyond Inverlochy Castle, the traveller can proceed as far as the lake on the back of a Highland pony."—*Anderson's Guide to the Highlands*, p. 268.

verlochy, and about three miles from the sea, on the river Lochy, are the ruinous walls of Tor Castle, the ancient seat of the clan Chattan. From Loch Eil to Loch Lochy the distance is eight miles. At Corpach are three locks, and a mile beyond, a series of eight locks called Neptune's Staircase. Each lock is 180 feet long, 40 broad, and 20 deep. Passing the villages of West and East Moy, the steamer, two miles farther, enters Loch Lochy, which is ten miles in length by about one in breadth; near the west end there is a fine bay, called the Bay of Arkaig, at a short distance from which is the mansion of Cameron of Lochiel, chief of that clan.

Between Loch Lochy and Loch Oich is the village of Laggan. The distance between the two lochs is nearly two miles. Loch Oich is about three and a half miles long by half a mile broad, and forms the summit level of the Caledonian Canal. Near the mouth of the river Garry, which discharges itself into this loch, are the ruins of Invergarry Castle, the ancient gathering-place of the clan Macdonell.

From Loch Oich, the steamboat descends to Loch Ness, by six locks; the distance between the locks being five and a half miles. At the south-western extremity of the latter and close upon the edge of the water, stands Fort Augustus. It was built shortly after the rebellion of 1715. In form it is quadrangular, with four bastions at the corners. The barracks contain accommodation for about 300 men.

Loch Ness is nearly twenty-four miles in length, and averages a mile and quarter in breadth. In many places it is of great depth and never freezes. The character of its scenery though highly interesting, is not so varied and striking as that through which we have already conducted the tourist.

A short distance from Fort Augustus, we pass the mouth of Glenmoriston, and the mansion of James Murray Grant, Esq., the proprietor, beautifully situated. A few miles farther on the right are Foyers House and the mouth of the river Foyers, where the steamer stops to afford passengers an opportunity of viewing the celebrated fall.

FALL OF FOYERS.

This famous cataract consists in reality of two falls, of which the lower is by far the most imposing. After being broken upon a projecting rock into a sheet of spray of dazzling whiteness, it is precipitated without further interruption, the stupendous depth of 212 feet. Nor is the sheet of water the sole attraction, for the banks on either side are diversified with the birch and the ash, and an undergrowth of copsewood, with those stupendous chasms and rocky eminences which confer additional grandeur on such a scene. About 2½ miles from this, on the left, are seen the ruins of Castle Urquhart, often noticed in the annals of the earlier Scottish monarchs. Glen Urquhart, which recedes behind the castle, is a beautiful Highland vale, containing many gentlemen's seats, and, at the mouth of the glen, there is a good inn called Drumindrochet. Glen Urquhart chiefly belongs to Grant of Grant. At the Ferry of Bona, 8½ miles from Drumindrochet, the steamer enters Loch Dochfour by a narrow channel about a quarter of a mile in length. At Lochend the steamer again enters the canal and proceeds to Muirton, where it descends by four locks to the level of Loch Beauly, an arm of the Murray Frith.

The Caledonian Canal was finally opened in October 1822. The whole distance ftom the Atlantic to the German Ocean is 60½ miles, of which 37 are through natural sheets of water, and 23 cut as a canal. The total disbursements up to the 1st of May 1831, were L.990,559. The revenue derived from the tonnage does not exceed L.3000 a-year.

For a description of Inverness, we refer to the Twelfth Tour.

TENTH TOUR.

STAFFA AND IONA.

Tourists wishing to proceed to Staffa usually leave Glasgow in a steamboat for Tobermory in Mull, touching at Oban in their way.

After leaving Oban, the steamer passes Kerrera, a narrow rugged island, forming a natural breakwater to the bay of Oban. It was here that Alexander II. died on his expedition in 1249, and here Haco, king of Norway, met the island chieftains, who assisted him in his ill-fated descent on the coasts of Scotland. Upon the south point of the island are the ruins of the Danish fort, Gylen. The boat now approaches Lismore,* a fertile island about nine miles in length and two in breadth. In ancient times it was the residence of the bishops of Argyle, who were frequently styled "Episcopi Lismorienses." Leaving Lismore on the right, the steamer enters the Sound of Mull, and passes the Lady Rock, visible only at low water, on which Maclean of Duart exposed his wife, a daughter of the second Earl of Argyle, intending that she should be swept away by the returning tide, but she was fortunately rescued by some of her father's people, who were passing in a boat. Maclean gave out that she had died suddenly, and was allowed to go through the ceremonial of a mock funeral, but was shortly afterwards put to death by the relations of his injured wife. This inci-

* *Leosmore*, that is, "the Great Garden."

dent has been made the subject of one of Joanna Baillie's dramas—the "Family Legend." On the brink of a high cliff on the shore of Mull is Duart Castle, formerly the seat of the chief of the warlike and powerful clan of the Macleans. The steamer now sails along through a narrow but deep channel. On the left are the bold and mountainous shores of Mull, on the right those of that district of Argyleshire called Morven, successively indented by deep salt water lochs running up many miles inland. To the south-eastward, arise a prodigious range of mountains, among which Ben Cruachan is pre-eminent. And to the north-east is the no less huge and picturesque range of the Ardnamurchan Hills. Many ruinous castles, situated generally upon cliffs overhanging the ocean, add interest to the scene. In fine weather a grander and more impressive scene, both from its natural beauties, and associations with ancient history and tradition, can hardly be imagined. When the weather is rough, the passage is both difficult and dangerous, from the narrowness of the channel, and in part from the number of inland lakes, out of which sally forth a number of conflicting and thwarting tides, making the navigation perilous to open boats. The sudden flaws and gusts of wind which issue, without a moment's warning, from the mountain glens, are equally formidable; so that, in unsettled weather, a stranger, if not much accustomed to the sea, may sometimes add to the other sublime sensations excited by the scene, that feeling of dignity which arises from a sense of danger.* Opposite to Duart, on the coast of Morven,

* Notes to the Lord of the Isles. The following sonnet was composed by Wordsworth in the Sound of Mull:

"Tradition, be thou mute! Oblivion, throw
Thy veil in mercy o'er the records, hung
Round strath and mountain, stamped by the ancient tongue
On rock and ruin darkening as we go,—

are the ruins of Ardtornish Castle, the scene of the opening canto of the "Lord of the Isles." "The situation is wild and romantic in the highest degree, having on the one hand a high and precipitous chain of rocks overhanging the sea, and on the other the narrow entrance to the beautiful salt water lake, called Loch Alline, which is in many places finely fringed with copsewood. The ruins of Ardtornish are not now very considerable, and consist chiefly of the remains of an old keep or tower, with fragments of outward defences. But in former days it was a place of great consequence, being one of the principal strongholds which the Lords of the Isles, during the period of their stormy independence, possessed upon the mainland of Argyleshire." Above the castle of Ardtornish, is Ardtornish House (Gregorson, Esq.) Another residence of the Island Kings next meets the eye in the Castle of Aros in Mull, a powerful rock-built fortress, situated about half-way from either end of the Sound.† A short way beyond on the Morven coast, is Killandine Castle. Holding on towards the head of the Sound, the steamer, seven miles beyond Aros, reaches Tobermory, (the well of our Lady St. Mary,) the only village of any note in Mull. It was founded in 1788 by the British Fishery Company and is finely situated at the head of the inner

Spots where a word, ghost-like, survives to show
What crimes from hate, or desperate love, have sprung;
From honour misconceived, or fancied wrong,
What feuds, not quenched but fed by mutual woe.
Yet, though a wild vindictive Race, untamed
By civil arts and labours of the pen,
Could gentleness be scorned by those fierce Men,
Who, to spread wide the reverence they claimed
For patriarchal occupations, named
Yon towering Peaks, 'Shepherds of Etive Glen*?'"

† From the village of Aros there is a road which leads across the island to Loch-na-Keal, and thence to Laggan Ulva, where there is a place of embarkation for Staffa and Iona.

* In Gaelic, *Buachaill Eite*.

recess of a well protected bay. In the immediate vicinity is Drimfin, the splendid mansion of Maclean of Coll. This romantic spot is well worthy the notice of the tourist. Quitting Tobermory, we enter Loch Sunart. Seven miles from Tobermory, on the Ardnamurchan coast, is the castle of Mingarry, which

> ——— ——— sternly placed,
> O'erawes the woodland and the waste.

The ruins, which are tolerably entire, are surrounded by a very high wall, forming a kind of polygon, for the purpose of adapting itself to the projecting angles of a precipice overhanging the sea, on which the castle stands. It was anciently the residence of the MacIans, a clan of MacDonalds, descended from Ian or John, a grandson of Angus Og, Lord of the Isles. Rounding the point of Cullich, the last promontory of Mull, we find ourselves moving freely on the bosom of the Atlantic, and at the same moment, if the weather is fine, the islands of Mull, including the Treshnish Isles, Tiree, Coll, Muck, Eig, and Rum, burst on the view, and, far to the north-west, the faint outlines of South Uist and Barra.

Staffa is about eight miles distant from the western coast of Mull. It is of an irregular oval shape, and about three-fourths of a mile in length by half a mile in breadth. The most elevated point is toward the south-west, where the rock attains an elevation of about 144 feet. The first cave approached is the Clam or Scallop-shell Cave, on one side of which the basaltic columns appear bent like the ribs of a ship, while the opposite wall is made up of the ends of horizontal columns, resembling the surface of a honeycomb. This cave is 30 feet in height, and 16 or 18 in breadth at the entrance, its length being 130 feet. Next occurs the noted rock Buachaille or the Herds-

FINGAL'S CAVE, STAFFA.

man, a conoidal pile of columns about 30 feet high. From this spot the pillars extend in one continued colonnade along the whole face of the cliff to the entrance of Fingal's Cave, by far the most impressive and interesting object in the island. The height from the water at mean tide to the top of the arch at the entrance is 66, its breadth 42, and its whole length is 227 feet. The sides within are columnar, and for the most part perpendicular, the columns being broken and grouped in many different ways. As the sea never entirely ebbs from this cave, the beautiful green water forms the only flooring, along which a boat may be pushed. Nothing can surpass the beautiful symmetry and grandeur of this wondrous pile. In the language of Sir Walter Scott:—

> "Where, as to shame the temples deck'd
> By skill of earthly architect,

Nature herself, it seem'd, would raise
A Minster to her Maker's praise!
Not for a meaner use ascend
Her columns, or her arches bend;
Nor of a theme less solemn tells
That mighty surge that ebbs and swells,
And still, between each awful pause,
From the high vault an answer draws,
In varied tone prolong'd and high,
That mocks the organ's melody.
Nor doth its entrance front in vain
To old Iona's holy fane,
That Nature's voice might seem to say,
'Well hast thou done, frail Child of clay!
Thy humble powers that stately shrine
Task'd high and hard—but witness mine!'"

"This palace of Neptune," the Poet adds in a note to these noble lines, "is even grander upon a second than the first view. The stupendous columns which form the sides of the cave, the depth and strength of the tide which rolls its deep and heavy swell up to the extremity of the vault—the variety of tints formed by white, crimson, and yellow stalactites, or petrifactions, which occupy the vacancies between the base of the broken pillars which form the roof, and intersect them with a rich, curious, and variegated chasing, occupying each interstice—the corresponding variety below water, where the ocean rolls over a dark-red or violet-coloured rock, from which, as from a base, the basaltic columns arise—the tremendous noise of the swelling tide, mingling with the deep-toned echoes of the vault,—are circumstances elsewhere unparalleled."* The Boat Cave, and Mackinnon's,

* On this cave Wordsworth has composed the following sonnet:

"Thanks for the lessons of this Spot—fit school
For the presumptuous thoughts that would assign
Mechanic laws to agency divine;

or the Cormorant's Cave, are two of less extent and beauty, which are usually visited after Fingal's Cave.

IONA.

Iona or Icolmkill, celebrated as an early seat of Christianity, is about nine miles to the south of Staffa. "In any other situation," says Dr. Macculloch, "the remains of Iona would be consigned to neglect and oblivion; but, connected as they are with an age distinguished by the ferocity of its manners and its independence of regular government; standing a solitary monument of religion and literature, such as religion and literature then were, the mind imperceptibly recurs to the time when this island was 'the light of the western world,' 'a gem in the ocean,' and is led to contemplate with veneration its silent and ruined structures. Even at a distance, the

And, measuring heaven by earth, would overrule
Infinite Power. The pillared vestibule,
Expanding yet precise, the roof embowed,
Might seem designed to humble man, when proud
Of his best workmanship by plan and tool.
Down-bearing with his whole Atlantic weight
Of tide and tempest on the Structure's base,
And flashing to that Structure's topmost height,
Ocean has proved its strength, and of its grace
In calms is conscious, finding for his freight
Of softest music some responsive place."

aspect of the cathedral, insignificant as its dimensions are, produces a strong feeling of delight in him who, long coasting the rugged and barren rocks of Mull, or buffeted by turbulent waves, beholds its tower first rising out of the deep, giving to this desolate region an air of civilization, and recalling the consciousness of that human society, which, presenting elsewhere no visible traces, seems to have abandoned these rocky shores to the cormorant and the sea-gull." Iona is nearly three miles in length and one in breadth. The origin of the celebrity of this island* is to be traced to its having become, about the year 565, the residence of Columba, an Irish Christian preacher. The monastery became, in subsequent years, the dwelling of the Cluniacenses, a class of monks who

* The following splendid and well known passage records the emotions excited in the breast of Dr. Johnson by the prospect of Iona, "We were now heading that illustrious island which was once the luminary of the Caledonian regions, whence savage clans and raving barbarians derived the benefits of knowledge, and the blessings of religion. To abstract the mind from all local emotion would be impossible, if it were endeavoured, and would be foolish if it were possible. Whatever withdraws us from the power of our senses—whatever makes the past, the distant, or the future predominate over the present, advances us in the dignity of thinking beings. Far from me and from my friends be such frigid philosophy as may conduct us indifferent and unmoved over any ground which has been dignified by wisdom, bravery, or virtue. That man is little to be envied whose patriotism would not gain force upon the plains of Marathon, or whose piety would not grow warm among the ruins of Iona." Wordsworth has composed the following sonnet upon landing at Iona:

"How sad a welcome! To each voyager
Some ragged child holds up for sale a store
Of wave-worn pebbles, pleading on the shore
Where once came monk and nun with gentle stir,
Blessings to give, news ask, or suit prefer.
Yet is yon neat trim church a grateful speck
Of novelty amid the sacred wreck
Strewn far and wide. Think, proud Philosopher!
Fallen though she be, this Glory of the west,
Still on her sons the beams of mercy shine;
And 'hopes, perhaps more heavenly bright than thine,
A grace by thee unsought and unpossest,
A faith more fixed, a rapture more divine
Shall gild their passage to eternal rest.'"

followed the rule of St. Bennet. At the Reformation, Iona, with its abbey, was annexed to the bishopric of Argyle by James VI. in the year 1617. The celebrated ruins consist of a cathedral, a nunnery, and St. Oran's Chapel. The latter, which appears to be the oldest building now standing, is of small extent (60 feet by 20) and rude architectural style, and was probably built by the Norwegians. It contains some tombs of different dates, and there are many carved stones in the pavement. The chapel of the nunnery is the next in the order of antiquity; it is in good preservation; the roof has been vaulted, and part of it remains. The nuns were not displaced at the Reformation, but continued, a long time after that event, to live together. They followed the rule of St. Augustine. The Cathedral Church of St. Mary is the principal edifice; it has obviously been erected at two distinct periods. Its present form is that of a cross, the length being about 160 feet; the breadth 24; the tower is about 70 feet high, divided into three stories. Most families of distinction in the Highlands had burying-places here, and many erected votive chapels in different parts of the island. On the west side of Martyrs' Street is Maclean's Cross, a beautifully carved pillar, and one of the 360 stone crosses which once adorned the island; but about the year 1560, they were thrown into the sea by order of the Synod of Argyle. Iona contains 450 inhabitants, and is the property of the Duke of Argyle.

"Homeward we turn. Isle of Columba's Cell,
Where Christian piety's soul-cheering spark
(Kindled from Heaven between the light and dark
Of time) shone like the morning-star, farewell!—

And fare thee well, to Fancy visible,
Remote St. Kilda, lone and loved sea-mark
For many a voyage made in her swift bark,
When, with more hues than in the rainbow dwell,
Thou a mysterious intercourse dost hold;
Extracting from clear skies and air serene,
And out of sun-bright waves, a lucid veil,
That thickens, spreads, and, mingling fold with fold,
Makes known, when thou no longer canst be seen,
Thy whereabout to warn the approaching sail."

ELEVENTH TOUR.

GLASGOW—BOTHWELL CASTLE AND BRIDGE—HAMILTON—LANARK—FALLS OF CLYDE.

Leaving Glasgow,* the tourist proceeds eastward, and passes Camlachie and Tollcross, where there are extensive coal and iron works. On the opposite side of the Clyde is the ancient royal burgh of Rutherglen, formerly a place of some importance, but now much reduced. In the church of Rutherglen a peace was concluded between the Scotch and English, 8th February 1297. All along the sides of the road are numerous elegant villas. Five and a half miles from Glasgow is Broomhouse Toll, where a road strikes off on the left to Holytown and Kirk of Shotts. A little farther on, the road crosses the North Calder by a bridge, and shortly after reaches the village of Uddingston, situated on an eminence commanding a delightful view. A short way beyond, on the right, are the magnificent ruins of

BOTHWELL CASTLE.

This noble structure is built of red freestone, and consists of a large oblong quadrangle, flanked towards the south by two huge circular towers, and covering an area of 234 feet in length and 99 feet in breadth. The origin

* There is another road from Glasgow to Hamilton on the other side of the Clyde, by Rutherglen, but it is by no means so interesting as the route described.

of the castle is unknown, but in the wars between Bruce and Baliol, Edward I. made a grant of it to Aymer de Valence, whom he had appointed governor of Scotland. In this fortress a number of the English nobility took refuge after the battle of Bannockburn, but were speedily obliged to surrender. Bruce bestowed Bothwell Castle

BOTHWELL CASTLE.

on Andrew Murray, who had married that monarch's sister. It next came into the possession of Archibald the Grim, Earl of Douglas, who married the grand-daughter of Andrew Murray. After the forfeiture of the Douglasses, in 1445, it was successively possessed by the Crichtons, John Ramsay, a favourite of James III., and the Hepburns, Earls of Bothwell. After the forfeiture of the infamous nobleman of that name, it passed through several hands, till it at last reverted to the noble family of Douglas.* The present residence of Lord Douglas is

* The following beautiful description of Bothwell Castle and the surrounding scenery, is given in the Notes to Wordsworth's Poems, Vol. v. p. 379:—" It was exceedingly delightful to enter thus unexpectedly upon such a beautiful region. The castle stands nobly, overlooking the Clyde. When we came up to it, I was hurt to see that flower-borders had taken place of the natural overgrowings of the ruin, the scattered stones and wild plants. It is a large and grand pile of red freestone, harmonising perfectly with the rocks of the river, from which, no doubt, it has been hewn. When I was a little accustomed to the unnaturalness

a plain mansion standing on a beautiful lawn near the

of a modern garden, I could not help admiring the excessive beauty and luxuriance of some of the plants, particularly the purple-flowered clematis, and a broad-leafed creeping plant without flowers, which scrambled up the castle wall, along with the ivy, and spread its vine-like branches so lavishly that it seemed to be in its natural situation, and one could not help thinking that, though not self-planted among the ruins of this country, it must somewhere have its native abode in such places. If Bothwell Castle had not been close to the Douglas mansion, we should have been disgusted with the possessor's miserable conception of *adorning* such a venerable ruin; but it is so very near to the house, that of necessity the pleasure-grounds must have extended beyond it, and perhaps the neatness of a shaven lawn and the complete desolation natural to a ruin might have made an unpleasing contrast; and, besides being within the precincts of the pleasure-grounds, and so very near to the dwelling of a noble family, it has forfeited, in some degree, its independent majesty, and becomes a tributary to the mansion; its solitude being interrupted, it has no longer the command over the mind in sending it back into past times, or excluding the ordinary feelings which we bear about us in daily life. We had then only to regret that the castle and the house were so near to each other; and it was impossible *not* to regret it; for the ruin presides in state over the river, far from city or town, as if it might have a peculiar privilege to preserve its memorials of past ages, and maintain its own character for centuries to come. We sat upon a bench under the high trees, and had beautiful views of the different reaches of the river, above and below. On the opposite bank, which is finely wooded with elms and other trees, are the remains of a priory built upon a rock, and rock and ruin are so blended, that it is impossible to separate the one from the other. Nothing can be more beautiful than the little remnant of this holy place: elm trees (for we were near enough to distinguish them by their branches) grow out of the walls, and overshadow a small, but very elegant window. It can scarcely be conceived what a grace the castle and priory impart to each other; and the river Clyde flows on, smooth and unruffled below, seeming to my thoughts more in harmony with the sober and stately images of former times, than if it had roared over a rocky channel, forcing its sound upon the ear. It blended gently with the warbling of the smaller birds, and the chattering of the larger ones, that had made their nests in the ruins. In this fortress the chief of the English nobility were confined after the battle of Bannockburn. If a man *is* to be a prisoner, he scarcely could have a more pleasant place to solace his captivity; but I thought that, for close confinement, I should prefer the banks of a lake, or the seaside. The greatest charm of a brook or river is in the liberty to pursue it through its windings; you can then take it in whatever mood you like; silent or noisy, sportive or quiet. The beauties of a brook or river must be sought, and the pleasure is in going in search of them; those of a lake or of the sea come to you of themselves. These rude warriors cared little, perhaps, about either; and yet, if one may judge from the writings of Chaucer, and from the old romances, more interesting passions were connected with natural objects in the days of chivalry than now: though going in search of scenery, as it is called, had not then been thought of. I had previously heard nothing of Bothwell Castle, at least nothing that I remembered; therefore, perhaps, my pleasure was greater, compared with what I received elsewhere, than others might feel."

old castle. It was built by the young Earl of Forfar, who was killed at the battle of Sheriffmuir. The scenery around Bothwell Castle is remarkably splendid, and is adorned with luxuriant natural wood. The Clyde here makes a beautiful sweep, and forms the fine semicircular declivity called Bothwell Bank, celebrated in Scottish song. The following interesting anecdote, which has been quoted from a work entitled, "Verstegan's Restitution of Decayed Intelligence," printed at Antwerp in 1605, is a proof of the antiquity of at least the air to which the song of "Bothwell Bank" is sung:—"So fell it out of late years, that an English gentleman, travelling in Palestine, not far from Jerusalem, as he passed through a country town, he heard, by chance, a woman sitting at her door, dandling her child, to sing, *Bothwel bank, thou blumest fair.* The gentleman hereat wondered, and forthwith, in English, saluted the woman, who joyfully answered him; and said, she was right glad there to see a gentleman of our isle: and told him, that she was a Scottish woman, and came first from Scotland to Venice, and from Venice thither, where her fortune was to be the wife of an officer under the Turk; who being at that instant absent, and very soon to return, she entreated the gentleman to stay there until his return. The which he did; and she, for country sake, to show herself the more kind and bountiful unto him, told her husband, at his home-coming, that the gentleman was her kinsman; whereupon her husband entertained him very kindly; and, at his departure, gave him divers things of good value."—Leyden makes the following allusion to this story in his Ode on Scottish music:—

"And thus the exiled Scotian maid,
By fond alluring love betrayed,
To visit Syria's date-crown'd shore,
In plaintive strains that soothed despair,
Did 'Bothwell's Banks that bloom so fair,'
And scenes of early youth deplore.'

Directly opposite to Bothwell Castle, on the south bank of the Clyde, are the ruins of Blantyre Priory, situated on the brink of a perpendicular rock.

Proceeding onwards, at the distance of a mile and a half, the tourist reaches Bothwell village and church. The old church which is still standing, is a lofty Gothic fabric, cased all over with a thin coating of stone. Within its walls, the unfortunate Robert Duke of Rothsay, who was starved to death by his uncle the Duke of Albany, in Falkland Palace, was married to a daughter of Archibald the Grim, Earl of Douglas.

At a little distance in front, the tourist crosses the Clyde by Bothwell Bridge, the scene of the famous battle which took place in 1679, between the royal forces under the Duke of Monmouth and the Covenanters. The royal army moved towards Hamilton, and reached Bothwell-moor on the 22d of June. The insurgents were encamped chiefly in the Duke of Hamilton's park along the Clyde, which separated the two armies. Bothwell Bridge was then long and narrow, having a portal in the middle with gates, which the Covenanters shut and barricadoed with stones and logs of timber. This important post was defended by 300 of their best men, under Hackston of Rathillet and Hall of Haughhead. The more moderate of the insurgents waited upon Monmouth to offer terms, and procured a promise that he would interpose with his Majesty on their behalf, on condition of their immediately dispersing themselves and yielding up their arms. The Cameronian party, however, would accede to no terms with an uncovenanted king, and while they were debating on the Duke's proposal, his field-pieces were already planted on the eastern side of the river to cover the attack of the footguards, who were led on by Lord Livingstone, to force the bridge. Here Hackston maintained his post with zeal and courage, nor was it until all his ammunition was expended, and every support denied him by the general, that he reluctantly abandoned the important pass. When his party were drawn back, the Duke's army slowly and with their cannon in front, defiled along the bridge and formed in line of battle as they came over the river. The Duke commanded the foot and Claverhouse the cavalry. It would seem that these movements could not have been performed without at least some loss, had the enemy been serious in opposing them. But the insurgents were otherwise employed. With the strangest delusion that ever fell upon devoted beings, they chose these precious moments to cashier their officers and elect others in their room. In this important operation they were at length disturbed by the Duke's cannon, at the very first discharge of which, the horse of the Covananters wheeled and rode off, breaking and trampling down the ranks of the infantry in their flight. Monmouth humanely issued orders to stop the effusion of blood, but Claverhouse, burning to avenge his defeat, and the death of his cornet and kinsman at Drumclog, made great slaughter among the fugitives, of whom 400 were slain. These events are thus described in *Clyde*, a poem by Wilson, reprinted in *Scottish Descriptive Poems*, edited by the late Dr. Leyden, Edinburgh, 1803 :—

"Where Bothwell's Bridge connects the margin steep,
And Clyde below runs silent, strong, and deep,
The hardy peasant by oppression driven
To battle, deem'd his cause the cause of Heaven;
Unskill'd in arms, with useless courage stood,
While gentle Monmouth grieved to shed his blood;
But fierce Dundee, inflamed with deadly hate,
In vengeance for the great Montrose's fate,
Let loose the sword, and to the hero's shade
A barbarous hecatomb of victims paid."*

Many of the fugitives found shelter in the wooded parks around Hamilton Palace.

Great changes have now been made on the scene of the engagement. The gateway-gate and house of the bridge-ward were long ago removed. The original breadth of the bridge was twelve feet, but in 1826, twenty-two feet were added to its breadth, the hollow which once lay at the Hamilton extremity was filled up, and an alteration was also made in the road at the other end. The open park in which the Covenanters were posted is now changed into enclosed fields and plantations, and the moor upon which the royal army advanced to the engagement, is now a cultivated and beautiful region.

The level grounds which stretch away from Bothwell Bridge along the north-east bank of the river, once formed the patrimonial estate of Hamilton of Bothwellhaugh, the assassin of the Regent Murray.

A mile and a half beyond Bothwell Bridge, and ten miles and a half from Glasgow, the tourist enters the town of

HAMILTON,

the capital of the Middle Ward of Lanarkshire. Hamil-

* See notes to the ballad of "The Battle of Bothwell Bridge," in the Border Minstrelsy. The reader cannot but remember the spirited description given of this engagement in the novel of Old Mortality.

ton is a burgh of regality, dependent on the Duke of Hamilton; it contains about 6000 inhabitants, of whom a considerable number are engaged in weaving. The principal object of attraction in this vicinity is Hamilton Palace, the seat of the Duke of Hamilton, which stands on a plain between the town and the river. It is a magnificent structure, and has been greatly enlarged and improved by the present Duke. Its interior is extremely splendid, and it contains a magnificent collection of paintings, which is supposed to be by far the best in Scotland. The most celebrated of these is *Daniel in the Lion's Den,* by Rubens.* Among other curiosities, Hamilton Palace contains the carbine with which Bothwellhaugh shot the Regent Murray.

Near Hamilton is the river Avon, a tributary of the Clyde. The vale which this stream waters is adorned with gorgeous old wood, and several ancient and modern mansions, the most famous of which is Cadyow or Cadzow Castle, the ancient baronial residence of the family of Hamilton, situated upon the precipitous banks of the Avon, about two miles above its junction with the Clyde. It was dismantled in the conclusion of the civil wars during the reign of the unfortunate Mary. The situation

* On this splendid picture Wordsworth has composed the following sonnet:

"Amid a fertile region green with wood
And fresh with rivers, well doth it become
The ducal Owner, in his palace-home
To naturalise this tawny Lion brood:
Children of Art, that claim strange brotherhood
(Couched in their den) with those that roam at large
Over the burning wilderness, and charge
The wind with terror while they roar for food.
Satiate are *these;* and still—to eye and ear;
Hence, while we gaze, a more enduring fear!
Yet is the Prophet calm, nor would the cave
Daunt him—if his Companions, now be-drowsed,
Outstretched and listless, were by hunger roused:
Man placed him here, and God, he knows, can save."

of the ruins, embossed in wood, darkened by ivy and creeping shrubs, and overhanging the brawling torrent, is romantic in the highest degree. In the immediate vicinity of Cadyow is a grove of immense oaks, the remains of the Caledonian forest which anciently extended through the south of Scotland from the Eastern to the Atlantic Ocean. Some of these trees measure twenty-five feet and upwards in circumference, and the state of decay in which they now appear, shows that they may have witnessed the rites of the Druids. The whole scenery is included in the magnificent and extensive Park of the Duke of Hamilton. The famous breed of Scottish wild cattle, milk-white in colour, with black muzzles, horns, and hoofs, are still preserved in this forest. They were expelled about 1760 on account of their ferocity, but have since been restored.* The following description of their habits is abridged from an article, by the Rev. W. Patrick, in the Quarterly Journal of Agriculture:—

"I am inclined to believe that the Hamilton breed of cattle is the oldest in Scotland, or perhaps in Britain. Although Lord Tankerville has said they have 'no wild habits,' I am convinced, from personal observation, that this is one of their peculiar features. In browsing their extensive pasture, they always keep close together, never scattering or straggling over it, a peculiarity which does not belong to the Kyloe, or any other breed, from the wildest or most inhospitable regions of the Highlands. The white cows are also remarkable for their systematic manner of feeding. At different periods of the year their tactics are different, but by those acquainted with their habits they are always found about the same part of the forest at the same hour of the day. In the height of

* See notes to the ballad of Cadyow Castle in the Border Minstrelsey.

summer, they always bivouac for the night towards the northern extremity of the forest; from this point they start in the morning, and browse to the southern extremity, and return at sunset to their old rendezvous; and during these perambulations they always feed *en masse.*

SCOTTISH WILD OX.

"The bulls are seldom ill-natured, but when they are so, they display a disposition more than ordinarily savage, cunning, pertinacious, and revengeful. A poor bird-catcher, when exercising his vocation among the 'Old Oaks,' as the park is familiarly called, chanced to be attacked by a savage bull. By great exertion he gained a tree before his assailant made up to him. Here he had occasion to observe the habits of the animal. It did not roar or bellow, but merely grunted, the whole body quivered with passion and savage rage, and he frequently attacked the tree with his head and hoofs. Finding all to no purpose, he left off the vain attempt, began to browse, and removed to some distance from the tree. The bird-catcher tried to descend, but this watchful Cerberus was again instantly at his post, and it was not till after six hours' imprisonment, and various bouts at 'bo-peep' as above, that the unfortunate man was relieved by some shepherds with their dogs. A writer's apprentice, who had been at the village of Quarter on business, and who returned by the 'Oaks' as a 'near-hand cut,' was also attacked by one of these savage brutes, near the northern extremity of the forest. He was fortunate, however, in getting into a tree, but was watched by the bull, and kept there during the whole of the night, and till near two o'clock next day.

"These animals are never taken and killed like other cattle, but are always shot in the field. I once went to see a bull and some cows destroyed in this manner—not by any means for the sake of the sight—but to observe the manner and habits of the animal under peculiar circumstances. When the shooters approached, they, as usual, scampered off in a body, then stood still, tossed their heads on high, and seemed to snuff the wind; the manœuvre was often repeated, till they got so hard pressed (and seemingly having a sort of half-idea of the tragedy which was to be performed), they at length ran furiously in a mass, always preferring the sides of the fence and sheltered situations, and dexterously taking advantage of any inequality in the ground, or other circumstances, to conceal themselves from the assailing foe. In their flight the bulls, or stronger of the flock, always took the lead; a smoke ascended from them which could be seen at a great distance; and they were often so close together, like sheep, that a carpet would have covered them. The cows which had young, on the first 'tug of war,' all retreated to the thickets where their calves were concealed; from prudential motives, they are never, if possible, molested. These and other wild habits I can testify to be inherent in the race, and are well known to all who have an opportunity of acquainting themselves with them."

Sir Walter Scott has made Cadyow Castle the subject of the following magnificent ballad, the perusal of which must gratify every lover of poetry and of historical recollections :—

"'Tis night—the shade of keep and spire
  Obscurely dance on Evan's stream,
And on the wave the warder's fire
  Is chequering the moon-light beam.

Fades slow their light; the east is grey;
  The weary warder leaves his tower,
Steeds snort; uncoupled stag-hounds bay,
  And merry hunters quit the bower.

The draw-bridge falls—they hurry out—
  Clatters each plank and swinging chain,
As, dashing o'er, the jovial rout
  Urge the shy steed, and slack the rein.

First of his troop, the chief rode on;
  His shouting merry-men throng behind;
The steed of princely Hamilton
  Was fleeter than the mountain wind.

From the thick copse the roe-bucks bound,
  The startling red-deer scuds the plain,
For the hoarse bugle's warrior sound
  Has roused their mountain haunts again.

Through the huge oaks of Evandale,
  Whose limbs a thousand years have worn,
What sullen roar comes down the gale,
  And drowns the hunter's pealing horn?

Mightiest of all the beasts of chase,
  That roam in woody Caledon,
Crashing the forest in his race,
  The Mountain Bull comes thundering on.

Fierce, on the hunters' quiver'd band,
  He rolls his eyes of swarthy glow,
Spurns, with black hoof and horn, the sand,
  And tosses high his mane of snow.

Aim'd well, the chieftain's lance has flown;
  Struggling in blood, the savage lies;
His roar is sunk in hollow groan—
  Sound, merry huntsmen! sound the *pryse!**

'Tis noon—against the knotted oak
  The hunters rest the idle spear;
Curls through the trees the slender smoke,
  Where yeomen dight the woodland cheer.

Proudly the chieftain mark'd his clan,
  On greenwood lap all careless thrown,
Yet miss'd his eye the boldest man,
  That bore the name of Hamilton.

'Why fills not Bothwellhaugh his place,
  Still wont our weal and woe to share?
Why comes he not our sport to grace?
  Why shares he not our hunter's fare?'

Stern Claud replied, with darkening face,
  (Grey Paisley's haughty lord was he)
'At merry feast, or buxom chase,
  No more the warrior shalt thou see.

'Few suns have set, since Woodhouselee
  Saw Bothwellhaugh's bright goblets foam,
When to his hearth, in social glee,
  The war-worn soldier turn'd him home.

There, wan from her maternal throes,
  His Margaret, beautiful and mild,
Sate in her bower, a pallid rose,
  And peaceful nurs'd her new-born child.

'O change accurs'd! past are those days;
  False Murray's ruthless spoilers came,
And, for the hearth's domestic blaze,
  Ascends destruction's volumed flame.

'What sheeted phantom wanders wild,
  Where mountain Eske through woodland flows.
Her arms enfold a shadowy child—
  Oh is it she, the pallid rose?

* The note blown at the death of the game.

'The wildered traveller sees her glide,
And hears her feeble voice with awe—
"Revenge," she cries, "on Murray's pride!
And woe for injured Bothwellhaugh?"

He ceased—and cries of rage and grief
Burst mingling from the kindred band,
And half arose the kindling chief,
And half unsheath'd his Arran brand.

But who, o'er bush, o'er stream and rock,
Rides headlong with resistless speed,
Whose bloody poniard's frantic stroke
Drives to the leap his jaded steed?

Whose cheek is pale, whose eye-balls glare,
As one, some visioned sight that saw;
Whose hands are bloody, loose his hair?—
—'Tis he! 'tis he! 'tis Bothwellhaugh.

From gory selle,* and reeling steed,
Sprung the fierce horseman with a bound,
And, reeking from the recent deed,
He dashed his carbine on the ground.

Sternly he spoke—' 'Tis sweet to hear
In good greenwood the bugle blown,
But sweeter to Revenge's ear,
To drink a tyrant's dying groan.

'Your slaughtered quarry proudly trod,
At dawning morn, o'er dale and down,
But prouder base-born Murray rode
Thro' old Linlithgow's crowded town.

'From the wild Border's humbled side,
In haughty triumph, marched he,
While Knox relaxed his bigot pride,
And smiled the traitorous pomp to see.

'But, can stern Power, with all his vaunt,
Or Pomp, with all her courtly glare,
The settled heart of Vengeance daunt,
Or change the purpose of Despair?

* Saddle. A word used by Spencer, and other ancient authors.

'With hackbut bent,* my secret stand,
 Dark as the purposed deed, I chose,
And marked, where, mingling in his band,
 Troop'd Scottish pikes, and English bows.

'Dark Morton, girt with many a spear,
 Murder's foul minion, led the van;
And clashed their broad-swords in the rear,
 The wild Macfarlanes' plaided clan.

'Glencairn and stout Parkhead were nigh,
 Obsequious at their regent's rein,
And haggard Lindesay's iron eye,
 That saw fair Mary weep in vain.

'Mid pennon'd spears, a steely grove,
 Proud Murray's plumage floated high;
Scarce could his trampling charger move,
 So close the minions crowded nigh.

'From the raised vizor's shade his eye,
 Dark-rolling, glanced the ranks along,
And his steel truncheon, waved on high,
 Seem'd marshalling the iron throng.

'But yet his sadden'd brow confess'd
 A passing shade of doubt and awe;
Some fiend was whispering in his breast,
 "Beware of injured Bothwellhaugh!"

'The death-shot parts—the charger springs—
 Wild rises tumult's startling roar!
And Murray's plumy helmet rings—
 Rings on the ground to rise no more.

'What joy the raptured youth can feel,
 To hear her love the loved one tell,
Or he who broaches on his steel
 The wolf, by whom his infant fell!

'But dearer to my injured eye,
 To see in dust proud Murray roll;
And mine was ten times trebled joy,
 To hear him groan his felon soul.

* Gun cock'd.

'My Margaret's spectre glided near:
  With pride her bleeding victim saw;
And shrieked in his death-deafen'd ear,
  "Remember injured Bothwellhaugh!"

'Then speed thee, noble Chatelrault!
  Spread to the wind thy bannered tree!
Each warrior bend his Clydesdale bow!—
  Murray is fallen, and Scotland free.'

Vaults every warrior to his steed;
  Loud bugles join their wild acclaim—
'Murray is fallen, and Scotland freed!
  Couch Arran! couch thy spear of flame!'"

Opposite Cadyow is Chatelherault, a summer residence of the Duke of Hamilton, so called from the estate and dukedom in France anciently possessed by his Grace's ancestors.*

Leaving Hamilton, the tourist proceeds in a south easterly direction, and at the distance of half-a-mile crosses the Avon. On the opposite bank of the Clyde is Dalziel House (General Hamilton,) surrounded by fine plantations. The views now obtained of the river and the surrounding scenery are extremely fine. This district, which is commonly termed "the Fruit Lands," and is eminently worthy of the appellation, has been justly characterized as "one uninterrupted series of grove, garden, and orchard,—a billowy ocean of foliage, waving in the summer wind, and glowing under the summer sun." A mile beyond Avon Bridge, the Carlisle road strikes off on the right towards Douglasdale. The road now descends gradually towards the margin of the river. On the opposite bank is Cambusnethan, (R. Lockhart, Esq.) a fine

* The banks of the South Calder, which lie at no great distance from Hamilton, are extremely romantic and adorned with a number of fine seats, the most remarkable of which are Wishaw Castle, (Lord Belhaven), Coltness (General David Stewart Denham,) Murdieston, (Admiral Sir A. Inglis Cochrane,) Allanton, (Sir Henry Stewart, Bart.) &c.

castellated mansion, shaded by splendid lime trees. Six miles from Hamilton, the tourist crosses the Clyde at Garrion Bridge, which derives its name from a seat of Lord Belhaven's in the immediate vicinity. At this spot the road from Edinburgh to Ayr crosses the Clyde. A mile beyond is the delightful bower-like village of Dalserf, celebrated for its excellent orchards. On the left is Dalserf House, (Hamilton, Esq.) and on the right, Millburn House, (Campbell, Esq.) On the opposite bank of the river is Brownlee, (Harvie, Esq.) and the stately mansion of Mauldslie Castle, the seat of the last Earl of Hyndford, now the property of Nisbet of Carfin.* A little farther on is Milton, (Captain Lockhart,) and Waygateshaw, (Steel, Esq.) Two miles and a half beyond Dalserf the tourist crosses the river Nethan by a bridge. On the right, near the junction of the Nethan and the Clyde, are the ruins of the Castle of Craignethan or Draphane, situated on a single rock overhanging the former stream. Craignethan appears to have been at one time a most extensive and important fortress. It was the seat of Sir James Hamilton, called the Bastard of Arran, a man noted for his sanguinary character in the reign of James V.; and here Queen Mary lodged for a few days after her escape from Lochleven. Craignethan has furnished the Author of "Old Mortality" with his description of Tillietudlem. It is now the property of Lord Douglas. The scenery around the Castle exhibits a striking mixture of the sublime and beautiful. A short way beyond, on the north bank of the river, is Carfin House, (Nisbet, Esq.) and soon after the road enters the

* Robert Bruce granted ten merks sterling out of his mills at Mauldslie for the purpose of keeping a lamp constantly burning upon St. Machute's tomb at Lesmahago. The lamp was kept burning till the Reformation.

plantations of Stonebyres, (Vere, Esq.) The channel of the river now becomes rugged and confined, and the banks more precipitous, and in a short time the tourist reaches the first of the Falls of the Clyde as he approaches from the west,

THE FALL OF STONEBYRES.

The river here makes three distinct falls, being broken by two projecting rocks. The scene is uncommonly magnificent.

Passing a number of elegant villas, the tourist, at the distance of a mile from the Fall of Stonebyres, crosses the Clyde by an ancient bridge of three arches, and soon after reaches

LANARK,

A royal burgh, and the county town of Lanarkshire, situated at the distance of twenty-five miles from Glasgow, and thirty-two from Edinburgh. Lanark is a town of no great importance in itself; till lately it was extremely dull, but the extension of the cotton-works in its neighbourhood, and the erection of several good public buildings, have considerably improved its appearance.* It

* It is said that the burgh of Lanark was till very recent times so poor that the single butcher of the town, who also exercised the calling of a weaver in order to fill up his spare time, would never venture upon the speculation of killing a sheep till every part of the animal was ordered beforehand. When he felt disposed to engage in such an enterprise, he usually prevailed upon the minister, the provost and the town-council, to take shares; but when no person came forward to bespeak the fourth quarter, the sheep received a respite till better times should cast up. The bellman or *skellyman*, as he is there called, used often to go through the streets of Lanark with advertisements such as are embodied in the following popular rhyme:—

Bell-ell-ell!
There 's a fat sheep to kill!
A leg for the provost,
  Another for the priest,
The bailies and deacons
  They 'll tak the neist;
And if the fourth leg we cannot sell,
The sheep it maun leeve and gae back to the hill!

CHAMBERS' *Rhymes of Scotland*, p. 140.

was in this place that the Scottish hero Wallace commenced his glorious exertions to free his country from a foreign yoke, and tradition points out a number of localities in the vicinity identified with his name and exploits.

About a quarter of a mile to the east of the town are the ruins of the very ancient church of Lanark, surrounded by the parish burying-ground.

There are a number of handsome seats in the neighbourhood of Lanark, the most splendid of which is Carstairs House, the seat of Henry Monteith, Esq.

In visiting the Falls of Clyde from Lanark, the tourist should at once proceed to the uppermost called Bonniton Linn, two miles from Lanark. A romantic path leads to it through the grounds of Bonniton House, (Lady Mary Ross.) Above this cataract the river moves very slowly, but all at once it bends towards the north-east, and throws itself over a perpendicular rock of about thirty feet. Immediately below the first fall the river hurries along with prodigious rapidity, boiling and foaming over its narrow and rocky channel. The banks are very steep, and at one point the river struggles through a chasm of not more than four feet, where it can easily be stepped over. Half a mile below Bonniton Linn is

CORRA LINN,

Where the river takes three distinct leaps, making altogether a height of about eighty-four feet. The best view of this magnificent fall is from the semicircular seat on the verge of the cliff opposite. Upon a rock above the fall on the southern brink of the river, is the old Castle of Corra; and to the right of this castle is Corra House, the seat of Lord Corehouse, half hid by trees. On the opposite bank of the river is a pavilion, erected in 1708 by Sir James Carmichael of Bonniton, upon an eminence overlooking the fall.

About half a mile below Corra Linn is the celebrated village of New Lanark, originally established in the year 1783 by Mr. David Dale of Glasgow, father-in-law of the famous Robert Owen. The inhabitants, who amount to about 2500, are exclusively engaged in cotton-spinning. They form a very singular community, and the internal economy of the establishment is conducted on very peculiar principles.

In Bonniton House are preserved two relics of Sir William Wallace, a portrait of the hero and a very curious chair on which he is said to have sat.

No traveller should leave this district without visiting Cartland Crags on Mouse Water, about a mile from Lanark. The stream flows through a deep chasm, apparently formed by an earthquake, instead of following what seems a much more natural channel a little farther to the east. The rocky banks on both sides rise to the height of about 400 feet. A few years ago a bridge was thrown across this narrow chasm, consisting of three arches of the height of 146 feet. At a little distance below is a narrow old bridge, supposed to be of Roman origin. On the north side of the stream, a few yards above the new bridge, is a cave in the face of the rock termed " Wallace's Cave," which is pointed out by tradition as the hiding-place of that hero after he had slain Haselrig the English sheriff.

About a mile and a half westward from Lanark, on the south side of the Mouse, is the ancient house of Jerviswood, the seat of the illustrious patriot who was murdered under the forms of law during the infamous government of Charles II. The attainder of Jerviswood was reversed by the Convention Parliament at the Revolution. On the opposite bank of the stream, situated amidst extensive plantations, is Cleghorn, the seat of William Elliot Lockhart, Esq. of Borthwickbrae.

About three miles below Lanark on the north bank of the Clyde is Lee House, the seat of Sir Norman Macdonald Lockhart, Bart. It is a fine mansion lately modernized in the castellated style, and contains a good collection of pictures. Here is kept the famous Lee Penny, the use made of which by Sir Walter Scott in his splendid tale of "The Talisman" must be familiar to every reader. The following curious extract is given in the introduction to that tale:—"Quhilk day, amongest the referries of the Brethren of the Ministry of Lanark, it was proponed to the Synod that Gavin Hamilton of Raploch had pursueit an Complaint before them against Sir James Lockhart of Lee, anent the superstitious using of an Stone, set in silver, for the curing of deseased Cattle, q[lk] the said Gavin affirmed could not be lawfully usit, and that they had deferrit to give ony decisionne thairin till the advice of the Assemblie might be had concerning the same. The Assemblie having inquirit of the manner of using thereof, and particularly understood, be examination of the said Laird of Lee and otherwise, that the custom is only to cast the stone in some water, and give the deseasit Cattle thereof to drink, and that the same is done without using any words, such as Charmers and Sorcereirs use in thair unlawfull practices; and considering that in nature thair are many things seen to work strange effects, whereof no human wit can give a reason, it having pleast God to give to stones and herbs a speciall vertue for healing of many infirmities in man and beast, advises the Brethren to surcease thair process, as therein they perceive no ground of Offence, and admonishes the said Laird of Lee, in using of the said stone, to take heid that it be usit hereafter with the least scandle that possibly maybe. Extract out of the Books of the Assemblie, holden at Glasgow, and subscribed at thair command.—M. Robert Young, Clerk to the Assemblie at Glasgow."

In the grounds of Lee there is a huge oak tree which is so completely hollowed out by age that it can hold half a dozen individuals standing upright.

The tourist may proceed from Lanark to Edinburgh (32 miles) by West Calder, Calder House, Lord Torphichen,) Mid-Calder, Dalmahoy, (Earl of Morton,) &c. For a description of this route see Itinerary.

TWELFTH TOUR.

EDINBURGH TO INVERNESS BY KINROSS—PERTH—DUNKELD—BLAIR ATHOLL.

LEAVING Edinburgh by the Queensferry Road, the tourist crosses the Water of Leith by Dean Bridge, a superb edifice of four arches, each ninety feet in span. Below, on the right, is St. Bernard's Well. On the left stands the village of the Water of Leith, and at a short distance are two buildings of great elegance—the Hospital endowed by John Watson, W.S. for the maintenance and education of destitute children, and the new Orphan Hospital, opened in 1833. The road now passes the new Episcopal Chapel, and on the right Dean House (Sir J. Nisbet); Craigleith (Bonar, Esq.); and Craigleith Quarry, from which the stone employed in building the New Town of Edinburgh was chiefly procured. At a short distance to the left is Craigcrook (Lord Jeffrey), and Ravelston (Lady Murray Keith). About four miles from Edinburgh stands Barnton House (W. R. Ramsay, Esq.) A mile farther on, the tourist crosses the Almond by Cramond Bridge, and passes, on the left, Craigiehall (Hope Vere, Esq.), and on the right, Newhall (Scott Moncrieff, Esq.) On the shore is the village of Cramond, and the entrance to Dalmeny Park (Earl Rosebery). The banks of the river Almond in this neighbourhood are very beautiful, and the scenery about the old bridge of Craigiehall is very romantic. Passing in succession Dalmeny Kirk, 7½ miles, and Ha's Inn, 8 miles from Edinburgh, you enter South Queensferry, which was erected into a royal borough by Malcolm Canmore, and derived its name from Margaret his queen. Here are some ruins of a monastery of Carmelite Friars, founded in 1330. On the left is Duddingstone House (G. H. Dundas, Esq.), and a little to the south, the ruins of Dundas Castle, a building of great antiquity, which has been in the Dundas family upwards of 700 years. The ferry across the Forth belonged, before the Reformation, to the Abbot of Dunfermline, and was at that period sold by his orders to a joint stock company.* Three miles west from Queensferry stands Hopetoun House, a building of great splendour, and possessing a delightful prospect. In the narrow strait at Queensferry, there is the little island of Inch Garvie, on which a fort was established during the last war. On this island, previous to the reign of Charles II., the principal state prison was placed. Upon a promontory, on the northern coast, stands the small village of North Queensferry. It is remarkable as the place where Oliver Cromwell first encamped on crossing the Forth, in 1651. On this promontory, which is called the Cruiks, there is a lazaretto, where goods landed on this part of the coast from tropical climates have to pass quarantine. In the immediate neighbourhood is Rosyth Castle, a huge square tower, situated close by the sea. It was the ancient seat of the Stuarts of Rosyth, a branch of the royal family, from which Oliver Cromwell is

* The agent appointed to dispose of the ferry divided it into sixteen shares, and offered the same for sale. The project was immediately successful; the shares were eagerly purchased; the agent continued to sell as long as he found persons willing to buy; and, scandalous to relate, there is evidence still in existence that he actually sold eighteen sixteenth shares of the Queensferry passage.

said to have been descended. The bay between the Cruicks and Rosyth Castle, is called St. Margaret's Hope, from the circumstance of the Princess Margaret, sister of Edgar Atheling, afterwards consort of Malcolm Canmore, having been wrecked there in her flight from England, immediately after the Norman conquest.

Two miles beyond North Queensferry, the road enters

INVERKEITHING,

a royal burgh of very great antiquity. By its first existing charter, which it received from William the Lion, the town obtained jurisdiction over a very extensive tract of country, but its importance is now greatly reduced. It was frequently the residence of David I. and of Queen Annabella Drummond, wife of Robert III., and an antique house is yet pointed out, which she is said to have inhabited. Great quantities of coal and salt are annually exported here. In the neighbourhood of Inverkeithing, a body of Scottish loyalists were defeated with great slaughter by a superior force under the command of Lambert, the English parliamentary general. In this engagement a foster father and seven sons sacrificed themselves for Sir Hector M'Lean of Duart; the old man, whenever one of his boys fell, thrusting forward another to fill his place, at the right hand of the beloved chief, with the words "Another for Hector." This incident has been introduced with great effect by Sir Walter Scott, in his description of the combat between the Clan Kay and Clan Chattan, in the Fair Maid of Perth.*

* At the distance of three miles from this part of the coast stands the ancient town of Dunfermline, which, about the time of Malcolm Canmore, became the seat of government, and continued to be a favourite residence of the Scottish kings down to the Union of the crowns.

"The king sits in Dunfermline town,
Drinking the blude-red wine."—*Ballad of Sir Patrick Spens.*

The most ancient of the antiquities of Dunfermline is the castle of Malcolm Can-

A short distance to the east of Inverkeithing, and close upon the shore, stands Donnibrissel House, a seat of the Earl of Moray. (See Fifth Tour, p. 172.) Passing in succession, on the right, Fordel (Sir J. Henderson, Bart.), Lochgelly (Earl of Minto), and Lochore (Sir W. Scott), the tourist reaches the Kirk of Beath, six miles from Inverkeithing, and 2½ miles beyond that Maryburgh, the birth-place of the two brothers Adam, the celebrated architects. The road crosses the Kelty Water at Gairney Bridge, where the poet, Michael Bruce, once taught a small school, and, twenty-five miles from Edinburgh, enters

more, the remains of which are still visible on a peninsular eminence jutting into a ravine near to the town. South-east of the town are the ruins of the later palace, which seems to have been a building of great magnificence. The south-west wall is all that remains of it. This palace was the birth-place of Charles I. The bed in which he was born is preserved in Broomhall, the seat of the Earl of Elgin, two miles from the town. The last monarch who occupied this palace was Charles II. who lived in it for some time during his campaign in 1650-51. The Abbey of Dunfermline was founded by Malcolm III. It was burned down, excepting the church and cells, by Edward I. in 1303. The parts thus spared were much injured at the Reformation. The founder, his queen, and seven other monarchs were interred within its precincts. The nave of the church, which is the only part that has been entire for a long time, has been used as a parish church ever since the Reformation. In 1818 it was judged expedient to abandon this part of the building, and it was resolved to provide a new parish church by rebuilding the chancel and transepts, which was accordingly done. It is to be regretted that the bad taste displayed in the erection has, in a great measure marred the beauty of the design. In clearing away the ruins of the ancient choir the tomb of Robert Bruce, who was buried here in 1329, was discovered. The skeleton of the illustrious monarch was found entire, together with the lead in which his body was wrapt, and even some fragments of his shroud. He was reinterred with much state by the Barons of the Exchequer, immediately under the pulpit of the new church. In the area of the church is shewn a large marble slab, broken into three pieces said to be the tombstone of Queen Margaret; also six large flat stones, affirmed to mark the graves of as many kings. The remains of the Abbey are very extensive, but it is generally asserted that the original buildings were much more so. The Fratery still retains an entire window, much admired for its elegant and complicated workmanship. Beneath the Fratery there were six and twenty cells, many of which still remain. The celebrated Ralph Erskine, one of the founders of the Secession Church, was for a number of years minister of Dunfermline. The tourist ought to ascend the old steeple of the church, from which a very extensive and magnificent prospect may be obtained. Dunfermline has greatly increased within the last thirty years, and is now distinguished by its activity in the manufacture of linen.

KINROSS,

the capital of the county of that name, and pleasantly situated on the banks of Loch Leven. Kinross House (Graham, Esq.), a large and elegant structure, erected in 1685, stands on the edge of the lake. The promontory on which it stands was once occupied by a stronghold, long the residence of the Earls of Morton. By far the most interesting object in the neighbourhood of Kinross is the lake, on whose banks it is situated. Loch Leven is well worthy of a visit from tourists, not only on account of the beautiful scenery with which it is surrounded, but especially on account of the historical associations with which it abounds. This lake is of an irregular oval figure, and extends from ten to eleven miles in circumference. It contains four islands, the chief of which are St. Serf's Isle, near the east end, on which there are yet to be seen some fragments of a religious house; and another, about two acres in extent, situated near the shore opposite Kinross, on which are the picturesque ruins of a castle, once the residence of the unfortunate Queen Mary. During the minority of David II., an English army, commanded by John de Strivilin, besieged the castle, and, by erecting a strong bulwark at the east end of the lake, where the river Leven issues out of it, expected to lay the island under water, and constrain Allan de Vipont, the commander of the castle, to surrender. The greater part of the besiegers, however, having gone to Dunfermline, to celebrate the festival of St. Margaret (June 19, 1335), the besieged seized the opportunity and broke through the barrier, when the water rushed out, overwhelmed the camp of the English, and forced them to raise the siege. Loch Leven Castle was afterwards granted to a branch of the Douglas family, and, in 1567, when Queen Mary was imprisoned there, it belonged to Sir Robert Douglas, stepfather to the famous Earl of Murray. Queen Mary escaped from the castle May 2, 1568, through the aid of young Douglas, and is said, by general tradition, to have landed at a place called Balbinny, at the south side of the lake, whence she was conducted, by Lord Seton, to Niddry Castle in West Lothian. Between the castle island and the nearest point of land at the churchyard, a causeway runs beneath the water, which is here so shallow, that in dry seasons it is possible to wade to the isle upon this strange pavement. Loch Leven is celebrated for the excellence of its trout. The rich taste and bright red colour are derived from a small red shell-fish upon which they feed. The silver grey trout is apparently the original native of the loch, and, in many respects, the finest fish of the whole. At the eastern extremity of the loch, there are some remains of the monasteries of Portmoak and Scotland's Well. In the little sequestered village of Kinnesswood, situated on the north-east shore of Loch Leven, Michael Bruce, the poet, was born. The house in which he first saw the light is still pointed out. His poem on Loch Leven Castle, his ballad of Sir James the Rose, and his verses in anticipation of his own death, are much admired. He died at the early age of twenty-one, before his poetical genius arrived at maturity.* The river Leven flows from the lake on the east side, and pursues an easterly course to the Firth of Forth. The vale of the Leven is beautiful and is ornamented with the woods around Leslie, the seat of the Earl of Rothes. About

* A most interesting biography of Bruce has lately been published by the Rev. Mr. M'Kelvie of Balgedie, who has satisfactorily proved that the Ode to the Cuckoo, and several of the paraphrases, published by Logan in his own name, were in reality written by Bruce.

two miles from Kinross, is the village of Milnathort, or Mills of Forth; and to the right, at some distance, are the ruins of Burleigh Castle, which gave title to Lord Burleigh, attainted in 1716. The road now enters Glenfarg, a romantic little valley, enclosed by the Ochils, which are clothed to their summits with verdure.

At the northern extremity of the glen is Ayton House (Murray,) and a short distance to the right the ancient village of Abernethy, once the capital of the Pictish kingdom, and a most extensive Culdee establishment, consisting of a university and a monastery, besides a church. Abernethy still contains a round tower similar to that of Brechin, supposed to have been erected by the Picts. Passing in succession Crossgates and the Kirk of Dron, the tourist reaches the Bridge of Earn, a village which affords accommodation to the strangers who resort in great numbers to Pitcaithly Wells in the neighbourhood. There is a ball-room and a library, with every other convenience that can be deemed requisite. The rules by which the society of this watering-place is regulated are of a peculiar, but very judicious kind. Shortly after passing Pitcaithly, the tourist will ascend the hill of Moncreiff, from which he will obtain the first view of Perth.*

* "One of the most beautiful points of view which Britain, or perhaps the world, can afford, is, or rather we may say was, the prospect from a spot called the Wicks of Baiglie, being a species of niche at which the traveller arrived, after a long stage from Kinross, through a waste and uninteresting country, and from which, as forming a pass over the summit of a ridgy eminence which he had gradually surmounted, he beheld stretching beneath him, the valley of the Tay, traversed by its ample and lordly stream; the town of Perth with its two large meadows, or Inches, its steeples, and its towers; the hills of Moncreiff and Kinnoul faintly rising into picturesque rocks, partly clothed with woods; the rich margin of the river studded with elegant mansions; and the distant view of the huge Grampian mountains, the northern screen of this exquisite landscape. The alteration of the road, greatly, it must be owned, to the improvement of general intercourse, avoids this magnificent point of view, and the landscape is introduced more gradually and partially to the eye, though the approach must be still considered as extremely beautiful. There is still,

The prospect from this hill has been much and deservedly admired. The fertile Carse of Gowrie,—the Firth of Tay, with the populous town of Dundee,—the city of Perth, and the beautiful valley of Strathearn, bounded by the hills of Menteith, are all distinctly seen from this eminence. Pennant calls this view "the Glory of Scotland."

PERTH,

An ancient royal burgh, and one of the most handsome towns in Scotland, is beautifully situated on the west bank of the Tay, at the distance of forty-four miles from Edinburgh. It occupies the centre of a spacious plain, having two beautiful pieces of public ground called the North and South Inches extending on each side of it.

A splendid bridge of ten arches and 900 feet in length, built in 1772, leads across the Tay to the north. Perth, or, as it used to be called from its church, St. Johnstoun, boasts of the most remote antiquity, and has been the scene of many interesting events. On account of its importance and its vicinity to the royal palace of Scone, it was long the metropolis of the kingdom before Edinburgh obtained that distinction. Here, too, the Parliaments and national assemblies were held, and many of the nobility took up their residence. Perth contains several beautiful streets and terraces, and a number of splendid public buildings. The oldest of these is St. John's Church, the precise origin of which is unknown. It has undergone various modifications, and is now divided into the East, West, and Middle Churches. It was in this

we believe, a footpath left open by which the station at the Wicks of Baiglie may be approached; and the traveller, by quitting his horse or equipage, and walking a few hundred yards, may still compare the real landscape with the sketch which we have attempted to give."—*Fair Maid of Perth*, vol. i. p. 21.

church that the demolitions of the Reformation commenced in consequence of a sermon which John Knox preached against idolatry. At the south end of the Watergate stood Gowrie House, the scene of a well-known mysterious incident in Scottish history called the Gowrie Conspiracy. The whole of that fine old building has unfortunately been removed, and the site is now occupied by the County Hall, a splendid building in the Grecian style. Perth contains also an excellent academy established in 1762, and a neat hall for the meetings of the Literary and Antiquarian Society, which was founded in 1784. Previous to the Reformation, Perth contained an immense number of religious houses. One of these, the Monastery of Greyfriars, stood at the end of the Speygate. In Blackfriars Monastery, which was situated at the north side of the town, James I. was assassinated by a band of conspirators. But of these and many other interesting buildings not a vestige now remains. Perth has been the scene of many important historical events. It was occupied by the English during the reign of Edward I. but was besieged and taken by Robert Bruce. In the time of the great civil war it was taken by the Marquis of Montrose after the Battle of Tippermuir. In 1715, and again in 1745, it was occupied by the rebel Highland army, who there proclaimed the Pretender as king. The Inches are two beautiful pieces of ground, each about a mile and a half in circumference, which afford most agreeable and healthy walks to the inhabitants. The North Inch is a bare green sward, but the South Inch is delightfully variegated with trees. On the North Inch there took place in the reign of Robert III. that singular combat between the Clan Kay and Clan Chattan, which Sir Walter Scott has introduced with so much effect into his novel of the Fair Maid of Perth. Perth is surrounded on all sides with the most beautiful and picturesque scenery, and the interesting objects in the neighbourhood are so numerous, that it would require a volume to notice them all. The view from the Hill of Moncreiff,—the walks on the hill of Kinnoul,—the battle-fields of Dupplin, Tippermuir, and Luncarty,—Scone, Dunsinnan-hill, and Birnam-wood, and the graves of Bessy Bell and Mary Gray may be mentioned as most worthy of attention. The population of Perth amounts to about 20,000.

Leaving Perth by the North Inch, the tourist passes on the left Tulloch Printfield and Few House, (Nicol, Esq.) and at the distance of two and a half miles from Perth sees Scone Palace, the seat of the Earl of Mansfield, who represents the old family of Stormont. It is a modern building occupying the site of the ancient palace of the kings of Scotland. Much of the old furniture has been preserved in the modern house, including, among other relics, a bed that had been used by James VI., and another of flowered crimson velvet, which is said to have been wrought by Queen Mary when imprisoned in Lochleven Castle. The gallery, which is 160 feet long, occupies the site of the old hall in which the coronations were performed. The situation of the palace is highly picturesque, and the view from the windows of the drawing-room is most splendid. At the north side of the house is a *tumulus* termed the Moat Hill, said to have been composed of earth from the estates of the different proprietors who here attended on the kings. The famous stone on which the Scottish monarchs were crowned was brought from Dunstaffnage to this Abbey. It was removed by Edward I. to Westminster Abbey, where it still remains, forming part of the coronation chair of the British monarchs. The Abbey of Scone was destroyed at the time of the Reformation by a mob from Dundee, and the only part now remaining is an old aisle, containing a magnificent marble monument to the memory of the first Viscount Stormont. The old market-cross of Scone still remains, surrounded by the pleasure grounds which have been substituted in the place of the ancient village. Three miles from Perth the road crosses the Almond near its junction with the Tay, and winds among plantations chiefly on Lord Lynedoch's estate. About a mile and a half in advance a road leads off from the left to Redgorton and Monedie, and a few paces farther on a road on the right conducts to the field of Luncarty, situated on the west bank of the Tay, about four miles from Perth, the scene of a decisive battle between the Scots and Danes in the reign of Kenneth III. The Scots were at first forced to retreat, but were rallied by a peasant of the name of Hay and his two sons who were ploughing in the neighbourhood. By the aid of these courageous persons, who were armed only with a yoke, the Scots obtained a complete victory. In commemoration of this circumstance the crest of the Hays has for many centuries been a peasant carrying a yoke over his shoulder. The plain on which the battle was fought is now used as a bleachfield. A mile in advance the road crosses the fine trouting streams of Ordie and Shochie.* A little farther on, a road turns off to the right to the Linn

* Perth suffered from a nocturnal inundation of the Tay in the year 1210, and it is predicted that yet once again it will be destroyed in a similar manner:

" Says the Shochie to the Ordie,
'Where shall we meet?'
'At the cross of Perth
When a' men are fast asleep.' "—*Popular Rhyme.*

of Campsie where the Tay forms a magnificent cascade, and the village of Stanley, famous for its extensive spinning-mills. The tourist next passes on the left the ruins of a residence of the family of Nairn and the Mill of Loak; and nine miles from Perth enters the village of Auchtergaven. Three miles farther on the tourist passes Murthly Castle, (Stewart, Bart.) and a short way north of it, the old Castle of Murthly. In the immediate neighbourhood is Birnam Hill, 1580 feet above the level of the sea, and Birnam Wood, so famous for its connection with the fate of Macbeth. The ancient forest has now disappeared, and been replaced by trees of modern growth. The traveller now passes the village of Little Dunkeld,* crosses the river Tay, and enters

DUNKELD.

"There are few places," says Dr. M'Culloch, "of which the effect is so striking as Dunkeld when first seen on emerging from this pass (a pass formed by the Tay, by which the traveller enters the Highlands), nor does it owe this more to the suddenness of the view, or to its contrast with the long preceding blank, than to its own intrinsic beauty; to its magnificent bridge and its cathedral nestling among its dark woody hills; to its noble river, and to the brilliant profusion of rich ornament. The leading object in the landscape is the noble bridge standing high above the Tay. The cathedral seen above it and relieved by the dark woods in which it is embosomed, and the town with its congregated grey houses, add to the general mass of architecture, and thus enhance its effect in the landscape. Beyond, rise the round and

* "Was there ere sic a parish, a parish, a parish,
Was there ere sic a parish as Little Dunkell?
They've stickit the minister, hang'd the precentor,
Dung down the steeple, and drucken the bell!!!"—*Old Song.*

rich swelling woods that skirt the river, stretching away in a long vista to the foot of Craiginean, which, with all its forests of fir, rises a broad shadowy mass against the sky. The varied outline of Craig-y-barns, one continuous range of darkly-wooded hill, now swelling to the light and again subsiding in deep shadowy recesses, forms the remainder of the splendid distance. The Duke of Atholl's grounds present a succession of walks and rides in every style of beauty that can be imagined, but they will not be seen in the few hours usually allotted to them, as the extent of the walks is fifty miles, and of the rides thirty. It is the property of few places, perhaps of no one in all Britain, to admit, within such a space, of such a prolongation of lines of access, and everywhere with so much variety of character, such frequent changes of scene, and so much beauty." The most interesting object in the town of Dunkeld, is the ancient and venerable cathedral. The great aisle measures 120 by 60 feet, the walls are 40 feet high, and the side aisles 12 feet wide. It is now roofless, but the choir was rebuilt and converted into a place of worship by the late Duke of Atholl, at an expense of L.5000. The new church is handsomely fitted up. In the vestry there is a statue in armour, of somewhat rude workmanship, which was formerly placed at the grave of the notorious *Wolf of Badenoch,* who burned the cathedral of Elgin. The early history of this establishment is obscure, but it is understood that there was a monastery of the Culdees here, which David I. converted into a bishoprick, A.D. 1127. Among its bishops were Gawin Douglas, famous for his poetical talents, and Bishop Sinclair, celebrated for his patriotic exertions in the reign of Robert Bruce. Immediately behind the cathedral, stands the ancient mansion of the Dukes of Atholl. A magnificent new mansion was commenced by the late Duke, but his death, in 1830, has suspended the progress of the building. At the end of the cathedral are the first two larches introduced into Britain. They were originally placed in flower-pots in a green-house, but are now ninety feet high, and one of them measures fifteen feet in circumference two feet above the ground. The walks through the policies of Dunkeld have been pronounced, by the late Dr. E. Clarke, to be almost without a rival. The larch woods alone cover an extent of 11,000 square acres; the number of trees planted by the late Duke of Atholl being about twenty-seven millions, besides several millions of other sorts of trees.

From the base of Craigievenean, a long wooded eminence projects, across which a path leads to Ossian's Hall, situated beside a cataract formed by a fall of the Braan. This is generally esteemed the greatest curiosity of Dunkeld. A hermitage or summer-house is placed forty feet above the bottom of the fall, and is constructed in such a manner that the cascade is entirely concealed by the walls of this edifice. Opposite to the entrance is a picture of Ossian playing upon his harp, and singing the songs of other times. At the touch of the guide, the picture suddenly disappears with a loud noise, and the whole cataract foams at once before the visitor, reflected in several mirrors, and roaring with the noise of thunder. The spectacle is exceedingly striking. About a mile higher up the Braan, is the Rumbling Bridge, which is thrown across a narrow chasm, eighty feet above the waterway. Into this gulf, the Braan pours itself with great fury, foaming and roaring over the massive fragments of rock which have fallen into the stream, and casting a thick cloud of spray high above the bridge.

"The most perfect and extensive view," says Dr. M'Culloch, "of the grounds of Dunkeld, is to be obtained opposite to the village of Invar, and at a considerable elevation above the bridge of the Braan; it affords a better conception of the collected magnificence and grandeur of the whole than any other place."*

ABERFELDY—KENMORE—TAYMOUTH CASTLE—KILLIN—LOCHEARNHEAD—COMRIE—CRIEFF.

THE tourist who wishes to survey the beautiful scenery of Kenmore and Killin, may either proceed to Blair Atholl, and thence to Kenmore, distant, by the common road, twenty-eight miles—over the hills, twenty miles—or he may adopt the route by Logierait and Aberfeldy. If he prefers the former, shortly after leaving Blair Atholl he reaches a chasm in the hill on the right hand, through which the little river Bruar falls over a series of beautiful cascades. These falls were formerly unadorned by wood, but, in consequence of the poetical address, written by Burns, entitled "Humble petition of Bruar Water," the Duke of Atholl has formed a plantation along the chasm. The river makes three distinct falls, the lowest of which forms an unbroken descent of 100 feet. The shelving rocks on both banks—the depth of the chasm—and the roughness of the channel through which the stream rushes, add greatly to the sublimity and interest of the scene. From these falls, the tourist may either proceed by the common road, or over the hill on the south side of the vale, to Tummel

* From Dunkeld the tourist may go off to the east by Cluny to Blairgowrie, distant twelve miles; a route which comprises some exquisitely beautiful scenery. The road winds along the foot of the Grampians, and passes in succession the Loch of Lowe, Butterstone Loch, the Loch of Cluny, with the ancient castle of Cluny, a seat of the Earl of Airlie on a small island near the southern shore, Forneth (Principal Baird), the Loch of Marlie, Kinloch (Hog, Esq.) Baleid (Campbell, Esq.); the House of Marlie (Farquharson, Esq.), and the church and inn of Marlie or Kinloch, much resorted to by parties from Perth and Dunkeld, and two miles farther Blairgowrie, situated on the west bank of the Ericht, containing a population of 1500.

Bridge and Inn. The scenery around this spot is extremely beautiful. In the midst of it stands Foss, the seat of — Stewart, Esq. From the Bridge of Tummel there is a road which leads through a gloomy and mountainous country to Loch Rannoch. This lake is about ten or eleven miles in length and two and a half in breadth, and is surrounded by lofty mountains covered with forests. In the neighbourhood is the steep mountain Schihallien, 3550 feet high, which afforded shelter to Robert Bruce after the battle of Methven. Leaving the Bridge of Tummel, an Alpine road of seven or eight miles length leads to Strath Tay. The ruins of a high square keep called Garth Castle, occupying a narrow rocky promontory at the confluence of two rivulets, form a prominent object in the landscape. The streams run in deep perpendicular channels, and the dell is richly wooded, and so deep that the roaring of the waters can scarcely be heard. The view from the confined channel of the burn, over-canopied by slanting trees, is peculiarly striking; and the whole scene presents an exquisite combination of beauty and terror. The tourist now descends along the edge of a deep and wooded dell, bordered by sloping cultivated ground, and passing Cusheville Inn, reaches Fortingal, as the lower part of Glen Lyon is called, and, crossing the Lyon by a boat, he turns the corner of a hill, and all at once alights upon the lovely village of Kenmore.

If, however, as is usually the case, the tourist should prefer the route by Logierait and Aberfeldy, on leaving Dunkeld he crosses the Tay by a magnificent bridge of seven arches, and a little farther on, reaches the village of Invar, where the Braan is crossed by a bridge, and a road strikes off upon the left to Amulree. Three miles beyond this, the road enters the village of Dalmarnock, then the village of Ballalachan, and a mile and a half beyond, passes Dalguise, (Stewart, Esq.) on the left. The road now leads along a wide cultivated valley, through which flow the combined waters of the Tay and Tummel. It abounds in the finest scenery, and extensive masses of larch and pine skirt the edges of the hills above. Six and a half miles from Dunkeld we pass Kinnaird House, (Duke of Atholl,) and one mile further, the village of Balmacneil,—opposite this spot the Tummel falls into the Tay. On a tongue of land, formed by the confluence of these rivers, stands the village of Logierait, (eight and a half miles from Dunkeld.) One mile from Balmacneil is Port village, and one mile further, Balnaguard Inn,—the opening scene of Mrs. Brunton's novel, entitled "Self Control." On the right, is Eastertyre, (Major M'Glashan.) Across the Tay is Ballechin, (Hope Stuart, Esq.) which appears to have been the scene of the slaughter of Sir James the Rose, in the original ballad of that name. A mile and a half beyond is Eastmill, and opposite, across the Tay, Fyndynet. After passing some Highland villages, the venerable Castle of Grandtully, (Stewart, Bart.) appears on the left, surrounded by rows of stately elms. It is an old structure, but kept in a habitable condition, and is said by Sir Walter Scott to bear a great resemblance to the mansion of Tullyveolan in Waverley. One of the square wings is completely encompassed with ivy. Three miles from Grandtully is the village of Aberfeldy, near which are the beautiful falls of Moness, said by Pennant to be an epitome of everything desirable in a waterfall. The description which Burns has given of these falls is not only beautiful in itself, but strikingly accurate:

"The braes ascend like lofty wa's,
The foaming stream deep roaring fa's,
O'erhung wi' fragrant spreading shaws,
The birks of Aberfeldy.

The hoary cliffs are crowned wi' flowers,
White o'er the linn the burnie pours,
And rising, meets in misty showers,
The birks of Aberfeldy."

The falls are three in number; the lowest is a mile from the village, the upper, half a mile beyond it. The glen is deep, and so exceedingly confined that the trees in some places almost meet from the opposite sides. The lowest fall consists chiefly of a series of cascades formed by a small tributary rivulet pouring down the east side of the dell. The next series consists of a succession of falls, comprising a perpendicular height of not less than a hundred feet. The last and highest cascade is a perpendicular fall of about fifty feet. Here the traveller may cross the dell by means of a rustic bridge, and return to the inn by a varied route. Opposite Aberfeldy the Tay is crossed by one of General Wade's bridges. About a mile in advance, on the north side, stands Castle Menzies, the seat of Sir Neil Menzies, the chief of that name, erected in the sixteenth century. It stands at the foot of a lofty range of rocky hills, and is surrounded by a park filled with aged trees. Weem Castle, the former seat of the family, was burnt by Montrose. About a mile farther is Balfrax, (Sir Neil Menzies, Bart.) and about a mile beyond, the Lyon water joins the Tay. Six miles from Aberfeldy the tourist reaches the beautiful little village of Kenmore, situated at the north-east extremity of Loch Tay. It consists of an inn and fifteen or sixteen houses, neatly whitewashed, and some of them embowered in ivy, honeysuckle, and sweet-briar. The most remarkable object in the vicinity of Kenmore, is Taymouth Castle, the princely mansion of the Marquis of Breadalbane, with its much admired environs. The castle is a magnificent dark-grey pile of four stories, with round corner towers and terminating in an airy central pavilion. Its interior is splendidly fitted up, and it contains one of the best collections of paintings in Scotland. The pleasure grounds are laid out with great taste, and possess a striking combination of beauty and grandeur. The hills which confine them are luxuriantly wooded and picturesque in their outlines, and the plain below is richly adorned with old gigantic trees. The view from the hill in front of the castle is reckoned one of the finest in Scotland. On the right is Drummond hill, and behind it the lofty Ben Lawers, with Ben More in the remote distance. On the left, two hills, partially wooded, rise from the water one above another. In the foreground, a portion of the lake is seen and the village and church of Kenmore, and to the north of them, the bridge across the Tay, immediately behind which is the little wooded island of Loch Tay, with the ruins of a priory founded by Alexander I. whose Queen, Sybilla, lies interred here.* Along the north bank of the river, there is a terrace sixteen yards wide and three miles in length, overshadowed by a row of stately beech trees, and, on the opposite side, there is a similar walk extending a mile from Kenmore. These promenades are connected by a light cast-iron bridge. Taymouth Castle was first built by Sir Colin Campbell, sixth knight of Lochaw, in the year 1580. It was then, and until lately, called Balloch, from the Gaelic *bealach*, a word signifying the outlet of a lake or glen. The builder being asked why he had placed his house at the extremity of his estate, replied, "*We'll brizz yont*," (press onward), adding that *he intended Balloch should in time be in the middle of it*. The possessions of the

* The last residents in this priory were three nuns who once a-year visited a fair in Kenmore, which, owing to that circumstance, is still called "Holy Women's Market."

family have, however, extended in the opposite direction. They now reach from Aberfeldy, four miles eastward, to the Atlantic ocean, a space upwards of one hundred miles, and are said to be the *longest* in Britain.

Leaving Kenmore, and Taymouth, the tourist proceeds along the shores of the Loch to Killin, which is sixteen miles distant at the opposite extremity. Both shores abound in beautiful scenery, but the southern is preferable, on account of the view which is thus obtained of the gigantic Ben Lawers, 4015 feet high, which borders the other side of the loch.* There is a good deal of cultivated ground on either side, with a prodigious number of rude and picturesque cottages. Two miles from Kenmore, on the south side of the lake, is the fine waterfall of Acharn, half a mile off the road. The cascade appears to be about eighty or ninety feet high, and a neat hermitage has been formed commanding an excellent view of the fall. Killin is a straggling little village on the banks of the Dochart, near its junction with the Lochy. It is much admired for the varied beauty of its landscapes. The vale of the Dochart is stern and wild, but that of the Lochy is peculiarly beautiful. At the village, the Dochart rushes over a strange expanse of rock, and

* "The northern shore of the lake presented a far more Alpine prospect than that upon which the Glover was stationed. Woods and thickets ran up the sides of the mountains, and disappeared among the sinuosities formed by the winding ravines which separated them from each other; but far above these specimens of a tolerable natural soil, arose the swart and bare mountains themselves, in the dark grey desolation proper to the season. Some were peaked, some broad-crested, some rocky and precipitous, others of a tamer outline; and the clan of Titans seemed to be commanded by their appropriate chieftains—the frowning mountain of Ben Lawers, and the still more lofty eminence of Ben Mohr, arising high above the rest, whose peaks retain a dazzling helmet of snow far into the summer season, and sometimes during the whole year. Yet the borders of this wild and silvan region, where the mountains descended upon the lake, intimated, even at that early period, many traces of human habitation. Hamlets were seen, especially on the northern margin of the lake, half hid among the little glens that poured their tributary streams into Loch Tay, which, like many earthly things, made a fair show at a distance, but, when more closely approached, were disgustful and repulsive, from their squalid want of the conveniences which attend even Indian wigwams. The magnificent bosom of the lake itself was a scene to gaze on with delight. Its noble breadth, with its termination in a full and beautiful run, was rendered yet more picturesque by one of those islets which are often happily situated in Scottish lakes. The ruins upon that isle, now almost shapeless, being overgrown with wood, rose, at the time we speak of, into the towers and pinnacles of a priory where slumbered the remains of Sibilla, daughter of Henry I. of England, and consort of Alexander the First of Scotland."—*Fair Maid of Perth.*

encircles two islands, one covered with magnificent pines, on one of which is the tomb of the Macnabs. From the upper end of the lower island there are three bridges across the stream. "Killin," says Dr. M'Culloch, "is the most extraordinary collection of extraordinary scenery in Scotland,—unlike everything else in the country, and perhaps on earth, and a perfect picture gallery in itself, since you cannot move three yards without meeting a new landscape. A busy artist might here draw a month and not exhaust it. * * * Fir trees, rocks, torrents, mills, bridges, houses, these produce the great bulk of the middle landscape, under endless combinations, while the distances more constantly are found in the surrounding hills, in their varied woods, in the bright expanse of the lake, and the minute ornaments of the distant valley, in the rocks, and bold summit of Craig Cailleach, and in the lofty vision of Ben Lawers, which towers like a huge giant to the clouds—the monarch of the scene." On the north side of Loch Tay, and about a mile and a half from the village of Killin, stand the picturesque ruins of Finlarig Castle, an ancient seat of the Breadalbane family. The castle is a narrow building of three storeys, entirely overgrown with ivy, and is surrounded by venerable trees. Immediately adjoining is the family vault. The following anecdote of the olden times is related by the Messrs. Anderson in their excellent Guide to the Highlands: "On the occasion of a marriage festival at Finlarig, in years gone by, when occupied by the heir apparent, intelligence was given to the company, which comprised the principal youth of the clan, that a party of the Macdonalds of Keppoch, who had just passed with a drove of *lifted* cattle, had refused to pay the accustomed *road* collop. Flushed with revelry, the guests indignantly sallied out and attacked the Macdonalds on the adjoining hill of Stronoclachan, but, from their irregular impetuosity, they were repulsed, and twenty young gentlemen left dead on the spot. Tidings of the affray were conveyed to Taymouth, and a reinforcement arriving, the victors were overtaken in Glenorchy, and routed, and their leader slain."

On leaving Killin, the tourist proceeds up Glen Dochart, and passes, on the right, the mansion house of Achlyne, a seat of the Marquis of Breadalbane. A little beyond, at a place called Leeks, a road strikes off to Crianlarich Inn, from which the tourist may either go by Tyndrum and Dalmally to Inverary, or he may descend Glenfalloch till he reach the head of Loch Lomond. The traveller now enters Glen Ogle, a narrow and gloomy defile, hemmed in by the rocky sides of the mountains, which are here strikingly grand, rising on the one side in a succession of terraces, and on the other, in a steep acclivity surmounted by perpendicular precipices. At the distance of eight miles from Killin, is the little village of Lochearnhead, with a good inn. From this point the tourist may turn southward by Balquhidder, the burial place of Rob Roy, and through the wild pass of Loch Lubnaig and Leny to Callander, a distance of thirteen miles. Loch Earn is about seven miles in length, and generally about one mile in breadth. "Limited as are the dimensions of Loch Earn," says Dr. M'Culloch, "it is exceeded in beauty by few of our lakes, as far as it is possible for many beauties to exist in so small a space. Its style is that of a lake of far greater dimensions,—the hills which bound it being lofty, and bold, and rugged, with a variety of character not found in many of even far greater magnitude and extent. It is a miniature and model of scenery that might well occupy ten times the space. Yet the eye does not feel this. There is nothing trifling or small in the details,—nothing to diminish its grandeur of style, and tell us we are contemplating a reduced copy. On the contrary, there is a perpetual contest between our impressions and our reasonings; we know that a few short miles comprehend the whole, and yet we feel as if it was a landscape of many miles,—a lake to be ranked among those of first order and dimensions.

"While its mountains thus rise in majestic simplicity to the sky, terminating in bold, and various, and rocky outlines, the surfaces of the declivities are equally bold and various, enriched with precipices and masses of protruding rock, with deep hollows and ravines, and with the courses of innumerable torrents, which pour from above, and, as they descend, become skirted with trees, till they lose themselves in the waters of the lake. Wild woods also ascend along their surface in all that irregularity of distribution so peculiar to these rocky mountains, less solid and continuous than at Loch Lomond, less scattered and romantic than at Loch Katrine, but from these very causes, aiding to confer upon Loch Earn a character entirely its own."

There is a road on each side of the lake, but the southern route is to be preferred. About a mile and a half from the inn, we come to Edinample, an ancient castellated mansion belonging to the

Marquis of Breadalbane. There is also a beautiful waterfall here, immediately below the road. The Ample, a mountain rivulet, pours in two perpendicular streams over a broad rugged rock, and uniting about midway, is precipitated again over a second precipice. The road now passes through continuous woods of oak, larch, ash, and birch. The view to the south is closed up by the huge Ben Voirlich (*i. e.* the Great Mountain of the Lake), which rises to the height of 3300 feet. About midway between Lochearnhead and the east end of the lake, is Ardvoirlich (Wm. Stewart, Esq.), the Darlinvaroch of the *Legend of Montrose.** The landscapes to the

* "During the reign of James IV., a great feud between the powerful families of Drummond and Murray divided Perthshire. The former, being the most numerous and powerful, cooped up eight score of the Murrays in the kirk of Monivaird, and set fire to it. The wives and the children of the ill-fated men, who had also found shelter in the church, perished by the same conflagration. One man, named David Murray, escaped by the humanity of one of the Drummonds, who received him in his arms as he leaped from amongst the flames. As King James IV. ruled with more activity than most of his predecessors, this cruel deed was severely revenged, and several of the perpetrators were beheaded at Stirling. In consequence of the prosecution against his clan, the Drummond, by whose assistance David Murray had escaped, fled to Ireland, until, by means of the person whose life he had saved, he was permitted to return to Scotland, where he and his descendants were distinguished by the name of Drummond-Eirinich, or Ernoch, that is, Drummond of Ireland; and the same title was bestowed on their estate.

"The Drummond-ernoch of James the Sixth's time was a king's forester in the forest of Glenartney, and chanced to be employed there in search of venison about the year 1588, or early in 1589. This forest was adjacent to the chief haunts of the MacGregors, or a particular race of them, known by the title of MacEagh, or Children of the Mist. They considered the forester's hunting in their vicinity as an aggression, or perhaps they had him at feud, for the apprehension or slaughter of some of their own name, or for some similar reason. This tribe of MacGregors were outlawed and persecuted, as the reader may see in the Introduction to Rob Roy; and every man's hand being against them, their hand was of course directed against every man. In short, they surprised and slew Drummond-ernoch, cut off his head, and carried it with them, wrapt in the corner of one of their plaids.

"In the full exultation of vengeance, they stopped at the house of Ardvoirlich, and demanded refreshment, which the lady, a sister of the murdered Drummond-ernoch, (her husband being absent,) was afraid or unwilling to refuse. She caused bread and cheese to be placed before them, and gave directions for more substantial refreshments to be prepared. While she was absent with this hospitable intention, the barbarians placed the head of her brother on the table, filling the mouth with bread and cheese, and bidding him eat, for many a merry meal he had eaten in that house.

"The poor woman returning, and beholding this dreadful sight, shrieked aloud, and fled into the woods, where, as described in the romance, she roamed a raving maniac, and for some time secreted herself from all living society,

east of the house are peculiarly beautiful. At the foot of Loch Earn, there is a small artificial islet covered with wood, which was at one time the retreat of a bandit sept of the name of Neish.

Some remaining instinctive feeling brought her at length to steal a glance from a distance at the maidens while they milked the cows, which being observed, her husband, Ardvoirlich, had her conveyed back to her home, and detained her there till she gave birth to a child, of whom she had been pregnant; after which she was observed gradually to recover her mental faculties.

"Meanwhile the outlaws had carried to the utmost their insults against the regal authority, which indeed, as exercised, they had little reason for respecting. They bore the same bloody trophy, which they had so savagely exhibited to the lady of Ardvoirlich, into the old church of Balquhidder, nearly in the centre of their country, where the Laird of MacGregor and all his clan being convened for the purpose, laid their hands successively on the dead man's head, and swore in heathenish and barbarous manner, to defend the author of the deed. This fierce and vindictive combination gave the late lamented Sir Alexander Boswell, Bart., subject for a spirited poem, entitled "Clan-Alpin's Vow," which was printed, but not published in 1811."

We give the spirited conclusion of the poem:—"The Clan-Gregor has met in the ancient church of Balquhidder. The head of Drummond-ernoch is placed on the altar, covered for a time with the banner of the tribe. The Chief of the tribe advances to the altar:—

"And pausing, on the banner gazed;
Then cried in scorn, his finger raised,
'This was the boon of Scotland's king;'
And, with a quick and angry fling,
Tossing the pageant screen away,
The dead man's head before him lay.
Unmoved he scann'd the visage o'er,
The clotted locks were dark with gore,
The features with convulsion grim,
The eyes contorted, sunk, and dim.
But unappall'd, in angry mood,
With lowering brow, unmoved he stood.
Upon the head his bared right hand
He laid, the other grasp'd his brand:
Then kneeling, cried, 'To Heaven I swear
This deed of death I own, and share;
As truly, fully mine, as though
This my right hand had dealt the blow;
Come then, our foemen, one, come all;
If to revenge this caitiff's fall
One blade is bared, one bow is drawn,
Mine everlasting peace I pawn,
To claim from them, or claim from him,
In retribution, limb for limb.
In sudden fray, or open strife,
This steel shall render life for life.'

Having on one occasion plundered some of the Macnabs, a party of that clan, commanded by the chieftain's son, carried a boat from Loch Tay to Loch Earn, surprised the banditti by night, and put them all to the sword. In commemoration of this event, the Macnabs assumed for their crest a man's head with the motto "Dreadnought."

At the east end of Loch Earn, stands the neat little village of St. Fillans. It was formerly a wretched hamlet, known by the name of Portmore, but through the exertions of Lord and Lady Willoughby de Eresby, on whose ground it stands, it has become one of the sweetest spots in Scotland. It derived its name from St. Fillan, a celebrated saint who resided in this place. He was the favourite saint of Robert Bruce, and one of his arms was borne in a shrine by the Abbot of Inchaffray at the battle of Banockburn. On the summit of a hill in this neighbourhood, called Dun Fillan, there is a well consecrated by him, which even to this day is supposed to be efficacious for the cure of many disorders. The St. Fillans Society, formed in 1819, holds an annual meeting in this place for athletic sports and performances on the bagpipe, and confers prizes on the successful competitors. These games are usually attended by great numbers of persons of condition, male and female, from all parts of the Highlands. The valley of Strathearn, which extends from this place nearly to Perth, contains many fine

"He ceased; and at his beckoning nod,
The clansmen to the altar trod;
And not a whisper breathed around,
And nought was heard of mortal sound,
Save from the clanking arms they bore,
That rattled on the marbled floor;
And each, as he approach'd in haste,
Upon the scalp his right hand placed;
With livid lip, and gather'd brow,
Each uttered, in his turn, the vow.
Fierce Malcolm watch'd the passing scene,
And search'd them through with glances keen;
Then dash'd a tear-drop from his eye;
Unbid it came—he knew not why.
Exulting high, he towering stood;
'Kinsmen,' he cried, 'of Alpin's blood,
And worthy of Clan-Alpin's name,
Unstain'd by cowardice and shame,
E'en do, spare nocht, in time of ill
Shall be Clan-Alpin's legend still!'"

Introduction to Legend of Montrose.

villas and wooded parks, and is celebrated for its beauty and fertility. Leaving St. Fillans, the road winds along the banks of the Earn, through groves of lofty trees, presenting here and there broken glimpses of the ridges of the neighbouring mountains. About two miles and a half from Loch Earn, we pass the mansion of Duneira, the favourite seat of the late Lord Melville, with its picturesque grounds and delightful pleasure walks. It is now the property of Sir David Dundas, Bart. A little further on, Dalchonzie (Skene, Esq.), and Aberuchill Castle* (Drummond, Esq.), are seen on the right; and, five miles and a half from St. Fillans, the tourist enters the village of Comrie, pleasantly situated on the north bank of the Earn, at its confluence with the Ruchill. Comrie is remarkable for the earthquakes with which it has occasionally been visited for a number of years. It is by many supposed to have been the scene of the dreadful battle between Galgacus and Agricola. Half a mile south of the village are the remains of a Roman camp. Close to the village stands Comrie House (Dundas, Bart.); on the east side of which the Lednoch Water flows into the Earn. On the summit of a hill called Dunmore, a monument seventy-two feet in height, has been erected to the memory of the late Lord Melville, overhanging a turbulent little stream called the "Humble Bumble." At the foot of Dunmore there is a place called the "Devil's Caldron," where the Lednoch, at the further extremity of a long, deep, and narrow chasm, is precipitated into a dark and dismal gulf. From the monument there is an extensive and interesting view of the adjacent country.

Leaving Comrie we descend towards Crieff, through a scene of the most enchanting beauty. A mile and a half beyond Comrie, we pass, on the left, Lawers' House (the mansion of the late Lord Balgray), the parks of which contain some of the largest pine trees in Scotland. A mile further on is Clathick (Colquhoun, Esq.), and half a mile beyond the road passes Monivaird Kirk. On an eminence to the south of this place there is an obelisk, erected to Sir David Baird, Bart. A mile and a half beyond is Ochtertyre (Sir William Murray), celebrated for the romantic beauty of its situation. The adjacent vale of the Turit exhibits a variety of romantic scenery, which has been rendered classical by the pen of Burns. The road now winds along the brow of a wooded hill, and about six and

* Aberuchill was built in 1602, and was the scene of many sanguinary battles between the Campbells and Macgregors.

a half miles from Comrie, enters the thriving town of Crieff, delightfully situated on a slope above the river Earn, backed by hills and crags, and the Knock of Crieff, all of considerable altitude. It contains about 5000 inhabitants, who are principally engaged in the manufacture of cotton goods. The environs of Crieff are exquisitely beautiful, and will amply repay the visit of the tourist. Three miles south from the town is the delightful little village of Muthil with its new church, an excellent specimen of the Gothic style. In the same direction, on the road to Dumblane, is Drummond Castle, the ancient residence of the noble family of Perth, now represented by Lady Willoughby d'Eresby. "If Drummond Castle," says M'Culloch, "is not all that it might be rendered, it is still absolutely unrivalled in the low country, and only exceeded in the Highlands by Dunkeld and Blair. Placed in the most advantageous position to enjoy the magnificent and various expanse around, it looks over scenery scarcely any where equalled. With ground of the most commanding and varied forms, including water and rock, and abrupt hill and dell, and gentle undulations, its extent is princely and its aspect that of ancient wealth and ancient power. Noble avenues, profuse woods, a waste of lawn and pasture, an unrestrained scope, every thing bespeaks the carelessness of liberality and extensive possessions, while the ancient castle, its earliest part belonging to 1500, stamps on it that air of high and distant opulence which adds so deep a moral interest to the rural beauties of baronial Britain."

North from Crieff, on the road to Amulree, is Monzie Castle (pronounced *Monée*), Campbell, Esq., situated amid splendid scenery. The paintings and armoury are well worthy of attention. Leaving Crieff for Perth, we pass in succession Fernton (Lady Baird); a mile beyond this Cultoquhey (Maxton, Esq.), then Inchbrakie (Græme, Esq.), and next on the right, Abercairney (Moray, Esq.) Further on is the village of Foulis, and a mile beyond this the ruins of the Abbey of Inchaffray, founded in 1200 by an Earl of Strathearn and his Countess, and the abbot of which carried the arm of St. Fillans at the battle of Bannockburn. A mile further on, the road passes Gorthy (Mercer, Esq.), and shortly after enters the plantations of Balgowan, the seat of Lord Lynedoch. A little further the road passes on the right Tippermalloch (Moncrief, Esq.) and between six and seven miles from Perth enters the village of Methven, containing a population of about 2000. In the immediate neighbourhood stands Methven Castle (Smythe, Esq.) Near Methven Robert Bruce was defeated, June 19, 1306, by the English, under the command of Aymer de Valence, Earl of Pembroke. About two miles and a half from Perth, the road passes the ancient castle of Ruthven, the scene of the memorable incident known in Scottish history by the name of the *Raid of Ruthven*. The building has now been converted into a residence for workmen, and its name changed to Huntingtower. A short distance to the north is Lynedoch Cottage, within the grounds of which is Burn Braes, a spot on the banks of Brauchieburn, where Bessie Bell and Mary Gray

> ———— "biggit a bower
> And theekit it ower wi' rashes."

Dronach Haugh, where these unfortunate beauties were buried, is about half a mile west from Lynedoch Cottage, on the banks of the river Almond. The road now passes Tulloch bleachfield and printfield, and shortly after enters the town of Perth.

KILLIECRANKIE—BLAIR-ATHOLL—INVERNESS.

Leaving Dunkeld, the road passes for some miles along the eastern bank of the Tay, and at the distance of five miles reaches Dowally Kirk. On the opposite side of the river are seen Dalguise (Stewart, Esq.) and Kinnaird House (Duke of Atholl.) A little farther on is Moulinearn Inn. A mile farther is Donavourd (Macfarlane, Esq.) on the right, and Dunfallandy (General Ferguson) on the western bank of the Tummel. A mile beyond is the village of Pitlochrie, and a little farther, on a low tongue of land formed by the junction of the Tummel and the Garry, is Fascally House, (Butter, Esq.) surrounded by wooded hills, forming a most romantic and attractive scene. Proceeding onward, at the distance of a mile, the traveller enters the celebrated pass of Killiecrankie, which stretches for the space of a mile or more along the termination of the river Garry. The hills which on both sides approach very near, are covered with natural wood, and descend in rugged precipices to the deep channel of the river. At the bridge over the Garry, near the entrance of the pass, a road leads on the left to the districts of the Tummel and Rannoch. The north end of this pass is the well known scene of the battle fought in 1689 between the Highland clans under Viscount Dundee and the troops of King William commanded by General Mackay. A stone is pointed out at Urrard House on the right which marks the spot where Dundee received his death-wound.* Several villas adorn the terraced sides of the

* "Dundee," says Sir John Dalrymple, "flew to the Convention and demanded justice. The Duke of Hamilton, who wished to get rid of a troublesome adversary, treated his complaint with neglect; and, in order to sting him in the tenderest part, reflected upon that courage which could be alarmed by imaginary dangers. Dundee left the house in a rage, mounted his horse, and with a troop of fifty horsemen, who had deserted to him from his regiment in England, galloped through the city. Being asked by one of his friends who stopped him, where he was going? he waved his hat, and is reported to have answered, 'Wherever the spirit of Montrose shall direct me.'"—*Memoirs*, 4to edit. vol. i. p. 287. Dundee immediately proceeded to collect the army with which he fought the battle of Killiecrankie. This incident has been commemorated by Sir W. Scott in the following spirited Song:—

"To the Lords of Convention, 'twas Clavers who spoke,
Ere the King's crown go down, there are crowns to be broke,
So each cavalier, who loves honour and me,
Let him follow the bonnet of bonnie Dundee.

Come, fill up my cup, come, fill up my can,
Come, saddle my horses, and call up my men;
Come, open the West Port, and let me gae free,
And it's room for the bonnets of bonnie Dundee.

Dundee he is mounted, he rides up the street;
The bells are rung backward, the drums they are beat;
But the provost, douce man, said, Just e'en let him be;
The town is weel quit of that deil of Dundee.
Come, fill up, &c.

valley approaching the pass, viz. Urrard House (Alston, Esq.); Killiecrankie Cottage, (Hay, Esq.); Strathgarey, (Stewart, Esq.) &c. Passing Lude, (M'Inroy, Esq.) the road descends into the valley and crosses the river at the

As he rode down the sanctified bends of the Bow,
Each carline was flyting and shaking her pow;
But some young plants of grace, they looked couthie and slee,
Thinking—Luck to thy bonnet, thou bonnie Dundee!
    Come, fill up, &c.

With sour-featured saints the Grassmarket was panged,
As if half of the west had set tryst to be hanged;
There was spite in each face, there was fear in each ee,
As they watched for the bonnet of bonnie Dundee.
    Come, fill up, &c.

The cowls of Kilmarnock had spits and had spears,
And lang-hafted gullies to kill cavaliers;
But they shrunk to close-heads, and the causeway left free,
At a toss of the bonnet of bonnie Dundee.
    Come, fill up, &c.

He spurred to the foot of the high castle rock,
And to the gay Gordon he gallantly spoke:
Let Mons Meg and her marrows three volleys let flee,
For love of the bonnets of bonnie Dundee.
    Come, fill up, &c.

The Gordon has asked of him whither he goes—
Wheresoever shall guide me the soul of Montrose;
Your Grace in short space shall have tidings of me,
Or that low lies the bonnet of bonnie Dundee.
    Come, fill up, &c.

There are hills beyond Pentland, and streams beyond Forth;
If there's lords in the Southland, there's chiefs in the North;
There are wild dunnniewassals three thousand times three,
Will cry *Hoigh!* for the bonnet of bonnie Dundee.
    Come, fill up, &c.

Away to the hills, to the woods, to the rocks,
Ere I own a usurper, I'll couch with the fox:
And tremble, false Whigs, though triumphant ye be,
You have not seen the last of my bonnet and me.
    Come, fill up, &c.

He waved his proud arm, and the trumpets were blown,
The kettle-drums clashed, and the horsemen rode on,
Till on Ravelston crags, and on Clermiston lee,
Died away the wild war-note of bonnie Dundee.

Bridge of Tilt, where there is a neat village and an excellent inn. The beauties of Glen Tilt and the Falls of Fender, formed by a burn falling into the water of Tilt, will amply repay a visit. A little further on, the road reaches the village and inn of Blair, and, in the neighbourhood the noble old castle of Blair, now called Atholl House, the ancient residence of the Dukes of that name. It is a long narrow building of three storeys. It was formerly much higher, and a place of considerable strength, but was reduced in height in consequence of the attacks of the Highlanders in 1716. Blair is celebrated for its noble old woods.

THE FALL OF BRUAR.

In the immediate neighbourhood there is a number of interesting waterfalls. Three miles to the westward are

Come, fill up my cup, come, fill up my can,
Come, saddle my horses, and call up my men;
Fling all your gates open, and let me gae free,
For 'tis up with the bonnets of bonnie Dundee.
Chambers's Songs, vol. ii. p. 689.

those of Bruar. The streamlet makes several distinct falls, and rushes through a rough perpendicular channel above which the sloping banks are covered with a fir plantation formed by the late Duke of Atholl, in compliance with the request of Burns in the well known "Petition." A walk has been cut through the plantation, and a number of fantastic little grottoes erected, and a carriage-road leads as far as the second set of falls. From Blair-Atholl a road leads through Glen Tilt, and over a wild mountainous district to the Braes of Mar. Leaving Blair Atholl the tourist passes through a wild Alpine territory, and proceeding along the banks of the Garry, at the distance of ten miles and a half, reaches the inn of Dalnacardoch. The country between Dalnacardoch and Dalwhinnie, (13 miles) presents a most desolate and cheerless aspect. Half way there are two mountains named the Badenoch *Boar* and the Athol *Sow*, at which the mountain streams part in opposite directions, some running eastward to join the Truim and the Spey, while others fall into the Tay. This spot is the proper separation between the counties of Inverness and Perth. The savage pass between Dalnacardoch and Dalwhinnie is called Drumouchter. The inn of Dalwhinnie is surrounded by a young plantation, the only green and pleasing object on which the eye can rest for many miles around. It is situated at the distance of about a mile from the head of Loch Ericht, on the north side of which is the mountain Benalder. A cave exists in this mountain in which Prince Charles Stuart found refuge for a short time after the battle of Culloden. At Dalwhinnie a road parts off by Laggan and Garviemore, and over the difficult hill of Corryiarick to Fort-Augustus. Leaving Dalwhinnie, at the distance of six miles, the road crosses the Truim, and four miles farther crosses the Spey. At Invernahavon, near the junction of these rivers, a celebrated clan battle was fought in the reign of James I. between the Mackintoshes and Camerons. Glen Truim is the property of Captain Ewen M'Pherson. The mountains which skirt the road on both sides are bleak and bare, and dull and uninteresting in their forms. Passing the village of Newton of Benchar,* commenced not long since by the late Mr. M'Pherson of Belleville, the tourist reaches Pitmain Inn, where he will enjoy an extensive view of the valley of the Spey and of the high black rock of Craig Dhu, the rendezvous of the M'Phersons. Badenoch was anciently the possession of the great family of the Cumings, who ruled here during the reigns of the early Scottish sovereigns. The remains of many of their numerous fortresses are still visible. The vast possessions of this family were forfeited on account of the part which they took in the wars between Bruce and Baliol. Badenoch now belongs to his Grace the Duke of Richmond. A mile beyond Pitmain is the village of Kingussie, opposite to which, on the other side of the Spey, are the ruins of Ruthven Barracks, destroyed by the Highlanders in 1746. On the same mount once stood one of the castles of the Cumings. It was at this place that the Highlanders re-assembled to the number of eight thousand two days after their defeat at Culloden, and here they received from Prince Charles the order to disperse. About two miles distant on the north side of the Spey, is Belleville, the seat of Macpherson, the transla-

* From Newton of Benchar the road to Fort-William by Loch Laggan strikes off. Here are relics of a Roman encampment, of which the lines are still discernible.

tor of Ossian, now occupied by Miss Macpherson. It stands on the site of the ancient castle of Raits, the principal stronghold of the Cumings. A little farther on, a view is obtained of Invereshie, the seat of Sir George Macpherson Grant of Ballindalloch, on the south bank of the Spey of Loch Insh, through which the river passes, and of some of the highest of the Grampians. A short way beyond is Kinrara, the favourite seat of the late Duchess of Gordon. The high rocky crag on the north bank of the Spey is Tor Alvie. On its eastern brow is a rustic hermitage, and at the other extremity of the ridge, an enormous cairn of stones, on one side of which is a tablet with an inscription to the memory of the heroes of Waterloo. On the left of the landscape is the beautiful Loch Alvie, with its neat manse and church. The magnificent scenery around Kinrara has been very correctly described by Dr. M'Culloch.—"A succession of continuous birch forest covering Kinrara's rocky hill and its lower grounds, intermixed with open glades, irregular clumps and scattered trees, produces a scene at once Alpine and dressed, combining the discordant characters of wild mountain landscape and of ornamental park scenery, while the variety is, at the same time, such as is only found in the most extended domains." Beyond Kinrara on the right are the great fir woods of Rothiemurchus,* (Sir J. P. Grant,) sup-

* The reader may, perhaps, recollect Sir Alexander Boswell's lively verses :—

"Come the Grants of Tullochgorum,
Wi' their pipers gaun before 'em,
Proud the mothers are that bore 'em.—
Feedle-fa-fum !

Next the Grants of Rothiemurchus,
Every man his sword and durk has,
Every man as proud 's a Turk is.—
Feedle-deedle-dum !"

posed to cover from 14 to 16 square miles. The Spey here takes several majestic sweeps, and supplies an elegant foreground to these forests. The road now enters Morayshire, and, thirteen miles from Pitmain, reaches Aviemore Inn, opposite to which is Cairngorm Hill, famous for a peculiar kind of rock crystals. The mountains on the left are extremely bare and rugged, but towards the west they terminate in the beautiful and bold projecting rock of Craig Ellachie (the *Rock of Alarm,*) the hill of rendezvous of the Grants. " Stand fast Craig Ellachie," is the slogan or war-cry of that clan, the occupants of this strath.—" From its swelling base and rifted precipices the birch trees wave in graceful cluster, their bright and lively green forming a strong contrast in the foreground to the sombre melancholy hue of the pine forests which in the distance stretch up the sides of the Cairngorms."* At Aviemore a road leads along the banks of the Spey to Grantown and Castle Grant, the residence of the Earl of Seafield. The road now leaves the Spey, and, at the Bridge of Carr, eight miles from Aviemore, crosses the Dulnain ; near this place another road strikes off on the right to Grantown. The country around is barren and uninteresting, but some burnt stumps sticking above the moor, and a few hoary and stunted pine trees are still to be seen, the solitary remains of those immense forests which once covered the surface of the country. The road now passes through the deep and dangerous pass called Slochmuichk, (the boar's den or hollow,) which was the favourite haunt of banditti even so late as near the close of last century. Four miles from the Bridge of Carr it re-enters Inver-

* Anderson's Guide to the Highlands, p 81.

ness-shire ; and two miles farther on crosses the rapid river Findhorn. The banks of the Findhorn are in general highly romantic, but at this spot they are by no means interesting. The road now passes Corybrough House (M'Queen, Esq.) and a short way beyond reaches the inn of

FREEBURN,

about nine miles from Bridge of Carr. Near it are the house and plantations of Tomatin (Duncan Macbean, Esq.) The small estate of Free is the property of John Macintosh, Esq. of Holm. All the rest of the adjoining lands, on the north side of the Findhorn, belong to the Mackintosh estate. Three miles and a half beyond this, on the right, is the castle of Moy, the ancient residence of Mackintosh, the chief of the clan Chattan, a confederation of the clans of Mackintosh, Macpherson, and others of less consequence. It stands on an island in the midst of a small gloomy lake, called Loch Moy, surrounded by a black wood of Scotch fir, which extends round the lake, and terminates in wild heaths, which are unbroken by any other object as far as the eye can reach. Near the southern end of the lake is a small artificial islet of loose stones, which the former chiefs of Moy used as a place of confinement for their prisoners. On the largest island a handsome granite obelisk, seventy feet high, has been erected to the memory of the late Sir Æneas Mackintosh, Bart. chief of the clan. On the west side of Loch Moy are the church and manse of Moy, and at the head of the lake, Moy Hall, the family residence of Mackintosh of Mackintosh. Here is preserved the sword of Viscount Dundee, and a sword sent by Pope Leo X. to James V. who bestowed it on the chief of clan Chattan, with the privilege of holding the king's sword at coronations. Leaving Loch Moy, the road enters Strathnairn, and passes for three miles through a bleak and heathery plain till it crosses the river Nairn, called in Gaelic *Kis-Nerane*, or the Water of Alders. The road now passes, on the right, Daviot House, the residence of Mackintosh of Mackintosh. Here stood the ancient castle of Daviot, founded, it is said, by David Earl of Crawford, who, by his marriage with Catherine, daughter of Robert II., acquired possession of the barony of Strathnairn. Passing Leys Castle, the seat of Miss Baillie of Leys, and various other mansions, the tourist, at the distance of six miles, enters the royal burgh of

INVERNESS,

situated on both sides of the river Ness, at the spot where the basins of the Moray and Beauly Friths and the Great Glen of Scotland meet one another. Inverness is a thriving sea-port, and is generally considered the capital of the Highlands. It is a tolerably handsome town, and contains a number of well built streets and elegant houses. The public buildings are spacious and some of them elegant. A handsome stone bridge of seven arches was erected over the Ness in 1685, between the second and third arches of which there is a vault, formerly used as a jail and latterly as a madhouse, which was only shut up about twenty years ago. Opposite the town-house is a strange blue lozenge-shaped stone, called Clach-na-Cudden, or "stone of the tubs," from having served as a resting-place on which the women in passing from the river, used to set down the deep tubs in which they carried water. It is reckoned the palladium of the town. In the wall above are the royal arms with those of the town beautifully carved. Inverness contains a flourishing academy, two public news-rooms, four banking-houses, several printing establishments, and two weekly newspapers, and carries on a respectable trade with London, Leith, &c. The tonnage of all the shipping belonging to the port is about 4300 tons, and the number of vessels sixty. In 1831, the population of the parish amounted to 14,324, that of the town alone being 9663. It joins with Forres, Nairn, and Fortrose in electing a member of Parliament. The present constituency is 489.

Inverness is a town of great antiquity, but the exact date of its origin is unknown. On an eminence to the south-east of the town stood an ancient castle, in which it was supposed that Duncan was murdered by Macbeth. This opinion is, however, now generally believed to be erroneous, but it is very probable that Macbeth had possession of this castle, and it is certain that it was destroyed by the son of the murdered king, Malcolm Canmore, who erected a new one on an eminence overhanging the town on the south. This latter edifice continued for several centuries to be a royal fortress. It was repaired by James I., in whose reign a Parliament was held within its walls, to which all the northern chiefs and barons were summoned, three of whom were executed here for treason. In 1562, Queen Mary paid a visit to Inverness, for the purpose of quelling an insurrection of the Earl of Huntly. Being refused admission into the castle by the governor, who held it for the Earl, she took up her residence in a house, part of which is still in existence. The castle was shortly after taken by her attendants, and the governor hanged. During the civil wars this castle was repeatedly taken by Montrose and his opponents. In 1715, it was converted into barracks for the Hanoverian soldiers, and in 1746, it was blown up by the troops of Prince Charles Stuart, and not a vestige of it now remains. On the north side of the town, near the mouth of the river, Cromwell erected a fort at an expense of £80,000. The stones employed in its construction were procured from the monasteries of Kinloss and Beauly, and the Greyfriar's Church. This fortress was demolished at the Restoration, but a considerable part of the rampart still remains. The environs of Inverness are remarkably fine, and the scenery on the banks of the river Ness presents a striking mixture of beauty and grandeur. At a little distance to the west of the town is a singular hill, called Craig Phadric, crowned by a splendid vitrified fort. The view from the summit is varied and extensive. The sides of the hill are covered by fine woods, in the midst of which stands the handsome house of Muirton, the seat of Mr. Huntly Duff, the great grandson of Catherine Duff, Lady Drummuir, in whose house both Prince Charles and the Duke of Cumberland lodged during their residence in Inverness.*

A mile to the south-west of Inverness is a strange wooded hill, called Tom-na-heurich (the hill of fairies), shaped like a ship with its keel uppermost. The walks all around it and on the banks of the Ness, are extremely beautiful.

One of the most interesting objects in the neighbourhood of Inverness is Culloden Moor, the scene of the final defeat of the Highland army under Prince Charles Stuart. This memorable spot lies about five miles to the south-east of the town. It is a vast and desolate tract of table land, traversed longitudinally by a carriage road, on the side of which are a number of green trenches marking the spot where the heat of the battle took place. On

* The bustle and confusion occasioned in the house by its distinguished tenants, made the proprietrix very testy; she used to say: "I have had twa kings' bairns for my guests, and trowth I never wish to hae another."

the north it is flanked by the Firth and the table land of the Black Isle. On the south-east by the ridges of Strathnairn, and its extremities are bounded on the westward by the splintered and serrated heights of Stratherrick. In the opposite distance, the moor is lost in a flat bare plain stretching towards Nairn,—one old square tower, the castle of Dalcross, a hold of the clan Chattan, rising upon the open waste with a unique and striking effect. The general smoothness of the ground rendered it peculiarly unfit for the movements of the Highland army, against cavalry and artillery. According to the general accounts, about 1200 men fell in this engagement. The number killed on both sides was nearly equal.

The victory at Culloden finally and for ever extinguished the hopes of the house of Stuart, and secured the liberties of Britain, but the cruelties exercised by the Duke of Cumberland on his helpless foes have stamped his memory with indelible infamy; and there are few who will not join in the sentiments expressed in the concluding stanza of Burns' pathetic song on the Battle of Culloden.

"Drumossie muir, Drumossie muir,
A waefu' day it was to me,
For there I lost my father dear,
My father dear and brethren three.

"Their winding sheet the bluidy clay,
Their graves are growing green to see,
And by them lies the dearest lad
That ever blest a woman's e'e.

"Now wae to thee, thou cruel Duke,
A bluidy man I trow thou be,
For monie a heart thou hast made sair,
That ne'er did wrang to thine or thee."*

* On the road leading from the battle-field to Inverness, there is an old farm steading with trees about it, like a small laird's dwelling. On the day succeed-

A mile to the north of Culloden Moor is Culloden House (Forbes, Esq.), which, at the time of the rebellion, belonged to the celebrated Duncan Forbes, Lord President of the Court of Session. Here Prince Charles lodged the night before the battle. Since 1745, it has been renewed in a very elegant style.

Fort-George, distant about twelve miles from Inverness, is another interesting object in this neighbourhood. It is situated on the extremity of a low sandy point which projects far out into the Moray Firth opposite

ing the battle, the body of a youth, of the better class, was carried here shrouded in a plaid: "My darling! my darling!" said the pitiful matron, to whom the stranger's corpse was brought, "some mother's heart is lying with thee." It was her own son, whom she fancied safe away with her relations in Glen Urquhart.—The following beautiful and pathetic song, of which Culloden is the scene, has never before (as far as we are aware) been in print. We have been unable to discover the name of the author, and shall feel obliged if any of our readers can communicate this information.

"Again the laverock seeks the skies,
And warbles dimly seen,
And summer views wi' sunny joys
Her gowden robe o' green.
But, ah! the summer's blythe return,
In flowery pride array'd,
Nae mair can cheer this heart forlorn,
Nor charm the Highland maid.

"My father's shielin' on the hill
Is cheerless now and sad,
The breezes round me whisper still,
I've lost my Highland lad.
His bonnet blue has fallen now,
And bloody is the plaid,
Where oft upon the mountain's brow
He row'd his Highland maid.

"The lee-lang night for rest I seek,
The lee-lang day I mourn,
The smile upon my wither'd cheek
Can never mair return.
Upon Culloden's fatal heath
He spak o' me they said,
And falter'd wi' his dying breath—
Adieu! my Highland maid."

Fortrose. At this spot the breadth of the firth is only about a mile. Fort-George was erected immediately after the suppression of the Rebellion, for the purpose of keeping the Highlanders in check. The fortifications, which are an exact resemblance of the great fortresses of the Continent, cover about fifteen English acres, and afford accommodation for about 3000 men. The establishment is kept in excellent order. At the bottom of the peninsula is Campbelton, a large modern village named from the Campbells of Cawdor.

A delightful excursion may be made to the little town of Beauly, situated at the head of the firth which bears its name, about twelve or thirteen miles west from Inverness. It has been justly said that there are not many rides of a more various and animating kind than that from Inverness westward to Beauly. Leaving Inverness, the tourist crosses the Caledonian Canal. The beautiful wooded hill in front is Craig Phadric, and the turreted mansion close by the road, embowered among trees, is Muirtown, the seat of Mr. Huntly G. Duff. The road now passes on the right the basin and village of Clachnaharry,* and enters on the Aird, the richest and most

* Clachnaharry derives it name (Clach-na-herrie, or the Watchman's Stone) from the rough impending rocks to the westward, where, in the days of black-mail and reivers, a watchman used to be stationed to give notice of the approach of the Highland clans from Ross or the west coast. On the highest pinnacle of the rock a column was erected by the late Major Duff of Muirtown, to commemorate a sanguinary engagement fought here between the Munroes of Foulis and the clan Chattan. It is thus described by Mr. Anderson in his *Historical Account of the Family of Fraser*, p. 54.—" The Munroes, a distinguished tribe of Ross, returning from an inroad they had made in the south of Scotland, passed by Moyhall, the seat of Mackintosh, leader of the clan Chattan ; a share of the booty, or road-collop, payable to a chief for traversing his dominions, was acceded to; but Macintosh's avaricious spirit coveting the whole, his proposal met with contempt, and Macintosh summoned his vassals to extort compliance. The Munroes pursuing their journey, forded the river Ness, a little above the island, and dispatched the cattle they had plundered across the hill of Kinmylies to Lovat's province. Their enemy came up to

beautiful district in Inverness-shire, and the land of the clan Fraser, studded with mansions, comfortable farm-houses, and snug cottages. The opposite shore of the firth is singularly rich and picturesque, and the background is occupied by the lofty mountains of Ross-shire. To the north is the huge form of Ben Wyvis and the heights of Strathglass and Strathconnan close the horizon to the west. The northern shore of the Firth, called the Black Isle, is adorned with the mansion of Redcastle, the seat of the late Sir William Fettes, anciently the property of a family sprung from the second son of the Laird of Kintail, chief of the clan Mackenzie. Three miles from Inverness is the wooded promontory of Bun-chrew, once the property and the favourite retreat of President Forbes of Culloden. It is now little more than a picturesque ruin in a dell or *cleugh,* covered by a perfect bewilderment of grotesque ancient trees, mossy springs, and tangled plants. The tourist now enters on the possessions of Lord Lovat; and on the next promontory will perceive the house of Phopachy, which has long been the property of an old branch of the clan Fraser, ancestors of the Frasers of Torbreck. At Bog-roy, seven miles from Inverness, a fine view is obtained of a ridge which rises from the bank of the river Beauly, crowned with luxuriant woods and adorned with elegant

them at the point of Clachnahayre, and immediately joined battle; the conflict was such as might have been expected from men excited to revenge by a long and inveterate enmity. Quarter was neither sought nor granted; after an obstinate struggle, Mackintosh was killed. The survivors of this band retraced their steps to their own country. John Munro, tutor of Foulis, was left for dead upon the field; his kinsmen were not long of retaliating. Having collected a sufficient force, they marched in the dead of the night for the Isle of Moy, where the chief of the Mackintoshes resided. By the aid of some planks which they had carried with them, and now put together, they crossed to the isle, and glutted their thirst for revenge, by the murder or captivity of all the inmates."

mansion-houses of gentlemen belonging to the clan Fraser. From Bogroy there are two roads which lead to Beauly,—the post-road, which keeps along the low ground, and passing the houses of Easter and Westr Moniack, surrounded by fine scenery, crosses the river Beauly by the handsome Lovat Bridge built in 1810, and reaches Beauly village. The old road passes several of the seats before alluded to, and the church and manse of Kirkhill, and leads over the summit of the hill where the old church of Wardlaw stood. The chapel which occupies the site of that building has been for many generations the burying place of the family of Lovat, and the walls are hung round with escutcheons and tablets, memorials of the chiefs of former days. From this spot a magnificent view is obtained of the valley of Beauly, traversed by the broad winding river, the village and the old priory, Beaufort Castle, and other mansions, embosomed in woods, and in the distance the rugged heights of Strathglass and Glenstrathfarrar.

Crossing the ferry, the tourist reaches the inn and village of Beauly, worthy of its name,—Beau-lieu, *fine place*. Close by the village, on the brink of the river, are the ruins of the priory founded by John Bisset of Lovat in 1230, and peopled at first by monks from France belonging to the order of Valliscaulium, a reform of the Cistercians. Only the walls and nave and transepts of the chapel now remain. The internal area is used as a burying-ground by the clan Fraser, the Chisholms, and other families in Strathglass. The north aisle belongs exclusively to the Mackenzies of Gairloch. The priory is overshadowed by some fine old trees which have a pleasing effect.

The tourist, while in this district, may visit Dingwall, nine miles north from Beauly, and the scenery around Strathpeffer. On quitting Inverness-shire the road at Beauly enters Ross-shire by a flat dull tract called the *Muir of Ord*, once the scene of the clan battles of the Frasers, Macleods, and Mackenzies, now distinguished for its large cattle-markets. About three miles farther on the tourist reaches the banks of the Conon, a stream flowing through a beautiful valley, richly studded with mansion-houses, woods, hamlets, and farms. On the left is Highfield (Gillanders, Esq.) beyond it Fairburn, (Miss Macpherson of Belleville,) and in the centre of the plain Castle Brahan, the seat of J. S. Mackenzie, Esq. of Seaforth, an imposing structure, with charming grounds.* Some delightful views are obtained of the grand scenery of Wester Ross-shire. The road now passes Conon House, the mansion of Sir Francis Mackenzie of Gairloch, and descends to the Bridge of Scuddel, where it joins the road from Inverness by Kessock Ferry, which is eight miles shorter than the road by Beauly. Here also a road strikes off to the west by Brahan to Contin inn (five miles distant) where it joins the road from Dingwall to Loch Carron. Three miles beyond, the road reaches the royal burgh of Dingwall, the capital of Ross-shire. Dingwall is a neat town, containing about 1000 inhabitants. It lies in a low situation near the opening of the valley of Strathpeffer. The scenery around is remarkably beautiful. In the neighbourhood of the town formerly

* Brahan Castle was built by Kenneth, the founder of the clan of the Mackenzies. The father, Kenneth, an Irishman, of the house of Geraldine, married the only daughter and heiress of *Coinneach Grumach, i. e.* 'Kenneth the morose,' chief of the clan Mathieson. Kenneth was named after his grandfather, and given up as heir-apparent to his management. According to clan traditions, Coinneach Grumach was assassinated through a perfidious plot of the chief of Glengarry with whom he was at feud about the lands of Lochalsh. At the same time nearly the whole of his clan were murdered by the Macdonalds in cold blood in their beds. Young Kenneth alone escaped through the affection and fidelity of his nurse. At a royal hunting match held in Kintail by Alexander III., the king having been accidentally separated from his attendants, was put in peril of his life by a stag, when young Kenneth sprung to the rescue of the monarch, exclaiming "*Cudich an Righ! Cudich an Righ!*" and getting between Alexander and the deer, the youth with his naked sword in his hand, severed its head from its body at one stroke. The *caber fae*, (the deer's head) ever after formed his crest, and his motto *Cudich an Righ!* Such was the respect of the clan for the roof-tree of Kenneth I. that it is said the heads of the different Mackenzie families at one time forcibly interfered to prevent the Earl of Seaforth from pulling down Brahan Castle.

stood the castle of the powerful Earls of Ross; but of that once princely structure scarcely a vestige now remains. From Dingwall the great road to the west coast of Ross-shire leads through a succession of valleys. Strathpeffer, the first of these, is a fair flat fertile valley, broad and open, stretching from Dingwall about four or five miles. At an obtuse angle it joins Strathconon, from which it is separated by Knockfarrel. On the other side of the open strath rises Ben Wyvis, the king of the mountains on this side of the island, divided from it by an advanced hill, on which hangs Tulloch Castle, (D. Davidson, Esq.) surrounded by fine plantations. At the head of Strathpeffer is an excellent and fashionable mineral well, and a number of villas and neatly built houses have lately sprung up around it. In the immediate vicinity of the Spa is the venerable baronial mansion the seat of the ancient Earls of Cromarty, and now the residence of the Hon. Mrs. Hay Mackenzie of Cromarty, to whom the greater part of Strathpeffer belongs. The surrounding scenery affords ample scope for excursions.*

Leaving Strathpeffer, the road leads us to the banks of the Conon, passing by the church and manse of Contin, standing on an island of the river embowered among trees and shrubs, and Coul House, the mansion of Sir George S. Mackenzie, Bart. the principal proprietor of this fine woodland district. A little to the east of Contin village the fine streams of the Conon and the Garve or Blackwater unite. At the church of Contin, the Parliamentary

* Strathpeffer was about the year 1478 the scene of a bloody conflict between the Macdonalds of the west coast and the Mackenzies. It is thus described by Messrs. Andersons in their Guide to the Highlands, p. 559.—" Strathpeffer, now the resort of the fair and the gay, as well as the sick and decrepit, was, in days of yore, about the year 1478, the scene of a bloody conflict between the Macdonalds of the west coast and the Mackenzies, who were aided by parties of their neighbours, the Dingwalls, Baynes, Maccullochs, and Frasers, in which the latter were victorious. Gillespie Macdonald, the nephew, or, as some say, the brother of the Lord of the Isles, headed one party, and the chief of the Mackenzies, whose residence stood on an island in the small adjoining lake of Kinellan, commanded his troops in person.

" This chief had, for a slight offence, repudiated his wife, a sister of the Macdonald, and married another lady, a daughter of Lord Lovat. The clan, in revenge for the injured honour of their chieftain, Macdonald, laid waste the lands of the Mackenzies. It is said they were challenged by the latter to meet them on the spot, and the combat which ensued was most desperate. A thousand of the islesmen are said either to have been killed or drowned in the river Conon while attempting to escape. This conflict is generally known as the battle of Blar-na-Parc."

road from Dingwall is joined by the other branch from Scuddel Bridge before noticed.* Exactly opposite the inn of Contin rises the shapely and graceful hill of Tor Achilty, lightly sprinkled with birches and pines, and young oak copses. From this spot a road strikes off to the west, which leads past Loch Achiltie and Comrie to Strath Conon, and the falls of the Conon. Passing Craigdarroch, the lovely villa of Colonel Murray, with its delightful pleasure grounds, the tourist reaches Loch Achiltie, "the most enchanting small lake in Great Britain," one of those exquisitely beautiful spots where, if

"Art ere come, 'tis with unsandalled feet."

"It is literally embosomed among hanging glades, and shrubby crags, and birchen knolls, rising in every light, graceful, and fanciful form, which, however, come not so near as to trouble or dim its bright loveliness there where it reposes

"A mirror in the depths of sylvan shelves,—
So fair a spot of earth, you might, I ween,
Have deemed some congregation of the elves,
To sport by summer-moons, had shaped it for themselves."

Loch Achilty is about three miles in circumference, its margin is broken into caves, islets, and promontories, luxuriantly clothed with trees, shrubs, and herbage, while in the extreme distance tower the "aerial or hazily empurpled summits" of Scuirvullin in Strath Conon. The road skirts the northern shore, and, leading past a series of little lochs, at the distance of two miles, enters the soft meadow holms of Comrie, and the sweet valley of Scatwell, watered by the combined streams of the Conon and Meig. The former river descends from Loch Luichart, the latter flows through Strath Conon, and rushes along at the bottom of a narrow savage gorge, presenting the appearance of a continuous cataract nearly a mile in length. There is a regular ferry boat which will conduct the tourist across the river, opposite Milltown of Scatwell. The road leads along the south side of the valley over a bare rocky ridge, and, at the distance of about a mile, enters Strath Conon, a narrow valley, the sides of which are fringed with alder trees and birch copse. This glen formed part of an estate which was forfeited on account of the participation of its proprietor in the rebellion of 1745. The numerous

* Contin is only sixteen or eighteen miles distant from two points where the Edinburgh and London steamers touch,—Invergordon, on the Cromarty Firth, and Kessock Ferry, opposite Inverness. From Kessock a coach (the *Caberfae*) proceeds to Dingwall every afternoon through the Black Isle.

patches of bright verdure which are seen here and there amidst the heathery or russet pasturages of the extensive sheep farms, show how populous this strath has once been. But it is now lone and desolate, and the interesting race who once peopled it have found a new Strath Conon beyond the western waters.

> "A noble race, but they are gone,
> With their old forests wide and deep
> And we have *fed our flocks* upon
> Hills where their generations sleep.
> *Their* fountains slake our thirst at noon;
> Upon *their* fields our harvest waves;
> Our shepherds woo beneath their moon,—
> Ah! let us spare at least their graves."

The tourist may either return to Contin by the way he left it, or he may proceed directly across the northern shoulder of Scuirvullin, and join the parliamentary road from Dingwall to Lochcarron, half way between Auchnanault and Auchnasheen.

Leaving the inn of Contin he proceeds up Strathgarve, winding through birch and pine woods. The picturesque Falls of Rogie, which have been likened to those of Tivoli in Italy, lie down the wooded steeps under the road. Loch Garve is a fine sheet of water about two miles in length. Near the head of the loch is the inn of Garve, which was sometimes the sojourn of Sir Humphrey Davy. The scenery beyond this point is uninteresting.

The most prominent object all through this tract of country is the mountain Ben Wyvis, not so much on account of its height as from its enormous lateral bulk. Sir Hugh Munro of Foulis, the principal proprietor of Ben Wyvis, holds his estate in Ross-shire by a tenure binding him to bring three wainloads of snow from the top of that mountain whenever his Majesty shall desire. It has never been entirely free from snow within the memory of man, except in September 1826.

About two miles west from Beauly are the lower falls of Kilmorack. They lie immediately under the garden of the manse, and are best viewed from it. The falls themselves are of no great consequence, " but the whole scene,—the full river toiling through the deep tortuous chasm, and escaping in smooth lapses,—the rough rocky steeps, and hanging woods and green margins,—is beautiful and striking." It is a favourite sport to catch the salmon at this place as they struggle to ascend the river over the rocky ledges; and it is said that the Lords Lovat of the olden time, by a particular contrivance, made the salmon leap into a boiling kettle which was kept suspended over the bank. On the opposite side of the river, close by the saw-mills, are the ruins of the old church and the deserted manse of Kiltarlity.

A little below the falls on the right bank of the river is Beaufort Castle, the seat of Lord Lovat, the chief of the clan Fraser. It was erected on the site of the old fortress of Beaufort, which belonged to the powerful family of Bizzet or Bisset. The possessions of this family extended over the Aird and a great part of Stratherrick and Abertarff on Loch Ness, but, being implicated in the rebellion of Donald Lord of the Isles, their estates were bestowed on the Frasers, who emigrated to the north from Peebles and Tweeddale about the year 1296. Beaufort was besieged by Edward I. in 1803, and also by Oliver Cromwell, who blew up the citadel. It was completely destroyed by the royal forces in 1746 after the battle of Culloden.

About three miles above the church and falls of Kilmorack, there is another succession of falls, at a place called "the Drhuim," where the valley has narrowed to a gorge, and completely shut out the view of frith and champaign. "The hilly banks, luxuriantly wooded, are lofty and steep, and high pyramids of rock, in every fantastic shape, shoot up like glaciers from the choked, though wide-spread, bed of the river, which here boils and chafes in fury, and there, when its rage is spent, sleeps in dreamy dark pools among the banks of the loveliest moss and freshest verdure, as if mustering its force for another fierce encounter.

"The broad rocky bed of this powerful river, in which are united the Glass and the Farrar, and many smaller tributaries, is studded by innumerable shrubby islets, which throw a wild profusion of intermingled boughs and plants into the translucent water, with exquisite effect in reflection and colouring." On one of these, (the island of Aigas,) which is, in fact, a river-girt and wooded hill, the notorious Simon Lord Lovat, in 1697, concealed the dowager Lady Lovat, whom he had forced to become his wife. Half way up the strath is an enchanting Highland residence, called Teanassie, often occupied in summer as a shooting lodge. Proceeding a few miles up the valley, the tourist reaches Erchless Castle, the seat of the late Laird of Chisholm, the chief of a small clan who, at a comparatively recent date, came from the Borders. The family estates lie on the north side of the Beauly, and in Strathglass. In front of Erchless Castle the Farrar and the Glass unite and form the river Beauly. Near the junction a handsome stone bridge of five arches was erected a few years ago, and adjoining it stands Struy House, till lately the seat of an ancient branch of the Frasers, next heirs of entail to the estate of Lovat after the present Lord and his heirs-male. Struy Bridge is about ten miles from Beauly. Here the valley or strath of the Beauly river divides itself into two glens, Glenstrathfarrar and Strathglass. The former extends along the base of the mountain Benevachart for a distance of about nine miles. It is lone and wild, rocky and lavishly wooded, but of exquisite beauty, and, alternately narrowing and expanding, presents a great variety of landscape. At its further extremity is Loch Miulie, in which is a small island that afforded shelter to Lord Lovat after the battle of Culloden.

Strathglass stretches nearly southwest, and is traversed by the stream whose name it bears. In ancient times large pine forests stretched along the valley up to the summits of the hills. These have long ago been destroyed, but the sides of the glen are still fringed with beautiful birch trees. About fifteen miles from Struy Bridge the tourist reaches the elegant mansion house of Guisachan, the seat of William Fraser, Esq. of Culbockie. The grounds are in a high state of cultivation, and their luxuriant vegetation is very unlike what we might have expected in such a remote district. The scenery around is uncommonly magnificent. The distance from Guisachan through Glen Affrick to Dornie in Kintail is only a forenoon's journey. The route lies along a series of lochs through a hoary primeval pine forest. The scenery is of a kindred nature to that of the Trosachs, but greatly surpasses it in magnificence, wildness, grandeur and extent.

Until the parliamentary road was opened through Glen Moriston and by Cluny into Glen Sheil, this was the principal route from Inverness and Ross-shires into Kintail and the surrounding parts of the west coasts.*

* It may be easily believed that no one was permitted in those days to enter Kintail whose visits were not perfectly acceptable to the natives. "When the estates of the Earl of Seaforth were forfeited after the rebellion of 1715, and the foolish attempt at invasion which succeeded it in 1719, it was found quite impracticable for the government to collect any rents in Kintail. A Mr. Ross, the first gentleman sent to make the attempt, was attended by a select party of soldiers, whom the Kintail men—to save them the needless trouble of coming through Glen Affrick, on a bootless errand—met at Lochan Cloigh, in the heights of Strathglass, where an admonitory bullet, sent from an overhanging thicket, grazed the neck of the collector of his Majesty's exchequer. He, however, was a Highlander, though a Whig; and he gallantly advanced three or four more

There are various roads which lead across the hills from Strathglass into Urquhart and Glen Moriston.

miles, when his son was fired at from another ambuscade, and mortally wounded. The *soldiers* became alarmed, and their leader capitulated, and retreated as wise as he came. Another attempt to enter Kintail next rent-time, made by a more northerly route, was met in the same manner: the military leader was wounded and forced to return. Yet all this while the rents were duly collected among the devoted tenantry of Seaforth—the Macraws of Kintail; and, by some means or other, duly transmitted to France to the forfeited Earl, by a Donald Murchieson, the memory of whose military and business talents, and attachment to the chief, are still embalmed in the hearts of the elders among the Kintail tribes. The natives felt not a little pride, that, though worsted in the open fight of Glenshiel, they for years contrived, by means of their fastnesses, and the mountain passes into their country, to baffle the agents and troops of the government.

"We were informed that it is not yet easy to execute even a civil process on this west coast, if against a popular character. The minions of the law coming from Inverness or Dingwall are as well known in the hills, and not much more beloved, than the *gaugers*. As soon as they are discovered descending the heights, their errand is guessed; and, though open deforcement is rarely ventured upon, the fiery cross is secretly speeded on to the individual in peril of the law, while the emissaries are detained at fords, ferries, and clachans, rivers, and arms of the sea. No boat tackle is ready,—ponies are on the hill and cannot be caught, until the safety of the party is secured; when the beagles, after beating about for some days, may return from whence they came, and draw out their bill of costs for travelling to Loch Broom or Loch Carron."—*Tait's Magazine.*

THIRTEENTH TOUR.

INVERNESS—BANKS OF THE CALEDONIAN CANAL—GLEN URQUHART —GLEN MORISTON—FORT AUGUSTUS—FORT WILLIAM—GLENCOE—TYNDRUM.

THE tourist may leave Inverness by a very delightful route, which leads along the banks of the Caledonian Canal. There are two roads along the opposite sides of Lochs Ness and Oich, but the north-west road is by far the most picturesque. Leaving Inverness by the old bridge, and passing the peculiarly-shaped hill called Tomnaheurich, the tourist, at the distance of about a mile from the town, crosses the canal, and ascends the undulating face of Torvain. On this hill, in 1197, there was fought a desperate battle, between Donald Bane of the Isles and a body of troops from the castle of Inverness. Passing the house of Dunain (W. Baillie, Esq.), the tourist comes in sight of the beautiful little lake—Dochfour. On its banks is Dochfour House, the seat of Evan Baillie, Esq. surrounded by fine parks and magnificent trees. Nearly opposite, in a lively sequestered bay which forms the narrow eastern extremity of Loch Ness, is Aldourie, the seat of W. F. Tytler, Esq. where Sir James Mackintosh spent several years of his childhood. For the first few miles along the shores of Loch Ness, the hills are bare and very steep. They are called Craig Derg or the Red Rocks, from their reddish tint. The inhabitants of these *braes* were formerly noted for smuggling whiskey. About fifteen miles from Inverness, Glen Urquhart opens up from the lake. This glen, which has been pronounced the fairest, the richest, and the most splendid in its beauty among Scotland's glens, is about ten miles in length, and is luxuriantly wooded. At the mouth of the glen there is an excellent inn called Drumindrochet. In the centre of the vale, there is a small but very pretty lake, having the mansions of Lakefield, Lochletter, and Sheuglie, scattered around its borders. About two miles from the inn, a small burn falls over a lofty ledge of rock forming the falls of Divach. A small bay runs up from the loch for about two miles into the valley, receiving the united waters of the Coiltie and Enneric. On the western promontory of this bay are the ruins of the castle of Urquhart, frequently noticed in the annals of the earlier Scottish monarchs. It appears to have been once a strong and extensive building. It was besieged and taken by the troops of Edward I. in 1303. In 1509, it fell, along with the barony of Urquhart, into the hands of the chief of the elan Grant, and it still continues in the possession of that family, who have a residence in it called Balmacaan. The road from Drumindrochet to Invermoriston—thirteen miles—is one of remarkable beauty. It is cut in the mountain side, plunging into hollows and climbing sharp acclivities, sometimes bordering the loch, but more frequently proceeding at a considerable elevation above its level, and winding through the most luxuriant woods of oak, birch, alder, and pine. It skirts the base of the high and naked mountain, Mealfourvonie, which separates the two glens of Urquhart and Moriston. Mealfourvonie rises almost perpendicularly from the lake to the height of 3060 feet. The opening of Glen Moriston is a very picturesque scene. In the foreground is the mansion of James Murray Grant, Esq. proprietor of the glen. The situation is very fine. On the opposite side of the river, and twenty-six miles from Inverness, is the inn of Invermoriston, a small but comfortable house. Immediately below it, the river Moriston falls over a considerable precipice, forming a very beautiful and picturesque waterfall. Glen Moriston is a quiet, serene, but extremely beautiful valley, watered by the Moriston, a wild, foaming, impetuous stream, which has its origin in Loch Cluny and the distant mountains of Glenshiel. From Invermoriston a road leads through the glen to Glenelg and the Isle of Skye. Proceeding along the side of Loch Ness, the tourist crosses the river Oich and reaches Fort Augustus, distant thirty-two miles from Inverness. This fort, which was built shortly after the rebellion of 1715, is situated at the west end of Loch Ness, on a high peninsula between the rivers Tarff and Oich, and commands a noble sweep of the lake and mountains. It forms a square with four bastions at the corners, and the barracks are constructed for one field-officer, four captains, twelve subalterns, and 280 rank and file. A few soldiers are stationed in the fort, but the guns have been removed to Fort-George, and the magazine is empty. Fort-Augustus is useless as a place of defence, being completely commanded by the surrounding hills and eminences. There is a pleasant little village in the neighbourhood. From Loch Ness to Loch Oich, the next and smallest of the chain, is a distance of five miles. The old road leads along the south side of Loch Oich, but the tourist should follow the new one on the opposite side. The scenery on the banks of this loch is finer than at any other part of the Great Glen.

Glen Garry, which opens upon Loch Oich, is a charming valley abounding in the most fascinating scenery. "Less splendid than Glen Urquhart, less diversified than Glen Moriston, it has in its beautiful Loch Garry, and its endless succession of birch-clad knolls and eminences, and, above all, in the magnificence of the mountain vista to the west, a character quite peculiar." In the birch-woods which adorn this romantic glen the trees have attained an extraordinary size and luxuriance equal to the finest of the pines of Rothiemurchus or the beeches of Athole. Near the mouth of the Garry, and close to the loch, are the ruins of the ancient castle of Invergarry, situated on a rock, which is the gathering place of the clan Macdonell, whose war-cry, now the motto of their chief, is "Craggan an Fhithich," "the rock of the raven." It was burnt by the Duke of Cumberland after the rebellion of 1745. In the immediate neighbourhood of the castle is Invergarry House, the modern residence of the chief of the Macdonells. Invergarry inn, which stands a little way up the glen, is about seven and a half miles from Fort Augustus, and about the same distance from Letterfinlay inn on the banks of Loch Lochy. A little way from Invergarry Castle is a small monument erected by the late Colonel Macdonell of Glengarry over the "well of seven heads," commemorating the summary vengeance inflicted by a former chief of Glengarry "in the swift course of feudal justice," on the perpetrators of the foul murder of the Keppoch family. The distance between Lochs Oich and Lochy is about two miles. Kinloch Lochy was the scene in 1544 of a most bloody battle between the Frasers and a much superior force of the Macdonalds of Clanranald. On account of the heat of the weather the combatants threw off their coats and fought in their shirts, whence the battle received the name of "Blar-na-leine" or "the Field of Shirts." Lord Lovat and his eldest son, together with most of the principal gentlemen of the clan, were slain in this engagement. Fourteen miles from Fort-Augustus is the inn of Letterfinlay on the south side of Loch Lochy. On the opposite side of the Loch is the bay of Arkaig, at a short distance from which, in Glen Arkaig, is the mansion of Lochiel, chief of the clan Cameron. It is delightfully situated, and completely embosomed in wood. The hills which environ Loch Lochy are wild and stupendous, and but scantily wooded. It is ten miles in length, and the depth is in some places from seventy to eighty fathoms. Seven miles from Letterfinlay the tourist crosses the deep and rocky channel of the Spean by a picturesque looking bridge, called High Bridge, which was built by General Wade. At this spot hostilities first commenced in the Rebellion of 1745. Here a road strikes off on the left to Glen Roy, celebrated for its parallel roads. Proceeding onward the road opens upon the river Lochy, and keeping along its banks, the tourist reaches the ruins of Inverlochy Castle about two miles distant from Fort-William. It consists of four large towers, the western and southern of which are nearly entire. Inverlochy is supposed to have been built by the powerful family of Cuming. It was the scene of a bloody engagement during the reign of James I. between Donald of the Isles, and the Earls of Mar and Caithness, in which the latter were defeated, and the Earl of Caithness slain. Here also in 1645, the Marquis of Argyle was defeated with great slaughter by the Marquis of Montrose. This engagement is described at great length in the "Legend of Montrose."

A mile and a half from Inverlochy Castle, the tourist reaches

FORT WILLIAM,

situated at a bend of Loch Eil, twenty-nine miles from Fort Augustus and sixty-one from Inverness. The fort was erected in the reign of William III. from whom it derived its name. It contains a bomb-proof magazine, and the barracks are intended to accommodate ninety-six private soldiers, with the proper number of officers. In 1715, and again in 1745, the Highlanders besieged it, but without success. The adjacent village of Maryburgh, named in honour of Queen Mary, contains a population of about 600 persons, who are for the most part engaged in the herring fishery. There is an excellent inn at Neptune's Staircase, at which most of the tourists prefer stopping rather than at Fort William. The celebrated mountain, Ben Nevis, 4370 feet high, rises from the plain to the east of Fort William. It stands out boldly from the adjoining hills, and has a peculiarly imposing appearance. On its northern side there are two distinct terraces, the lowest of which contains a lake, and on the north-east side there is a tremendous precipice of at least 1500 feet. The view from the top is remarkably grand and extensive. It is supposed that the horizon is not less than 120 miles distant in all directions from the spectator. The ascent of Ben Nevis usually occupies three hours and a half, but it ought never to be undertaken by strangers without a guide.

The road from Fort William to Oban, along the shores of Lochs Eil and Linnhe, is a continued succession of romantic scenery.

A parliamentary road leads from Fort William to Arisaig, distant forty miles, where there is a ferry to Skye.

This road passes through the lovely vale of Glenfinnan, in which there is an inn, remarkable as the place where Prince Charles Stuart first raised his standard, August 19, 1745, and at Borrodale, on the shore of Loch na Nuagh, he first disembarked on the mainland of Scotland, and from the same spot he finally embarked for France, after the failure of his unfortunate attempt.

Leaving Fort William, the road proceeds along the south side of Loch Linnhe, and, at the distance of nine miles, reaches Coran Ferry; thence it leads a short way along the north shore of Loch Leven, a branch of Loch Linnhe, extending in a straight line between the counties of Inverness and Argyle. "From its mouth to its further extremity," says Dr. M'Culloch, "Loch Leven is one continued succession of landscapes." On both sides it is bounded by lofty mountains. Fourteen miles from Fort William the tourist crosses Loch Leven at Ballachulish Ferry. About two miles from the ferry are the celebrated slate quarries of Ballachulish, which give employment to about 200 people. The road now proceeds for about four miles along the southern shore of Loch Leven, and enters the vale of

GLENCOE,

celebrated both for the grandeur of its scenery and its historical recollections. The lower part of the glen, next Loch Leven, is covered with rich verdure, while the character of the upper portion is unmingled wildness and grandeur. In the middle of the valley is the small lake Treachtan, from which issues the wild stream of Cona, celebrated by Ossian, who is said to have been born on its banks. On both sides of this river the hills shoot up perpendicularly to a tremendous height, casting a deep gloom on this wild vale, calculated to strike the traveller with the deepest awe. From one end of the vale to the other only one solitary farm-house is to be seen. The well known massacre of Glencoe, which casts so deep a stain on the character of King William and his ministers, happened at the north-west end of the vale. At the farthest extremity of Glencoe is the rugged mountain of Buchael Etive, the road over which, from its steepness, has been denominated *The Devil's Staircase.* Proceeding onward through a barren district, the tourist arrives at King's House, distant twenty-eight miles and a half from Fort William. The road then crosses a tedious hill called the Black Mount; and, nine and a half miles from the King's House, reaches Inverouran, on the banks of Loch Tulla. Two miles beyond this, the road crosses the river Orchy, which waters the pretty valley of Glenorchy, and, seven miles farther, reaches

TYNDRUM,

situated at the head of Strathfillan, in Perthshire. A short distance from Tyndrum, at a place called Dalrigh, or the King's Field, King Robert Bruce was encountered and repulsed after a very severe engagement by the Lord of Lorn. "Bruce's personal strength and courage," says Sir Walter Scott, "were never displayed to greater advantage than in this conflict. There is a tradition in the family of the MacDougals of Lorn, that their chieftain engaged in personal battle with Bruce himself, while the latter was employed in protecting the retreat of his men; that MacDougal was struck down by the king, whose strength of body was equal to his vigour of mind, and would have been slain on the spot, had not two of Lorn's vassals, a father and son, whom tradition terms M'Keoch, rescued him, by seizing the mantle of the monarch, and dragging him from above his adversary. Bruce rid him self of these foes by two blows of his redoubted battle-axe, but was so closely pressed by the other followers of Lorn, that he was forced to abandon the mantle, and broach which fastened it, clasped in the dying grasp of the MacKeochs. A studded broach, said to have been that which King Robert lost upon this occasion, was long preserved in the family of MacDougal, and was lost in a fire which consumed their temporary residence."* Ac-

* This exploit is celebrated by Sir Walter Scott in the following song, entitled "The Broach of Lorn," supposed to be sung by the bard of Lorn at his chieftain's request:—

"Whence the broach of burning gold,
That clasps the chieftain's mantle-fold,
Wrought and chased with rare device,
Studded fair with gems of price,
On the varied tartans beaming,
As, through night's pale rainbow gleaming,
Fainter now, now seen afar,
Fitful shines the northern star?

"Gem! ne'er wrought on Highland mountain,
Did the fairy of the fountain,
Or the mermaid of the wave,
Frame thee in some coral cave?
Did in Iceland's darksome mine
Dwarf's swart hands thy metal twine?
Or, mortal-moulded, comest thou here,
From England's love, or France's fear?

"No!—thy splendours nothing tell
Foreign art or faëry spell.
Moulded thou for monarch's use,
By the overweening Bruce,
When the royal robe he tied
O'er a heart of wrath and pride;
Thence in triumph wert thou torn,
By the victor hand of Lorn!

"When the gem was won and lost,
Widely was the war-cry toss'd!
Rung aloud Bendourish fell,
Answered Douchart's sounding dell,
Fled the deer from wild Teyndrum,
When the homicide, o'ercome,
Hardly 'scaped with scathe and scorn,
Left the pledge with conquering Lorn!

cording to the account given by Barbour, three of the strongest among Lorn's followers resolved to rid their chief of this formidable foe. "They watched their opportunity until Bruce's party had entered a pass between a lake (Loch Dochart probably) and a precipice, where the King, who was the last of the party, had scarce room to manage his steed. Here his three foes sprung upon him at once. One seized his bridle, but received a wound which hewed off his arm; a second grasped Bruce by the stirrup and leg, and endeavoured to dismount him, but the King, putting spurs to his horse, threw him down, still holding by the stirrup. The third taking advantage of an acclivity, sprung up behind him upon his horse. Bruce, however, whose personal strength is uniformly mentioned as exceeding that of most men, extricated himself from his grasp, threw him to the ground, and cleft his skull with his sword. By similar exertion he drew the stirrup from his grasp, whom he had overthrown, and killed him also with his sword as he lay among the horse's feet."

Two miles from Tyndrum is St. Fillan's Church. Here

"Vain was then the Douglas brand,
Vain the Campbell's vaunted hand,
Vain Kirkpatrick's bloody dirk,
Making sure of murder's work;
Barendown fled fast away,
Fled the fiery De la Haye,
When this broach, triumphant borne,
Beam'd upon the breast of Lorn.

"Farthest fled its former Lord,
Left his men to brand and cord,
Bloody brand of Highland steel,
English gibbet, axe, and wheel.
Let him fly from coast to coast,
Dogg'd by Comyn's vengeful ghost,
While his spoils, in triumph worn,
Long shall grace victorious Lorn!"

Lord of the Isles, Canto II. Stanza 11, and Notes.

there is a linn in the river Etterick, called St. Fillan's Pool, in which a considerable number of lunatics are annually immersed, and then bound hand and foot, and laid all night in the churchyard of St. Fillans in the expectation of effecting a cure. Two miles farther is Crianlarich inn, from which the tourist may either proceed through Glenfalloch to the head of Loch Lomond, or by Glen Dochart and Glen Ogle to Lochearnhead, and join the route described p. 311.

FOURTEENTH TOUR.

STEAMBOAT TOUR FROM NEWHAVEN TO ABERDEEN, INVERNESS, WICK, ORKNEY AND SHETLAND ISLANDS.

After leaving Newhaven, the first object of interest is the island of Inchkeith, which received its name from the ancient family of Keith, to whom it formerly belonged. It was fortified by the English in the reign of Edward VI., but the fortifications were afterwards demolished by order of the Scottish Parliament. During the regency of Mary of Guise it was occupied by the French, who designated it L'Isle des Chevaux, because the grass which it produced formed a nutritious food for horses. Inchkeith possesses several fine springs of water, and maintains a few sheep and rabbits. The lighthouse on this island is a work of great neatness, and the machinery which causes the lights to revolve is very interesting. A fine view is obtained from the middle of the Firth, of the city of Edinburgh, with the harbours of Leith and Newhaven, and the coast of Fife thickly studded with towns. In allusion to this striking characteristic of Fife, King James VI. is said to have likened it to "a gray cloth mantle with a golden fringe." A little to the west is Burntisland, nearly opposite is the inn of Pettycur,* and

* Pettycur is supposed to have derived its name (petit corps) from the landing of a small body of French troops during the regency of Mary of Guise.

a little farther east is the royal burgh of Kinghorn,* which gives a title of Earl to the Earls of Strathmore. About half a mile west of the town is a precipice called King's Woodend, where Alexander III. was thrown from his horse and killed 16th March 1285. Below Kinghorn is a square tower, the remains of Seafield Castle. A short way farther on is the "lang town of Kirkaldy," a royal burgh of great enterprise and trade. Its streets are extremely irregular, narrow, crooked, ill-paved, and dirty. Dr. Adam Smith, author of the "Wealth of Nations," was a native of this town. Balwearie, in this neighbourhood, was the birth-place of Sir Michael Scott, the famous wizard immortalized in the Lay of the Last Minstrel. The ruins of the old tower of Balwearie are still to be seen. On a rising ground behind Kirkaldy is Raith House, the handsome seat of Robert Ferguson, Esq. M.P. Lord Lieutenant of Fife. The situation is commanding, and the pleasure grounds are extensive and very beautiful. At a short distance is Dunnikier House, the seat of Sir John Oswald. To the east of Kirkaldy is Ravenscraig Castle, the property of the Earl of Rosslyn, situated upon a rock overhanging the sea. It has been in the possession of the St. Clair family since the reign of James III., and was entire and habitable till the time of Cromwell. About half a mile farther on is Dysart House, a seat of the Earl of Rosslyn, and close to it is the town of Dysart,† a royal burgh of

* The parish church of Kinghorn is without a spire. This and some other circumstances, supposed to be characteristic of the town, has given rise to the following couplet:

"Here stands a kirk without a steeple,
A drucken priest, and a graceless people."

† "The canty carles o' Dysart,
The merry lads o' Buckhaven,
The saucy limmers o' Largo,
The bonny lasses o' Leven."—*Old Song.*

great antiquity, and two or three centuries ago a place of considerable trade. It now exports coals and salt. Two miles farther on is West Wemyss, a burgh of barony, containing about 600 inhabitants. It is a most dingy, dirty, ruinous looking place. The steamer now passes Wemyss Castle, the seat of Captain Erskine Wemyss, M.P. situated on a steep rock overhanging the sea. In this Castle Darnley was first introduced to Queen Mary. Farther on is Easter Wemyss, a burgh of barony principally occupied by weavers. Wemyss derives its name from the number of caves on this part of the coast,—Weem or Weemyss being the Gaelic word for a cave. One of these, called the King's Cave, received its designation from an adventure related of James IV. Travelling through Fife on foot and incognito, that monarch happened to be benighted, and was obliged to enter a cave for shelter. He found it already occupied by a band of robbers, but having gone too far to retreat, he was under the necessity of joining the company. After some time, supper having been served up, two of the gang approached him with a plate on which lay two daggers,—a signal that he was to be put to death. He instantly snatched a weapon in each hand, laid the two robbers prostrate at his feet, and rushed through the rest toward the mouth of the cave. Having fortunately succeeded in making his escape, he returned next day with a sufficient force and captured the whole band. A short way farther east are the ruins of Macduff's castle, said to have been built by Macduff, created Thane of Fife about the year 1057. A mile farther down is Buckhaven, a curious antique fishing village, inhabited by a most extraordinary race who are supposed to be the descendants of the crew of a vessel from the Netherlands, which was wrecked near this place in the reign of Philip II. They were severely ridiculed more than a century ago in a celebrated satirical pamphlet called the "History of the College of Buckhaven, or the Sayings of Wise Willie and Witty Eppie," well known to the book stall collectors of pamphlets and broadsides. Buckhaven is however a place of considerable wealth. A mile farther on is the small village of Methill, and, at the distance of another mile, the thriving village of Leven, situated at the mouth of the river of the same name, which issues from Loch Leven. Though it has a course of only twelve miles, it receives an immense number of tributary streams. The principal of these are enumerated in the following rhyme:—

Lochtie, Lochrie, Leven, and Orr,
Rin a' through Cameron Brig bore.

Leven contains about 1200 inhabitants, who are principally engaged in weaving linen. A short way in the interior is Durie House, the seat of C. M. Christie, Esq. of Durie. The steamer is now in Largo Bay, familiar to every Scotsman from the allusion made to it in the fine old song "Weel may the boatie row." In the centre of the bay is the village of Lower Largo, the birth-place of Alexander Selkirk, whose singular adventures form the groundwork of Defoe's charming novel of "Robinson Crusoe." The chest and cup which he used on the uninhabited island are still in possession of his family, and the gun with which he killed his game, now belongs to Major Lumsden of Lathallan. Upper Largo was the birthplace of Sir Andrew Wood, the celebrated Scottish Admiral, who received the barony of Largo from James IV. as a reward for his services at sea against the English. Largo also gave birth to Sir John Leslie, the celebrated philosopher. Near Upper Largo, in the midst of a beautiful park, and surrounded by trees, stands Largo House, the seat of General Durham. To the north of the village, the fine hill called Largo Law rises to the height of 1000 feet above the level of the sea. A short way to the west of Largo, in the midst of a park, are three straight sharp stones, several yards high, called "the Standing Stanes o' Lundie." They have attracted considerable notice, and are supposed to be of Roman origin. Four miles east from Largo is a neat little town called the Elie. Elie House, the seat of Sir W. C. Anstruther, stands close to the town. Two miles farther on is St. Monance, noted for its curious little old Gothic church. The ruins of Newark Castle, the seat of the famous General Leslie, stands on a bold part of the shore about a mile to the west of the village. A mile to the east is the ancient royal burgh of Pittenweem. Here are the ruins of some curious antique religious buildings. Pittenweem contains the house in which Wilson and Robertson committed the robbery upon the Collector of Excise which led to the famous Porteous Mob. A mile from Pittenweem there are two or three towns placed together in a cluster. The first is Wester Anstruther, or Anster, a royal burgh, with a population of about 420,* then Easter Anstruther, also a royal burgh, with a population of 1000.

Anstruther was the residence of the renowned "Maggie Lauder," commemorated in the popular song of that name, and "Anster Fair," has been made the subject of an amusing poem by Mr. Tennant, Professor

* It is said that a minister of Easter Anster during the last century used to say of the Magistrates of Wester Anster, that instead of their "being a terror to evil doers," evil doers were a terror to them.

of oriental languages in the University of St. Andrews. Opposite to this part of the coast is the Isle of May. It is about three miles in circumference, and was formerly the seat of a considerable religious establishment. It is now inhabited only by the persons who attend upon the lighthouse, which was first built here in the reign of Charles I. A fine view is obtained here of North Berwick Law, the Bass, and the coast of East Lothian. About a mile farther down the coast stands Kilrenny, another royal burgh, with a population of about 1500. The next town to the east is Crail, a venerable and decayed burgh, formerly a place of considerable importance, but now greatly diminished. It contains about 2000 inhabitants. It was in the church of Crail that John Knox, on the 29th of May 1559, preached a sermon against popery, which so inflamed the populace, that they immediately rose and, in a very short time, demolished all the churches in Crail, Anstruther, and the adjacent towns along the coast. Crail was famous for its *capons*, a kind of haddocks prepared by a peculiar mode of cookery. The notorious Archbishop Sharpe was at one time minister of this parish. About a mile to the east of Crail is the East Neuk of Fife, which gives name to a popular Scottish air. Beyond this promontory the coast stretches away towards the northwest, forming the extensive bay called St. Andrew's Bay. At the bottom of this bay, on a ridge of rock projecting into the sea, stands the ancient city of St. Andrews, with its venerable towers and numerous spires.

ST. ANDREWS

was formerly a place of great importance, and was the seat of the primate of Scotland. It is about a mile in circuit, and consists of three principal streets, intersected by a few considerable lanes. Of late years a number of elegant houses have been erected, and the streets have been repaired and lighted with gas. The principal street, it has been justly said, for length, straightness, and uniformity, may be reckoned as, even at this day, one of the best in Scotland. It is entered at the west end by a massive antique portal, which the magistrates have with great taste preserved unimpaired,—its other extremity terminates in the ruins of the cathedral, church, and monastery. The city abounds in curious antique houses, which were once occupied by persons of rank, both in church and state, and it has an air of seclusion and quiet that, together with its colleges and memorials of antiquity, gives it an appearance not unlike some of the cathedral towns of England. The surrounding scenery is extremely beautiful. The origin of St. Andrews is involved in obscurity, but it is justly believed to have been at a very early period the seat of a religious establishment. It was originally denominated Muckross. According to the common tradition, about the end of the fourth century it became the residence of St. Regulus, who was shipwrecked here. The ruins of his chapel, and an entire tower, known by the name of St. Regulus or St. Rule, are still to be seen near the cathedral. On the union of the Scottish and Pictish kingdoms, the name of the city was changed to St. Andrews. The famous priory of St. Andrews was erected by Bishop Robert in the reign of Alexander I. about the year 1120. It was made a royal burgh by David I. in the year 1140. The charter of Malcolm II., written upon a small bit of parchment, is preserved in the tolbooth. In 1471, it was erected into an archbishopric by Sextus IV. at the request of James IV. It is not known with certainty at what time its church became metropolitan, but it must have been at a very early period. St. Andrews contains many interesting memorials of antiquity. The chapel of St. Regulus is, without doubt, the oldest relic of ecclesiastical architecture in the kingdom. The oldest Scottish writers agree in admitting, that it is at least as ancient as the end of the fourth or beginning of the fifth century. The tower is a square prism 108 feet in height, the side of the base being twenty-four feet. A winding stair leads to the summit, from which a most delightful view is obtained. The stone of which this building is composed, is of so excellent a texture that although it has been exposed to the weather for so many centuries, it still remains quite entire and unimpaired. The chapel to the east of the tower, which was the principal one, remains, but of a small chapel to the west, which formerly existed, there is now no trace. The cathedral was founded in the year 1159, by Bishop Arnold, but it was not finished till the time of Bishop Lamberton, who completed it in 1318. This magnificent fabric, the work of several ages, was demolished in a single day by an infuriated mob, excited by a sermon of John Knox against idolatry, preached in the parish church of St. Andrews.* It was an edifice of

* This event is graphically described by Professor Tennant in his poem entitled " Papistry Stormed; or the Dinging Doun o' the Cathedral." We may give a short extract as a specimen of the poem :—

" I sing the steir, strabash, and strife,
Whan bickerin' frae the towns o' Fife
Great bangs o' bodies, thick and rife,
Gaed to Sanct Andro's town.

" And wi' John Calvin in their heads,
And hammers in their hands, and spades,
Enraged at idols, mass, and beads,
Dang the Cathedral down.

great extent; the length being 350 feet, the breadth 65, and the transept 180 feet. The eastern gable, half of the western, part of the south side wall, and of the transept, are all that now remain of this once splendid pile. The annexed wood engraving gives a view from the sea of the square tower of St. Regulus, and the east end of the cathedral.

ST. ANDREW'S CATHEDRAL.

The other religious houses in St. Andrews were the convent of the Dominicans, founded, in 1274, by Bishop Wishart; the convent of Observantines, founded by Bi-

"I wot the bruilzie then was dour,
Wi' sticks, and stanes, and bluidy clour,
Ere Papists unto Calvin's power
Gaif up their strongest places.

"And fearfu' the stramash and stour
Whan pinnacle cam down, and tow'r,
And Virgin Marys in a shower
Fell flat, and smash'd their faces.

"The copper roofs that dazzlit heaven,
Were frae their rafters rent and riven,
The marble altars dasht and driven,
The cods wi' velvet laces;

"The siller ewers and candlesticks;
The purple stole and gowden pyx;
And tunakyls and dalmatycks
Cam tumbling frae their cases.

shop Kennedy, and finished by his successor, Patrick Graham, in 1478, a collegiate church, which stood immediately above the harbour, and a priory. Slight vestiges of the latter, which was the most important of these foundations, may be traced to the south of the cathedral. It was of great extent and richly endowed. Its boundary wall is still nearly entire, and seems to have enclosed all the east quarter of the town. The prior of St. Andrews had precedence of all abbots and priors, and on festival days had a right to wear a mitre and all Episcopal ornaments.

"On the east side of the city are the remains of the castle, on a rock overlooking the sea. This fortress was founded about the year 1200, by Roger, one of the bishops of St. Andrews, and was repaired towards the end of the 14th century by Bishop Trail, who died in it in 1401. He was buried near the high altar of the cathedral, with this singular epitaph:

> Hic fuit ecclesiæ directa columna, fenestra
> Lucida, thuribulum redolens, campana sonora.

"James III. was born in the Castle. It was the residence of Cardinal Beaton, who, after the cruel execution of the celebrated reformer George Wishart in front of it, was afraid of the fury of the people; and his knowledge of this, joined to his apprehension of an invasion from England, induced him to strengthen the fortifications, with a view of rendering the castle impregnable. In this fortress he was surprised and assassinated by Norman Lesley, aided by fifteen others. Early in the morning of May 29, 1546, they seized on the gate of

> 'The devil stood bumbazed to see
> The bonnie cosie byke where he
> Had cuddlit monie a century,
> Rip't up wi' sic disgraces."

the castle, which had been left open for the workmen who were finishing the fortifications; and having placed sentinels at the door of the Cardinal's apartment, they awakened his numerous domestics one by one, and, turning them out of the castle, without violence, tumult, or injury to any other person, inflicted on Beaton the death he justly merited. The conspirators were immediately besieged in this castle by the regent, Earl of Arran; and although their strength consisted of only 150 men, they resisted his efforts for five months, owing more to the unskilfulness of the attack than the strength of the place, for in 1547, the castle was reduced and demolished, and its picturesque ruins serve as a land-mark to mariners. The entrance to the castle, and the window out of which it is said Cardinal Beaton leaned to witness the cruel martyrdom of George Wishart, are still pointed out."*

The University of St. Andrews, which is the oldest establishment of that nature in Scotland, was founded in 1411 by Bishop Wardlaw. It consisted formerly of three colleges:—1. St. Salvator's, which was founded in 1458 by Bishop Kennedy. The buildings of this college formed an extensive court or quadrangle about 230 feet long, and 180 wide, and a gateway surmounted by a spire 156 feet high. On one side is the church, on another what was the library of St. Salvator's, the third contains apartments for students, the fourth is unfinished. The buildings connected with this college have fallen into a state of decay, and a grant was made by Parliament for erecting a new structure. One half of the proposed buildings for the United College have been erected, but

* Encyclopædia Britannica, Seventh Edition, Vol. III. p. 121.

the rest of the funds appointed to complete the works having unfortunately been diverted to another purpose, the structure remains incomplete. 2. St. Leonard's College, which was founded by Prior Hepburn in 1532. This is now united with St. Salvator's, and the buildings sold and converted into private houses. 3. New, or St. Mary's College, which was established by Archbishop Hamilton in 1552, but the house was completed by Archbishop Beaton. The buildings of this college have lately been repaired with great taste.

In the United College the languages, philosophy, and the sciences are taught. St. Mary's, which stands in a different part of the town, is reserved exclusively for theology. The classes and discipline of the two colleges are quite distinct, each having its respective Principal and Professors. They have a common library, containing upwards of 35,000 volumes, which, till lately, was entitled to a copy of all new books entered in Stationers' Hall, but by an Act of Parliament passed in 1837, that right was abolished, and in lieu of it, the library receives from the Treasury the sum of £600 annually for the purchase of books.

Seventy-one bursaries or endowments are connected with the university, and are conferred upon the students. Of these, sixteen are foundation bursaries belonging to the college, and fifty-five were established at different times by various benefactors, and are in the gift of different patrons. In St. Mary's College there are nine foundation bursaries, which extend their benefit to about twenty individuals.

The system of instruction carried on in the United College is excellent. From the sequestered character of the town, the absence of all manufacturing establishments, and of those temptations incident to large cities, there are few seminaries where youth are better protected from idle and vicious habits, or where greater facilities are afforded for acquiring a sound and comprehensive education. The moderate number attending the College enables the Professors to become personally acquainted with each of the students; and, while advancing their literary and scientific proficiency, their instructors at the same time exercise a wholesome control over their moral habits. Previous to 1824, the attendance at the United College averaged about 70. In session 1824-5 there were 220 students. Since that period the numbers have gradually declined, though they are still far above what they were in former times. The average number of students attending St. Mary's College is about 30.

The Madras College was established in the year 1833 by the late Dr. Andrew Bell, a native of St. Andrews, and inventor of the monitorial system of education which bears his name, who bequeathed the munificent sum of £120,000 in three per cent. stock for its establishment. The buildings, which are very splendid, stand on the site of the Blackfriar's monastery, and in front of it is the fine old ruin of the chapel connected with that monastery. The system of education followed, comprises the classics, the English, and other modern languages, mathematics, and drawing. The fees being low, and in many cases not exacted, the institution has been very successful, the number of scholars averaging about eight hundred.

St. Andrews contains five places of worship—the parish church, the college church, and an episcopal, secession, and independent chapel. A new chapel in connection with the established church is at present in progress. The parish church is a spacious structure, 162 feet in length, by 63 in breadth, and is large enough to accommodate 2500 persons. It contains a lofty monument of white marble, erected in honour of Archbishop Sharpe, who, in revenge for his oppressive conduct, was murdered by some of the exasperated covenanters. On this monument is a bas relief representing the tragical scene of the murder. To the north is situated the college church, which belongs to the united college of St. Salvator and St. Leonard. It was founded in 1458 by Bishop Kennedy, and contains a beautiful tomb of its founder, who died in 1466. It is a piece of exquisite Gothic workmanship, though much injured by time and accidents. About the year 1683, on opening this tomb, six highly ornamented silver maces were discovered, which had been concealed there in times of trouble. Three of these maces are still preserved in the university, and one was presented to each of the other three Scottish universities. The top has been ornamented by a representation of our Saviour, with angels around, and the instruments of his passion; with these are shewn some silver arrows with large silver plates affixed to them, on which are inscribed the arms and names of those who were victors in the annual competitions of archery, which, after having been discontinued for half a century, were again revived in 1833. Golf is now the reigning game in St. Andrews. It is played on a piece of ground called the Links, which stretches along the sea-shore to the extent of nearly two miles. A considerable number of golf-balls are manufactured in St. Andrews. Besides the consumption of the town, about 9000 are annually exported to various other places.

The trade of St. Andrews was once very considerable. The shipping of the port now consists of a few vessels which are employed in the coasting trade. The harbour is guarded by piers, and is safe and commodious; but it is difficult of access, having a narrow entrance, and being exposed to the east wind, which raises a heavy sea on the coast. The shore of the bay is low, and in severe storms, vessels are frequently driven on it and lost. St. Andrews unites with Cupar, Anstruther, Pittenweem, Crail, and Kilrenny in returning a member to Parliament. The population of the town is 4300.

About two miles from St. Andrews is the estuary of the river Eden; and a short distance inland the village of Leuchars. A little beyond this is Tentsmoor Point, the south-eastern point of the frith of the Tay, and on the opposite shore, in Forfarshire, is Button Ness, the north-eastern point of the same estuary. There are two light-houses on this promontory. About six miles up the Firth of Tay, on the north shore, is

DUNDEE.

"The history of Scotland narrates many sackings and burnings of this town. The last of these was by General Monck; and such was its wealth at that time, that every soldier in Monck's army is said to have received £60 sterling as his share of the plunder. Dundee was erected into a royal burgh by William the Lion in 1165. It is governed by a provost, four bailies, a dean of guild, a treasurer, and fourteen councillors, and sends a member to parliament. The market-place, or High Street, is a spacious square, 360 feet long by 100 broad, from which diverge the Nethergate, Seagate, Overgate, and Murraygate, the principal streets, which run from east to west, parallel to the river. Castle Street leads from the south-east end of the High Street to the new docks on the south, and contains, among other neat buildings, an episcopal chapel and a theatre. At the south-east corner is an elegant building in the Grecian style, erected for an exchange and reading-room. On the south side of the market-place or square stands the town-hall, surmounted by a steeple, and having piazzas below; it was built in 1743. Opposite to this building is a spacious new street, named Reform Street; at the north end of which, and fronting the town-hall, is an elegant edifice, in the Grecian style of architecture, for an academy and public schools. At the east end of the High Street, and rather obstructing the entrance to the Murraygate, stands the Trades' Hall, a plain edifice, with pilasters of the Ionic order, the principal apartment of which is used as a reading-room, and it contains, besides, apartments for each of the nine incorporated trades. A little to the west of the High Street is the Nethergate, in which are the remains of an old cathedral, containing four places of worship, one of which, the most entire, is built in the finest Gothic style, the groining of the arches being much admired. This structure is said to have been originally built by David, Earl of Huntingdon, in 1185. On the west end of these churches stands a magnificent Gothic tower 156 feet high. There are several other churches and chapels connected with the Establishment, besides two Episcopal chapels, and various other places of worship for Dissenters, who form no inconsiderable part of the population. Among the public institutions may be mentioned a Lunatic Asylum, an Infirmary, a Dispensary for out-patients, and an Orphan Institution; a Chamber of Commerce, the Society of Writers, incorporated by royal charter, and a Mechanics' Institution. Dundee has four joint-stock banking establishments, viz. the Dundee Bank, the Union Bank, the New Bank, and the Commercial Bank. Besides these, there are agencies for the British Linen Company, the National Bank of Scotland, and the Bank of Scotland. There is a native establishment for fire insurance, and one for sea insurance. There are three weekly newspapers published in the place. The trade of Dundee has long been extensive, and it has rapidly increased of late years. Its manufactures are chiefly brown and bleached linens for the home and foreign market, great quantities of which are exported directly to North and South America. It also carries on a great trade to the Baltic, and has a number of vessels employed in the whale-fishery. In the London trade, besides a number of sailing smacks, there are two splendid steam-vessels, having each two engines of 125 horse power. A railway was opened some years ago between Dundee and Newtyle, a village in Strathmore, about ten miles distant, which lays open the traffic of that extensive agricultural district. This town has now become the principal seat of the linen trade of great Britain, and the great emporium of flax and hemp. In 1835 its imports of flax and hemp amounted to 24,243 tons, and in 1836 to 37,216 tons. The exports of linens in 1835 were 618,707 pieces, and in 1836 710,944 pieces. In the town and neighbourhood there are about fifty spinning-mills, all worked by steam; and the steam-power employed in the different establishments exceeds 1400 horse-power. There are several extensive iron founderies and establishments for the manufacture of steam-engines and machinery. The grandest and most important feature of Dundee is its harbour, with its magnificent wet docks, and a number of spacious quays, graving dock, &c. spreading along the margin of the Tay, and terminated on the west by the Craig Pier, which is exclusively appropriated to the use of the ferry. The increase of the trade of Dundee within the last eighteen years has been greater than that of any other place in the empire, if we except Liverpool and Glasgow. The population in 1821 was 30,575, and in 1831 it was 45,355, exclusive of the seamen belonging to the port. It is now understood to exceed 60,000."*

About twelve miles east from this part of the coast is the famous Bell Rock, or Inch-Cape Rock, which, from a very remote period, has been the cause of a vast number of wrecks. The top of this rock only being visible at low water, one of the abbots of Aberbrothock attached to it a frame-work and a bell, which, being rung by the waves, warned mariners to avoid the fatal reef. A story which is current respecting this bell has been embodied by Dr. Southey in his ballad called "Ralph the Rover." A famous pirate of this name is said to have cut the bell from the frame-work "to plague the Abbot of Aberbrothock," and some time after to have received the just punishment of being shipwrecked on the spot. An elegant light-house, 115 feet high, has now been erected by Government at an expense of £60,000. It is one of the most prominent and serviceable beacons on the Scottish shores, and has been the means of preventing innumerable shipwrecks.† About nine miles from Button Ness is the royal burgh of Aberbrothock or

* Encyclopædia Britannica, Seventh Edition, Vol. VIII. p. 281-2.

† The following beautiful lines were written by Sir Walter Scott in the Album kept in this light-house:—

PHAROS LOQUITUR.

Far on the bosom of the deep,
O'er these wild shelves my watch I keep:
A ruddy gem of changeful light,
Bound on the dusky brow of night:
The seaman bids my lustre hail,
And scorns to strike his tim'rous sail.

ARBROATH,

a neat and thriving sea-port town, situated at the distance of 58 miles N.N.E. from Edinburgh. The harbour is an artificial one, and though neither safe nor spacious, possesses considerable trade. Here are the ruins of a magnificent abbey founded by William the Lion in 1178, and dedicated to the celebrated primate Thomas-à-Becket. The founder was interred within its precincts, but there are no remains of his tomb. The last abbot was the famous Cardinal Beaton, who was at the same time Archbishop of St. Andrews. King John of England granted this monastery most uncommon privileges, for, by a charter under the Great Seal, he exempted it from taxes in trading to every part of England, except London. The ruins of the Abbey are greatly dilapidated. The Scottish nobility met here in 1320, and drew up a spirited remonstrance to the Pope against the claims made by Edward II. upon the sovereignty of the kingdom. Arbroath is a royal burgh, and unites with Forfar, Inverbervie, Montrose, and Brechin in sending a member to the British Parliament. The population of the parish in 1831 was 11,211.*

* Fifteen miles north-west of Arbroath lies Forfar, the county town. It is a burgh of great antiquity, and was a royal residence in the time of Malcolm Canmore. It is a neat and clean looking town, and the inhabitants are principally engaged in weaving and the manufacture of *brogues*. About a century ago, Forfar was the scene of the murder of the Earl of Strathmore. That nobleman was returning with a party of gentlemen from attendance upon a *dredgie*, or funeral entertainment, when one of them, Mr. Carnegie of Finhaven, being tossed by another into the gutter, rose, bespattered and blinded with mire, and mistaking the Earl for the offender, ran him through the body. He was tried for the crime and narrowly escaped the gallows. On a mount to the north of the town, was the castle in which King Malcolm resided, and his queen lived in a nunnery which stood on a small artificial island near the north side of the loch. In the steeple of Forfar is preserved a curious instrument, called "the Witches' Bridle," which was placed on the head of the miserable creatures who were burnt in Forfar for the imaginary crime of witchcraft, and acted as a gag to prevent their cries during the dreadful process of incremation. There are a

Leaving Arbroath, at the distance of two miles and a half is Carlinheugh Bay, and a short way farther on,

number of pleasant anecdotes connected with Forfar, but it is somewhat curious, as has been noticed by Chambers, that they all refer to drinking or to public houses. The legal gentlemen of this town, indeed, are characterized as the "drucken writers of Forfar." Their tippling habits are finely illustrated by an anecdote of the late Earl of Strathmore. The town is a good deal annoyed with a lake in its neighbourhood, which the inhabitants have long had it in contemplation to drain, and which would have been drained long ago but for the expensiveness of such an undertaking. At a public meeting, held some years ago for the discussion of this measure, the Earl said that he believed the cheapest method of draining the lake would be, to throw a few hogsheads of good mountain dew into the water, and set the *drucken writers* of Forfar to drink it up.*

The chief magistrate of Forfar, in the time of King James VI., kept an alehouse. His Majesty, in the course of his first journey to London, having been entertained with great splendour by the mayor of an English town, who, in honour of the occasion, kept open house for several days, some of the courtiers hinted that such examples of munificence must be very rare among the civic dignitaries of Scotland. "Fient a bit o' that are they," cried the king, "the provost o' my burgh of Forfar, whilk is by nae means the largest town in Scotland, keeps open house a' the year round, and aye the mae that comes the welcomer."

It was in Forfar that the famous case occurred which led to the decision of the Court of Session, that no charge could be made for a stirrup-dram. A brewster-wife in Forfar, previous to the Restoration, having one day "brewed a peck o' maut," and set it out to the door to cool, a neighbour's cow passing by, drank the whole browst. The injured alewife had recourse to the law for satisfaction, and in process of time the case came before "The Fyfeteen," when that learned body decided, that as by the immemorial custom of the land, nothing is ever charged for a standing drink, otherwise called a *deoch-an-dorras* or stirrup-dram, the defendant ought to be absolved from the charge of dependence, seeing that she swallowed the browst standing and at the door.

Forfar is situated in the beautiful valley of Strathmore, which gives title to the noble family of Lyon. The seat of this family, the celebrated castle of Glammis, stands near the village of the same name, about five miles and a half south-west of Forfar. It is situated in the midst of a park, one hundred and sixty acres in extent, and containing a considerable number of fine old trees. The castle is an edifice of great antiquity, and has a princely and antique appearance. The walls in some places are fifteen feet thick, and the height is such that the stair which leads to the top contains 143 steps. Glammis was anciently used as a royal residence, and was the scene of the death of Malcolm II. who was mortally wounded by assassins on the Hunter's Hill in this neighbourhood. Macbeth, as the readers of Shakspeare know, was Thane of Glammis, and after his death it reverted to the Crown. It was given by Robert II. to John Lyon, who married the king's second daughter by Elizabeth Mure, and became the founder of the present family of Strathmore. On the barbarous and unjust execution of the young and beautiful Lady Glammis for witchcraft, in 1537, Glammis was once more forfeited to the Crown, and was for some time a residence of James V. (*the Gudeman of Ballengeich*), but was afterwards restored to the family. It contains an extensive and valuable museum of ancient curiosities,

* Chambers' Rhymes of Scotland, p. 117. Picture of Scotland, vol. ii. p. 220.

Ethie House, the seat of the Earl of Northesk. About a mile beyond is the promontory of Redhead, 250 feet high. The coast now bends inward, forming the fine bay of Lunan. Six miles from Redhead is the mouth of the South Esk river, and near it the new parish church of Craig, on an elevated situation, and Rossie Castle, (Horatio Ross, Esq.) On the north side of the mouth of the South Esk stands the royal burgh of

MONTROSE,

twelve miles north from Arbroath. Behind the town the river expands into a spacious basin, which forms a sort of road-stead to the port. At high water it has a peculiarly striking and beautiful effect. The South Esk is crossed by a very magnificent suspension bridge,—the distance between the points of suspension being 432 feet. Mon-

old armour, and a collection of portraits, amounting to about a hundred in number, principally of the most distinguished characters in the reign of Charles II. The view from the top of the castle is remarkably splendid and extensive. Near the castle stand the figures of four lions rampant, each supporting in their fore paws a dial facing the four cardinal points. The figures are extremely curious, and well deserve the attention of the tourist.

GLAMMIS CASTLE.

Finhaven Castle, the once magnificent residence of the powerful family of Lindsay, is frequently visited by tourists. It is situated about six miles from Forfar on the new road to Brechin. The ruins, which now consist of little more than a square tower, stand on a steep bank of the small river Lemno, near the place where it joins the South Esk. To this castle, Alexander, Earl of Crawford, popularly known by the appellation of Earl Beardie, retired in disgrace after the battle of Brechin, in 1452, and here he feasted James II. in the most magnificent style after his reconcilement to that monarch.

trose is a remarkably neat town, and carries on a considerable trade. It has been connected with a number of interesting and important events in Scottish history. From this place Sir James Douglas embarked in 1330 on a pilgrimage to the Holy Land, carrying along with him the heart of Robert Bruce. It was the birth place of the celebrated Marquis of Montrose. It was the first port made by the French fleet in December 1715, with the Chevalier St. George on board; and that personage embarked at the same place 14th February 1716, having spent the previous night in the house in which Montrose was born. The principal public buildings are the town hall, the parish church, the episcopal chapel, the public schools, the academy, the lunatic asylum, and the office of the British Linen Company. In 1831 the population of Montrose was 12,055.*

About four miles and a half from Montrose, the North Esk joins the ocean, and immediately beyond it commences Kincardineshire or the Mearns. The scenery along the coast is peculiarly desolate. Passing the fishing village of Miltown, and the manufacturing village of Johnshaven, the royal burgh of Inverbervie is seen, situated on the river Bervie. It received its charter from David II. in 1362, on account of the kindness which the poor fishermen of Bervie dis-

* Eight miles west from Montrose is the ancient royal burgh of Brechin, it is romantically situated on the banks of the South Esk. In ancient times there was an abbey of Culdees in this place, and a bishopric was established here by David I. in 1150. On the edge of a precipitous bank descending towards the river, stood the Cathedral, a stately Gothic fabric, but its architectural symmetry has of late been almost entirely destroyed by the wretched taste displayed in repairing it as a modern place of worship. Brechin contains one of those round towers, which, like that of Abernethy, has proved such a stumbling block to antiquaries. Brechin Castle, the ancient seat of Lord Panmure, stands on a precipitous rock in the immediate neighbourhood of the town. It underwent a siege of twenty days, in 1303, from the English army under Edward I. and only surrendered on Sir Thomas Maule, its brave governor, being killed.

played to him when forced to land here by stress of weather. About two miles and a half farther on are the remains of Whistleburg Castle, and, in the immediate vicinity, the church of Kinneff, beneath the pulpit of which the regalia of Scotland were concealed, when they had been secretly conveyed from Dunnotar Castle.

All along this district the coast is bold and precipitous. Upon the top of a stupendous insulated rock, 160 feet above the level of the sea, stand the ruins of the celebrated castle of Dunnotar, the seat of the ancient family of the Keiths, Earls Marischal. The area of the castle measures about three acres, and the rock bears a considerable resemblance to that on which Edinburgh Castle is built. It is divided from the land by a deep chasm, and the only approach is by a steep path winding round the body of the rock. Dunnotar was built by Sir William Keith, then Great Marischal of Scotland, during the wars between England and Scotland in the reign of Edward I. In 1296 it was taken from the English by Sir William Wallace. Edward III. re-fortified it in his progress through the kingdom in 1336, but as soon as he quitted the kingdom, it was again captured by Sir Andrew Murray, Regent of Scotland. During the time of the Commonwealth, it was selected as the strongest place in the kingdom for the preservation of the regalia. The garrison, under the command of Ogilvy of Barras, made a vigorous resistance to the English army, but were at length compelled to surrender by famine. Previously to this, however, the regalia had been secretly conveyed away, and buried beneath the pulpit of the church of Kinneff, by Mrs. Grainger, the wife of the minister of that parish. At the Restoration, all the persons connected with this affair were amply rewarded.

Ogilvy was made a baronet; the brother of the Earl Marischal was created Earl of Kintore; and Mrs. Grainger was rewarded with a sum of money. During the reign of Charles II. Dunnotar was used as a State prison for confining the Covenanters. It was dismantled soon after the Rebellion of 1715, on the attainder of its proprietor, James Earl Marischal. "The battlements with their narrow embrasures, the strong towers and airy turrets, full of loop-holes for the archer and musketeer; the hall for the banquet, and the cell for the captive, are all alike entire and distinct. Even the iron rings and bolts that held the culprits for security or torture, still remain to attest the different order of things which once prevailed in this country. Many a sigh has been sent from the profound bosom of this vast rock,—many a despairing glance has wandered hence over the boundless wave,—and many a weary heart has there sunk rejoicing into eternal sleep."*

About a mile and a half from Dunnotar is the seaport of Stonehaven, situated in the bottom of a bay at the mouth of a stream called the Carron. It has a safe and commodious harbour, and contains a population of upwards of 2000. The tract of country which extends between Stonehaven and Aberdeen is remarkably bleak and sterile, presenting, for the most part, barren eminences and cold swampy moorlands. The only object worthy of notice is the fishing village of Finnan, remarkable for its dried fish called Finnan Haddocks.† At the

* A Summer Ramble in the North Highlands.

† In a very amusing and well written work just published, entitled "The Book of Bon Accord: or a Guide to the City of Aberdeen," we find the following glowing apostrophe to these far famed fish:—"FINNAN, *magnum et venerabile nomen!* 'To abstract the mind from all local emotion,' says the moralist, 'would be impossible if it were endeavoured, and would be foolish if it were possible. Far from me and from my friends be such frigid philosophy. That man is little to be envied, whose patriotism would not gain force upon the plain

northern extremity of this barren tract is Aberdeenshire, and passing Girdleness, the eastern termination of the great chain of the Grampians, on which an elegant light-house has recently been erected, the tourist reaches the city of

ABERDEEN,

situated on the river Dee. Aberdeen is reckoned the third city in Scotland, and in point of population, wealth, and commerce,—ranks as the chief town in the north of the kingdom. It is a spacious and well built city, and possesses many handsome streets and elegant public buildings. Union Street, which forms a splendid approach from the south and west, extends about a mile in a straight line, and crosses a deep ravine by a magnificent bridge of one arch 130 feet in span with a rise of only 22. Aberdeen is a place of great antiquity, having been a seat of population since the third century, and a privileged borough since the ninth, and has long been distinguished for its commerce, having in this respect got the start by many centuries of every

of *Marathon*,' or whose appetite would not grow keener among the huts of *Finnan*. Its unlettered sages will impart wisdom which will be vainly sought in elaborate dissertations on culinary science. 'Finnan Haddocks,' says a lady who cooks upon principles of economy, 'are served at breakfast in Scotland to eat with bread and butter, either *cold* or *just warmed* through, and moistened with one or two *drops of sweet oil!*' This nauseous and abominable libel may be forgiven in an author born on the wrong side of the Tweed; but it is not easy so leniently to overlook the blunders of Mrs. Margaret Dods of St. Ronan's, whose recommendation is, that 'Finnan's be taken from the gridiron when just done, and *dipped in hot water*, *if dry or hard*, and wrapped in a cloth to *swell and soften them!*' With becoming diffidence, it is surmised that mine Hostess of the Cleikum knows as much about Finnans, as a bare-legged Nereid of Port Lethen knows of Parisian *entremets*, or of the Chinese luxury of edible birds'-nests. Before your Finnan becometh 'dry or hard,' or needeth to be recovered by blankets and hot-baths, you shall nose him as you go up stairs, and may rely that a certain convocation of politic worms are e'en at him. Worthy Mrs. Margaret must have mistaken him for a *Pin-the-Widdie*, or other member of the same dessicated family. A similar mistake has led Sir Walter Scott to protest, in the name of his country, against Dr. Johnson's taste; but the philosopher's 'disgust' was virtuous,—for it was expressed against *Buckie* haddocks."

other commercial town in Scotland. Its manufactures and trade are in a flourishing condition. The most important branches of manufacture are cotton, woollen, and linen goods. Aberdeen granite is famous for its durability, and is shipped to a great extent. The harbour has undergone great improvements of late by a series of expensive works. The pier now runs out into the sea to the length of 1206 feet. The aggregate tonnage of the vessels belonging to the port of Aberdeen was in 1838 above 30,000.

The object most worthy of attention in New Aberdeen is Marischal College, founded, in 1593, by George Keith, Earl Marischal. It is attended by nine professors, and has a good library, an observatory, and an excellent apparatus of philosophical instruments. The principal hall contains an extensive museum of curiosities, and the walls are hung with portraits. The foundation of a splendid new building for this college was laid in 1837. A great number of distinguished persons have been educated in Marischal College, among others may be mentioned Dr. Arthur Johnson, Bishop Burnett, Dr. Gregory, Dr. Arbuthnot, Colin Maclaurin, Dr. Campbell, Dr. Beattie, Dr. Gerard, Dr. Reid, Sir James Mackintosh, and Robert Hall. The other public buildings are the town-house and jail, which is surmounted by a handsome spire 120 feet in height, and connected with it there has been erected a new court-house, which combines the advantages of elegance, convenience, and comfort. In a fine oblong square, denominated Castle Street, and fronting the town-house, stands the cross, which is adorned with busts, cut in stone, of the kings of Scotland, from James I. to James VII. and is surmounted by a unicorn rampant, on a fine Corinthian column.

The charitable institutions of Aberdeen are numerous, and it contains about thirty places of worship.

The population, inclusive of Old Aberdeen, is upwards of 60,000.

Old Aberdeen stands about a mile north from the modern city, at the mouth of the river Don. It was formerly the seat of a bishop, and had an extensive cathedral, commonly called St. Machar's, the only relics of which are two very antique and lofty spires of stone, and the nave which is used as a church. They are finely ornamented, and are in a state of complete repair. The principal building in Old Aberdeen is King's College, a large and stately fabric on the south side of the town. It is built in the form of a square with cloisters on the south side. The chapel is very ruinous within, but there still remains some woodwork of exquisite workmanship. The steeple is vaulted with a double cross arch, above which is an imperial crown, supported by eight stone pillars, and closed with a globe and two gilded crosses. King's College was founded, in 1494, by Bishop Elphinstone. The library is considerable, and now contains upwards of 25,000 volumes. The first principal of this college was Hector Boethius. The professorships are Humanity, Greek, and Oriental Languages, Moral and Natural Philosophy, Mathematics, Divinity, Medicine, and Civil Law, and there are a considerable number of bursaries for the poorer students. The average attendance at both collages is about 500.

The Dee, which falls into the sea on the south side of New Aberdeen, is a river of great note in Aberdeenshire. It has its source in Lord Fife's forest, in the parish of Crathy, at the point where the south-western extremity of Aberdeenshire unites with Inverness-shire. The total length of the Dee, from its source to its mouth, following its various windings, is about eighty miles. It is distinguished by its rapidity, its broad and capacious channel, and the limpid clearness of its waters. It is skirted with fine natural forests and extensive plantations. There is but little alluvial land on its banks, but its salmon fisheries are very valuable. Hence the old rhyme—

> "A rood o' Don's worth twa o' Dee,
> Unless it be for fish and tree."

The Don rises on the skirts of Ben Avon, on the confines of Aberdeenshire and Banffshire. Its total course is about sixty-one miles. It is a much less rapid river than the Dee, and flows for a considerable part of its course through rich valleys. About a mile from Old Aberdeen the Don is crossed by the "Brig of Balgownie," celebrated in Byron's Don Juan. It was built by Bishop Cheyne in the time of Robert Bruce, and consists of one spacious Gothic arch, which rests on a rock on each side.*

After leaving Aberdeen, and passing a number of fishing villages and Cruden Boy, the old castle of Slaines is seen standing on a steep precipice overlooking the sea. This fortress was destroyed in 1594, when James VI. marched north after the battle of Glenlivat, to reduce

* A very interesting tour may be made from Aberdeen up the Dee to Ballater and Castleton of Braemar. It has been said by Dr. M'Culloch, that Strath Dee is "superior to any other in Scotland, in the displays of its wildly Alpine boundary, and yields to none in magnificence and splendour." The upper portion of this district is peculiarly wild, exhibiting those awful wildernesses which pervade the central Highlands. About a fifth part of the surface of Aberdeenshire is composed of high mountainous tracts, and these, with hills, extensive moors, mosses, and other waste lands, occupy nearly two thirds of the entire county. These immense moors, which form a very peculiar feature in Scottish scenery, are calculated to impress the mind with feelings of the deepest loneliness and awe. They are generally rented in such portions as circumstances may require, by gentlemen from the southern parts of the kingdom, for the purpose of shooting, and they promise to afford refuge and shelter to the moorfowl and the blackcock, for many an age after they have been extirpated by the sportsmen from the more accessible moors of the south.

Huntly and Errol to obedience. The Errol family then removed to their present habitation a collection of low houses forming a quadrangle, one side of which is built on the very verge of the precipice overhanging the ocean. The coast here is very rocky, but, the rocks being soft, are wasted and corroded by the constant action of the waves, and the fragments which remain where the soft parts have been washed away, have assumed the appearance of old Gothic towers. In this neighbourhood is that wonder of nature, the Buller of Buchan. It is a huge rocky caldron, into which the sea rushes through a natural arch or rock. There is a path around the top which in one place is only two feet wide, with a monstrous precipice on either side. In the side of the caldron there opens a huge black cavern. In high gales the waves rush in with incredible violence, and fly over the natural wall of the Buller, which is at least two hundred feet high. Rounding the promontory of Buchanness,—the most easterly point of land in Scotland,—the tourist comes in sight of Peterhead,—the fifth sea port in Scotland, and, as a whale fishing, inferior only to Hull. It possesses a highly accessible, safe, and commodious harbour, and its inhabitants are remarkable for their activity and public spirit. The chevalier St. George landed at Peterhead in the disguise of a sailor, on his fruitless expedition to Scotland in 1715. Eighteen miles north from Peterhead is Fraserburgh, a considerable town, and burgh of regality, of which Lord Saltoun is superior, and chief proprietor. It has risen into considerable importance in consequence of the construction here, during last war, of a large harbour for the reception of ships of war. The old castle of Fraserburgh, which is now converted into a light house, stands on Kinnaird-head about a mile north of the town, and is a picturesque object from the sea. Twenty-one miles from Fraserburgh is the royal burgh of Banff, the capital of the county which bears its name. It is an old fashioned but clean and neat town, and contains about 3000 inhabitants. At the distance of a mile, on the opposite bank of the Deveron, is the modern village and seaport of Macduff. In the immediate neighbourhood is Duff House, the magnificent mansion of the Earl of Fife, surrounded by extensive plantations. The park is fourteen miles in circumference. About a century ago Banff was the scene of the execution of a noted robber, named Macpherson, whose "farewell" has been made the subject of a spirited song by Burns.

About seven miles from Banff is Portsoy, a small irregularly built town, with a thriving port. A few miles farther is the royal burgh of Cullen, where the queen of Robert Bruce died, and was buried in the eastern aisle in the old church. Behind the town is Cullen House, the splendid mansion of the Earl of Seafield. It contains a valuable collection of paintings. The other towns round the coast are Garmouth, a neat modern town on the left bank of the Spey; Burghead, a thriving seaport with a considerable trade in ship-building, and herring fishing; Nairn, a royal burgh, and capital of the county. After leaving Aberdeen, the Orkney steamer does not touch at any intervening place till it reaches Wick, a royal burgh, and the county town of Caithness. It is a thriving town, and is the principal seat of the herring fishery in the north of Scotland.

After leaving Wick, the steamer proceeds to Kirkwall, the principal town in the Orkney Islands. The Orkney and Shetland Islands lie in two groups to the north of Scotland, and form between them a county which returns a member to Parliament. The former, which are the most southerly, are separated from the county of Caithness by the Pentland Firth, which is about six miles broad. Their number is estimated at sixty-seven, of which twenty-seven are inhabited. They comprise an area of about 281,600 acres, and their population, in 1831, amounted to 28,847. There are about a dozen principal islands, of which Pomona or the mainland is decidedly the largest. Kirkwall, the chief town, contains upwards of 3000 inhabitants. The most important public building is St. Magnus's Cathedral, a stately pile, which was founded about the year 1138, and is still quite entire. There are also some interesting remains of the Bishop's Palace, and of the Earl's Palace, built by the infamous Patrick Stuart, who obtained the earldom in 1600. The general aspect of the country is bare and dreary, and there is a total absence of trees. In some places, however, the land is fertile and produces good crops. The herring fishery has greatly increased of late, and strawplaiting for bonnets is carried on to a considerable extent. The total amount received in Orkney, in 1833, for the exports of farm produce, manufactures, fisheries, &c. was £60,114.

The Shetland or Zetland Isles, supposed to be the *Ultima Thule* of the ancients, are separated from the Orkneys by a channel 48 miles across. They exceed 100 in number, but of these only between 30 and 40 are inhabited. Lerwick, which is the capital, contains about 2700 inhabitants. In the Lowlands it would be only entitled to the name of a thriving village, very irregularly built. " The opposite island of Bressay forms Bressay Sound, one of the finest harbours in the world, and the rendezvous of all the vessels destined for the north and the whale fishery. Off Bressay is the most remarkable of the rock phenomena of Shetland ; the Noss, a small high island, with a flat summit, girt on all sides by perpendicular walls of rock."* It is only 500 feet in length, and 170 broad, and rises abruptly from the sea to the height of 160 feet. The communication with the coast of Bressay is maintained by strong ropes stretched across, along which a cradle or wooden chair is run, in which the passenger is seated. It is of a size sufficient for conveying across a man and a sheep at a time. The purpose of this strange contrivance is to give the tenant the benefit of putting a few sheep upon the Holm, the top of which is level, and affords good pasture. The animals are transported in the cradle, one at a time, a shepherd holding them upon his knees in crossing.

NOSS HOLM, SHETLAND.

"The temptation of getting access to the numberless eggs and young of the sea-fowl which whiten the surface of the Holm, joined to the promised reward of a cow, induced a hardy and adventurous fowler, about two centuries ago, to scale the cliff of the Holm, and establish a connection by ropes with the neighbouring main island. Having driven two stakes into the rock, and fastened his ropes, the desperate man was entreated to avail himself of the communication thus established in returning across the gulf. But this he refused to do, and in attempting

* Murray's Encyclopædia of Geography. Lon. 1834.

to descend the way he had climbed, he fell, and perished by his fool-hardiness."*

There are scarcely any roads in Shetland, and travelling is usually performed on those hardy, spirited little horses known by the name of *shelties,* which are bred in Shetland, and are exported in considerable numbers.

SHETLAND PONEY.

The trade and exports of Shetland are much the same as those of Orkney. These islands formerly belonged to the kingdom of Denmark, but, in 1468, on the marriage of James III. with the Princess Margaret of Denmark, they were given in pledge for the payment of her dowry, and have never since been disjoined from Scotland. They were at various times bestowed by the Crown on different persons, some of whom subjected the inhabitants to great oppressions. At length, in 1707, James Earl of Morton obtained them from the Crown in mortgage, which was rendered irredeemable in 1742, and in 1766 he sold the estate for £60,000 to Sir Lawrence Dundas, the ancestor of the Earl of Zetland, their present proprietor.

* Anderson's Guide to the Highlands.

ITINERARY.

ITINERARY.

I. EDINBURGH.—GALASHIELS.—MELROSE.—JEDBURGH.—51 Miles.

ON RIGHT FROM EDIN.	From Jed.	EDINBURGH.	From Edin.	ON LEFT FROM EDIN.
		Leave Edinburgh by Newington.		
Grange House, Sir Thos. Dick Lauder, Bart.	49	Powburn.	2	
	48	Libberton vill. & Kirk.	3	
	47	Gilmerton.	4	Eldin, —— Clerk, Esq.
In the neighbourhood is Roslin Castle and Chapel.	45	Lasswade.	6	Melville Castle, Lord Melville.
Hawthornden, once the seat of Drummond the Poet; under the house are several curious caves.	43	cr. South Esk.	8	Newbattle Abbey, Marquis of Lothian.
		Dalhousie.		
	42	Kirkhill vill. & Kirk.	9	Powder Mills, the oldest in Scotland.
Dalhousie Castle, Earl of Dalhousie, an ancient seat modernized.	39¾	Fushie Bridge.	11¼	Ruins of Borthwick Castle, with Borthwick Kirk. The Castle is very entire, and was inhabited for a short time in 1567 by Queen Mary and Bothwell.
	38	Middleton.	13	
Arniston, —— Dundas, Esq.	31	Crookston.		
Heriot House.		cr. Heriot Water.		
Heriot Kirk and Manse.		cr. Crookston Wat.		
Bowland, —— Walker, Esq.	27	Gala bank Inn.	24	
		Torsonce Inn.	25	Crookston House, —— Borthwick, Esq.
Torwoodlee and Fernielie, —— Pringle, Esq.	25½	Stow vill.	25½	Pirn, —— Tait, Esq.
Galashiels is separated from this line of road by the Gala, which joins the Tweed about a mile below.		Buckholm Farm.		
	20½	Laudhopeburn House.	30½	
		Langhaugh.		Langlee House, —— Bruce, Esq.
Gala House, —— Scott, Esq.		cr. Allan Water.		Pavillion, L. Somerville.
Across the river may be seen Abbotsford, the seat of Sir Walter Scott.		cr. Tweed.		The vale of the Allan is supposed to be the "Glendearg" of the Monastery.
		Darnick vill.		
Melrose Abbey, the finest specimen of Gothic Architecture in Scotland.	15	MELROSE.	36	Near Melrose are the Eildon Hills, on which are the remains of Roman Camps.
		Eildon vill.		
In St. Boswell's Village a great annual fair is held on the 18th of July for horses, cattle, sheep, &c.	13	Newton, Dryburgh.	38	Dryburgh Abbey is beautifully situated on the left bank of the Tweed. Sir Walter Scott was interred here. Farther down the Tweed is Mertoun, the seat of Lord Polwarth.
	10	St. Boswell's.	41	
Ancrum House, Sir Wm. Scott, Bart.	3	Ancrum, where the Ale joins the Teviot.	48	
Near Ancrum the Battle of Lilliards Edge was fought in 1545, where a body of English troops, under Lord Evers and Sir Brian Latoun, were completely defeated by the Earl of Angus.	2	Teviot Bridge.		Near Ancrum the Roman road from York to the Firth of Forth passes.
		cr. Teviot.		
		Bonjedward.	49	
		cr. Jed Water.		
		JEDBURGH.	51	

Jedburgh is situated on the west bank of the Jed, in the midst of a country beautifully wooded. It is a royal burgh of very ancient erection, and was one of the chief Border towns, and a place of considerable importance before the Union. After that period its trade was, in a great measure, destroyed; it has now, however, greatly revived. The remains of the Abbey form the principal object of curiosity in Jedburgh. It was founded either in 1118 or 1147, and, after various damages in the course of the Border wars, was burnt by the Earl of Hertford in 1545. It is a magnificent ruin, and is considered the most perfect and beautiful specimen of the Saxon and early Gothic in Scotland. Part of the west end is fitted up as a parish church. The Castle of Jedburgh, situated on an eminence at the town head, was a fortress of very great strength. The ground is now occupied by a Jail. The environs of Jedburgh abound in rich woodland scenes. Some remains of the famous ancient forest are to be seen in the neighbourhood of the half ruined castle of Ferniehirst, belonging to the Marquis of Lothian, and the original seat of his ancestors, the Kers. Jedburgh contains above 4000 inhabitants, and joins with Haddington, North Berwick, Dunbar, and Lauder, in electing a member of Parliament.

II. EDINBURGH.—DALKEITH.—LAUDER.—KELSO.—42 Miles.

ON RIGHT FROM EDIN.	From Kelso.	EDINBURGH.	From Edin.	ON LEFT FROM EDIN.
		Leave Edinburgh by Hope Park Chapel.		
	$41\frac{3}{4}$	Gibbet Toll.	$\frac{1}{4}$	
Inch, Little Gilmour, Esq.	41	Salisbury Green.	1	
	$40\frac{3}{4}$	cr. Pow Burn.	$1\frac{1}{4}$	
Said to have acquired its name from the French attendants of Queen Mary.	$39\frac{1}{2}$	Little France.	$2\frac{1}{2}$	Ruins of Craigmillar Castle, a residence of Queen Mary.
Drum, Miss Innes, formerly a seat of the Somerville family.	36	cr. N. Esk River and enter Dalkeith.	6	Population 5586; votes with the county for M.P.
Melville Castle, Lord Melville.		cr. South Esk.	$6\frac{1}{4}$	Dalkeith Palace and grounds, Duke of Buccleuch.
Newbattle Abbey, Marquis of Lothian.	32	Cranston Kirk.	9	Oxenford Castle, Sir J. Dalrymple.
Near, Crichton Castle, once the residence of Chancellor Crichton.	30	Pathhead.	$10\frac{1}{2}$	
		cr. Fala Water.		
		Fala vill.		
	27	Blackshiels Inn.	15	Soutra Hill, 1200 feet above the level of the sea, where there was once an hospital built in 1164 by Malcolm IV.
		cr. Soutra.		
		Enter Berwickshire.		
		cr. Red Brae.		
		cr. Leader Wat.		
	$20\frac{3}{4}$	Carfrae Mill Inn.	21	
	$20\frac{1}{2}$	cr. Leader Wat.	$21\frac{1}{4}$	
Lauder is a royal burgh. Population 2063. Joins with Haddington, North Berwick, Dunbar, and Jedburgh in electing M.P.	$16\frac{3}{4}$	LAUDER.	$25\frac{1}{4}$	Cochrane, Earl of Mar, and other favourites of James V. were hanged by the factious nobles over Lauder bridge.
		cr. Leader Wat.		
	$14\frac{1}{4}$	Thirlestane.	$27\frac{3}{4}$	Close beside Lauder stands Thirlestane Castle, an ancient and spacious edifice, the seat of the Earl of Lauderdale.
—— Spottiswoode, Esq. lineal descendant of Archbishop Spottiswoode the historian.	$12\frac{3}{4}$	Spottiswood.	29	
	$12\frac{1}{2}$	Whitburn Inn.	$29\frac{1}{4}$	
	$10\frac{3}{4}$	Legerwood Kirk.	$31\frac{1}{4}$	Hume Castle seen on a height to the left. Also Mellerstain House, Geo. Baillie, Esq. of Jerviswood.
The original residence of the Gordon family, and from which their title of Duke was derived.	$7\frac{3}{4}$	Gordon Kirk, and vill. of West Gordon.	$34\frac{1}{4}$	
		cr. Eden.		
The scene of the boyhood of Sir Walter Scott.	$6\frac{3}{4}$	Smailholm vill. and Tower.	$35\frac{1}{4}$	
	4	Nenthorn vill. & Kirk.	38	Nenthorn House, Roy, Esq; formerly possessed by a branch of the powerful family of the Kers.
Fleurs, Duke of Roxburghe.		cr. Eden.		
		KELSO.	42	

Kelso is a handsome town, containing a spacious square or market-place, in which stand the town-house, and many elegant houses and shops. The Tweed is here crossed by a handsome bridge of Rennie's construction, from which the view, looking westward, and taking in Fleurs, the seat of the Duke of Roxburghe, is extremely beautiful. Kelso Abbey is well deserving of attention for its venerable antiquity, and the purity of its Saxon architecture. It was founded in 1128 by David I. who dedicated it to the Virgin Mary and St. John, and endowed it with immense possessions and privileges. In this Abbey James III. was crowned in 1460. The ruins of Roxburgh Castle, so celebrated in Scottish history, are situated about a mile from Kelso, near the junction of the Tweed and Teviot. Kelso contains above 4000 inhabitants; it votes with the county for M.P.

III. EDINBURGH.—SELKIRK.—HAWICK.—LONGTOWN.—85¾ Miles.

On right from Edin.	From Longtown	For the space between Edinburgh and Galashiels, 30½ miles, see No. 1.	From Edin.	On left from Edin.
		A new road from Galashiels to Selkirk was formed in 1829, now crossing the Tweed and Ettrick by two handsome bridges. It leaves the old road at Crosslee toll-bar, three miles from Galashiels.		
A little above Yair is Ashiestiel, formerly the residence of Sir W. Scott.	53	Whitebank.	29	
		cr. Gala Water.		
Near Selkirk is Bowhill, a seat of the Duke of Buccleuch.	50	cr. Tweed at Yair Bridge.	32	
	49	Sunderland.	33	Sunderland Hall, Plomer.
Philiphaugh, a plain to the north of the junction of the Ettrick and Yarrow, was the scene of the famous battle between the army of the Marquis of Montrose, and a body of horse commanded by General Leslie, in which the former was completely defeated.	46	cr. Ettrick Wat. and enter SELKIRK.	39¼	Selkirk is a royal burgh, containing a population of 1800. A band of Selkirk burgesses behaved with great gallantry at Flodden. A standard was taken by them, which is still preserved by the corporation. A great business in shoemaking was formerly carried on. The electors of Selkirk vote with those of the county.
		Immediately beyond Selkirk, pass the Haining, —— Pringle, Esq.		
	41	cr. Ale Water.	44¼	
Wool, Scott, Esq.	40½	Ashkirk.	44¼	Sinton, Scott, Esq.
Thirlestane, Lord Napier.				
Wilton House, across the Teviot.	34½	Wilton Kirk.	50¼	
Near Hawick, on the banks of the Teviot, stands Branxholm Castle, belonging to the Duke of Buccleuch, and the chief scene of the Lay of the Last Minstrel.	34	cr. the Teviot, and enter HAWICK.	50¾	Population 4970; a remarkably active manufacturing town, chiefly producing hosiery. Votes with the county.
		Junction of Borthwick and Teviot.		
	32	cr. the Teviot.	52¾	Goldiland's Tower, celebrated in Border ballads.
Here Johnny Armstrong and his men were hanged by the summary justice of James V.	26	Carlinrig Ch. in ruins.	58¾	
	22	Mosspaul Inn.	63½	On the heights where the counties of Roxburgh and Dumfries meet.
Mickledale, Beatty, Esq.	16	Ewes Kirk.	69½	
Langholm Lodge, a minor seat of the Duke of Buccleuch.		cr. Ewes Bridge.		
	11¼	Langholm vill.	73¾	Broomholm, —— Maxwell, Esq.
	9½	cr. Esk River.	75½	The banks of the Esk are here romantically beautiful.
Near Hollows is Gilnockie Tower, the ruined stronghold of Johnny Armstrong.	8	Hollows vill.	77	
		cr. Canobie Wat.	78	
	6	Canobie vill.	79	
		Scots Dyke toll-bar,	81½	
	3½	Where English ground commences.		Across the Esk is Netherby, the beautiful seat of Sir James Graham.
	2½	Kirk Andrews.	82½	
		cr. the Esk,		
		and enter LONGTOWN.	85¾	

IV. EDINBURGH.—MUSSELBURGH.—HADDINGTON.—DUNBAR.—BERWICK.

$57\frac{3}{4}$ MILES.

ON RIGHT FROM EDIN.	From Berwick.	EDINBURGH. Leave Edinburgh by Regent Bridge.	From Edin.	ON LEFT FROM EDIN.
		Jock's Lodge.		Restalrig. Lochend House.
Fine view of Arthur's Seat and St. Anthony's Chapel.		Portobello.	3	Piershill Barracks, with accommodation for 1000 Cavalry.
		Duddingstone Salt Pans.		Portobello, much resorted to by the inhabitants of Edinburgh for sea-bathing.
New Hailes, Miss Dalrymple.		cr. Esk Bridge.	$5\frac{3}{4}$	
Pinkie House, Sir John Hope, near the spot where the battle of Pinkie was fought in 1547.	52	Fisherrow and MUSSELBURGH.	6	Musselburgh Race-course, upon which the Edinburgh Races are run annually.
Coalston, Earl of Dalhousie.	48	Tranent.	10	On the coast, Prestonpans village.
Lennox Love, L. Blantyre.	45	Gladsmuir.	13	Gosford House, Earl of Wemyss.
In Haddington the chief object of interest is the old Franciscan Church. Here, according to some writers, John Knox was born.	41	HADDINGTON. A royal burgh; population 5583.	17	The battle of Preston, in which the Royal troops, under Sir John Cope, were defeated by the Highlanders under Prince Charles Stuart, was fought in this neighbourhood. The house of Colonel Gardiner, and the spot where he fell, as well as the tree under which Prince Charles stood during the battle, are still pointed out.
Amisfield, E. of Wemyss.				
Ruins of Hailes Castle, the seat of the Earl of Bothwell, husband of Queen Mary.	$37\frac{1}{4}$	Hailes.	$20\frac{3}{4}$	
	$35\frac{1}{2}$	Linton.	$22\frac{1}{4}$	
		cr. River Tyne.		
A mile to the south is Traprain Law.	$33\frac{3}{4}$	Gateside Inn.	24	
Biel, Mrs. Ferguson Nisbet.	$31\frac{3}{4}$	West Barns.	26	
Belton Place, —— Hay, Esq.		cr. Belton Water.		
		Belhaven vill.		A short distance from Dunbar is Broxmouth, a large mansion of the Duke of Roxburghe, surrounded with wood.
Lochend House, Sir G. Warrender, Bart.	$29\frac{3}{4}$	DUNBAR.	28	
Two celebrated battles have been fought in the neighbourhood of Dunbar, the first in 1296, when the Scotch were defeated by the English under Earl Warren, and the second in 1650, when they were defeated by Cromwell.	27	East Barns vill.	$30\frac{3}{4}$	The ruins of Dunbar Castle, about 200 yards west of the town. Here Edward II. found refuge after his defeat at Bannockburn.
	$26\frac{1}{4}$	cr. Dryburn Wat.	$31\frac{1}{2}$	
	$24\frac{3}{4}$	Thornton Bridge.	33	
		cr. Innerwick Wat.		
	$22\frac{1}{4}$	cr. Dunglas Burn, and enter Berwickshire.	$35\frac{1}{2}$	To the north of the town is Dunbar House, a seat of the Earl of Lauderdale.
Dunglas House, Sir John Hall, Bart. situated amidst beautiful plantations. It stands on the site of an old castle which was originally a strong fortress of the Earls of Home.	$18\frac{1}{4}$	cr. Penmanshiel Bridge.	$39\frac{1}{2}$	
		cr. Peas Burn.		
	$16\frac{1}{2}$	Grant's Inn.	$41\frac{1}{4}$	A little below, on the old road, is the celebrated Pease Bridge, consisting of two arches 300 feet long, and 240 feet in height, supported in the centre by one of the loftiest piers in the world.
	$12\frac{1}{2}$	Houndwood.	$45\frac{1}{4}$	
Houndwood House, Mrs. Coulson, said to have been a hunting seat of the Scottish monarchs.	$7\frac{3}{4}$	Ayton vill.	50	
		cr. Ay Water.		
	$6\frac{3}{4}$	Fleemington.	51	
Remains of Lamerton Kirk, where James IV. of Scotland was married by proxy to Margaret, eldest daughter of Henry VII. of England.	3	Liberties of Berwick.	55	
		BERWICK.	58	

The town of Berwick is more remarkable for its historical recollections than for its present importance. It is 23 miles distant from Kelso, and 58 from Edinburgh, and is a respectable looking town, containing about 9000 or 10,000 inhabitants. It is still surrounded by its ancient walls, which only of late years ceased to be regularly fortified. Its principal trade is the export of salmon.

V. EDINBURGH.—LINLITHGOW.—FALKIRK.—STIRLING.—$35\frac{1}{4}$ MILES.

ON RIGHT FROM EDIN.	From Stirling.	EDINBURGH.	From Edin.	ON LEFT FROM EDIN.
		Leave Edinr. by west end of Prince's Street.		
Corstorphine Hill, richly wooded and studded with gentlemen's seats and villas.	$33\frac{3}{4}$	Coltbridge.	1	
	$33\frac{1}{4}$	cr. Water of Leith.	2	
	$31\frac{1}{4}$	Corstorphine vill.	4	On the right bank of the Almond, before crossing the bridge, is a rude monument, called the Catstane, commemorative of a battle fought in 995.
	$27\frac{3}{4}$	cr. Almond Water, and enter Linlithgowshire.	$7\frac{1}{2}$	
	$26\frac{1}{4}$	Kirkliston vill.	9	
At Winchburgh, Edward II. first halted after his defeat at Bannockburn.	$23\frac{3}{4}$	Winchburgh vill.	$11\frac{1}{2}$	Ruins of Niddry Castle, where Queen Mary first slept after her escape from Lochleven.
		cr. Union Canal.		
	$22\frac{1}{4}$	Three-Mile-Town.	13	
		cr. Haugh-burn.		Linlithgow Bridge was the scene of a battle fought between the Earls of Arran and Lennox in the minority of James V.
Champfleurie, Johnston of Straiton. Linlithgow, a town of great antiquity. In its streets the Regent Moray was shot. The palace is the chief object of interest. In it Queen Mary was born. The church is a fine specimen of Gothic architecture.	$18\frac{1}{2}$	LINLITHGOW.	$16\frac{3}{4}$	
	$17\frac{1}{4}$	cr. Avon by Linlithgow Bridge and enter Stirlingshire.	18	Callander Ho., Forbes, Esq., formerly the seat of the Earl of Kilmarnock.
	14	Polmont vill.	$21\frac{1}{4}$	Falkirk, an ancient town, celebrated for a defeat sustained in its neighbourhood by Wallace, in a battle with Edward I. Also the scene of an engagement between the rebel and the royal armies in 1746, when the latter was defeated. The town has now acquired a more peaceful celebrity, by its trysts or cattle markets. At a short distance from the village of Bannockburn, is the field of Bannockburn, where Robert Bruce, with 30,000 men, defeated Edward II. with 100,000. At Milton, in the same neighbourhood, is the scene of James Third's assassination after his defeat at Sauchie.
		cr. Castle Water.		
	$13\frac{1}{2}$	Lauriston.	$21\frac{3}{4}$	
		cr. Burn Water.		
	$10\frac{3}{4}$	FALKIRK.	24	
	$10\frac{1}{4}$	cr. under Canal.	25	
	$9\frac{1}{4}$	Camelon vill.	26	
A mile from Camelon the Carron Iron Works are easily distinguishable by the smoke and flames.		cr. Carron Water.		
	$8\frac{1}{4}$	Larbert.	27	
At Torwood stood the tree in which Wallace used to conceal himself when hard pressed by his enemies. Here Mr. Cargill, in 1680, excommunicated King Charles II. the Duke of York, and the Ministry.	$6\frac{1}{4}$	Torwood.	29	
	$1\frac{3}{4}$	Bannockburn vill.	$33\frac{1}{2}$	
		cr. Bannockburn.		
	1	St. Ninian's vill.	$34\frac{1}{4}$	
		STIRLING.	$35\frac{1}{4}$	

The central and original part of Stirling bears an appearance rather antique than elegant, but there are several good streets, and a great number of neat villas in the outskirts. The church is a handsome old Gothic fabric, and includes two places of worship called the East and West Churches. The former was erected by Cardinal Beaton, the latter by James IV. in 1494. The celebrated Ebenezer Erskine, founder of the Secession Church, was for some time minister of the West Church.

The most conspicuous object in Stirling is the Castle. It was a favourite residence of the Scottish monarchs, and a stronghold of great importance. Many events of historical interest are associated with this fortress. Here James II. murdered William Earl of Douglas for refusing to withdraw himself from a rebellious association with other Scottish nobles; in revenge for which the friends of Douglas burnt the town. Here also James IV. was born, and James V. crowned. The prospect of the surrounding country from the castle is magnificent, combining every element of beauty and of grandeur. A visit to Demyat, one of the Ochils, will amply repay the labour of the tourist, as this hill commands one of the noblest views any where to be met with.

*** *Tourists proceeding from Stirling to Callander and the Trosachs, are referred to page 183 for a description of the route.*

VI. EDINBURGH.—PEEBLES.—MOFFAT.—DUMFRIES.—74 MILES.

ON RIGHT FROM EDIN.	From Dumfries.	EDINBURGH. The road leaves Edinburgh by Nicolson Street.	From Edin.	ON LEFT FROM EDIN.
Morton Hall, —— Trotter, Esq.	72	Powburn.	2	At a little distance, the ruins of Craigmillar Castle.
Burdiehouse House, a corruption of Bourdeaux House, some French Protestants having emigrated hither from Bourdeaux after the revocation of the edict of Nantes in 1685.	71	Libberton Kirk.	3	Gracemount, Mrs. Hay.
	70½	Burdiehouse.	3½	St. Catherine's, Sir Wm. Rae.
	69	Straiton vill.	5	Near Straiton was fought the second of three conflicts which took place in one day in 1303, styled the battle of Roslin.
	68	Pass Bilston Toll-bar, where road to Roslin parts off to left.	6	
At a little distance, Woodhouselee, F. Tytler, Esq.	67	Greenlaw.	7	Dryden House, G. Mercer, Esq.
Glencorse House and Church.		Auchindinny.		
	64	Penicuik.	10	Built as a depot for French prisoners during the late war.
Penicuik, Ho., Sir George Clerk, Bart.	63	cr. North Esk.	11	
	62	Wellington Inn.	12	
Where the direct road to Dumfries parts off on the right.	61	Leadburn Inn.	13	
Early Vale.	60	Kingside Edge.	14	Pass through a considerable tract of moorish country.
		cr. Eddleston Wat.		
	56	Eddleston vill.	18	Close to the village is Darnhall, a seat of Lord Elibank.
An ancient royal burgh beautifully situated on the Tweed. Population of the parish 2750. Votes with the county for a Member of Parliament. From this is six miles along the north bank of the Tweed to Innerleithen, a village much resorted to for its mineral springs, and for rural recreations.	52	PEEBLES.	22	A little beyond is the Cottage, Mackenzie of Portmore, Esq.
	51		23	
	49	cr. Lyne Wat.	25	On the left Nidpath Castle, nearly in ruins, a most romantic situation.
	46½	Stobo Kirk.	27½	
	46	Stobo Castle, Montgomery, Bart.	28	Barns, Burnet, Esq.
	44½	New Posso, Nasmyth, Bart.	29½	Across the Tweed, the Vale of Manor, in which lived David Ritchie, the original of the Black Dwarf.
Drummelzier Castle was formerly the property of the powerful family of Tweedie, from whom it went to the family of the Hays. It is now the property of White, Esq.	42½	Drummelzier Kirk.	31½	Oliver Castle Ruins, Tweedie, Esq.
	37	Crook Inn.	37	Polmood House, Captain Forbes.
	28	Tweed Shaws.	39	
			46	On the left, the remarkable hollow called the Devil's Beefstand.
	21	cr. Annan.	48	
		MOFFAT.	53	Moffat is a pleasant town, noted for its medicinal waters. Population about 1400.
There is another road from Edinburgh to Moffat and Dumfries, which leads by the Pentland Hills, Glencross, Linton, and Broughton villages, and joins the other road about 31 miles from Edinburgh. The distance between Edinburgh and Dumfries by this road is 71 miles.	19½	Beatoch Inn.	54½	
	17½	Kirkpatrick Juxta.	56½	
	6½	cr. Water of Æ.	67½	Amisfield is the seat of the ancient family of Charteris.
	5	Amisfield House, with the old ruined tower of Amisfield.	69	Tinwald was the birthplace of Paterson, the projector of the banks of England and Scotland, and likewise of the Scottish expedition to Darien.
	3	Tinwald Kirk.	71	
		DUMFRIES.	74	

Dumfries was made a royal burgh in the thirteenth century. It contains few monuments of antiquity, except an excellent bridge of three arches, which has stood for nearly 600 years. The most interesting circumstance connected with Dumfries is its having been the residence and burial place of Burns. St. Michael's church yard contains an extraordinary number of monuments of fine proportions and decorations. Dumfries unites with Annan, Kirkcudbright, Lochmaben, and Sanquhar, in returning a Member of Parliament. Population 11,606.

VII. EDINBURGH.—MID CALDER.—STRATHAVEN.—GALSTON.—KILMARNOCK.—AYR.—72 MILES.

ON RIGHT FROM EDIN.	From Ayr.	EDINBURGH. Leave the city by Princes St.	From Edin.	ON LEFT FROM EDIN.
Near Merchiston Ho., Walker, Esq.	69½	Gorgie Mills.	2½	Dalry House, Walker, Esq.
		cr. Wat. of Leith.		
Saughton Hall, Baird, Bart.		Loanend.		
Saughton, Watson, Esq.	66	Long Hermandston vill.	6	Riccarton, Sir James Gibson-Craig, Bart.
	64	Addiston. } Earl of Morton.		
	63¼	Dalmahoy.	7¼	
		cr. Gogar Burn.		
Hatton, Captain Davidson; formerly a residence of the Lauderdale family.	63	Burn Wynd Inn.	9	
	61¾	Wester Cocksiedean.	10¼	
		East Calder.		
The Church of Mid Calder is a fine specimen of an old parochial place of worship in the Gothic style. The father of Archbishop Spottiswoode officiated here, being Minister of Calder.	60	MID CALDER.	12	
		From Mid Calder proceeds also the southern line of road to Glasgow. See No. XII.		Close to Mid Calder is Calder House, the seat of Lord Torphichen, where John Knox preached, and where the only authentic portrait of him exists. The scenery around Mid Calder is of a very romantic description.
		cr. Almond Wat.		
	55½	West Calder vill.	16½	
		Here commences an extensive moor, unenlivened by any object of interest. At length, after passing near the extensive iron work of Shotts, the road begins to descend by the minor vale of Calder into the valley of the Clyde.		
A new road leads from this to Strathaven, crossing the Clyde by the Garion Bridge; another road, somewhat less direct, leads by Hamilton. The former is used by the stage coaches to Ayr.	44	Allanton, Lady Seton Stuart.	28	
	43	Bonkill.	29	
	42	Newmains Inn.	30	
		On left of Garion Bridge the vill. of Dalserf.		
		Stonehouse vill.		The road now passes over a long tract of moorish land, enlivened only by the towering form of Loudon Hill, where Ayrshire is entered.
Wallace's Cairn, marking the scene of a conflict between that hero and a party of English.	32	STRATHAVEN.	40	
	22	Priestland.	50	
	21	Darvel vill.	51	The more direct road to Ayr from this point, leads by Fail and St. Quivox, saving two miles.
A mile and a half to the right is Drumclog, the scene of the battle of that name, in May 1679, in which Claverhouse was defeated by the Covenanters.	17	Newmills vill.	55	
		GALSTON.		
	12	KILMARNOCK.	60	Kilmarnock is eminent as a seat of various branches of woollen manufacture. It now rivals Kidderminster in the manufacture of carpets. The cotton manufacture has also been introduced with marked success, and the town now produces shawls, gauzes, and muslins of the finest quality. The external appearance of Kilmarnock is very pleasing.
Loudon Castle, the magnificent seat of the Countess of Loudon, Dowager Marchioness of Hastings.	11	cr. Irvine Water, and pass through	61	
		Riccarton vill.		
	7	Symington Kirk.	65	
For the Description of Ayr, see No. XVII.	4	Monkton vill.	68	
	2¾	Priestwick vill.	69¼	
		AYR.	72	

VIII. EDINBURGH.—CARNWATH.—DOUGLAS MILL.—CUMNOCK.—AYR.—76¾ Mi.

ON RIGHT FROM EDIN.	From Ayr.	EDINBURGH.	From Edin.	ON LEFT FROM EDIN.
Merchiston Castle, Lord Napier.		Leave the city by the Lothian Road and Port-Hopetoun.		Craig Ho., Gordon.
		Pass under the Union Canal.		
	73¾	Slateford vill.	3	Overhung by a splendid aqueduct bridge of the Union Canal, which here crosses the Water of Leith.
Baberton, Christie. Charles X. and his family occupied this house for some time as shooting quarters.	70¾	Currie vill.	6	
	69	Ravelrig.	7¾	At a little distance on the left, Colinton village.
At a little distance, Riccarton, Gibson-Craig, Bart.	65¾	Little Vantage Inn.	11	Lennox Castle in ruins, on a fine situation, commanding an extensive view. It has been a place of great strength.
Lumphoy Castle, ruins.	64¾	Morton Castle Ruins.	12	
Malleny, General Scott. Dalmahoy Crags, 866 feet above the sea.	62¾	Causewayend Inn.	14	
Meadowbank, Maconochie, Lord Meadowbank.	61¾	cr. Linhouse Wat.	15	
	59¼	Crosswood Hill.	17½	Easter Colzium, Linning, Esq.
		cr. Dryburn Burn.		
	54¾	cr. Medwen Wat.	22	For many miles before and after this point, the road passes over a dismal moor.
	51¾	Carnwath vill.	25	
	48¼	Carstairs vill.	28½	Kersewell, Capt. Bertram.
Carnwath Ho., Macdonald Lockhart, Bart.	47¼	Ravenstruther Toll.	29½	Carstairs Ho., Monteith, Esq.
		cr. Clyde.		At the distance of 2½ miles is Lanark, an ancient royal burgh; population of the parish 7672. The falls of the Clyde at Bonnington and Cora are about 2 miles from Lanark, approached by a road leading through New Lanark village, where the celebrated cotton mills, formerly conducted by Mr. Robert Owen, are to be seen.
	44¾	Hyndford Bridge Inn.	32	
	41¼	Hecklebirny.	35½	
Here was the original seat of the family of Douglas. In the vicinity of the town stands Douglas Castle, a seat of Lord Douglas. A part of the old church is still kept in repair, on account of the monuments in it and the burying vault.	38¼	Douglas Mill Inn.	38½	
	36¼	Douglas.	40½	
		cr. Douglas Wat.		
	25¾	Muirkirk.	51	
		Muirmill Bridge.		Between Cumnock and Muirkirk lies the extensive morass denominated Aird's Moss, where, on July 20, 1680, a skirmish took place between a body of dragoons, commanded by Bruce of Earlshall, and sixty-six Covenanters, under the conduct of Hackstoun of Rathillet and Mr. Richard Cameron.
	20¾	cr. Ayr Wat.	56	
Cumnock is celebrated for the manufacture of those curious little cabinets known by the name of Cumnock snuff-boxes.	15¼	CUMNOCK.	61½	
	9¾	Ochiltree.	67	
		cr. Burnock Wat.		
	5¾	Drongan House.	71	
	4¾	cr. Kyle Wat.	72¾	
For the Description of Ayr, see No. XVII.	1	Shawwood.	75¾	
		AYR.	76¾	

IX. EDINBURGH.—QUEENSFERRY.—INVERKEITHING.—KINROSS.—PERTH.—
44 MILES.

ON RIGHT FROM EDIN.	From Perth.	EDINBURGH.	From Edin.	ON LEFT FROM EDIN.
St. Bernard's Well.		Leave Edinburgh by Queensferry Road.		
Dean House, Sir J. Nisbet. Craigleith Park, Bonar, Esq. Craigleith Quarry.		cr. Wat. of Leith by Dean Bridge, a superb edifice of four arches, each 90 feet in span.		The old road passes between John Watson's Hospital, and the Orphan Hospital both buildings of great elegance.
Newhall, Scott Moncrief, Esq.	40	Barnton.	4	Craigcrook, Lord Jeffrey.
Village of Cramond on the shore to the right.	39	cr. Almond by Cramond Bridge.	5	Ravelston, Lady Murray Keith. Barnton, W. R. Ramsay, Esq.
Dalmeny Park, Earl Rosebery.	36½	Dalmeny Kirk.	7½	Craigiehall, Hope Vere, Esq.
A little to the south are		Hawes Inn.		
the ruins of Dundas Castle, a building of great antiquity, which has been in	34¾	QUEENSFERRY.	9¼	Queensferry was erected into a royal burgh by Malcolm Canmore, and derived its name from Margaret his Queen, sister of Edgar Atheling. Here are the ruins of a monastery of Carmelite Friars, erected in 1330.
the Dundas family upwards of 700 years.		Cross Ferry.		
Donnibrissel House, Earl of Moray. Donnibrissel House was the scene, in 1592, of the murder of the Earl of Moray by the Marquis of Huntly. This	33¾	North Queensferry Inn.	10¼	
melancholy event is commemorated in the ballad	31½	INVERKEITHING.	12½	A very ancient royal burgh, erected, it is said,
of "The bonnie Erle of Moray."	25½	Kirk of Beath.	18½	by William the Lion. The bay is large and safe. Great
Fordel, Sir J. Henderson, Bart.	23	Maryburgh.	21	quantities of coal and salt are annually exported here.
Lochgelly, Earl of Minto. Lochore, Sir Walter Scott.		cr. Kelty Wat.		Population 3189. Its neighbourhood was, in 1651, the
Here the Poet, Michael Bruce, once taught a small school.	21	Gairney Bridge vill.	23	scene of a battle between the English Parliamentary army under General Lambert, and that of the Scottish loyalists, in which the latter were defeated.
The two brothers Adam, the distinguished architects, were natives of Maryburgh.	18½	KINROSS. Population 2017.	25½	
	17	Milnathort.	27	Blair Adam, Sir Charles Adam.
Kinross is situated on the beautiful banks of	11¼	Drumhead Inn.	32¾	The road now enters
Lochleven. Lochleven	6¼	Crossgates, Dron Kirk.	37¾	Glenfarg, a beautiful little
Castle, remarkable for its great antiquity, and as being the place where Queen Mary was imprisoned. The trout produced in Lochleven are of acknowledged excellence.	4	Bridge of Earn. Moncrief Hill, On whose shoulder the traveller first comes in sight of Perth.	40	valley, enclosed by the Ochils. To the right Abernethy, the capital of the Pictish kingdom. In the neighbourhood of Bridge of Earn is Pitcaithly
		PERTH.	44	Well, celebrated for its medicinal waters.

Perth is one of the handsomest and most ancient towns in Scotland. It is beautifully situated on the west bank of the Tay, having the spacious plains of the North and South Inches extending on each side. On account of its importance, and its vicinity to the royal Palace of Scone, it was long considered the capital of Scotland, before Edinburgh acquired that distinction. Here, too, the Parliaments and national assemblies were held, and many of the nobility took up their residence. A splendid bridge of ten arches, and 900 feet in length, leads across the Tay to the north. Perth contains several beautiful streets and terraces, and a number of splendid public buildings. It is peculiarly rich in objects of historic and picturesque interest. Of Gowrie House the scene of a well known mysterious incident in Scottish history, most unfortunately not a vestige remains. In Blackfriars Monastery, which once stood at the north side of the town, James I. was assassinated by a band of conspirators. The principal and oldest public building is St. John's Church, in which the demolitions of the Reformation commenced, in consequence of a sermon preached by John Knox.

X. PERTH.—CUPAR-ANGUS—FORFAR.—BRECHIN.—STONEHAVEN.—67 MILES.

ON RIGHT FROM PERTH.	From Stoneh.	PERTH. Leave Perth by Bridgend.	From Perth.	ON LEFT FROM PERTH.
	$65\frac{1}{4}$	Pass through Scone vill.	2	Scone Palace, Earl of Mansfield. It is a heavy modern building, occupying the site of the ancient palace, where the kings of Scotland at an early period used to be crowned. In the modern house much of the old furniture has been preserved. At the north side of the house is a small eminence said to have been composed of earth from the estates of the different barons who here attended the early kings. About 50 yards from the house there is an old aisle, the last remaining portion of the Abbey of Scone.
Dunsinnane Hill, on the top of which the circumvallations of what is said to have been Macbeth's Castle may still be traced. It commands an extensive view.	$61\frac{3}{4}$	St. Martin's vill.	$5\frac{1}{4}$	
	$60\frac{1}{2}$	Dunsinnane.—Nairn. The road now passes through the valley of Strathmore, having on the right the Sidlaw Hills, on the left the Grampians.	$6\frac{1}{2}$	
Belonging to Lord Willoughby D'Eresby.	57	Burrelton vill.	$9\frac{1}{2}$	
Cupar-Angus is a neat town of about 6000 inhabitants, situated on the border of Forfarshire, and partly within Perthshire.	54	CUPAR-ANGUS.	13	
Belmont Castle, Lord Wharncliffe.	$50\frac{1}{2}$	Junction of the Isla and Ericht.	$16\frac{1}{2}$	Kinloch—Kinloch, Esq. Here is obtained a fine view of Strathmore.
Meigle is remarkable on account of some very antique monuments in the church-yard, which the common people assert to denote the grave of Queen Vanore, the wife of King Arthur. The stones bear a variety of hieroglyphical figures with representations of animals and men.	48	Meigle vill.	19	
	$43\frac{1}{2}$	Essie Kirk.	$23\frac{1}{2}$	
	$41\frac{1}{4}$	Glammis vil.	$25\frac{3}{4}$	The celebrated Castle of Glammis, the seat of the Earl of Strathmore, is situated within a park of 160 acres. It is an edifice of princely and antique appearance. Glammis was the scene of the murder of Malcolm II. in 1034. The armoury contains a vast assortment of ancient armour. The rooms contain about 100 portraits of great value. The view to be obtained from the *leads* of the Castle is splendid and extensive.
Forfar, the county town of Forfarshire has a pleasant appearance. It is a burgh of great antiquity, and was a royal residence in the time of Malcolm Canmore. About a mile to the east of Forfar stand the ruins of the ancient Priory of Restennet, one of the three churches founded in Scotland by Boniface at the beginning of the 7th century.	36	FORFAR. Popularly denominated "Brosie Forfar."	31	
	30	Finhaven Castle ruins.	37	
		cr. South Esk.		
	$25\frac{3}{4}$	Cariston.	$41\frac{1}{4}$	Finhaven Castle, the once magnificent residence of the powerful family of Lindsay, is an object much visited by the tourist.
The ancient royal burgh of Brechin is romantically situated on some high ground overhanging the north bank of the South Esk. The Cathedral was a stately Gothic fabric 166 feet in length and 61 broad. Brechin was one of the seats of the Culdees. (Brechin Castle, the seat of Lord Panmure, is in the immediate neighbourhood of the town.) Population 6503.	$23\frac{1}{2}$	BRECHIN.	$43\frac{1}{2}$	
	22	Keithock Hall-Know.	45	
	20	Strickathrow vill.	47	In the church-yard of Strickathrow King John Baliol was divested, by command of Edward I. of all the ensigns of royalty.
	$18\frac{3}{4}$	North Esk Bridge.	$48\frac{3}{4}$	
	13	Laurencekirk vill.	54	Laurencekirk was the birth place of Dr. Beattie. The illustrious Ruddiman was once schoolmaster there. The town is remarkable for a manufacture of snuff-boxes.
		STONEHAVEN. Thence to Aberdeen, as No. XV.	67	

XI. PERTH.—DUNKELD.—BLAIR ATHOLL.—INVERNESS.—112 Miles.

On Right from Perth.	From Inverness.	PERTH. Leave Perth by the North Inch.	From Perth.	On Left from Perth.
Balhousie.	109½	Palace of Scone.	2½	Tulloch Printfield. Earl of Mansfield.
Luncarty Bleachfield, near which is the scene of the battle of Luncarty, between the Scots and the Danes.	109	cr. Almond Wat.	3	Fen House,—Nicol, Esq.
		cr. Shochie Wat.		Near Birnam Hill and Birnam Road.
	106	New Inn.	6	The walks through the policies of Dunkeld are upwards of 50 miles.
Near Stanley Mills, celebrated for their enormous wheels, and the Linn of Campsie.	103	Auchtergaven vill.	9	
	100	Murthly Castle. (—— Stewart, Bart.)	12	
Another road parts off directly east to Blairgowrie. The present route passes for some miles along the east bank of the Tay.		Little Dunkeld.		From this point a road proceeds by the west side of the river to Logierait, and thence by Aberfeldie to Kenmore.
		cr. the river Tay.		
	98	DUNKELD. Dunkeld Ho., Duke of Athole.	14	
Dunkeld is a place of great antiquity, and was at one time the capital of ancient Caledonia. One of the principal objects of curiosity here, is the ruined Cathedral. It must have been a fine pile of building. The architecture is partly Gothic, partly Saxon.	93	Dowally Kirk.	19	Eight miles above Dunkeld the united waters of the Tummel and Garry fall into the Tay.
		Near Dalguise Ho., Stewart, Esq.		
		Kinnaird House.	20	The site of Faskally is of a peculiarly romantic character. It stands at the junction of three deep and confined valleys, and is encircled on all sides by diverging mountains.
	92	Logierait, where Prince Charles kept the prisoners whom he had taken at Prestonpans.	22½	
	90¾	Moulinearn Inn.		
The road now enters the pass of Killiecrankie, a narrow glen, at the bottom of which runs the Tummel water.	84	Faskally, Butter, Esq.	28	
		Lude, M'Inroy, Esq.	30½	In front, on the ascent to Urrard House, is the scene of the battle of Killiecrankie, fought July 26, 1689, between the Highlanders under Dundee, and the forces of King William under Mackay, the former being killed, and the latter defeated.
	81½	cr. the Tilt Wat.	33	
	77	BLAIR ATHOLL.	35	
The vale of the Tilt is celebrated for its fine scenery, and for geological wonders. At the Bridge of Tilt is an excellent inn.		The road now passes through a wild Alpine territory, almost to Inverness.		
The noble old Castle of Blair, (Duke of Atholl,) is in the neighbourhood.	69½	Dalnacardoch Inn.	42½	
		Dalnaspidal.		From Dalwhinnie the mountain of Benalder may be seen, situated on the north side of Loch Ericht.
About two miles from Blair Atholl, the road crosses the Bruar, where that river makes a series of cascades, which enjoy extensive celebrity.	67½	cr. Edendon Wat.	44½	
		Enter Inverness-shire.		
		Drumochter Forest.		
	56½	Dalwhinnie Inn.	55½	Here a road parts off by Laggan and Garvamore, and over the difficult hill of Corriarrack to Fort Augustus.
		In front is Ben Chruben.		
Near Etrish there is a beautiful waterfall.	50	Etrish.	62	
		cr. Truim Wat.		From Pitmain may be seen the rocky barrier of Craig Dhu towards the west, the gathering-place of the M'Phersons.
Across the Spey, ruins of Ruthven Castle and Barracks, destroyed by the Highlanders in 1746.	46	Bridge of Spey.	66	
		Newton of Benchar.	66½	
	43½	Pitmain Inn.	68½	
Across Spey, Invereshie, Sir Geo. M'Pherson Grant of Ballindalloch.	42	Kingussie Kirk & vill.	70	Belville, the seat of M'Pherson, the translator of Ossian, now possessed by Miss M'Pherson.
Rothiemurchus, Grant, Esq.	37	Kincraig, Built on the site of an ancient monastery.	75	
Opposite Aviemore is Cairngorm Hill.	20½	Aviemore Inn.	91½	Inverness is a royal burgh of the first reformed class, joining with Forres, Fortrose, and Nairn in electing a Member of Parliament. Population 14,834. Inverness is considered the capital of the Highlands, being the only town of importance beyond Aberdeen. For further description see page 408.
Near Moy Hall, M'Intosh of M'Intosh. Here Prince Charles Stuart was nearly taken by surprise in February 1746.		cr. the Dolnain.	99	
	13	Freeburn Inn.		
	6	Daviot Kirk.	106	
		INVERNESS.	112	

XII. EDINBURGH.—MID CALDER.—KIRK OF SHOTTS.—HOLYTOWN.—GLASGOW.—44 MILES.

ON RIGHT FROM EDIN.	From Glasgow.	EDINBURGH. For a description of the road from Edinburgh to Mid Calder, see No. VII.	From Edin.	ON LEFT FROM EDIN.
	32	Howden.	12	
	29	Kirk Livingston.	15	
		Cowsland.		
	26¾	Seafield.	17¼	
	25¼	Blackburn.	18¾	
	25	Lathbrae.	19	
	24	Swan Inn.	20	
Polkemmet House, Baillie, Bart. ; remarkable for the quantities of game in the neighbourhood.	23	Whitburn vill.	21	
	22	Half-way-house.	22	
	19	Badweather.	25	
	17	Kirk of Shotts Inn.	27	Here the traveller is on the highest ground between the Forth and Clyde in this direction.
	13¾	Newhouse Inn.	30¼	
Lachup House, Robertson, Esq. Woodhall, Campbell of Shawfield.	11	HOLYTOWN, Where a road turns off to Hamilton.	33	
		cr. Shirle Water.		
Tollcross, Ho. Dunlop, Esq.	9	Bellshill vill.	35	
	2¾	cr. Calder Wat.	41¼	One mile to the left, are the Clyde Iron Works, where 12,500 bars of iron were produced in 1835, a greater amount than the aggregate production of any other work in Scotland.
Jeanfield, Finlayson, Esq.		Tollcross vill.		
Newlands and Borrowfield Houses, Hozier, Esq.	1½	Parkhead.	42½	
		Camlachie.		
		GLASGOW.	44	

XIII. EDINBURGH.—LINLITHGOW.—FALKIRK.—CUMBERNAULD.—GLASGOW.—46¾ MILES.

ON RIGHT FROM EDIN.	From Glasgow.	EDINBURGH. For a description of the road between Edinburgh and Falkirk, see No. V.	From Edin.	ON LEFT FROM EDIN.
Larbert Ho., Stirling, Bart. Dunipace, Spottiswoode, Esq.		Camelon.	26	
Underwood House.		Cumbernauld Inn.		
Knowhead Ho., Patrick, Esq.		cr. Bonny Wat.		Merchiston Hall. Woodside Ho., Russell, Esq.
Castle Cary House. Cumbernauld House, Admiral Fleming.	14¼	CUMBERNAULD.	32½	Bankhead Ho., Cuthill, Esq.
		cr. Logie Water.		
Dunbeath Tower in ruins, once the property of the Kilmarnock family.	9¾	Bedlay Inn.	37	Mayothill Ho., Graham, Esq.
	8¼	Christon vill.	38½	Frankfield Loch.
Frankfield Ho., Millar, Esq.	4¼	Frankfield House.	42½	Kennyhill Ho., Stewart, Esq.
Rosemount Ho., Millar, Esq.	2¾	Provan Mill.	44	Whitehill Ho., Graham, Esq.
Garnkirk, Sprott, Esq.		cr. Monkland Canal.		Dunchattan and Cudbear Manufactories.
Riddry Park, Miss Provan.		GLASGOW.	46¾	Broom Park.

XIV. EDINBURGH.—UPHALL.—BATHGATE.—AIRDRIE.—GLASGOW.—42¾ Miles.

ON RIGHT FROM EDIN.	From Glasgow.	EDINBURGH. Leave the city by Princes St.	From Edin.	ON LEFT FROM EDIN.
Murrayfield, W. Murray, Esq.		For 4½ miles the road is the same as in No. V.		Rosebery House, Balfour, Esq.
Beechwood, Dundas, Bart.	37¾	North Guile.	5	Saughton House, Baird, Bart.
Corstorphine House, Keith, Bart.				Milburn Tower.
Clermiston, Paterson, Esq.	36¾	Nether Gogar.	6	Gogar Camp, Osborne, Esq.
		cr. Gogar Burn.		
Gogar House, Ramsay, Esq.	36¼	Mount Gogar.	6½	Wardlaw, Esq.
Ingliston, Gibson, Esq.		Golf Hall.		Norton House, Norton, Esq.
Newliston, James Hog, Esq., once the seat of the great Earl of Stair.	35¼	Middle Norton.	7½	
		cr. Almond Wat.		Clifton Hall, Sir A. Gibson Maitland, Bart.
Kirkhill, the ancient family seat of the Earl of Buchan.	32¾	cr. Broxburn.	10	
	31¾	Broxburn.	11	Kinpunt House, which once gave the title to an Earl. It is now the property of Earl Hopetoun.
In Uphall Kirk lie interred the Hon. Henry Erskine, and Lord Erskine, his brother.	30¾	UPHALL.	12	
		West Mains.		Middleton, Thriepland, Esq.
A thriving burgh of barony; population 5593, supported mostly by weaving, and partly by the adjacent coal and lime works.	24¾	BATHGATE.	18	Houston, Shairp, Esq. Robert Bruce gave the barony of Bathgate as a portion with his daughter Marjory, who married Walter, the High Steward, in 1315. Walter died at his castle here, the remains of which are still pointed out.
	20¾	Armadale Inn.	22	
Bedlormie, Livingstone, Bart.		cr. Craigs Water.		
Auchingray, Haldane, Esq.		West Craigs Inn.		
The road is here skirted by a fine sheet of water, from which the Canal is supplied.	18¾	Auchingray.	24	The country is here generally a moorish upland, variegated by few objects.
		Blackrig.		
Woodhall, Campbell of Shawfield.	13¾	Pass Calder Water.	29	Moffat Hills in the south.
Airdrie is a thriving modern town which has been called into existence chiefly by the neighbouring iron works and collieries. It is situated between two rivulets on a rising ground, and is a handsomely built town. The parish of New Monkland, in which Airdrie is situated, contains 9867 inhabitants.		Clerkston vill.		Airdrie Place, Miss Mitchelson.
	10¾	AIRDRIE.	32	
	9½	Cairnhall.	33¼	
	7¾	Longloan.	35	Drumpellier, Ho. Buchannan, Esq.
	6¾	Drumpellier.	36	Barracknie, Hamilton, Esq.
	3	Shettlestone.	39¾	Glenduff Hill, Tod, Esq.
Summerlee House, M'Braire, Esq.		Joins the Mid Calder road.		Larch Grove, Scott, Esq.
Bailliestoun Ho. Maxwell, Esq.		Camlachie.		Wellhouse, Millar Esq. Greenfield, M'Nairn, Esq.
Mount Vernon, Buchannan, Esq.		GLASGOW.	42	Carntyne House, Gray, Esq.

V. EDINBURGH.—KIRKALDY.—CUPAR.—DUNDEE.—ARBROATH.—STONEHAVEN.—ABERDEEN.—109¼ MILES.

ON RIGHT FROM EDIN.	From Aberdeen.	EDINBURGH. Newhaven to Pettycur by steamboat.	From Edin.	ON LEFT FROM EDIN.
	100¼	Kinghorn.	9	
At the east end of the town Ravenscraig Castle in ruins, formerly the seat of the family of St. Clair.	98¼	KIRKALDY.	11	An ancient royal burgh. Population of the parish 2579.
	97¼	Pathhead vill.	12	
	95¼	Galatown.	14	
	89¾	Plasterer's Inn.	19½	Raith, Robert Ferguson, Esq.
Near Markinch Kirk, where General Leslie, the leader of the Covenanting army, lies interred.		cr. Leven Wat.		Leslie House, Earl of Rothes.
	87¼	New Inn	22	Balbirnie, Gen. Balfour.
Cults Kirk. Cults Manse, the birth place of Sir David Wilkie, R.A.	85¼	Kettle vill.	24	On left, two miles distant, bye road to Perth, Falkland, and Falkland Palace.
	84¼	Pitlessie.	25	
		cr. Eden Wat.		Rankeillour, Maitland M'Gill, Esq.
The Mount, the patrimonial estate of Sir David Lindsay, is about four miles to the west of Cupar, but no old building exists at the place.	79¼	CUPAR.	30	Crawford Priory, Earl of Glasgow.
	76	Dairsie Kirk.	33¼	
	75½	Osnaburgh vill.	33¾	Cupar is a handsome town of modern and thriving appearance. The Town Hall and County Hall are elegant buildings. An eminence at the east end of the town was the site of a fortress of considerable importance, of which no trace now exists.
	72¼	St. Michael's Inn.	37	
	69¼	Newport, Where embark in a steamboat, and cross the Tay to	40	
Dundee is the chief seat of the linen manufacture in Britain, and one of the most prosperous towns in the empire. The principal objects are the Town Hall, Exchange Reading Rooms, (open to strangers,) Academy, the Howf or Burying Ground, the Tower of the old Church, and the Law, from which a most extensive view is to be seen.	67¼	DUNDEE.	42	
	65¼	cr. Dighty Wat.	44	
	54¼	Muirdrum vill.	55	Near Cupar, in ruins, Airdit Ho., Stewart, Esq.
		Panbride Kirk.		Fintry, Graham, Esq.
		cr. Elliot Wat.		
	50¼	ARBROATH.	59	The most interesting object in Arbroath is the venerable ruins of the Abbey. It was founded by William the Lion, who is interred here.
	44¼	Chance Inn.	65	
		cr. Lunan at Lunan Kirk.		
		cr. South Esk to		The rock on which the Bell Rock Lighthouse is founded, is about 12 miles from the shore at Arbroath
Ethic, Earl of Northesk.	37½	MONTROSE.	71¾	
The road, for some miles, passes near the sea coast.		cr. North Esk.		Montrose is a remarkably neat, and even handsome town. The river is crossed by a fine suspension bridge. Population 12,055.
	32¼	St. Cyrus Kirk.	77	
Kaim of Mathers, Adam.	28¼	Johnshaven.	81	
Ruins of Dunnotar Castle. Dunnotar was built by an ancestor of the Marischal family about the time of the contest between Bruce and Baliol. Before the use of fire arms, it was considered as almost impregnable, and was used as the deposit of the Regalia of Scotland, to preserve them from the English army under Cromwell, in 1651.	24¼	INVERBERVIE.	85	
		cr. Bervie Wat.		Aberdeen is a large and elegant city of great antiquity, possessing many handsome streets and splendid public buildings. The large proportion of eminent Scotsmen who have been produced in this city, is very remarkable, and can only be attributed to the presence of its Universities. In Old Aberdeen are to be seen the remains of the Cathedral. The scenery in the neighbourhood is remarkably interesting.
	15	STONEHAVEN.	94¼	
		cr. Carron and Cowie Waters.		
	11	Muchals House.	98¼	
		cr. Dee, and enter		
		ABERDEEN.	109¼	

XVI. INVERNESS—BEAULY—TAIN—WICK—THURSO.

ON RIGHT FROM INVERN.	From Thurso.	INVERNESS.	From Invern.	ON LEFT FROM INVERN.
Chachnaharry Basin, the end of the Canal. Fopachie, Fraser.		Leave Inverness by the Bridge over the Ness, and cross the Caledonian Canal.		Muirtown, Duff.
Across Beauly Firth, Redcastle, the seat of the late Sir William Fettis, Bart.	170	Bunchrew, Forbes.	2	Bunchrew, or Bunchrive, was long the residence of President Forbes.
Near the road, at the point where it enters Ross-shire, are two upright stones, standing in a due line east and west, which mark the scene of a conflict between the Frasers and M'Kenzies.	$165\frac{1}{2}$	Kirkhill Kirk.	$7\frac{1}{2}$	Near Auchnagairn, Relig, Warrenfield, and Fingask.
		☞ cr. Beauly river,		
	162	and enter BEAULY.	10	Beauly, a pleasant village, with the ruins of Beauly Priory, and at no great distance Kilmorack waterfalls. Farther up the Beauly, Beaufort Castle, the seat of Lords Lovat.
Tannadale, Baillie. Road to Fortrose. Highfield, M'Kenzie.		Enter Ross-shire.		
One of the most remarkable things in the eye of a stranger, all through this tract, is the enormous mountain Ben Wyvis. Sir Hector Munro of Foulis, the proprietor of this mountain, holds his estate in Ross-shire, by a tenure from one of the early Scottish kings, binding him to bring three wain-loads of snow from the top of the hill, whenever his majesty shall so desire. *	160	Gilchrist Kirk.	12	Ord House, M'Kenzie.
	158	Urray Kirk.	14	
	154	Bridgend vill.	18	Brahan Castle, Lady Hood M'Kenzie.
	153	Pitglassie vill.	19	Conon, M'Kenzie.
Dingwall Castle was formerly the residence of the Earls of Ross.	$150\frac{1}{2}$	Dingwall.	$21\frac{1}{2}$	Dingwall was erected into a royal burgh by Alexander II. in 1226. Near the town are the ruins of the ancient residence of the Earls of Ross. Near the church is an obelisk, fifty-six feet high, though only six feet at the base, intended to distinguish the burial-place of the Cromarty family.
Incheulter, Fraser; and Culcairn and Novar, Munro.	$148\frac{1}{2}$	Ardulie, and	$23\frac{1}{2}$	Near Tulloch, Davidson.
	147	Foulis, Munro, Bart.	25	At the head of Strathpeffer, about four miles from Dingwall, there is an excellent and well-frequented mineral well, round which are congregated a considerable number of buildings.
Near Castle Leod, the ancient seat of the Cromarty family, and Cowl House, M'Kenzie, Bart.	$142\frac{1}{2}$	Alness Kirk.	$29\frac{1}{2}$	
	138	Rosskein Kirk.	34	
Invergordon Castle, M'Leod, Esq.	$136\frac{3}{4}$	Invergordon vil. & seaport.	$35\frac{1}{4}$	There are some fine views of the opposite coast through the Sutors of Cromarty.
	135	Kilmuir Kirk.	37	
Tarbet House was once the seat of the Cromarty family, and whence the first Earl took his first title of Viscount Tarbet.	134	Tarbet House.	38	
	$128\frac{1}{2}$	Knockbreck House.	$43\frac{1}{2}$	

* The top of Ben Wyvis was never known to be uncovered by snow, till the memorably warm summer of 1826, when it was quite bare.

INVERNESS TO THURSO—*Continued.*

ON RIGHT FROM INVERN.	From Thurso.		From Invern.	ON LEFT FROM INVERN.
The road from Tain to Dornoch is a very singular one. The distance between the two towns, straight across the firth, is only four miles, but, instead of going directly across the water, the coach winds round the bed of the firth, a distance of thirty-one.	125	TAIN.	47	Tain is an irregularly built town, with several new and handsome houses. It is situated on the margin of the Dornoch Firth. The ancient church of Tain was collegiate, and dedicated to St. Duthus. James IV. performed pilgrimage to the shrine of this Saint, to whose honour several churches were at different times built in this place.
	123	On right Meikle Ferry of Dornoch, which, if adopted, cuts off 19 miles of road. The mail proceeds by the route now described.	49	
The Castle of Lochlin is a remarkable building; it has stood 500 years. Sir George M'Kenzie, (popularly denominated *The Bloody M'Kenzie,*) King's Advocate in the reign of Charles II., was born there.	122	Edderton Kirk.	50	
	115	West Fearn.	57	Near Fearn, there are the ruins of an abbey of great antiquity, founded by the first Earl of Ross. Patrick Hamilton, an abbot of this place, was the first who suffered in this country for the Reformed religion. Near the abbey is a high square column, covered with Saxon characters.
	114½	Kincardine Inn.	58½	
Bonar Bridge is a strong and magnificent structure, composed of iron. It cost £14,000.		cr. Firth of Dornoch, by Bonar Bridge.		
Near Crach Church is an obelisk, eight feet by four, erected in memory of a Danish chieftain. Here, on the summit of a hill, which juts out into the firth, is a noted vitrified fort, called Dun Creech.	112¼	Bonar Inn.	59¾	
	100¾	Clashmore Inn.	71¼	Near Skibo, Dempster, Esq.
	97¾	Dornoch.	74¼	Dornoch is, without exception, the most miserable of all our royal burghs. It is nevertheless, the county town of Sutherland, and formerly was the seat of the bishopric of Caithness. Part of the cathedral still serves as the parish church.
	95	cr. Loch Fleet, By a stupendous mound, built to dam out the sea—Cost £9000.	77	
From Golspie, all the way to Brora, the road is skirted with neat cottages, surrounded by shrubberies and covered with honeysuckle. Brora is one of the new villages built by the Duke of Sutherland. It is situated at the mouth of the river Brora, which descends from a vale of the most romantic and savage character.	86¾	Golspie vill.	85¼	Dunrobin Castle, the seat of the Duke of Sutherland, occupies an eminent site upon the shore, a little beyond Golspie, and is surrounded by some fine old wood, besides extensive modern plantations. It is said to have been founded in the 13th century by one of the earliest Earls of Sutherland. About a mile farther on, between the road and the beech, stands one of those unaccountable relics of antiquity, called Picts Houses.
	83	Brora.	89	
	82	Kirk of Clyne.	90	
	80½	Kinkradwell.	91	
	77	Loth Kirk.	95	
	71¼	Helmsdale.	100¾	Adjoining Helmsdale, are the ruins of a romantic old castle, once the seat of an extensive proprietor of the name of Gordon.

ON RIGHT FROM INVERN.	From Thurso.		From Invern.	ON LEFT FROM INVERN.
In the immediate neighbourhood of Berridale, on a high crag, stand the remains of a castle, once the residence of the Sutherlands of Langwell, the ancient Lords of Berridale, and, according to tradition, a very gigantic race. One of them, William More Sutherland, is reported to have been upwards of nine feet high.	61½	Berridale Inn.	110½	
		cr. Dunbeath water.		
	60¾	Dunbeath Inn.	116¼	
	52	Kirk of Latheron.	120	Latheron House, Sinclair.
Swiney, Gordon.	49	Swiney Inn.	123	Nottingham House, Sutherland.
	48		124	Near Stempater and Rangog Lochs. Near the former is a Druidical temple and the Arch-Druid's house.
	46	Clyth, Henderson.	126	
	37	Hempriggs, Dunbar, Bart.	135	
	36	Newton.	136	
		cr. the Wick river, by a to		
From Wick, the mail-road to Thurso proceeds from a point south of the river, keeping by the south side of the Loch of Watten, and twenty-one miles in extent, Watten Inn being situated about midway. The road by Duncansbay Head and John O'Groat's House, proceeds by the coast. On right, upon the coast, the ruins of Girnigo and Sinclair Castles. Also, Akergill Tower, Dunbar, Bart.	34½	WICK.	137½	Wick is the principal seat of the herring fishery in the north of Scotland. It is a thriving and fast increasing town. Piers and other erections have lately been built at the harbour, costing upwards of £13,000.
	32	Werter House and Loch.	142	
	25	Miltown.	147	Kliss House, Macleay, and Kliss Castle ruins, formerly the seat of the Earl of Caithness.
	23	Freswick, Sinclair.	149	
Near Duncansbay Head and John O'Groat's House.	18	Houna Inn.	154	Bucholis Castle ruins.
Ratter, Earl of Caithness.	16½	Cannisbay Kirk.	155½	Moy Castle, Stirling, Bart.
	8	Dunnet Kirk.	164	
Thurso is a burgh of barony, holding of Sir George Sinclair of Ulbster. Thurso Castle, his residence, is in the neighbourhood, along with a highly ornamental structure, which the late Sir John built to the memory of Harold Earl of Caithness, who was slain and buried on the spot upwards of six centuries ago. The coast to the west increases in terrific wildness and grandeur till it terminates at Cape Wrath.	1	Thurso Castle.	171	
		THURSO.	172	

XVII. GLASGOW.—PAISLEY.—GREENOCK.—LARGS.—KILWINNING.—AYR.—
72 MILES.

ON RIGHT FROM GLASGOW.	From Ayr.	GLASGOW.	From Glasgow.	ON LEFT FROM GLASGOW.
	70	Leave Glasgow by the New Bridge, and pass through Tradestown.	2	Parkhouse, Walkinshaw, Esq.
	69		3	
Paisley, a celebrated seat of manufacturing industry. Placing the factories out of view, the most interesting object of curiosity in Paisley is the Abbey church, which is still a magnificent and impressive object. Attached to its south side there is a small chapel, where it is said Marjory, daughter of King Robert Bruce, was interred. This chapel possesses a remarkably fine echo.	$64\frac{1}{4}$	PAISLEY.	$7\frac{3}{4}$	Cardonald Lord Blantyre.
	61	Johnston vill. where cr. Black Cart River.	11	Crookston Castle in ruins. A place deriving interest from its connection with Queen Mary.
	$58\frac{1}{2}$	Kilbarchan vill.	$13\frac{1}{2}$	
		Bridge of Weir; where		A thriving village, engaged in the cotton manufacture.
	58	cr. Gryfe Water.	14	The course of the Gryfe, to its junction with the Cart, is a tract of beautiful scenery.
	$53\frac{1}{4}$	Kilmalcolm vill.	$18\frac{3}{4}$	
Greenock is a large and populous town, the first seaport in Scotland. The situation of Greenock is remarkably beautiful. The principal branches of its commerce have reference to the East and West Indies, the United States, and British America. The Custom House is a beautiful building. There is also an elegant Exchange.	$49\frac{1}{4}$	Port Glasgow.	$22\frac{3}{4}$	A populous sea-port erected by the merchants of Glasgow, as an appropriate place for the shipping of goods. On the shore, at a little distance to the east, is situated the deserted Castle of Newark, formerly a place of great strength.
	$46\frac{1}{2}$	GREENOCK.	$25\frac{1}{2}$	
	$43\frac{1}{2}$	Gourock.	$28\frac{1}{2}$	
	$40\frac{1}{2}$	Innerkip vill.	$31\frac{1}{2}$	Near Innerkip, Ardgowan, Shaw Stewart, Bart. and Kelly, Wallace, Esq.
	$38\frac{1}{2}$	cr. Kelly Water.	$33\frac{1}{2}$	
	$32\frac{3}{4}$	cr. Nodle Water.	$39\frac{1}{4}$	
Largs stands on a beautiful plain, surrounded by mountains on the land side. Near this place, in 1263, in the reign of Alexander III., was fought the battle of Largs between the Scots and Danes.	32	LARGS.	40	Brisbane Ho., Brisbane, Bart. Kelburn Ho., Earl of Glasgow.
	$29\frac{3}{4}$	Fairley.	$42\frac{1}{4}$	Fairley Castle in ruins.
		cr. Rye Water.		
	$26\frac{1}{4}$	West Kilbride.	$46\frac{3}{4}$	Near ruins of Ardrossan Castle. The Harbour of Ardrossan possesses advantages superior to all the other harbours in the Frith of Clyde.
A few miles to the north of Ardrossan, stands the ruined Castle of Portincross, rendered memorable by the frequency of the visits of the first Stuart sovereign to it. Its situation on a bare rock projecting into the sea, is singularly wild and picturesque.	20	Ardrossan.	52	
	$18\frac{1}{2}$	Saltcoats.	$53\frac{1}{2}$	
	14	KILWINNING.	58	Eglinton Castle, Earl of Eglinton; a splendid structure.
		cr. Garnoch Wat.		
	11	Irvine.	61	Irvine was the birth-place of John Galt, and James Montgomery, the poet. Burns was, for a short time, engaged in business in Irvine as a flax-dresser.
		cr. Irvine Water.		
Kilwinning is remarkable as the first settlement of Free Masons in Scotland.	3	Monkton.	69	
		AYR.	72	

Ayr is a handsome old-fashioned town, skirted with modern streets of considerable elegance. It dates as a royal burgh from 1202, and was the scene of several remarkable exploits of Sir William Wallace. Many of the localities of Ayr and its vicinity are rendered interesting by their association with the life and poems of Burns. The poet was born in a clay-built cottage, about two miles and a half from the town. At a little distance are the ruins of Alloway Kirk, the Auld Brig of Doon, Burns' Monument, &c.

XVIII. GLASGOW.—AYR.—MAYBOLE.—GIRVAN.—PORTPATRICK.—94 MILES.

ON RIGHT FROM GLASGOW.	From Portpat.	GLASGOW. Glasgow to Ayr, see No. XVII.	From Glasgow.	ON LEFT FROM GLASGOW.
The native cottage of Burns, his monument, the old bridge of Doon, and other objects deriving interest from the life and writings of the poet.	60½		33½	Blairston, Cathcart.
	59	Alloway Kirk.	35	Maybole is a burgh of barony, and obtained its privileges in 1516. It carries on a woollen manufacture to a considerable extent. The Mansion House of the Cassilis family is the finest surviving specimen of the twenty-eight winter seats of noble and baronial families formerly existing in Maybole. It is said to have been the residence of the repudiated Countess of Cassilis, whose story was the subject of the well known ballad of Johnny Faa.
		cr. Doon by new Bridge, and skirt along Brown Carrick Hill.		
	56	Grange House. Torrence, M'Micken, Esq.	38	
Crossraguel Abbey, founded in 1244; part of the cloisters remain, and the Abbot's house is entire. The last Abbot was famed for his disputation with John Knox. The ruin is preserved with great care.	51½	MAYBOLE. Population 6287.	42½	
	49	Ruins of Crossraguel Abbey.	45	
	47	Kirkoswald.	47	
Some miles to the right of Kirkoswald, is Colzean Castle, the splendid mansion of the Marquis of Ailsa. It is built on the brink of a perpendicular precipice; under it are the celebrated caves of Culzean, penetrating 200 feet into the rock.	41	Chasel House.	53	Burns received part of his education in Kirkoswald.
		cr. Girvan Wat.		Girvan, a place of considerable antiquity, situated at the mouth of Girvan Water, the banks of which abound in fine scenery, and in fine seats.
	39	Girvan vill. The road now keeps close by the coast for many miles.	55	
On the coast, the ruins of Turnberry Castle, a seat of Robert Bruce when Earl of Carrick.	36½	Ardmillan. Crawford, Esq.	57½	Carleton Castle, ruins, Cathcart, Bart. Stinchar Castle ruins, an ancient seat of the Kennedys of Bargany.
	34	Carleton Bay.	60	Such is the irregularity of the rivulet which runs through Glenap, that the road crosses it at least half a dozen of times within the extent of half a dozen miles.
The village of Ballantrae is situated close to the mouth of the Stinchar water, and picturesquely overhung by the ruins of an old castle. It was formerly a great haunt of smugglers. It has a good sea and salmon fishery.	26½	Ballantrae vill.	67½	
		cr. Stinchar Wat.		
	24	Glenapp, A romantic glen.	70	Near Stranraer, Castle Kennedy and Culhorn, Earl of Stair.
View of the beautiful Bay of Lochryan, celebrated in the fine old pathetic ballad, entitled "The Lass of Lochryan."	16½	Enter Wigtonshire.	77½	Stranraer is a thriving and handsome seaport town, uniting with Wigton, New Galloway, and Whithorn, in returning a Member to Parliament. In the centre of it stands a tall strong edifice, originally a castle. There are several seats in the neighbourhood adorned with all the charms of nature and of art.
	15	Cairn.	79	
Portpatrick is a thriving town of considerable size, The channel between Great Britain and Ireland is here only 21 miles across. Portpatrick possesses an excellent harbour and reflecting lighthouse.	9	Stranraer. Population 3320.	85	
	6	Lochan's Bridge.	88	
		PORTPATRICK.	94	Dunskey Castle ruins, finely situated on a very high rock overhanging the sea.

XIX. GLASGOW.—RUTHERGLEN.—HAMILTON.—LANARK.—PEEBLES.—SELKIRK—HAWICK.—83½ MILES.

ON RIGHT FROM GLASGOW.	From Hawick.	GLASGOW.	From Glasgow.	ON LEFT FROM GLASGOW.
		Leave Glasgow by the Calton. At Barrowfield take to the left.		
Near the ancient royal burgh of Rutherglen, of date 1126, now chiefly occupied by weavers. Population of the parish in 1831, 5503.		cr. Clyde at Dalmarnock Bridge.		On the left, at a distance, Clyde Iron Works.
	80	Cambuslang vill.	3½	Remarkable for a great revival of religion, which occurred there in consequence of the preaching of Whitefield.
Dechmont Hill is here a conspicuous object, it commands a very extensive view.	75½	Blantyre vill. and Priory on the left.	8	The remains of Blantyre Priory are delightfully situated on the banks of the Clyde, opposite to Bothwell Castle. In the neighbourhood there is a large cotton mill, which gives employment to 900 persons.
Numerous neat villas on both sides of the road.	74¼	HAMILTON.	9¼	
Hamilton unites with Falkirk, Airdrie, Lanark, and Linlithgow in sending a representative to Parliament. Population of the parish in 1831, 9513. Close to the town is Hamilton Palace, the superb seat of the Duke of Hamilton. The interior of the palace is fitted up in the most gorgeous style; and the collection of paintings has long been considered the best in Scotland. Within the grounds, on the banks of the river Avon, the ruin of the ancient Castle of Cadzow is perched on the top of a rock 200 feet above the water.	67	Dalserf vill.	16½	
	60¾	Nethanfoot.	22¾	Near Mauldslie Castle, Nisbet, Esq. once the seat of the Earls of Hyndford.
		Soon after pass Stonebyres Fall.		Stonebyres Fall, so named from the adjacent estate of Stonebyres, a cataract of eighty-eight feet in height.
	59¼	cr. Clyde Water by Lanark Bridge.	24¼	
	58½	LANARK.	25	Lanark is a very ancient royal burgh containing about 4000 inhabitants.
Twenty-two miles from Glasgow stands Craignethan Castle, on a lofty eminence near the conflux of the Nethan and the Clyde. This fortress, now in ruins, was once the seat of the celebrated personage called the Bastard of Arran.		cr. Clyde by Hyndford Bridge.		About a mile from Lanark, there is a profound ravine through which the Mouse water descends to join the Clyde. The precipitous sides of the ravine are the celebrated Cartland Crags, in which Wallace found refuge on several occasions.
	48	Biggar.	35½	
		cr. Biggar Water.		
	41	Broughton.	42½	
	39½	Stobo Castle.	44	Montgomery, Bart.
Vale of Manor, in which lived David Ritchie, the original of the Black Dwarf.	39	Stobo Kirk.	44½	
		cr. Lyne Water.		Nidpath Castle, nearly in ruins, a most romantic situation.
	33	PEEBLES.	50½	
Innerleithen, a favourite resort of the citizens of Edinburgh, is a handsome village full of neat houses; its situation is very beautiful.	27	Innerleithen vill. and Mineral Wells.	56½	Horsburgh Castle in ruins. Cardrona, Williamson, Esq.
Traquair House, Earl of Traquair.	18	Fernalie or Yair Bridge.	65½	
	12	SELKIRK.	71½	
		For the route between Selkirk and Hawick, see No. III.	83½	

XX. GLASGOW—DUMBARTON—TARBET—TYNDRUM—FORT WILLIAM.—103 MILES.

ON RIGHT FROM GLASGOW.	From Fort Wil.	GLASGOW.	From Glasgow.	ON LEFT FROM GLASGOW.
		Leave Glasgow by Anderston.		
Cranston Hill, Houldsworth, and numerous other villas, belonging to the wealthy citizens.		cr. Kelvin Water.		
	99½	White Inch.	3½	Dalnottar.
Jordanhill, Smith, Esq.	93½	Kilpatrick vill.	9½	
	92	Dunglas Castle ruins.	11	Near the termination of the Forth and Clyde Canal.
Dumbarton is one of the four fortresses stipulated by the articles of Union to be kept up, and accordingly is still in repair, and occupied by a garrison.	88¾	DUMBARTON.	14¼	
Cordale Ho., Stirling, Esq.		cr. Leven Water.		Levenside, Ewing.
Bonhill, Smollet, Esq.	86¼	Renton vill.	16¾	Near Smollet's monument, and Dalquhurn House, where he was born.
Balloch Castle Stott.	85	Alexandria.	18	Broomley, Miss Alston. Tillichewen Castle, Horrocks.
Loch Lomond is on the right for many miles.	84	Lower end of L. Lomond.	19	Woodbank, Miss Scott. Bellretiro, Miss Rowet.
Cameron Ho., Smollet, Esq.	82	Arden, Buchannan.	21	
Rossdow, Colquhoun, Bart.	78	cr. Fruin Water.	25	Glen Fruin was the scene of a bloody conflict between the M'Gregors and Colquhoun in 1602.
Luss is beautifully situated; the waters of the Luss run through it, and fall into Loch Lomond.	76¼	Luss vill. and Inn.	26¾	
	72¾	Inveruglas Ferry.	30¼	For crossing Loch Lomond to Rowardennan, where the ascent to Ben Lomond is usually commenced.
Nearly opposite Inveruglas Island, in a hollow above a small cascade, are the ruins of Inversnaid Fort, an old military station, chiefly designed to keep the Clan Gregor in check.	68¾	Tarbet Inn.	34¼	
		Keep along the side of Loch Lomond.		Three miles above Tarbet is a small wooded island called Inveruglas, and about two miles farther, another called Eilan; on each of which are the ruins of a stronghold of the family of Macfarlane.
	65	Across the loch is Inversnaid Mill.	38	
	60	Head of Loch Lomond.	43	
	58	Auldtarnan Inn.	45	
About half way between Crianlaroch and Tyndrum, there is a linn in the river called the Pool of St. Fillan's, which is to this day not unfrequently the scene of the observance of a degrading superstitious rite. Here St. Fillan, so noted in the Highlands for works of piety and sacred gifts, is said to have lived.	57	Glenfalloch, Campbell.	46	
	52	Proceed up Glenfalloch to Crianlaroch Inn.	51	On the right a road proceeds to Killin.
		Take to the left up Strathfillan.		Strathfillan was the scene of a battle of Robert Bruce.
	47	Tyndrum Inn.	56	Tyndrum Ho., Marquis of Breadalbane.
	38	Inverouran Inn.	65	Between Inverouran and King's House, the road crosses a lofty hill called the Black Mount. From the top an extensive view is obtained of the Moor of Rannoch, the largest tract of the kind in Scotland.
In the neighbourhood of Ballachulish, is a cavern of such difficult access, that nobody of late has ventured to explore it.	28½	Mountainous scenery to King's House Inn.	74½	
	26	Foot of the steep road to Fort William, called the Devil's Staircase.	77	
		Enter Glencoe.		Glencoe is famous for its singularly wild Alpine scenery, and the historical event connected with it. The massacre of Glencoe in King William's reign, took place at the north-west end of the vale.
	14½	Ballachulish Inn.	88½	
So called from the tradition of Patrick, a Danish Prince, having been drowned there.	13	The Ferry of Calas-ic Phatric.	90	
Fort William is situated on the shore of Loch Eil, at the distance of about two miles from the termination of the canal of Corpach. It was erected in the reign of William III. for the purpose of keeping down the Jacobite clans of the west.	11	ONICH.	92	Maryburgh contains about 1500 inhabitants, and two respectable inns.
	7¾	Coran Ferry across Loch Eil.	95¼	It contains a bomb-proof magazine, and the barrack is calculated to accommodate 96 men. The fort was besieged in 1745-6 by the Camerons, but without success. It is now almost in a state of disuse.
	½	Maryburgh.	102½	
		FORT WILLIAM.	103	

XXI. ABERDEEN.—KINTORE.—INVERURY.—HUNTLY.—KEITH.—FOCHABERS.—57 Miles.

ON RIGHT FROM ABERD.	From Focha.		From Aberd.	ON LEFT FROM ABERD.
		ABERDEEN.*		
Mugiemoss, L. Ja. Hay. Caskieben, Dr. Henderson.		Cross the hill of Tyrebagger, *i.e.* Tirebegger.	4½	Craibstone, Mrs. Dr. Scott. Glasgow Forest, Mrs. Brebner.
Glasgowego, Wilson, Esq. Greenburn Inn. Balbethan, Gen. Gordon. Keith Hall, Earl of Kintore.	45	KINTORE, A borough of considerable antiquity.	12	Benachie rises to the height of 1420 feet. On the east end is a remarkable rock, rising perpendicularly on three sides 180 feet,
The Bass, a conical mount of considerable elevation, said to be artificial. The river Ury runs close to it. Tradition says the pestilence was buried in it. Thomas the Rhymer has predicted: "Dee and Don shall run in one, And Tweed shall run and Tay, And the bonnie water of Ury Shall bear the Bass away." The first part of the prediction was fulfilled by the Inverury Canal. Pitcaple, Lumsden, Esq.	41¾	Cross Don by a handsome of 3 arches, built in 1798.	15¼	it is only accessible on one side; it has been fortified, tradition says, by the Picts.
	41½	INVERURY. Pitcaple Inn. At some distance, on the opposite side of the Ury, the battle of Harlaw was fought. "July 24, St. James's even, Harlaw was fought fourteen hundred and eleven."	15½	A borough of considerable antiquity. Here Robert Bruce gained a victory over the English. Here, in 1745, the rebels defeated a party of the King's troops. Maner, Gordon, Esq. Balquhain, Leslie, Esq. Pittodrie, Erskine.
Logie, Elphinstone, Bart.	36	The Church of Oyne to the west 1 mile.	21	Old castle of Harthill.
	35	cr. the Gadie. "Oh an I were where Gadie rins, At the back o' Benachie."	22	Worthall, Captain Dalrymple.
Pitmachie Inn. Newton, Gordon, Esq.	33		24	
Williamston, Fraser, Esq.	31	Vill. of Old Rain.	26	At a distance may be seen the hill of Dunideer,
Freefield, Gen. Leith.	30½	cr. Kelloch.	26½	*i.e.* Dun d'Ore; on the top of which are the ruins of an old castle, said to have
Enter the Glens of Fondland, through which the road passes for some miles. In stormy weather it is frequently shut up.	25	cr. the Ury, Here called the Glen Wat. On the left is the hill of Fondland, celebrated for its slate quarry, some of which are of the finest quality.	32	been the palace of King Gregory the Great about 300. It has been surrounded by a double rampart. The walls, after encountering 1000 winters, are so hard that the smallest
Huntly Castle, a ruin partly built by George first Marquis of Huntly, whose name, and that of his wife, Hen. Stewart, daughter of Esme Duke of Lennox, are in the hall. The extensive estates of the Gordon family have now devolved upon the Duke of Richmond.	19	cr. Bogie. "I'll o'er Bogie wi' my love." HUNTLY, pop. 3000. Once celebrated for its linen manufacture, and still for its bleaching. Huntly Lodge.	38	stone will break rather than be separated from the mass; large masses of vitrified stone are scattered over the level top of the hill, and marks of many buildings. Many years the residence of the last Duke of Gordon when Mar. of Huntly.
A handsome Church.	18	cr. Deveron.	39	
About a mile distant, the vill. of New Mills.	9	Keith vill. cr. Isla.	48	A short way below the Deveron is joined by the Bogie, and afterwards by
Shortly after leaving Keith, the road enters upon the property of the Duke of Richmond, and continues to Fochabers; close to which stands Gordon Castle, 560 feet in length. The park is 18 miles in circumference.	8	Fife Keith vill. Barren moor to FOCHABERS.	49 57	the Isla, and after a course of 20 miles it falls into the Moray Firth at Banff.

* The Great North Road from Aberdeen to Inverness, at the distance of 3½ miles from the former divided into two, one branch by Turriff, Banff, and Cullen, being 72 miles; the other by Kintore, Inverury, Huntly, and Keith, being 57 miles to Fochabers, where the roads again unite. The latter being the shortest line, is the mail coach road, and is now chiefly used by travellers.

XXII. ABERDEEN.—BANFF.—CULLEN.—ELGIN.—FORRES.—NAIRN.—INVERNESS.—126 Miles.

ON RIGHT FROM ABERD.	From Inver.		From Aberd.	ON LEFT FROM ABERD.
Persley, Haddin, Esq. Woodside, Kilgour, Esq. Waterton, Pirie, Esq. Parkhill, Skene, Esq.		Leave Aberdeen, and pass for several miles along the bank of the Inverury Canal.		Hilton, Johnston, Bart.
		Dyce vill.	6	Kirkhill, Bannerman, Esq. Fintry House, Forbes, Bart. Kinmundy, E. of Aberdeen. Elrick House, Burnett, Esq.
		cr. the Don.		
		New Macher Kirk.	9	Straloch, Ramsay, Esq. Barra, Ramsay, Esq.
Tillygreig, Harvey, Esq. Pittrichie, Milne, Esq. Udney Castle, Col. Udney. Kilblein, Manson, Esq.	111	Leithfield.	14½	Fingask, Elmslie, Esq. Tulloch, Kilgour, Esq.
	108	Old Meldrum vill.	18	
Haddo House, Earl of Aberdeen.		Meldrum Ho., Urquhart, Esq.		
	101½	Fyvie Kirk.	24½	
	99½	Fyvie Castle, Gordon of Fyvie, on the right.	26½	Fyvie Castle is a princely looking building, beautifully situated on a small eminence in the centre of a large amphitheatre of fine grounds, skirted with woods on the heights around, and the river winding through the centre.
Hatton Castle, Duff, Esq.	95½	Towie, The native place of the father of Barclay de Tolly, *i.e.* Towie, the Russian general.	30½	Gask, Earl of Fife.
"When ye're at the Brig o' Turay, Ye're half-way between Aberdeen and Elgin o' Murray."		cr. Turriff Water. Muiresk, Spottiswood, Esq. Laithers, Stuart, Esq.		
Delgatty Castle, Earl of Fife, a mile from Turriff; not seen from the road.	93	Turriff. Pronounced Turay. Forglen House, Abercromby, Bart., about a mile from Turriff.	33	
Craigston Castle, Urquhart, Esq.	91½	On the left Montblairy, Morison, Esq. and Eden, Duff, Esq.	35½	Banff, the county town, is agreeably situated on the side of a hill at the mouth of the river Deveron. It was founded by Malcolm Canmore in 1163. There have been large additional piers built to the harbour here, but, owing to the sandy bottom, the bar is often much filled up.
Forglen Church on the north side of the river Deveron.	88	cr. King Edward.	38	
	79	cr. Deveron River, and enter BANFF.	47	
Between Boyndie and Portsoy are the ruins of Boyne Castle, Lord Seafield, once the finest seat in the North of Scotland, but destroyed in the civil war.	75½	New Kirk of Boyndie.	50½	On the left on entering the town is Duff House, the elegant mansion of the Earl of Fife. Durn Park, Gordon, Esq.
		cr. Boyne Streamlet by cr. of Broadlie.		
Along this line of road the Earls of Fife and Seafield, and the Duke of Richmond, are the chief proprietors.	70	Portsoy, A small irregularly built town, with a thriving port; population 2000.	56	Durn, Earl of Seafield. Glasshaugh, Abercromby, Esq.
From Banff to Fochabers (26 miles) the road passes at no great distance from the sea-coast.	65	CULLEN, A royal burgh in the Elgin district, population 1593.	6	Birkenbog, Abercromby, Bart. Cullen House, Earl of Seafield, a large and venerable building. The grounds are fine.
Near village of Buckie.	61	Letterfourie, Gordon, Bart.	65	Cairnfield, Gordon, Esq.
Near village of Port Gordon.	52	Fochabers vill.	74	Near Fochabers is Gordon Castle, Duke of Richmond; a magnificent mansion, erected by Alexander Duke of Gordon, who died in 1827. The ancient seat of the family was Huntly Castle, now in ruins; near it Huntly Lodge, Duchess of Gordon.
Speymouth Kirk.		cr. Spey River, enter Morayshire.		
The royal burgh of Elgin is an old fashioned and impressive place. The remains of the Cathedral form the chief object of attraction in Elgin. It was founded in 1224 by the Bishop of Moray. The great tower fell in 1711. The Cathedral, when entire, was exactly a model of Lichfield. Elgin has been much improved of late years by the erection of various public buildings.	48	Urquhart vill.	78	
	46	Kirk of St. Andrews.	80	
	43	ELGIN Joins with Banff, Cullen, Inverary, Kintore, and Peterhead, in electing an M.P.; population 4500.	83	

ABERDEEN to INVERNESS—*Continued.*

ON RIGHT FROM ABERD.	From Inver.		From Aberd.	ON LEFT FROM ABERD.
		cr. the Lossie.		
	40	Newton House, Forteath; a little farther, Thunderton, Dunbar, Bart.	86	A little to the east of Forres, and near the road, stands the remarkable obelisk, usually called Sweno's Stone; it is above 20 feet high; it has a number of figures cut on it, which are still remarkably distinct. There are various traditions respecting it; one is, that it was erected to commemorate the murder of King Duffus in the castle of Forres, and the execution of the murderers; another, that it commemorates a victory over the Danes under Sweno, in the time of Malcolm II., about the year 1010. The character of the figure seems to favour the former tradition, the name of the obelisk the latter.
	38	Kirk of Alves.	88	
On the right, ruins of Abbey of Kinloss. The genius of Shakspeare has immortalized the town of Forres. It was on a waste in the neighbourhood that Macbeth and Banquo were said to have met the weird sisters.		Burgie Castle, Brodie. At distance, see Findhorn vill.	91	
	31	FORRES, A royal burgh, in the Inverness district. Population 3895.	95	
On a small conical hill, about a mile south of Forres, is erected a tower to commemorate the victory of Trafalgar.	30	Moy, Grant, on the right.	96	
	29½	cr. Findhorn River.	96½	
Darnaway Castle, Earl of Moray, not seen from the road. It is four miles from Forres. The great hall was built by the celebrated Regent Randolph, the nephew of Bruce. It contains the *dais* of feudal times. The original roof, which is of dark oak, still remains. The Findhorn flows by it through a well wooded park. Immense plantations of oak, pine, larch, &c. cover the whole country side, and conceal the castle from view.	27½	Kirk and vill. of Dyke, enter Nairnshire.	98½	Brodie House, Brodie, Esq.
	22½	Auldearn vill.	104	Auldearn was the scene of a victory gained, May 4, 1645, by the Marquis of Montrose over an army of the Covenanters, under Sir John Hurry.
		cr. Nairn Water.		
	20	NAIRN, A royal burgh of very old fashioned appearance. Population 3266.	106	In the neighbourhood of Nairn is Cawdor Castle, the seat of the Earl of Cawdor. It is one of the most ancient and entire baronial residences in Scotland. It stands upon a low rock overhanging the bed of a torrent, and is surrounded by the largest sized forest trees. It is enclosed within a moat, and is approachable only by a drawbridge. Macbeth was "Thane of Cawdor."
	18	Firhall.	108	
	14	Ardersier Kirk.	112	
	12	Campbellton vill.	114	At no great distance is Fort George, remarkable as the only regular fortification in the island, and as a complete architype in miniature of the great fortresses of the continent. Fort George is a mile N.W. of Campbellton, 8 miles from Inverness.
On right 5½ miles from Inverness, Castle Stewart, Earl of Moray, a ruin.	11	Connage.	115	
		Culloden House.		
Inverness contains a number of goodly streets and has the usual public buildings of a large county town. The whole environs are beautiful in a high degree, and there is no town in Scotland which enjoys so many fine walks. The famous Castle of Inverness, which was the property and residence of Macbeth, stood on an eminence to the east of the town, termed the Crown. This castle was destroyed by Malcolm Canmore, who soon after built another to serve as a royal residence and fortress. This edifice was destroyed, in 1746, by the troops of Prince Charles Stuart, and only the wall of an interior rampart now remains.		INVERNESS. The remains of the Fort which Oliver Cromwell built at Inverness are to be seen at the place where the Ness joins the sea. The most remarkable natural curiosity in the neighbourhood of Inverness is a strange oblong mound called Tom-na-heurich (hill of the fairies.) Inverness joins with Forres, Nairn, and Fortrose in electing an M.P. The population of the town in 1831 was 9663.	126	The scene of the Battle of Culloden is a mile to the left of Culloden House, about 4 miles from Inverness. The most distinguished seats in the neighbourhood of Inverness are, Culloden House, Raigmore (Mackintosh, Esq.), Derroch Villa (Dowager Lady Saltoun), Leys (Miss Baillie), and Muirton (Mr. Huntly Duff).

INDEX.

Now Publishing,

IN MONTHLY HALF VOLUMES, PRICE EIGHTEEN SHILLINGS,

Durably and Elegantly Bound in Embossed Cloth,

THE

ENCYCLOPÆDIA BRITANNICA,

SEVENTH EDITION,

EDITED BY PROFESSOR NAPIER.

THE republication of this great National Work, in Monthly Half-Volumes, has now reached the Eighth Volume. This accelerated rate of publication enables present purchasers to complete the book simultaneously with the original Subscribers.

The high reputation which the ENCYCLOPÆDIA BRITANNICA has maintained throughout the Six Extensive Editions which have already been disposed of, and more especially the peculiar favour with which the present Edition, remodelled in all its departments, has been received, render alike unnecessary any detailed explanation of its plan, or commendation of the manner in which it has been executed. A provision of twelve thousand pages of stereotype plates, and of four hundred engravings on steel, affords ample security that the publication will proceed with the most rigid punctuality to its completion.

A very large proportion of the matter is entirely new. Wherever any of the text of the former Edition or Supplement has been retained, it has been amended in style, improved in arrangement, and in every respect accommodated to the actual state of knowledge and the general design of the Work. In paper, typography, and beauty of embellishment, as well as in the literary value of its contents, the present Edition will be found very far superior to any which have preceded it. In every department, indeed, no expense has been spared to render the work worthy of the improved taste of the age and of the national name. The Proprietors, therefore, have the most confident expectation that the SEVENTH EDITION of the ENCYCLOPÆDIA BRITANNICA will form a most important addition to the well-selected Library, and will prove an nvaluable substitute to such as are denied access to a general collection of ooks.

Part CVIII. which is just published, contains RAILWAYS, by LIEUTENANT ECOUNT of the London and Birmingham Railway—RELIGIOUS MISSIONS, by MES DOUGLAS, Esq. of Cavers—Biographies of RABELAIS, RACINE, Mrs. ANN DCLIFFE, ERASMUS RASK, RENNIE the Engineer, and many others; with the icles REFORMATION, REGISTRATION and the commencement of REPTILIA.

Folio 415 incorr…

GEOGRAPHICAL WORKS,

GUIDE BOOKS FOR TOURISTS,

AND TRAVELLING MAPS.

I.

In 9 vols. 8vo., with a comprehensive Index of 44,000 Names, price £7.

A SYSTEM OF UNIVERSAL GEOGRAPHY. By M. MALTE BRUN, Editor of the "Annales des Voyages," &c. &c.

"We think the translators of M. Malte Brun's Geography have done good service to the public by rendering so valuable a work accessible to the English reader."—*Edinburgh Review.*

"M. Malte Brun is probably known to most of our readers as the author of a systematic work on Geography; he is, besides, the Editor of a periodical digest under the title of "*Nouvelles Annales des Voyages de la Geographie et de l' Histoire;*" the first is as much superior to the compilations of our Guthries and Pinkertons, as the other is to the garbled productions of our Truslers and Mavors."—*Quarterly Review.*

"Infinitely superior to any thing of its class which has ever appeared."—*Literary Gazette.*

II.

In post 8vo. price 6s. illustrated with Woodcuts, Maps, and other Engravings, including Humboldt's Map of the Geographical Distribution of Plants,

PHYSICAL GEOGRAPHY. By THOMAS STEWART TRAILL, F.R.S.E., Regius Professor of Medical Jurisprudence in the University of Edinburgh, &c. &c.

"A most elaborate digest of facts judiciously arranged, and, as a great exposition, perhaps the most complete that has yet appeared."—*Leeds Mercury.*

III.

Preparing for Publication, in one very thick volume 8vo.

AN ABRIDGMENT OF BALBI'S AND MALTE BRUN'S SYSTEMS OF GEOGRAPHY. Compiled from the original Works, as well as from the French Abridgment and English Translations of Malte Brun, with a careful comparison of later authorities; containing numerous Tables of Population and Statistics; together with much important information of a date subsequent to the publication of the French editions. To which will be added, a copious Index of the Countries, Towns, and Miscellaneous Information contained in the body of the Work, affording that facility for reference which forms the chief recommendation of a Gazetteer.

IN PREPARATION.

In a pocket volume, price 3s. 6d.

BLACK'S ECONOMICAL TOURIST OF SCOTLAND; Containing an accurate Itinerary and Travelling Map, with Descriptive Notices of all the interesting objects along the several roads, and Four Engraved Charts of those localities which possess peculiar Historical or Picturesque interest.

In a closely printed and portable volume, with many Illustrations,

BLACK'S PICTURESQUE TOURIST OF SCOTLAND; Containing a highly finished Map engraved by Sydney Hall, Four Engraved Charts, an accurate Itinerary, and a profusion of Engravings on Wood and Steel.

In a neat portable case, price 2s. 6d.

BLACK'S TRAVELLING MAP OF IRELAND, Engraved by Sydney Hall, and beautifully coloured. (*In preparation.*)

In a neat pocket volume,

BLACK'S ECONOMICAL GUIDE THROUGH EDINBURGH, Arranged in Four Walks; with Plates and a Map.

In a pocket volume, closely printed and illustrated with a Map of the Lake District,

BLACK'S ECONOMICAL GUIDE TO THE LAKES OF WESTMORELAND, CUMBERLAND, AND LANCASHIRE; with an Itinerary, and Charts of all the important districts. (*In preparation.*)

In a neat portable case, price 2s. 6d.

BLACK'S TRAVELLING MAP OF SCOTLAND, Engraved by Sydney Hall, and beautifully coloured.

In a neat portable case, price 2s. 6d.

BLACK'S TRAVELLING MAP OF ENGLAND, Engraved by Sydney Hall, and beautifully coloured.

WORKS
ILLUSTRATIVE OF
SCOTTISH CHARACTER AND SCENERY.

I.

In two volumes 8vo., price One Guinea,

With seven Illustrative Etchings by W. Dyce, Esq.,

HIGHLAND RAMBLES, AND LONG LEGENDS TO SHORTEN THE WAY. By Sir THOMAS DICK LAUDER, Bart.

Author of "An Account of the Morayshire Floods," "Lochandu," "Wolfe of Badenoch," &c. &c.

"We heartily recommend these volumes to all tourists to the 'Land of the Mountain and the Flood,' who are now setting forth on their delightful trip."—*Bentley's Miscellany.*

"Full of legend, full of adventure, full of interest."—*Athenæum.*

"Sir Thomas evinces an intense sympathy with our Highland landscapes, people, and traditions."—*Inverness Courier.*

"Admirable, and admirably narrated. . . . . . Full of the true perceptive feeling of the beautiful in nature."—*Dublin University Magazine.*

II.

In small octavo, price 7s. 6d.

SCENES AND LEGENDS OF THE NORTH OF SCOTLAND. By HUGH MILLER.

"A well imagined, a well written, and a somewhat remarkable book."—*Athenæum.*

"A very pleasing and interesting book; his style has a purity and elegance which remind one of Irving, or of Irving's master, Goldsmith."—*Spectator.*

"A highly amusing and interesting book, written by a remarkable man, who will infallib[ly] be well known."—*Leigh Hunt's Journal.*

III.

In small 8vo., price 4s.

TALES AND SKETCHES OF THE SCOTTISH PEASANT[RY]. By ALEXANDER BETHUNE, Labourer.

"Alexander Bethune, had he published anonymously, might have passed for a regular littérateur."—*Spectator.*

"It is the perfect propriety of his taste, no less than the thorough intimacy with the unobtrusive subjects he treats of, which gives Mr. Bethune's little book a great charm in [our] eyes."—*Athenæum.*

"The work is an extraordinary one. * * * * His pictures of rural life and char[acter ap]pear to us remarkably true, as well as pleasing."—*Chambers' Journal.*

IV.

Price Two Shillings,

TWO VIEWS OF FINGAL'S CAVE, STAFFA. Engraved for the Seventh Edition of the Encyclopædia Britannica.

These Views were pronounced by the late Proprietor of Staffa, (Sir Reginald Macdonald Seton,) to be the only Engravings which conveyed any adequate idea of this extraordinary cavern. They are beautifully engraved on steel, and equally well adapted for framing, or for the portfolio.

V.

Price 7s. boards, or 8s. neatly bound,

PICTURE OF EDINBURGH, containing a Description of the City and its Environs. By JOHN STARK, F.R.S.E. With a New Plan of the City, and Forty-eight Views of the Principal Buildings. Sixth Edition, Enlarged and Improved.

VI.

In two volumes 12mo. price 8s.

THE SCOTTISH SONGS Collected and Illustrated by ROBERT CHAMBERS.

VII.

In one volume 12mo. price 4s.

THE SCOTTISH BALLADS Collected and Illustrated by ROBERT CHAMBERS.

PLANS & DRAWINGS

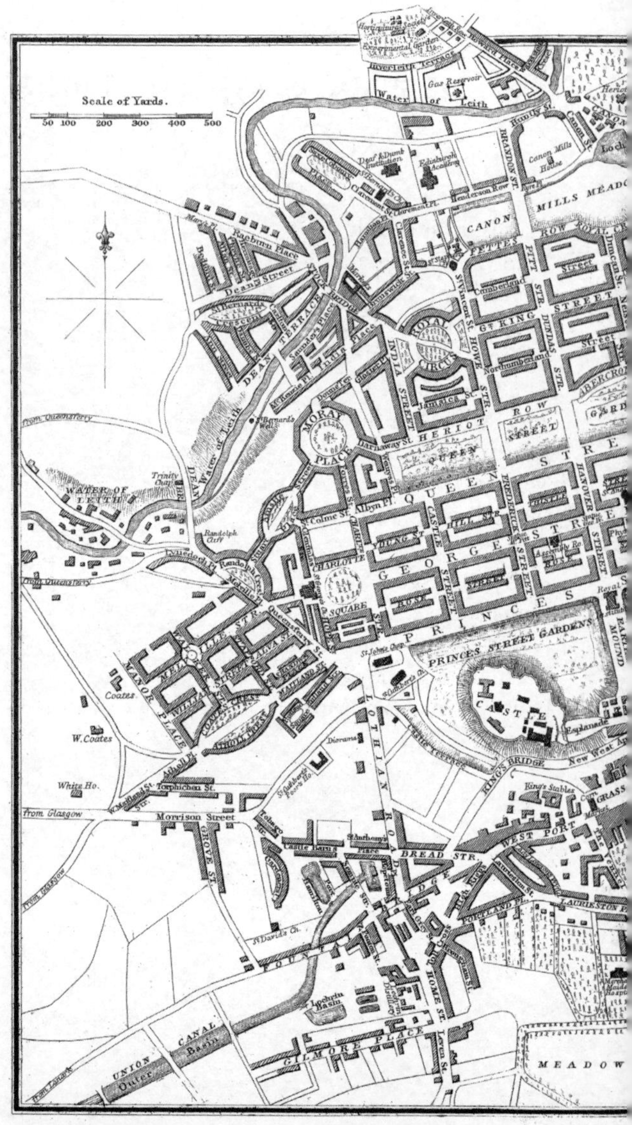

Scale of Yards.
50 100 200 300 400 500
Horticultural Society's Experimental Garden
Inverleith Terrace
Howard Place
Gas Reservoir
Water of Leith
Huntly St.
Canon St.
Deaf & Dumb Institution
Edinburgh Academy
Canon Mills House
MILLS MEADO
Henderson Row
BRANDON ST.
Claremont Pl.
CANON
ROW
FETTES
Clarence St.
Brunswick St.
Raeburn Place
Dean Street
STOCK BRIDGE
St. Bernards Crescent
DEAN TERRACE
India Place
ROYAL CIRCUS
INDIA STREET
St. Vincent St.
HOWE STR.
PITT STR.
Cumberland
Gt. KING STREET
DUNDAS STR.
Northumberland
Jamaica St.
MORAY PLACE
Darnaway St.
HERIOT ROW
QUEEN STREET
ABERCROM
from Queensferry
St. Bernard's Well
Water of Leith
DEAN
WATER OF LEITH
Trinity Chap.
Randolph Cliff
Lynedoch Pl.
Randolph Cres.
St. Colme St.
Albyn Pl.
CHARLOTTE SQUARE
CASTLE STREET
FREDERICK STREET
HANOVER STREET
HILL STR.
YOUNG ST.
GEORGE STREET
ROSE
PRINCES STREET
PRINCES STREET GARDENS
St. John's Chap.
St. Cuthbert's Ch.
CASTLE
Esplanade
New West Ap
KING'S BRIDGE
King's Stables
GRASS
WEST PORT
LAURISTON PL
PORTLAND PL.
High Riggs
BREAD STR.
St. Anthony's Place
LOTHIAN ROAD
Castle Barns
Morrison Street
GROVE ST.
Torphichen St.
W. Maitland St.
Atholl Pl.
MELVILLE STR.
MANOR PLACE
MAITLAND ST.
Queensferry St.
Coates
W. Coates
White Ho.
from Glasgow
Diorama
St. Cuthbert's Poor's Ho.
St. David's Ch.
FOUNTAIN
Lochrin Basin
HOME ST.
Leven St.
GILMORE PLACE
UNION CANAL
Outer Basin
from Lanark
MEADOW

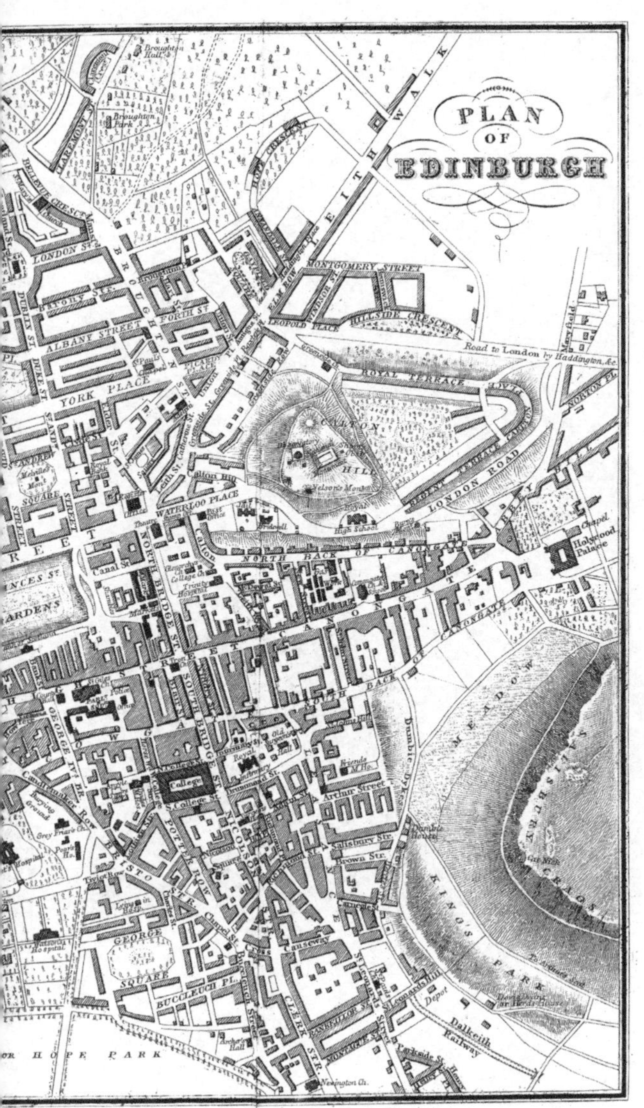

PLAN
OF
EDINBURGH
Broughton Hall
Broughton Park
LEITH WALK
HOPE CRESCENT
BELLEVUE CRESCT
LONDON ST.
BROUGHTON ST.
MONTGOMERY STREET
WINDSOR ST.
ELM ROW
LEOPOLD PLACE
HILLSIDE CRESCENT
Road to London by Haddington &c.
Mary field
ROYAL TERRACE
NORTON PL.
ALBANY STREET
FORTH ST.
DUBLIN ST.
DUKE ST.
YORK PLACE
PICARDY PLACE
St. Paul's Chapel
CALTON HILL
Nelson's Mont.
REGENT TERRACE
LONDON ROAD
ABBEY HILL
Chapel
Holyrood Palace
WATERLOO PLACE
Post Office
Bridewell
High School
Theatre
NORTH BACK OF CANONGATE
CANONGATE
SOUTH BACK OF CANONGATE
Canal St.
NORTH BRIDGE ST.
Trinity Hospital
PRINCES ST.
GARDENS
MELVILLE'S Mont.
ST. ANDREW SQUARE
HIGH STREET
COWGATE
SOUTH BRIDGE ST.
Royal Infirmary
College
S. College St.
Drummond St.
Arthur Street
Salisbury Str.
Brown St.
Friends M. Ho.
NICOLSON ST.
Nicolson Square
POTTER ROW
BRISTO ST.
Grey Friars Ch.
Burying Ground
Heriot's Hospital
Lying in Hosp.
Watson's Hospital
GEORGE SQUARE
BUCCLEUCH PL.
Buccleuch Street
Chapel St.
Cross Causeway
CLERK STR.
St. Leonards Street
St. Leonards Hill
Depot
Dalkeith Railway
Newington Ch.
Archers Hall
Montague Street
Parkside St.
Dumbie Dykes
Dumbie House
KING'S PARK
SALISBURY CRAGS
Cat Nick
Deanhaugh or Herds House
HOPE PARK
MEADOW

HUMES MONUMENT,

from Leith Wynd.

ST. ANTHONY'S CHAPEL.

CASTLE.

from the graſs Market.

HERIOT'S HOSPITAL
from the Grafs Market.

THE UNIVERSITY.

G.M. Kemp invt et delt R. Scott Sculpsit

THE SCOTT MONUMENT

D. McKenzie G. Aikman

ROSLIN CASTLE.

Drawn by G.Barret. Engraved by J.Mc Gahey.

MELROSE.

MUSSLEBURGH TOLBOOTH.

STIRLING CASTLE.

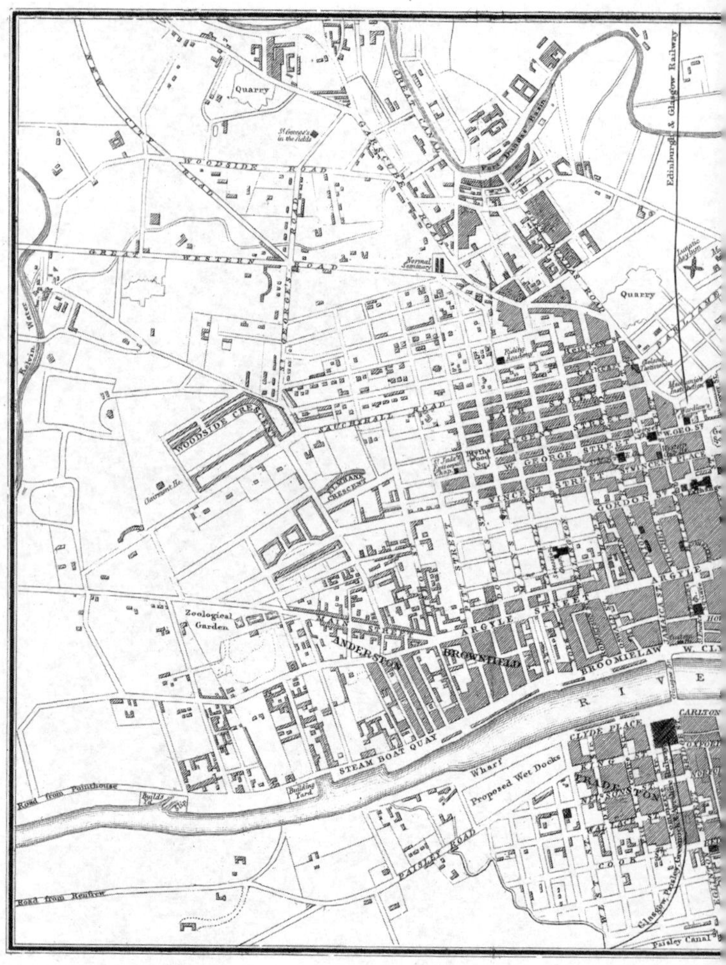

Quarry
St George's in the Fields
NEW CITY ROAD
WOODSIDE ROAD
GARSCUBE ROAD
GREAT CANAL
Port Dundas Basin
Edinburgh & Glasgow Railway
GREAT WESTERN ROAD
Normal Seminary
Lunatic Asylum
Quarry
Kelvin Water
Riding Academy
WOODSIDE CRESCENT
SAUCHYHALL ROAD
BATH STREET
W. GEORGE STREET
ST VINCENT STREET
ST VINCENT PLACE
GORDON ST
Clairmont Pl.
ELMBANK CRESCENT
Zoological Garden
MAIN STREET
ARGYLE STREET
ARGYLE
ANDERSTON
BROWNFIELD
BROOMIELAW
JAMAICA ST.
RIVER
STEAM BOAT QUAY
CLYDE PLACE
CARLTON
Wharf
Proposed Wet Docks
TRADESTON
KING ST.
NELSON ST.
WALLACE ST.
COOK ST.
Road from Pointhouse
Building Yard
PAISLEY ROAD
Road from Renfrew
Paisley Canal

PLAN
OF
GLASGOW
Monkland Canal
Garnkirk & Glasgow Railway
Asylum for the Blind
New Burial Ground
Royal Infirmary
Cathedral
NECROPOLIS
Knox's Monument
DRYGATE ST
ROTTENROW
STIRLING'S ROAD
DUKE ST
GEORGE STREET
COCHRANE ST
Canon St
Cattle Market
Hunterian Museum
COLLEGE
College Church
Moncurlands Chs
ROAD
GALLOWGATE
KING ST
Millroad St
Rose St
CALTON
KIRK ST
Stevenson St
TRONGATE
GREAT HAMILTON ST
MONTEITH ROW
CANNING ST
LOW GREEN
HIGH GREEN
Nelson's Monument
STREET
E. CLYDE ST
CLYDE
Pelham St.
ADELPHI ST.
GORBALS
HUTCHESONTOWN
GOVAN STREET
ROAD TO RUTHERGLEN
BRIDGETON
KING'S PARK
FLESHERS HAUGH
Proposed Cemetery
G. Aikman, Sc. Edin.

Drawn with Camera Lucida, by Thos. Allan, Esqr. F.R.S.E.

FINGAL'S C.

Engd. by G. Aikman, Edinr.

VE, STAFFA.

FALL OF THE CLYDE AT STONEBYRES.

LOCHLEVEN CASTLE.

LOCH ASSYNT_ BEN MORE IN THE DISTANCE.